LOVERS OF SOPHIA

MW00856246

LOVERS OF SOPHIA

JASON REZA JORJANI

Copyright © 2019 by Arktos Media Ltd.

All rights reserved. No part of this book may be reproduced or utilised in any form or by any means (whether electronic or mechanical), including photocopying, recording or by any information storage and retrieval system, without permission in writing from the publisher.

ISBN	978-1-912975-47-1 (Paperback)
	978-1-912975-48-8 (Hardback)
	978-1-912975-49-5 (Ebook)
COVER & LAYOUT	Tor Westman

CONTENTS

"Nothing is true; everything is permitted."

— Hassan Sabbah, Medieval Iran

"Hassan Sabbah is the only spiritual teacher with anything to say in the Space Age."

— William Burroughs, Postmodern America

This book is dedicated to my best student,
my dear friend, and fellow Assassin,
Selwyn Griffith.

INTRODUCTION

This mammoth volume is a collection of twenty distinct philosophical reflections written over the course of a decade. Most of them are essays, some almost of book length. Others would be better described as papers. A few are well-structured notes. There is also one lecture. A magnum opus like *Prometheus and Atlas* does not emerge from out of a vacuum, and an alternative title to these collected works could have been "The Path to *Prometheus and Atlas*." While there are a few pieces that postdate not only that book but also *World State of Emergency*, most of the texts included here represent the formative phase of my thought. Consequently, concepts such as "the spectral revolution" and "mercurial hermeneutics" are originally developed in these essays.

In addition to revealing the context for the genesis of specific concepts that I have developed, these reflections also have certain stylistic features and central concerns that, when taken together with my two published books, make it possible to discern the key characteristics of my philosophical standpoint. For example, I reject any subdivision of Philosophy into distinct and specialized fields such as Ontology, Epistemology, Aesthetics, Ethics, and Politics. The main reason that I have included "An Introductory Lecture on Ethics" is because it exemplifies my integral conception of what it means to philosophize. From the essay "Philosophy, Science, and Art," it becomes clear that beyond a rejection of specialization within Philosophy, I go so far as to argue against any fundamental differentiation of Philosophy from the arts and sciences. It is my contention that philosophers (such as Aristotle and Descartes) determine the deep structure of successive scientific paradigms, at least at their inception, and that philosophical thought can take place in an artistic and literary medium. This is why several of the pieces here are interpretations of literary or cinematic works, such as *The Trial* of Franz Kafka, or two films based on the writings of Philip K. Dick. In my view, aesthetic intuition is a necessary (but not a sufficient) condition for being a philosopher.

While on the subject of what it means to be a philosopher, let me point out that it is only with the publication of these essays that I reconcile myself to making the claim that I am one. Thus far I have described myself only as "an aspiring philosopher." In addition to the aforementioned "Introductory Lecture on Ethics" and reflection on the relationship between "Philosophy, Science, and Art," my diatribe "Against Perennial Philosophy" makes it quite clear that I do not recognize the majority of academics in the field of Philosophy as "philosophers" even though they disrespect the great thinkers of the past by referring to themselves as that. "Against Perennial Philosophy" actually disqualifies the majority of so-called "philosophers" in the Canon as well, and it suggests that there has hardly been any philosophy worthy of the name outside of the Indo-European civilizations (including the Aryan heritage of Buddhist Asia).

A philosopher is someone whose thought engages with fundamental questions concerning Truth, Beauty, and Justice, in a way that leads to the discovery of concepts with a potential to catalyze scientific and political revolutions. The philosopher's ethics and politics must be grounded on his ontology and epistemology, and, as I have already suggested, this integral thought has to be guided by an aesthetic intuition comparable to that of the most extraordinary geniuses in literature and the arts. This is a definition that disqualifies scientists as innovative as Khayyam, Galileo, and Newton, political theorists like Cicero

Rousseau, and Strauss, or artists such as Ferdowsi, Dostoyevsky, and Kubrick. That I reflect philosophically on the brilliant works of Franz Kafka and Philip K. Dick, does not mean that I consider them philosophers. On this definition, there are probably not many more than two dozen philosophers known to recorded history.[1] On account of the development of at least four original concepts thus far, namely the "spectral revolution" and "mercurial hermeneutics" in *Prometheus and Atlas*, the concept of a "world state of emergency" in the book by that name, and the terrifying idea of a "destructive departure in worldview warfare" from the essay "Black Sunrise" that appears in this volume, I now see myself as (just barely) having joined the ranks of these fellow lovers of Sophia.

The backbone of this collection is constituted of critical, and in some cases iconoclastic, contemplation of the work of my predecessors in the Canon: Plato, Aristotle, Spinoza, Kant, Hegel, Nietzsche, James, and Wittgenstein. The interpretation of Plato ventured in "The Pharmakon Artist" and that of Aristotle in "Building the Theater of Being" are totally original and extremely destabilizing to received tradition. The essay on Hegel's "Paranormal Phenomenology," which also adopts and adapts certain ideas from Maurice Merleau-Ponty, is the point of origin for the concept of "mercurial hermeneutics" further developed in *Prometheus and Atlas*.

However, it is by no means the case that these philosophical reflections are limited to the Western Canon. Rather, one of the distinguishing characteristics of *Prometheus and Atlas* as well as *World State of Emergency* is the cosmopolitan scope of my thought. My "Critique of Shiite Esotericism" and exegesis of "Verse 4:34" from the *Quran*, are incisive philosophical critiques of Islam. They were instrumental scholarly exercises on the way to the anti-Islamic argument of *World State of Emergency*. Essays like "Serpent Power of the Superman,"

---

1   This qualifier "recorded history" is important since I am certain that we have
     lost a great deal of legitimate philosophy to vicissitudes such as the burning of

where I argue that Hindu Tantra is more Nietzschean than Nietzsche, reaffirm that I recognize no distinction between "Western" and "Eastern" philosophy. Although most of what could be called philosophical thought in the East is Indo-European or Aryan in origin, my "Notes on the Tao of Bruce Lee" suggest that Aryan traditions like Buddhism can be augmented by assimilating elements of non-Aryan traditions such as Taoism. As I argued in both *Prometheus and Atlas* and *World State of Emergency*, I see this innovatively evolving cosmopolitan humanism as one of the most distinctive qualities of the Indo-European community. Bruce Lee is Aryan, not Chinese—and I say that mainly on account of the form of his thought, rather than his partly German genetic inheritance or his upbringing in the British colonial culture of Hong Kong.

By the way, as "Trial Goddess" strongly suggests, I also consider Franz Kafka to be an Aryan. Fragmentary as his writings may be, in my view Kafka is the peak of German literature—or rather the cathedral gloom of its most horrifyingly abyssal depth. How integral Jews have been to defining the most Aryan of attitudes and ideas in the Western Canon is also clear from the overwhelming influence of Baruch Spinoza on the development of the core structure of Nietzsche's thought, which I trace in the essay, "Spinoza, the Untimely One." Nietzsche, the progenitor of the Aryan Superman, himself recognized the Jews as a world-historical community who, as compared to their small numbers, have demonstrated an incomparable genius in every field of human endeavor, producing some of the most brilliant philosophers, scientists, artists, and mystics.

To the horror of those who consider cosmopolitan Jews to be nothing other than crafters of corrupting golem, in the essay "Prisoners of Property and Propriety" I argue that Karl Marx was a devotee of Prometheus—the most Aryan of all divinities. Moreover, it is in this essay on Marx and other radical Marxists that I first developed the concept of the "spectral revolution" as early as 2010. I synthesized Prometheus and Atlas from this essay with Deleuze's idea of concen-

understanding of spectrality as I interpret it in "Paranormal Phenomenology," in order to produce the core structure of my magnum opus. Reflecting on Ludwig Wittgenstein's concept of language games was also instrumental to arriving at the idea of "worlds at war over Earth" in *Prometheus and Atlas*. My thinking defies all binaries. More than that — it mocks them. Those who know how to read esoterically, as I know how to write esoterically, ought to have discerned that in *Prometheus and Atlas*. Hermes or Mercury, the Trickster, is not the book's villain. Like the figure of the Joker in the essay "Gotham Guardian," he (or she, another false binary) is an agent of chaos and a de-structuring force required for any new world order. This is what the Alt-Right never understood about Pepe, the incarnation of the ancient Egyptian god Kek. Of all the figures in the leadership of the Alt-Right, I was Kek's most faithful emissary.

This brings me to "Black Sunrise," which is by far the most disturbing essay in this collection and the only one in which I develop a new concept beyond those of my first two books. This concept is "destructive departure in worldview warfare" — a loose translation from the much more evocative German phrase that I coined to express this idea: *Abbauende Aufbruch ins Weltanschauungskrieg*. This is not a hypothetical idea. It is, in practice, the most radical form of psychological warfare imaginable. It presupposes an anarchical existential ontology on the basis of which one can captivate entire societies through the manipulation of false binaries that form the fabric of their *Weltanschauung*. The societies are broken down and then re-conquered by a breakaway civilization, in comparison to which the target societies are simulacra with programmable mytho-poetic variables. "Black Sunrise" also explores some radical ideas about the nature of space-time and the possible non-linearity of human history reaching all the way back to the antediluvian civilization of Atlantis.

These questions about Time, and specifically whether it is possible for the future to re-write the past, are at the heart of the debate over

it is central to at least four of the pieces in this book: "Free Will vs. Logical Determinism," "Rewriting God's Plan," "Changing Destiny," and "An Introductory Lecture on Ethics." Readers who are familiar with *Prometheus and Atlas* will know that my argument for Free Will, which draws heavily on the metaphysics of William James, also featured prominently in that text. Consequently, this concern with the metaphysical preconditions of human freedom, conscientious action, and genuine creativity can rightly be seen as one of the most defining characteristics of my thought. These four essays on free will should leave no doubt that I am, above all, a freedom fighter. It is because, like Zarathustra and Buddha before me, I recognize that superhuman gods are real but unjust and deceptively manipulative that I reject democracy as a political form that is capable of protecting the creative power of the precious individual genius. Democracies will always be instruments of these master manipulators, whether through their direct power over the psyche of the ignorant mob or through their dealings with oligarchs who hide behind the façade of democracy in order to outlast other more forthright forms of tyranny.

My philosophical project ultimately represents a rebellion against all forms of tyranny, including tyranny of the majority. Its goal is the highest human self-consciousness and the most creative self-determination. One reason that this has not been understood is that my detractors, and those who have defamed me, are not capable of seeing past their own noses. At its deepest and most esoteric level, my thought, like that of Plato or Nietzsche, is scaled to thousands of years of human and post-human evolution. People who think that John Rawls is a philosopher and waste their time writing about him are ants laboring in the shadow of my obelisk. What is written in these pages is not for them. It is for you, lovers of Sophia — all of you, across the ages into the distant future, into the lighthouses of a galactic Alexandria. From Zarathustra onwards, we are all flames of the same undying cosmic fire. We are the glowing forge of futures past.

AN INTRODUCTORY LECTURE ON ETHICS

At the risk of stating the obvious, let me begin by asking you to recognize that whatever the specific content of any ethical standpoint may be there is a very basic form of ethical action that is independent of this content: a person can act ethically only if that person is an agency that is responsible for the action in question. If a person is no more responsible than a rolling rock, it is utterly senseless for anyone to judge that a person has acted ethically or ought to be held responsible for acting unethically. The guilty conscience would also be an absurd experience. When an avalanche happens due to natural causes and one rock rolling down the mountain impacts another, sending it on a trajectory other than the one that was its heading before being hit, that is a radically different kind of action or interaction than an "ethical" one. Hopefully we can all agree on this simple but important observation.

The problem is that the contemporary view held by the scientific establishment is that the kind of action at play when one rock impacts another is basically the only kind that there is. Together with Metaphysics, Epistemology, Politics, and Aesthetics, Ethics has been a major concern of Philosophy since its origin 2,500 years ago in Greece. Ethics is concerned with the question of "the good life." Metaphysics asks about the ultimate nature of reality. Epistemology is concerned with the theory of knowledge or how it is that we can know what we claim to have knowledge of. Politics is concerned with the art of statecraft and the applied understanding of the concept of Justice. Aesthetics is a study of the nature of the beautiful, for example, as contrasted with the merely pleasant in judgments of taste. Until about 250 years ago all of what we now study and practice as the various empirical sciences were considered types of natural Philosophy, falling within the domain of Metaphysics or Epistemology. Science or Scientia simply means "knowledge," which is part of what philosophers sought in their "love of wisdom." Beginning with Physics in the mid-1700s, then Chemistry and Biology in the 1800s, and finally Psychology in the early 1900s, the various sciences attempted to distinguish themselves from Philosophy. Yet, in fact, what had happened was that a certain type of metaphysics had become dominant in Physics and ever since most other scientists have tacitly deferred to it.

This dominant metaphysics grew out of a reductive and materialist interpretation of the mechanistic approach to understanding Rene Descartes (1596–1650), whose Latin name was Cartesius, and so it is often referred to as the Cartesian paradigm or conceptual frame of reference. A paradigm is broader than any given theories and is the context of background assumptions without which theories cannot be formed in the first place. The assumptions are cultural and historical in character and they condition what counts for empirical or "experiential" data regarding natural phenomena and the proper method of obtaining it.[1]

Until very recently, scientists did not realize that they work within a paradigm and that the theories generated by one paradigm are incommensurate with those of another paradigm. Most still refuse to acknowledge this. Consequently, even biologists and psychologists who deal with natural phenomena that are very different from loose rocks hitting each other on a mountainside want to claim that everything in Nature happens either by chance or is determined in a mechanical way. From the perspective of Ethics, this amounts to the same thing. In either case, a person cannot be held responsible for having done anything. What we think of as a "person" in a psychological sense is actually an organism that biologists are willing to concede can further be reductively analyzed (or "broken down") as certain elementary particles or quantum wave-functions whose interactions are either determined in a chain-link of causality going back to the initial expansion of the universe or they are somewhat probabilistic, but not in a way that allows any one a chance to influence or affect the probabilities. In the 17th century, when this view of Nature was developed, the fairly explicit model for it was the machinery then being invented and implemented in industry. Julien Offray de La Mettrie, a reductionist reader of Descartes, captures this zeitgeist best in *Man a Machine* (1748).

For the last couple of centuries there have been an almost universal marginalization and exclusion of work in the sciences that does not suit the metaphysical doctrine that there is only matter and that the smallest or most elementary constituents of matter interact with each other in a mechanical way. Yet this dominant metaphysics of the scientific establishment makes nonsense out of Ethics. This remains true even if many have tried to worm their way out of recognizing it. Some establishment scientists try to speak as if from out of the grey matter of the brain and the various mechanical processes that make it function there is an "emergence" of mind, including its ability to make choices that are free enough so that the individual making them can be held responsible for the actions that embody those choices. Yet mind as an "emergent property" is completely empty and superfluous rhetoric unless the mind that emerges can do things not reducible to the elementary particles or waves — or, these days, superstrings — that themselves have none of the agency that is attributed to persons

So, one of the first things I am going to try to get you to realize is that the sciences, as often learned from High School textbooks, do not allow for Ethics — any Ethics, at all. This does not mean that Science precludes Ethics, simply that the dominant worldview and methodologies in the modern scientific establishment would have to change to allow for Ethics. You cannot believe both in the reductively materialistic and mechanistic worldview prevalent in the sciences and also think that people can be ethical or unethical.

If in the back of your mind you have been mistakenly hearing this as an underhanded defense of religion, then it is high time to disabuse you of that impression. The dominant form of religious belief in the Western world, and for that matter also in the Islamic world, is just as incompatible with Ethics as the mechanistic worldview of the scientific establishment. In Judeo-Christianity, just as in Islam, the overwhelmingly accepted and established doctrine concerning the Creator is that God is both omniscient or "all-knowing" and omnipotent or "all-powerful." Whatever else a Judeo-Christian or Muslim believes, this is part of it.

There is a long-standing theological debate over something known as "the problem of evil," namely if God is omniscient and omnipotent then why does God allow for all of the evil in the world? This classic formulation misses the point as far as the problem that God's omniscience and omnipotence poses for Ethics. The real question is this: If God always knows everything that can and will happen, then the entire domain of possible events is already scoped-out and defined in detail so that it can be accessible to God's mind. Moreover, if God is also all-powerful then God is really the motivating force behind the actualization of each of these predefined possibilities. These possibilities that are predefined for God's mind and actualized by God's power include all of the actions that we mistakenly attribute to our agency. The problem is not simply that God is acting when we take ourselves to be acting, but that we never choose anything if God already knows everything, because to choose is — at least on some minimal scale — to create. A world of predefined possibilities accessible to an eternal mind outside of time is a world that is already completed and cannot be added to. No finite agency exists in such a world as an agent capable of transforming that world in ways that she or he is responsible for. The world of the Almighty Creator leaves no place for any creative act on our part.

Granted both Judeo-Christianity and Islam are full of rules to follow. These have been "revealed" by the Creator and they are to be "obeyed." In fact, the fundamental presupposition of religious revelation as such is that the Law needs to be given by authority and accepted on faith. From the perspective of the revealed religions, to think that one's own contemplation and exercise of conscience could suffice for living a good life is the worst kind of sin. But unquestioning obedience to a prescribed code of conduct is not Ethics. It is certainly Law and you can call it Morality if you wish, but Ethics derives from the Greek word *ethos*. This means the dynamic "character" or vital "constitution" of a person or group of people. The very concept of Ethics presupposes choice, introspective assessment, creative interpretation, consideration of context, and, above all, personal responsibility. The major difference between the two can be seen when one reflects on religious law from the perspective of the omnipotence and omniscience of the Creator. All reward and punishment — as well as gracious divine forgiveness — is purely at the discretion of the Creator and the individual has no responsibility whatsoever for the actions that, from the perspective of chronological time, appear to have preceded it. This moral begins to become apparent in the book of Job, and its fatalism ultimately becomes most explicit in Islam.

However many times and in whatever ways Judeo-Christians and Muslims claim that their scriptures enjoin individuals to act responsibly and that each will be held responsible for their own deeds, all that such insistences can do is entangle the one making them in absurd contradictions. Remember, God is omnipotent and omniscient. We do nothing at all. The heavenly reward of the faithful and hellish retribution of sinners is a farcical puppet show.

So, looking at it from the perspective of our cultural-historical conditioning, we are between a rock and a hard place as far as Ethics is concerned. You must realize that the very idea of Ethics is incompatible with both Modern scientific materialism and Abrahamic religious revelation. Until you sort that out for yourself, anything else discussed in this area is really pointless.

It is not true that Ethics does not make claims about the way the world is. A world in which ethical or unethical action makes sense cannot be a world wherein there is nothing other than mechanistic causality acting on microscopic material structures that make up everything in nature without an irreducible remainder. Nor can it be a world wherein everything that we might do — or rather that we might misperceive ourselves as initiating — is already an event mapped out in a completed logical space accessible to the eternal mind of God, a mind capable of now surveying every possible future. Either these possible futures collapse into a single predefined future, in which case we have no free will, or there are an infinity of parallel universes in which doppelgangers of ourselves live lives in many cases nearly identical to our own and in other cases somewhat more different, in which case none of these parallel selves are any more unique or uniquely responsible for the minutely different iterations of their actions than we are for ours in this one of many possible worlds.

I would make the case that a world where Ethics has any meaning at all must be a finite world where no one has an infinite or eternal perspective let alone unlimited power. So, Ethics — in its very form and irrespective of its content — makes claims that explicitly conflict with those of certain widely accepted scientific theories and religious doctrines. It is rootless idiocy to teach Ethics as if it could be applied in business or medicine or whatever field without recognizing this, and making it seem as if it had nothing to do with one's scientific outlook or religious standpoint. Ethics as such implicitly endorses a scientific and religious orientation different from the ones dominant in our place and time. That orientation is very open to question as far as its details are concerned, but we can know enough about it to realize that it makes a different demand of us than the one made by reductionist scientists or God Almighty.

Just as Ethics is often uprooted from metaphysical considerations about the nature of reality that it presupposes, it is also artificially abstracted from the socio-political context that it needs in order to be meaningful. A person is not ethical or unethical in a vacuum. Ethics is concerned with one's relationship to others in a society, and whether or not this society is a just one — in a political sense — has everything to do with whether and to what extent it is possible for those who constitute it to cultivate virtuous conduct. Also, societies generally feature internal differentiation, so there is a question about whether it is possible for everyone in a society to be virtuous in the same ways and to the same degree.

First of all, consider how many of the virtues cannot be practiced in isolation. For example, generosity requires someone to be generous to and courage presupposes a situation of shared danger within the context of which to be courageous. This social context also helps us to determine whether someone is generous or simply squanders his wealth, or whether a supposedly courageous person is actually rash. There is a great difference between righteous anger and an expression of sheer wrath, but discerning the distinction between them in any given case would involve a consideration of the status and character of the offending and offended parties, their respective histories and values.

In a certain context killing is murder, in another it is just retribution, in another an act of valor in the defense of one's country. To be ethical is to tell the difference, for example, between enlisting in a just war and being party to mass murder. "I was just following orders" is the excuse of a slave. Depending on context, might it not also sometimes be ethical to do other things that under different circumstances

would be considered unethical? For example, is it sometimes justified to lie? If the Nazis come banging on your door looking for some innocent people of Jewish descent who are hiding in your attic, is it ethical to tell a lie and say you've never seen them? What about lying to an entire nation in order to protect it from an enemy or even from its own worst impulses?

In light of these fine distinctions, it is certainly fair to say that a person raised by wild animals would not be virtuous and we would even have to wonder whether he were a "person." Practice of the virtues probably requires some degree of habituation from childhood, and one of the things we are going to look at in the second unit is to what degree this is the case. In addition to proper upbringing, the development and sustenance of a virtuous ethos requires continual practice. As we will see, Aristotle suggests that the mirror of friendship is indispensable to maintaining virtue as an active disposition and gaining insight into one's own character.

There are, however, all kinds of "friendships." Some are associations for the sake of successful business and others are based on commonly enjoying certain pleasures, like participation in a sport or a hobby. There might even be friendships predicated on the common pursuit of a vice. Consider this: Even in the case of what seem to be the best friendships grounded on the virtuous character of those in the relationship, how many people would wish that their best friends become god-like in their degree of virtue or excellence? It is virtuous to wish the best for one's friends, but who would wish such excellence for their friends that it opened a chasm between them and their friends as great as that between mere mortals and gods?

What would such god-like virtue look like? What if it were possible to get away with anything whatsoever in stealth — to steal anything, indulge any lust, maneuver oneself into any position of power that commands respect? Suppose one could become invisible while secretly committing every manner of criminal and unethical deed and that doing so allowed one to publicly command ever more respect and even to be praised as virtuous by the masses. Imagine also that persecution and even a torture worse than death were the reward for actually being virtuous, rather than merely seeming so while raping and plundering in stealth. Who would prefer to actually be virtuous rather than seem so while being wicked? Even if we grant that being ethical requires habituation from childhood and the mirror of personal relationships throughout life to sustain, could the god-like virtue required to be this ethical be a matter of habit or having the right kind of friends?

If there are individuals who seem to have a transcendent virtue, people who are ethically exemplary, it also seems that for any one of them there are many others who are at the opposite extreme: people whom no amount of proper habituation can render ethical and who are incapable of entering into any but the crassest and most convenient friendships. We are going to contemplate whether, as Plato and Aristotle think, sometimes entire societies are dominated by such people — societies so viciously oppressive that the cultivation of virtue is impossible in them. If a society needs exemplary individuals even in order to cultivate ethical habits in others, doesn't it make a very great difference whether the political system is one that encourages exemplary leadership or one where the most vicious elements in a society are allowed to harness the vilest impulses in the masses to create conditions that make life impossible for ethical paragons? Can a true democracy ever be ethical?

The United States of America is often mistakenly considered a democracy. Even some of our recent Presidents have spoken as if this is a democracy and one of them called for spreading the fire of democracy around the world. Well, we have seen what kind of fire that policy has spread in the Middle East. In fact, the United States is not a true democracy and most of the founding fathers of America considered "democracy" a dirty word. They were students of classical Greek and Roman thinkers like Plato, Aristotle, Xenophon, and Cicero who reasoned that democracy was pretty near to the worst form of government there is. Only tyranny is more vicious than democracy from a classical perspective, and the founding fathers viewed democracy as a "tyranny of the majority." Those with a poor education in history think that democracy was some shining accomplishment of the Greeks, when in fact almost all Greek intellectuals were harsh critics of democracy.

Analysis of the *Declaration of Independence*, the *Bill of Rights*, and the various writings (including the private letters) of the founding fathers make it clear that rather than being a democracy, this nation is grounded on the concept of Natural Right — sometimes also known as the Rights of Man. This has been more recently reframed by the United Nations as Universal Human Rights but in a way that is less clear and coherent than the Natural Right conception of the founders. The founders of the American constitutional Republic, and by the way also some of their French revolutionary colleagues, saw Natural Right as a universal ethical standard. In his book *The Rights of Man*, Thomas Paine, who set off the American Revolution with his more widely read pamphlet *Common Sense*, explicitly and publicly states what others of the founders privately believed: Natural Right is so universal that it applies even to all of the other intelligent beings throughout the Universe, so that the bell of liberty rung by the American Revolution is not even limited to all of the oppressed individuals on the planet Earth — it reverberates throughout the Cosmos.

For Deists and Freemasons such as Benjamin Franklin, Thomas Jefferson, George Washington, and other key founders, the "Creator" in the Declaration of Independence was not the God of the Bible but the macrocosmic rational order reflected in the microcosm of reason that allows us to perfect ourselves. This relationship between a reason inherent in Nature at large and the rational faculty characteristic of human nature is at the core of the idea that we have certain rights that are "inalienable" — in other words, not given by any government and therefore not justly ignored, withdrawn, or violated by any government. Even if a 99% majority of people in this country were to vote through their elected representatives to strip individuals of their natural rights, their votes would be null and void. Military officers who have sworn to uphold the constitution could legitimately disempower a congress or President that acknowledged such a majority vote. So, again, the United States is very far from a democracy. It is a constitutional government dedicated to the protection of the Natural Rights of Man, where "man" means not just men and women but each and every intelligent being in the Universe.

This basic conception of Natural Right or a universal Ethics was most carefully crystalized by Immanuel Kant in his argument for a Categorical Imperative. Kant thinks that his universal ethics would be truly universal, namely that it would apply to every form of extraterrestrial intelligence regardless of their biological differences from *Homo sapiens*. How tenable is this claim considering what we now know about evolution? Couldn't there be forms of extraterrestrial intelligence that are much more similar to terrestrial insects with a hive mind than they are to humans on Earth, and given the horrifying amorality of interactions within insect colonies wouldn't it be absurd to claim that the beings constituting them would be bound by the ethical standards of anything like the *Bill of Rights* or the *Universal Declaration of Human Rights*?

Furthermore, aren't emergent biotechnologies giving us the power to so radically alter the human genome that a speciation of our own race could present us with beings of a common ancestry that are as alien to us as any extraterrestrials? In the second half of the third unit we will look together with Francis Fukuyama at how the technologies of embryo selection, cloning, genetic engineering, and genetic hybridization call into question whether there is any essence or metaphysical nature that we all share as humans in the first place — the kind of nature that would ground Natural Right or Human Rights. If our so-called "nature" is only an evolutionarily contingent and technologically malleable biological nature, what legitimacy do such conceptions of universal ethics have in the first place? We may be able to use legislation to keep these technologies at bay (although that is unlikely), but even so such legislation only covers over the power of such technologies to reveal something much more fundamental to us about ourselves—something with profound ethical implications. Emergent biotechnologies even give us the power to create new forms of intelligent life, to be the designers of new species of sentient beings. What if we were to find out that we ourselves are the artifacts of more advanced beings? Is there something about each of us that is uncreated and a bearer of pre-political ethical rights, irrespective of whether or not the human race was someone else's pet project? Prometheus created the human race in his own image; what are the ethics of a Promethean, of a superman alien to the human condition?

THE PHARMAKON ARTIST

"The safest general characterization of the
European philosophical tradition is that it consists
of a series of footnotes to Plato."

— ALFRED NORTH WHITEHEAD

For too long now has this quote from Whitehead sounded like a
cliché. Historically, doctrinally, and temperamentally, there are many
branches in the tree of *Philosophia* — between Neo-Pythagorean
Platonists and Aristotelian Neo-Platonists before Descartes, between
analytic and continental thought after Kant, between Marxist and
Existentialist thinkers after Hegel. Nevertheless, they all recognize
their common heritage in the solid trunk of the dramatic dialogues
of Plato before disappearing into subterranean Pre-Socratic roots. A
radical reinterpretation of Plato, then, has an obvious bearing on any
attempt to revolutionize the philosophical tradition as a whole. If it
could be shown that the dialectical development from out of Platonic
idealism and into other forms of rationalism and intuitive understanding was in some way anticipated by Plato himself, even designed by
him as a vast social conditioning mechanism, the whole of intellectual
history would have to be rethought. I do not claim to attain this aim in

the present essay, but I do paint in broad strokes some indispensable path marks to that end.

The essay is divided into five sections. The first three sections are closely related and form the initial phase of my argument. In them I interpret Plato's development of the Theory of Forms in terms of the metaphysics of the two foremost Pre-Socratic Greek thinkers, Heraclitus and Parmenides. The first section offers a concise sketch of the life-affirming worldview of Heraclitus and of the Eleatic school's transcendentalist reaction against it, beginning with Parmenides. In the interests of a point made later in the essay, I preface this with an even briefer evocative glimpse at the Greek mind in the Homeric age.

Since this essay is already ambitious in the scope of its treatment of Plato, to give more attention to the Pre-Socratics than I do here would seriously compromise its coherence. For the reader who is basically unfamiliar with this background to Plato's thought, and who needs more than the refreshers that I offer in the first section of this paper, I recommend Friedrich Nietzsche's lectures on *The Pre-Platonic Philosophers*[1] as well as his *Philosophy in the Tragic Age of the Greeks*[2] — a very short posthumously published book that he wrote contemporaneously with his famous study of Greek drama. My own understanding of the Pre-Socratics, or as Nietzsche called them the "Pre-Platonic" philosophers, has been profoundly influenced by these two works, especially his view therein of the relationship between Heraclitus and the Eleatic school of Parmenides.

The second section argues that the Platonic "form" or "idea" (*eidos*) was something devised with a view to Parmenidean notions of enduring unity, and on the basis of a tacit acceptance of a Heraclitean view of the world of sensuous experience as a perpetual flux. In itself, this is no great revelation, but what I suggest is something more. Namely,

---

1   Friedrich Nietzsche, *The Pre-Platonic Philosophers* (Chicago: University of Illinois Press, 2001).

2   Friedrich Nietzsche, *Philosophy in the Tragic Age of the Greeks* (Washington,

that Plato deliberately misinterprets the ontology of Heraclitus, privileging Becoming to the total exclusion of Being whereas for Heraclitus Becoming is a concealing or sheltering aspect of Existence. Likewise, he perversely distorts the meaning of Non-Being in Parmenides from a negatively infinite ontological Nothingness to a finite cipher in the context of indexical reference (i.e. as that which is not being presently referred to, but which nonetheless exists as a counterfactual referent).

Following clues in certain remarks made by Aristotle concerning Plato's Heraclitean pedigree, I excavate the Heraclitean world-view tacitly accepted by Plato from between the lines of the dialogues *Theaetetus*, *Cratylus*, and *Phaedo*. I then turn to the dialogues *Parmenides* and *The Sophist* to see how Plato appears to respond to this vision of a world in perpetual flux, a world where certain knowledge of definite objects is impossible, by taking recourse to a rationally apprehensible transcendental realm that endows each object with its distinctive cohesive unity. The reader unfamiliar with academic philosophy will be duly forewarned that this exposition is by far the most abstract and abstruse section of the essay, and may seem — to those who even invest the effort in following it — to consists of platitudes concerning the relationship between the One and the Many and other fundamental points of Logic. The simplicity is, however, a deceptive one and carefully following Plato on these points is important for appreciating the more substantive claim of the next section.

That claim is the following: The Theory of Forms can be seen as arising out of an attempt to find a middle way between uprooted and straw-man versions of Heraclitean and Parmenidean ontology, one which acknowledges the Heraclitean realm of sensuous experience, which Parmenides rejected as sheer illusion, while also securing the Parmenidean unity and simplicity indispensable to the definitions required for rational knowledge of objects. To this end, as we see perhaps most clearly in *Timaeus*, Plato develops the concept of a plurality of perfect unities — "forms" or "ideas" — that formatively define pure matter which would otherwise be in an ungraspable state of perpetual flux. The soul on a quest for knowledge is at the crux of the mixture of form and matter, and is consequently impure. Nevertheless, she may seek purification through the rational element within her. However, Plato admits that perfect knowledge—which is the indispensable standard or *sine qua non* of any inferior "knowledge" as such—cannot be attained insofar as intellection remains mediated by sensuous experience. I show how at one point in *Phaedo*, Plato makes the bold claim that knowledge by means of the pure intellect apart from anything bodily or sensory is possible after death, but he quickly contradicts this claim by consoling his disciples with a sensory account of the afterlife.

I then insist that the metaphysics implicit in the latter statement cannot simply be dismissed—apart from its consoling moralistic content—because it is on a continuum with the tale of Er, which plays a key role in *Republic*, with its Pythagorean account of the unambiguously sensory state between death and (even the highest) rebirth (as a philosophical Guardian). Remaining in *Republic*, two key sets of passages on "the Good" are then examined toward the end of showing how Plato actually conceived of the "forms" as constructs or postulates akin to those employed by geometers, and that these cannot even be viewed as leading one to a rational comprehension of the form of the Good. This "form of forms" is itself incomprehensible and inexplicable. So, briefly put, the forms are not only inescapably contaminated by matter where it counts, namely in the soul, but rational knowledge of that which the forms are postulated in order to apprehend is itself basically impossible.

The third section concludes with significant citations from two of Plato's private *Letters*, which suggest that the upshot of his entire method of dialectical inquiry in terms of the forms is actually a moment when mystical insight flashes upon the mind confronted with paradoxes that are bound to seem irresolvable within the limits of conceptual understanding or rational analysis. This requires as a prerequisite not only a fine-tuning of intellect through contemplation of the postulated forms and dialectical discourse with others, but also an intimately communal life among devoted seekers.

That is the point of departure for the second part of the essay, which consists of its fourth and fifth sections. Together they forward the proposal that this irrational intuition that Plato is trying to provoke is essentially an *aesthetic* intuition. The fourth section explores this in terms of the account of the pursuit of the form of the Beautiful in *Symposium*, with a focus on the relationship between that dialogue and another text named after *Alcibiades* — who is the most significant character in *Symposium* besides Socrates himself. It is argued that through Alcibiades' eulogy, amidst an unprecedented honesty of intoxication, Plato offers us an insight into the profoundly Dionysian character of Socrates. We also have a shocking admission from Socrates himself, that *eros* or "erotic love" is the *only* thing that he really understands!

A review of the egregious flaws of logic in the dialogue *Alcibiades*, which Plato obviously intended to be cross-referenced with *Symposium*, attests to the truth of many of Alcibiades' charges that Socrates is actually a Great Deceiver and Seducer — a satyr playing enchanting flute tunes. With reference to Friedrich Nietzsche's analysis of Apollonian and Dionysian archetypes in *The Birth of Tragedy*, I work to undermine Nietzsche's own view of "Socrates" as an Apollonian figure responsible for the degeneration of Dionysian dramatic art. Instead I interpret the closing of *Symposium* as a call for a new art form, namely Philosophy, which would strike a dynamic balance between the Dionysian and the Apollonian.

Alcibiades compares being seized by Socrates' philosophy to being bitten by a poisonous snake. In ancient Greece snake poison was among a class of dangerous medicinal cures known as *pharmakea*. The person who administers a *pharmakon* — which is a poison but can be a cure in the right dosage and at the right time — is a *pharmakeus*, a "witch doctor" or "black magician." Drawing on Jacques Derrida's treatment of this question in his essay "Plato's Pharmacy," I build on what has already been elaborated to push beyond where even Derrida dares to go. I conclude by suggesting that Plato's entire philosophical project may be a *pharmakon* — a poison that is also a cure, and that the history of occidental rationalism may have been set in motion as one man's attempt to deliberately mislead people so as to force them to develop certain latent mental faculties.

In the end, I return to the question of Plato's Homeric context, situating his opposition to the poetry and art of his time in the context of its all-pervasive *mimesis* — an unreflective and imitative embodiment of traditional views, customs, and values. In light of the essay's argument as a whole, one is led toward the startling realization that far from being an enemy of art, this man who began his career as a tragic poet, was combating an uncreative and stagnant traditional "art" form with an avant-garde *Art* of his own creation. *Philosophy*, as it began with Plato, is a fundamentally different endeavor than the naively earnest Truth-seeking of Heraclitus, or Parmenides, or any number of Oriental sages.

1. THE HISTORICAL BACKDROP OF PLATONIC THOUGHT

One cannot understand Plato without recognizing his complex appropriation of Heraclitus and Parmenides, and to that end it is necessary to first consider the doctrines of these two thinkers in their own right. Yet in order to appreciate the dawn of Philosophy among the pre-Socratics we need to take the even more preliminary step of briefly envisioning the Homeric age of the Greeks, which stands as its backdrop. This will also be important for our ultimate evaluation of Plato's motives for composing his dialogues in the diabolically deceptive manner that he did.

In Greece during the second millennium BC, we see a culture completely absorbed in an ancient mythology whose origins are lost in the dark ages of man. It is a grim mythology where the might of heroes makes right, and man is always trying to find reprieve from the jealously and wrath of feuding gods by offering sacrifices of animals and riches of gold and jewels up to appease them. As is well known the pantheon of ancient Greek Gods was a dramatically exaggerated reflection of the realm of mortals, replete with sexual and feudal intrigue, murder and war. More disturbing is that, especially in the *Iliad*, this human drama has a particularly soulless quality.[3] In *The Origin of Consciousness in the Breakdown of the Bicameral Mind*, Julian Jaynes notes that Greek words like *psyche*, *phrenes* and *noos* that much later develop the connotation of "mind," "heart" and "soul" are rendered anachronistically as such by modern translators. They have a more physical sense in the older language of the *Iliad*. No one, neither mortal nor god, could escape Fate, and a "god" intervenes whenever a mortal must make a crucial decision. Jaynes argues that we would be making a mistake to interpret these incidents as metaphorical, for the subtlety involved in the use of metaphor was not yet grasped by the Greeks of the late 2nd millennium BC. Rather, we ought to take the absolute power of fate and the constant intercession of the gods as evidence of a startling lack of a sense of personal agency and rational deliberation.[4] The ultimate Fate consigned to archaic Greek man was death conceived of in the earliest traditions as a passage to *Hades,* the eternal abode of shades. It was an underworld of shadows where good and bad would wander equally bereft. In light of this woeful end the only purpose of life, brilliantly fulfilled by heroes, was to win a fame that would promise immortality through dramatic deeds worthy of remembrance in the songs of poets. In short, we find a society completely mesmerized by its reflection in the distorting mirror of its own mythology.

For six centuries, from at least the Trojan War in 1230 BC to Hesiod's *Theogony* in 650 BC, we see essentially no change in the

---

3   Julian Jaynes, *The Origin of Consciousness in the Breakdown of the Bicameral Mind* (New York: Mariner Books, 1990), 69–71.

mythic world-view of the Greeks. Hesiod's "Theogony," which according to Jonathan Barnes had "no serious rivals," is a genealogical story that sees the world proceed from Chaos and Earth. On the one side Chaos gives birth to Night and Erebos, which in turn produce aether and day. On the other side, Earth produces heaven, mountain and seas, which in turn give rise to a series of Gods (Oceanus, Thethys, Theia, Hyperion, Kreios, Eurybie) that in union with each other produce the Rivers, Sun, Moon, and Dawn. Finally, the union of Dawn and Astraios (a grandchild of sea and earth) produces the wind and stars.[5] There were other less significant, perhaps more natural, cosmological speculations contemporary to the one above recounted by Hesiod. However, as classicist M.L. Mills notes, these speculations were very primitive:

> [P]hysical speculation existed in Hesiod's time. It seems, however, to have been limited to the interpretation of man's immediate environment. Man is earth and water. Thunder and lightening are somehow caused by wind. Rain and moisture are drawn up from the rivers [by a god] and conveyed across land by the wind. Ask what the stars are, and the only answer is that they are children of Eos and Astraios. Ask about night and day: Night is the daughter of Chaos, the sister and wife of Erebos, the mother of Aither and Day, death and sleep, and various others. Night and Day go in and out of a certain house, in turn, crossing a great bronze threshold, at appointed times. What is the sun made of, or makes it rise and set? No answer.[6]

By "Philosophy" I understand most basically an inquiry into the *Truth* concerning the ultimate nature of reality or the structure of existence (Metaphysics/Epistemology) in order to discover the principles of *the good life* in accordance with this Truth, or how people may live "rightly" rather than "wrongly" (Ethics/Politics). On that definition, the first metaphysical and ethical thinker of ancient Greece, whose

---

5   Jonathan Barnes, *Early Greek Philosophy* (New York: Penguin Books, 1971), 203–204.

6   M.L. Mills, *Early Greek Philosophy and the Orient* (Oxford: Carendon Press,

own work has come down to us, is Heraclitus of Ephesus. All we have left of his writings are *Fragments*.[7] Piecing them together, we arrive at something like the following worldview.

The thought of Heraclitus begins in a rejection of the folk understanding of the polytheistic gods and traditional mythological answers to fundamental cosmological and ethical questions, like how the world was created, why, how we should live with each other in it, and what lies beyond it. More daringly, he rejects the authorities that embodied these views and the regimes that sanctioned them (and whose rule was sanctioned *by* them) — i.e. the priesthood and all contemporary forms of government (be it the oppression of the people by the undeserving few or the tyranny of the mob over the deserving few). Heraclitus did not reject these pat answers and schemes in order to replace them with new ones. Rather, he chose to leave fundamental questions open, either by evoking a mysterious terminus to understanding, or by offering deliberately contradictory answers that try to force one beyond the limits of rational thinking.

In this first metaphysical vision of the Greeks, the world is comprehended as an abstract process of Becoming, whose closest tangible analogy is that of an Eternal Fire. This Becoming is one with Being, as the manifested expression of its ineffable potentiality, and also as one with the Nothingness of Death, which is what Being would be reduced to if Becoming did not shelter it. Again, in this we do not see the world as an effect of some primordial cause or causes (as it would be portrayed in Mythology or Religion); rather it has always come forth from itself and always will. The Eternal Fire is a Oneness that *is* Plurality and all of the discordant strife of the dimension of plurality generatively conceals a deeper harmony of cosmic communion. The right-order of the cosmos — the *Logos* — is an expression of a supreme Intelligence that Heraclitus calls "the Wise One" and that is the Consciousness of Being.

---

7   Charles H. Kahn, *The Art and Thought of Heraclitus* (New York: Cambridge

This Metaphysics is the ground for an ethics that revolves around Conscience. Heraclitus rejects moral Law, which in his time was intimately bound up with ritualism. The notion of Conscience is fundamentally different from morality or religious duty and is absent from the most ancient Greek Mythology. It is concerned with the greater concept of "soul," which is equally absent from ancient mythologies that speak only of a "spirit" more or less equivalent with the breath (*pneuma*). For Heraclitus, the phenomenological experience of the world's *presence* nakedly shining-forth like an eternal revelation (a Sun "which never sets") should compel one to thoughts, words and deeds that accord with each other that personal authenticity. Human beings should not deceive themselves and each other by hiding in their own fanciful thoughts and opinions. This would be an affront to Being, which lays itself out before us without reservation. Yet precisely because the Sun of Truth is so scintillating in its presence, it hides itself by making us want to turn away so as not to be blinded.

Ultimately, Being is ever one with us (our source and end), and moreover since it is conscious and intelligent, there is a sense in which it perceives our deceitfulness from within. This discerning presence of Being within us, which perceives our own folly of deceit before it, is the Conscience. We sense it as an almost visceral feeling of inner discord (a burning of the heart), because the right order is deep within ourselves, but our lack of self-transparency blocks its manifestation. By the same token, if we open and clear our conscience through authenticity, the agency of Being within us will align us with the right-order that it sustains throughout the cosmos. Thus at the dawn of Philosophy, we have a metaphysical truth that consists in the phenomenological experience of the world's presencing, and an ethical notion of the opening of conscience through a truthfulness synonymous with ruthless honesty before oneself and others.

Responding directly to the Heracliteans, in his *Way of Truth*[8] Parmenides of Elea follows a profound urge to sever Being from Becoming, regarding the former alone as an all-pervasive "One" that is inherently posited by consciousness while denying the latter as total illusion. "Thinking and the thought 'it is' are the same"—this is his basic axiom. Parmenides also severs the mind from the body and urges us to use the former in order to transcend the latter's depraved delusions and know the unseen ideal. Here for the first time we have an epistemological conception of "Truth," one that consists in a knowing subject and a non-sensible object from which it is separated by the veil of illusion that is the sensible realm. This discrepancy between what lies before one's eyes and what exists in an unseen reality within the grasp of Reason, opens the door to the dialectical arguments or proofs which come to characterize Western Philosophy after Parmenides.

That Parmenides' move is indeed an idealist and rationalizing revolution is attested to by the fact that it effects a fundamental change in the pseudo-scientific speculations of the Pre-Socratics. Before Parmenides these "natural" speculations were implicitly grounded in a phenomenological conception of Truth epitomized by Heraclitus. *What is* was taken for granted as "true" so that all of the elements conjured up to explain the creation and composition of the world were transmutations of various substances actually existing in the world of experience: water, earth, fire and air in their manifestations as primordial oceans and mud or as the fiery stars and aether. We see this in Thales, Anaximander, Anaximenes, and Xenophanes.

Suddenly, after Parmenides philosophical thought is redefined in terms of abstraction. Zeno's tract of *Paradoxes* consists of a set of *ad absurdum* proofs rationally demonstrating that common-sense phenomenological notions of "space and time" do not possess absolute reality and because what is relative does not possess "Being"—they possess no reality at all. Anaxagoras tells us of eternal qualities which cannot be seen (or hardly even conceived) but which nonetheless give rise to the forms of the world by impressing themselves upon the primordial mass of Chaos through motion. Empedocles banishes the Intellect as unnecessary in this process, replacing it with the "random combination of elements of which some are purposive and capable of life."

From here it is only a short step to the apex of idealist abstraction in Atomism. Responding to Zeno's paradox of motion Democritus argues that for there to be Being at all it must not be infinitely divisible because otherwise it would collapse into Not-Being. Thus Being is reduced to a plurality of indivisible units. Democritus explains that these "atoms" hover in eternal motion in infinite space, forming things by "purposeless causality." We do not perceive much of what is perceptible (in the atomic realm) because our senses are not suited for it. Our impressions are mediated, they do not reach our eyes directly but only via refraction and distortion by air atoms, our eyes then also further modify the image. Similarly, sound is a delusion that arises from the rapid motion of air atoms. Both the proto-Platonic metaphysics of Anaxagoras and the proto-Aristotelian empiricism of Democritus share common roots in Parmenides' conception of an *ideal* dimension beyond the illusory world of the senses but within the grasp of the intellect.

2. CRAFTING THE FORMS BETWEEN BEING AND NOTHINGNESS

Aristotle tells us that in his youth Plato studied with a Heraclitean teacher and that he maintained the Heraclitean world-view that he accepted at that time throughout his life. According to Aristotle, it is based upon an acceptance of the Heraclitean view pertaining to the sensible world of becoming, that Plato proposed his Theory of Forms. In his *Metaphysics*, Aristotle writes of his own teacher:

For as a young man Plato was originally an associate of Cratylus and Heraclitean opinions, to the effect that all perceptible things were in a permanent state of flux and that there was no knowledge of them, and these things he also later on maintained.[9]

Now the starting point for those who came up with the Theory of Forms was a conviction of the truth of the Heraclitean considerations to the effect that all perceptible objects are in a permanent state of flux, so that a condition on the very possibility of knowledge and understanding was the existence in addition to the perceptible ones of certain other natural entities which are not in a state of flux, on the assumption that entities in flux were not possible objects of knowledge.[10]

In order to verify Aristotle's claim I will search for the Heraclitean basis of Plato's philosophy between the lines of the relevant dialogues *Theaetetus, Cratylus,* and *Phaedo.* Through various participants in these dialogues Plato paints a picture of what the world would be like if there were *no* ideal forms beyond the sensible realm, at times directly and at times implicitly attributing such a view of the world to Heraclitus and his followers. Plato does this in order to make the case that in such a terribly unreliable world of perpetual Becoming rational knowledge of definite objects would be impossible.

So as to present the most coherent picture I will abstract relevant statements from their differing contexts and interweave them in an explication that aims to elucidate the unspoken assumption forth from which Plato philosophizes. This pastiche does not do injustice to the contexts of these Heraclitean statements because I admit that they are being made by Plato's Socrates for argument's sake and are to be proven wrong in the course of each dialogue. However, what is important is that in every case the only way that these Heraclitean views are discredited is by demonstrating that the existence of forms that lie *beyond* the world is a prerequisite for rational knowledge. Plato's

---

9   Aristotle, *The Complete Works of Aristotle.* Two Volumes. (Princeton, NJ: Princeton University Press, 1995), *Metaphysics*: Alpha6, 987a.

narrative in effect reads: "If there were no *forms* the world would be *like this*…so there must be forms." The validity of the Heraclitean view of the world is not challenged but only restricted to not being the whole story. Time and again it is embraced as the ground of arguing for a Parmenidean transcendence of the physical world. This Parmenidean aspect should be kept in mind until I turn to explore it explicitly as the template for the *forms*, once I have completed an explication of the Heraclitean element of Plato's ontology.

First a brief overview of the original context of these spliced passages. *Theaetetus* is a discussion of the nature of knowledge, which stems from the belief of one of its participants in the truth of Protagoras' view that "knowledge is perception" and truth is relative to the perceiver. Plato equates the views of Protagoras and Heraclitus in this respect and embarks on a detailed exposition of how a world of Becoming could "come to be" without necessitating independently de-limited "beings" either as subjects or as objects. *Cratylus*, named in honor of the young Plato's Heraclitean teacher, is an argument over the appropriateness of names to their objects and the very possibility of naming things at all, which is of course a precondition for the existence of Logic. During the course of a discussion on the significance of names Plato embarks on a profound elaboration of the meaning of Justice, which he himself implies is Heraclitean. The dialogue ends with Socrates' advice to Cratylus not to so easily accept Heracliteanism because its view of the world defies the possibility of rational knowledge. Finally, *Phaedo* takes place on the day that Socrates executes his death sentence by drinking hemlock. During the course of his arguments for why the philosopher should not fear death, but should rather long for it, we are presented with an exposition on the interdependence of mental and physical opposites towards the end of proving that rebirth follows life. Let us begin reading between the lines of the various dialogues…

The world is an ever-changing Becoming in that all things are always simultaneously undergoing two kinds of change: 1) movement from place to place or revolving in the same place and 2) seeming to remain fixed in position while changing qualitatively (as in growing old, changing color, or hardening, etc).[11] Since everything is always changing no thing can be properly named as such; i.e. the mirroring of simple concept (name) and simple object, which is the very foundation of Logic, is impossible.[12] Thus such a world of becoming defies knowledge (*episteme*) because there is neither a fixed object to be known nor a unified subject to be a knower.[13] We can see this to be the case through an examination of how the perceived "object" and the structure suited to perception mutually define each other when they approach one another in the overall motion of nature. This definition occurs without necessitating a unitary "perceiver" or "subject." Something can "become so" only to someone, but also someone can become so only for something. All beings in the movement of nature become for each other and in this way a Necessity binds all things in the universe together, and so also in the same breath does not allow anything or anyone to be "bound to itself" as a unitary subject or object that can be isolated from others.[14]

In this definition of the world through the mutual perception of that which comes to be, that which is perceived is never a quality, for example "redness" or "hotness," but merely an example or degree of a quality that does not itself exist. This seeming contradiction is resolved in that "Opposites come from opposites — wherever there is an opposite."[15] This is true for both physical and moral qualities. For example, anything deemed "large" or "heavy" in comparison to one thing will always also be "small" in comparison to something else. Thus we can never speak of "largeness" or "heaviness" but only of

---

11 Plato, *The Collected Dialogues of Plato* (Princeton, NJ: Princeton University Press, 1999), *Theaetetus*: 181c–182a.

12 Ibid., 182d–183b.

13 Ibid., *Cratylus*: 440a–e.

14 Ibid., *Theaetetus*: 156a–157c; 160b–c.

larger than… , heavier than… , smaller or lighter than…. This 'than…' yet again underlines the greater unity of all things within the relativity of Becoming.[16] Similarly, pleasure and pain seem to yield to one another at their extreme thresholds. One always follows, or is the ground of, the other.[17] In saying that when one seeks the one the other follows, Plato is probably also implying emotional pain, for example, the pain of being abandoned after selfishly seeking pleasure in a relationship.[18] Fear and bravery are also aspects of the same phenomenon, because the man who defines his character by his willingness to die courageously for some alleged cause does so above all out of fear of cowardice — although the very definition of bravery is to be free from fear.[19]

What all of these examples of the mutual generation of opposites imply is that seeming opposites are on the same spectrum and precisely when they approach the greatest extremity of distance from each other they at once become each other. One of the two seeming opposites can only be seen as such by being defined against the other as an abstracted aspect of this spectrum, thereby simultaneously defining the other as well. The finite spectrum within which they can be distinctly judged collapses at its extremities — and so really throughout — into infinity. It is the indifference of this free space, of a oneness that is void, which alone makes the spectrum of opposites in the drama of Becoming both possible and necessary. This drama is the means by which the tension of existence satisfies itself. We could call such satisfaction Justice and conceive of it as an abstract (neversetting) Sun or Fire. This Justice is different from the relative quality by the same name; it has no opposite of "injustice." The moving universe is receptive to the penetrating force of Justice, which is not only

---

16   Ibid., *Theaetetus*: 152d–e.

17   Plato's mundane example is Socrates' feeling of pleasure in his leg after the fetter that has been causing it pain is released.

18   Ibid., *Phaedo*: 60c.

the agent of its perpetual creativity but also its cause and end. That it "must pass by other things as if they're standing still" means that since the other things are in fact a movement of Becoming, this Fire or Sun of Justice is the stillness of Being that incandescently burns through and beyond them.[20] There you have the elements of Plato's tacit Heraclitean ontology.

The influence of Parmenides on the development of Plato's Theory of Forms is even clearer than that of Heraclitus, the man who Parmenides saw as his philosophical adversary. We are not required to read between the lines. Two of Plato's dialogues explicitly deal with Parmenides, the dialogue bearing the latter's name as well as *The Sophist*. In these works, Plato goes so far as to quote whole passages of Parmenides' *The Way of Truth* word for word. The *Parmenides* is staged as a dialogue that is supposed to have taken place between an elderly Parmenides and a "Socrates" still in his youth. As we shall see, Plato probably intends this dramatic situation to imply that his own early confrontation with Parmenides was a key factor in his development. The Theory of Forms can be seen in part as an answer to the problem that Plato has Parmenides bring to bear on the young "Socrates" in this dialogue. A glimpse into what the beginning of that answer must have been comes in *The Sophist*. I will start with the *Parmenides*.

In order to provide an example of the method young Socrates should follow in investigating his own philosophical problems, Parmenides sets about to examine whether or not his idea of the existence of "the One" withholds tight scrutiny. To this effect, Parmenides engages in three main arguments. The first two concern the existence of the One, and the third its non-existence.

In the first argument Parmenides demonstrates that a true (simple) unity such as the One must not have parts and cannot be spatial or have place; can be neither in motion nor at rest; neither the same as or different from itself or anything else, nor equal to, greater or less than itself; as it is immeasurable it also cannot have anything whatsoever to do with Time; because it is not within Time and so neither comes to be nor passes away, we cannot even say that it *"is,"* therefore neither can it be the object of knowledge nor can it be spoken of.[21]

In the second argument Parmenides demonstrates the consequences of positing that the One as a truly simple unity does in fact exist or "have being." If this is so then the One is both like and unlike other things (the many) and itself; it both touches and does not touch itself and the many; it is at once equal to, greater than, and less than itself and the many; in respect to Time it is both becoming older and younger than itself at the same time as it neither becomes older nor younger than itself, and it would be both younger and older than the many and at once neither younger nor older than them.[22] Parmenides goes on to explain that in this case the One would undergo all of these transitions between seemingly contradictory conditions in a certain timeless "instant" (i.e. the moment) that always endures between and beyond the contradictory states. It is out from within and back into this instant "situated between the motion and the rest" that the One "passes from being in existence to ceasing to exist or from being nonexistent to coming into existence" and "from one to many or from many to one," etc...[23]

If the many were "parts" of "the whole" that is *the One*, the latter would bring *the many* into being through giving each thing its cohering unity by limiting (the being of) unlimitedness. Thus *the many* would come to be like each other in respect of their original unlimited nature but unlike each other in the contrary characteristics they are allowed to possess by each having a distinct unity from the others.[24] However, since no true "one" (i.e. — an irreducibly simple unity) can

---

21   Ibid., *Parmenides*: 137d–142a.

22   Ibid., 142b–155a.

23   Ibid., 156c–157b.

ever have "parts," the One and the Many are totally distinct. Thus the many's unlimitedness cannot be tamed by the coherence of unity and therefore "the many" cannot exist at all because for there to be two or three things, each of them has to first be *one* thing, but the simple nature of the One refuses the many participation in its quality of oneness.[25]

The point that Plato makes by juxtaposing these two arguments is that if we want to preserve the validity of the relative concepts by which we comprehend and judge the world, we cannot admit — either in thought or speech — that the One has being or *is*. For if we do admit that there *is* a One, then in light of its reality all that seems evidently true and logical of our world is in fact reduced to an unreal illusion.

The dialogue now goes on to examine the consequences of denying that the One *is*. Before doing so Parmenides makes clear that by saying the One "is-not" we mean that it *is* (has Being) in no way whatsoever (and not that it is in one way but not in another).[26] In that case it will be as void of measure, without quality and impossible to think on or discourse over, as the One was shown to be according to the first argument above. In consequence it would seem that since the many could not partake of its unity because it exists in no way at all, everything in the world — while appearing to be distinct — will on closer examination collapse into infinite divisibility.[27] Parmenides then corrects himself to say that in fact the situation would be still more dire than this, because even a semblance of a "many" is inconceivable without there being a *One*. So if the One is not, then everything else is also *no-thing*.[28] Plato concludes the dialogue with these words from

25 Ibid., 159c–160b.

26 Ibid., 163c.

27 Ibid., 164d–165c.

the mouth of Parmenides: "Thus in sum, we may conclude, if there is no one, there is nothing at all."[29]

In the conclusion of this dialogue we see the problem that Parmenides' philosophy must have posed for Plato. He has tremendous, even "awful," reverence for Parmenides and explicitly says so himself through the mouth of Socrates on several occasions in his dialogues. He follows Parmenides in his idealist reaction against Heracliteanism by using the power of the mind over and against the senses. However, he is not satisfied with Parmenides' stark insistence that there is either Being, conceived of as Oneness without distinction, or utter Nothingness. Plato needs to find some way of accounting for the semblance of the world of Becoming while still subjugating it to an ideal realm of Being so as to secure the possibility of rational knowledge. Though many scholars allege that the *Sophist* is one of Plato's later dialogues, within it Plato portrays what must have been the first step on his way to the Theory of Forms by reinterpreting the meaning of Nothingness in Parmenides.

The dramatic context of *The Sophist* is that Socrates and a couple of friends are acquainted with a "stranger" from Elea who belongs to Parmenides and Zeno's school. Together with this "stranger" Socrates and friends, mainly Theaetetus, seek to discover the nature of the practitioners of sophistry and deceptive rhetoric that were often hired by the wealthy of Athens — especially as tutors for their children or as legal counsel. This allows Plato to once again vent his contempt for a traditional enemy of his project. The main argument of the dialogue begins when Parmenides' claim that "*what-is-not* never *is*" is stated and there is a proposal to investigate its truth. Socrates asks for the concrete signified of the signifier "that which is not." The "stranger" explains that this cannot be "something," so a person who talks about it is not really saying anything at all. One could say that it is even "unthinkable." In light of this the dialogue's own pursuit seems self-contradictory.[30] Semblances are offered as a compelling example suggesting that what-is-not has some sort of being.

It is at this point that Plato makes explicit his chief concern, which as in his attacks on Heracliteanism, is to secure the possibility of rational knowledge. The participants realize that if any judgment or statement can ever be false then it must be possible to think things that are not; therefore if "not-being" never "is," no statement is ever false. Through the Eleatic "stranger" Plato argues that in order to overcome this crisis of knowledge, revered Parmenides' claim that "not-being" never "is," must be challenged.[31] Plato reiterates this in terms explicitly relevant to our concerns when he has the stranger explain that if "reality" were either totally changeless as Parmenides holds, or everchanging as the Heracliteans hold, in both cases "intelligence" [i.e., rational knowledge] would be impossible.[32]

Plato goes about challenging Parmenides' claim by explaining that when we say "something is *not* such-and-such" the negation does not refer to non-existence but only to something in existence other than what follows the "not." Certainly, in this sense "what-is-not" can still *be*. Through the "stranger" Plato then goes on to claim that this refutes Parmenides' statement that: "Never shall this be proved, that what-is-not *is*, restrain yourself from this way of inquiry."[33] Plato interprets "that which is not" merely as the part of "that which is" that is not presently indicated in, or is bracketed off by, any given statement.[34] Then he explicitly addresses the more profound interpretation of "what-is-not" (i.e. as Nothingness) by reaffirming his previous dismissal of it on the ground of its being inconceivable:

---

30 Ibid., *Sophist*: 237b–238c–d.

31 Ibid., 240–241.

32 Ibid., 249b–d.

33 Ibid., 257b–258d.

Then let no one say that it is the contrary of the existent that we mean by
'what is not,' when we make bold to say that 'what is not' exists. So far as
any contrary of the existent is concerned, we have long ago [in 237e–238d
above] said good-bye to the question whether there is such a thing or not
and whether any account can be given of it or none whatsoever.[35]

The dialogue then concludes with Plato's salvation of knowledge based
upon this reinterpretation of "what-is-not." The "stranger" explains
that since words, like forms, can and cannot be combined in various
ways, true *and false* statements exist and the false statement will be
something different from what presently is indicated, but something
that nevertheless has existence.[36] Since thinking is just like discourse
but in silence, there can in the same way be false perception and
judgment.[37]

The answer that the *Sophist* gives to the problem posed in the
Parmenides must make us question Plato's appropriation of both
Heraclitus and Parmenides. Plato invents the personage of a "stranger"
who belongs to Parmenides' Eleatic school in order to "authoritatively"
reinterpret what Parmenides meant by "Nothingness" in *The Way of
Truth*. In the same breath as this superficial reinterpretation of "not-
being," Plato for the first time explicitly vanquishes the contemplation
of true Nothingness from the discourse in Western Philosophy. Yet the
dilemma of "either Being or Nothingness" could have been resolved
by understanding Being and Nothingness to be reciprocally necessary
manifestations of each other, whose contradiction is resolved in the
realm of Becoming. The metaphysics of Heraclitus arises out of just
such an abyssal understanding. Is it possible that Plato did not really
understand Heraclitus? In his *Metaphysics*, Aristotle tells us the following about the young Plato's Heraclitean teacher, Cratylus:

---

35   Ibid., 258e–259a.
36   Ibid., 261–263d.

[T]hey observed that all nature around us undergoes change and held that one cannot speak the truth about that which is undergoing change. So *a fortiori* nothing true could be said about what was changing at all points in all ways. ... This is the position of those who appropriated the legacy of Heraclitus, notably of Cratylus. His mature position was that speech of any kind was radically inappropriate and that expression should be restricted exclusively to the movement of the finger. He was appalled that Heraclitus had claimed that you could not step *twice* into the same river. In his, Cratylus,' opinion it was already going too far to admit stepping into the *same* river *once*.[38]

Could it be that Plato was misled by Cratylus' shallow Neo-Heracliteanism into a false interpretation of Heraclitus? Does he fail to understand that Heraclitus concerns himself with the contradictions of Becoming only as a manifestation of the harmony of Being and Nothingness that lies beyond them? That many of the Heraclitean passages in Plato's dialogues (which were cited above) emphasize Becoming to the detriment of Being, and that Plato sometimes uses this as a means of discrediting the Heracliteans, seems to suggest that he might have made such a mistake. If so, it may be the greatest "mistake" in the history of thought, one with the most disastrous consequences. However, other of Plato's Heraclitean passages suggest a more profound understanding of Heraclitus and at one point "Socrates" even cautions Theodorus from making the superficial assessment of the Heracliteans which Plato himself sometimes seems to make.[39] Passages like these, taken together with Plato's evident brilliance as a thinker and the fact that, though he had Cratylus for a guide in his Heraclitean period, he must have read Heraclitus for himself, would suggest that Plato intentionally distorts or reinterprets the meaning of Becoming in Heraclitus, as he does the meaning of Nothingness in Parmenides.

---

38 Aristotle, *The Complete Works of Aristotle, Metaphysics*: Gamma, 1010a.

Parmenides' idealism, reinterpreted and appropriated by Plato, lies at the heart of the latter's metaphysics as we find it in the dialogue *Timaeus*. Here we see once again the dichotomy between an ideal realm of perfection and a chaotic realm of formless matter, which we are left with in the *Parmenides*. On the one hand there are the eternal Forms or Ideas (*eidos*). Here they are presented as perfect concepts, such as that of a perfect circle, or perfect square, or perfect fast or slow or perfect heaviness, heat or cold. These concepts are not imagined, they are not mental "images" and thus they have no characteristics or qualities. Rather, each perfect form is one given quality in its absolute. In other words, the perfect circle is not a round image nor is the concept of perfect heaviness *heavy*. For the purposes of the *Timaeus*, "Perfection" means *final, absolute*, and thus also unchanging. Since these forms are unchanging they are constant, timeless and eternal — they have always existed. Furthermore one must not imagine them to exist in any "place," for example above the physical plane. Instead the forms exist within themselves. On the other hand there is the material substance: absolute physicality with no form whatsoever. It is pure matter in a state of total chaos and is devoid of any characteristics, or perhaps more accurately, it represents all characteristics without giving dominance to any one over another so that it may be individually distinguishable. Due to such complete consistency in this Matter we can say that it is as absolute as the perfect forms, which would make it equally eternal as well.

However, this chasm between ideal and material, which we are left with in the *Parmenides*, is bridged by altering the nature of the ideal from one of unity to one of plurality. Plato describes all of his forms in the very same terms as Parmenides describes "the One": within-itself, simple, immaterial (non-spatial), unchanging and timeless. Yet now there is an ideal for every quality that exists within the material world. This preserves the Parmenidian dismissal of the world as illusory and corrupt, but at the same time it opens a way between the sensual and ideal realms. Plato envisions this new "space" between them as a "receptacle," a metaphorical vacuum of emptiness that may be the necessity of being. Matter cannot simply fill this necessity on its own because due to its absolute nature it is as non-becoming as forms, yet it has or is the ultimate potential to become. The forms alone cannot fill this void either because of course they are also absolute in nature. Thus the void of "space" as a matter of principle (or what Plato calls a "god") lends itself to the shaping of Matter according to the design of the Eternal Forms such that this very crafting can serve as the Becoming, the change, that will fulfill the receptacle's need for material existence. In this crafting, and the resulting dual realm of part-form/part-substance, there is not one form for every entity. Rather, diverse forms to various degrees have some stake in the composition or form-ation of each entity.

Thus in Platonism, as it has been scholastically understood by academics for centuries, though the ultimate reality is not our immediate experience, it can become our experience. This follows from the fact that our "shadow" world (the immediate data of consciousness) is in part from, or of, the eternal forms — and thus so too are we. The basic scholastic interpretation has it that Plato believed that reason is put into the soul which is put into the body, and that the "soul," the place where our material substance meets with the "forms," is tainted by this contact with matter, while the reason within the soul is always perfectly pure and of the eternal forms. Thus we have a dual-nature in which there is a pathway to the eternal forms through the use of the reason within us, in leading what Plato calls "the philosophic life."

This enterprise consists of using our rational faculties in the constant pursuit of the perfect forms through analysis of their reflections in the immediate data of consciousness and through persistent reasoning so as not to be deceived by the delusion of the senses. To questioningly scrutinize the objects in physical reality is possible because the reason within us is of the *Logos* — the prime matrix of Logic — just as the forms are, and so it is in a way at the same time to descend stage by stage to the innermost depth of what is within oneself and is one's own source and end.

In his *Way of Truth* Parmenides had demanded: "In order to attain truth, one should not follow stupid eyes, nor with ringing ears or the tongue, but rather one must grasp with the power of thought." However, his utter rejection of our world's existence and his insistence that there is either the One Being or Nothing, made it difficult to find a way to an ideal reality so different from our own. By finding a means to explain the supposed delusion of the sensuous realm, Plato made it possible to look through the world's shadows and into the forms instead of simply closing one's eyes to the world altogether. Or so it would seem.

3. PLATO'S NAUSEA OVER AN ESOTERIC PARRICIDE

Plato's treatment of Parmenides' doctrine in the *Sophist* is the crescendo of Jacques Derrida's essay entitled "Plato's Pharmacy."[40] Derrida notes that Plato regards Parmenides as an authoritative father figure, just as he does Atum in the *Phaedrus* myth of the invention of writing by Thoth (Hermes). However, in the *Sophist* Theaetetus and the Stranger agree that they must "now dare to lay unfilial hands on that paternal pronouncement" of "father Parmenides."[41] This "paternal pronouncement" is of course Parmenides' demand, in his *Way of Truth*, that anything but the pure unity of Being is to be considered totally non-existent. Derrida calls Plato's violation of this injunction (in order to admit a realm of shadows that partakes of both Truth & Untruth, Being & Non-Being) a "parricide" (murder of one's father). He writes:

40 Jacques Derrida, "Plato's Pharmacy" in *Dissemination* (Chicago: University of Chicago Press, 1981).

[W]hat the parricide in the *Sophist* establishes is not only that any *full*, *absolute* presence of what *is* (of the being-present that most truly 'is': the good or the sun that can't be looked in the face) is impossible; not only that any full intuition of truth, any truth-filled intuition, is impossible; but that the very condition of discourse — *true or false* — is the diacritical principle of the *sumploke*. If truth is the presence of the *eidos*, it must always, on pain of mortal blinding by the sun's fires, come to terms with relation, nonpresence, and thus nontruth.[42]

As Derrida realizes, once Plato allows the realm of pure Being in which the forms reside to mix with base and chaotic matter in the receptacle of space, thereby giving rise to our mediate "world of shadows," he can no longer logically privilege Being over Becoming, presence over withdrawal, the world of forms over our sensual world. For Plato Being *needs* Becoming, otherwise he would have had no need to allow the formless chaos of non-being to play a role in explaining the transient world of human experience. He could have simply rejected the latter altogether in one grand gesture of transcendence, as Parmenides had done. Instead, he subjugates the ideal Being of the world of forms to the transient Becoming of the sensuous world, upon which it is logically dependent. Plato could not have been unaware of the consequences of this conflation. This is why in the *Sophist* he repeatedly emphasizes the treachery involved in violating Parmenides' injunction and why he explicitly invites the comparison of this philosophical violation to a parricide, the most heinous crime in Greek society. Parmenides is not the only fatality; Plato murders Being itself in its transcendent isolation as The Father.[43]

The doctrine that Plato presents in his dialogues invites its own reversal. We should not be surprised that Plato neither writes about the moment of reversal itself, nor explains what may lie beyond it, for in the *Seventh Letter* he issues this warning:

---

42 Derrida, "Plato's Pharmacy," 166.

[T]his much at any rate I can affirm about any present or future writers who pretend to knowledge of the matters with which I concern myself, whether they claim to have been taught by me or by a third party or to have discovered the truth for themselves; in my judgment it is impossible that they should have any understanding of the subject. No treatise by me concerning it exists or ever will exist. …

If I thought that any adequate spoken or written account could be given to the world at large, what more glorious life-work could I have undertaken than to put into writing what would be of great benefit to mankind and to bring the nature of reality to light for all to see? But I do not think that the attempt to put these matters into words would be to men's advantage, except to those few who can find out the truth for themselves with a little guidance. …

That is why any student of serious realities will shrink from making truth the helpless object of men's ill-will by committing it to writing. In a word, the conclusion to be drawn is this; when one sees a written composition, whether it be on law by a legislator or on any other subject, one can be sure, if the writer is a serious man, that his book does not represent his most serious thoughts; they remain stored up in the noblest region of his personality.[44]

Plato reiterates this shocking revelation at the close of his *Second Letter* to Dionysus of Syracuse, the tyrant whom he attempted to manipulate into actualizing a Neo-Pythagorean utopian political project along the lines of *Republic* or the *Laws*. Derrida quotes this passage as the ominous conclusion of his critique in "Plato's Pharmacy":

Take precautions lest this teaching ever be disclosed among untrained people. … It is impossible for what is written not to be disclosed. That is the reason why I have never written anything about these things, and why there is not and will not be any written work of Plato's own. … Farewell and believe. Read this letter now at once many times and burn it.[45]

---

44 Ibid., *Seventh Letter*: 341–; 344.

So it seems that no forthright and literal expression of Plato's true doctrine is to be found in the corpus of his writings that has been handed down to us. Instead, we are left to search the dialogues for traces of it. This is why the speaker is always Socrates or some other straw man, and Plato does not so much as even mention his own name in these texts — *except* on two *very significant* occasions. The first is Socrates' defense of his way of life when he stands trial and is ultimately sentenced to death in the *Apology*. The second is his discourse on the immortality of the soul as he awaits death in the *Phaedo*, and it is to this that I will now turn, as if following traces of blood that lead to the scene of Plato's unfilial crime against the Being of "father Parmenides."

The only way that Plato could in some way preserve the aloof utter ineffability of the ideal realm of Parmenides' One, once he has allowed the forms and matter to touch in the receptacle and without making any concessions to Becoming, is to defer the experience of perfection — devoid of all physicality — to a place and time beyond death. In the *Phaedo*, Socrates argues that by leading a life of using one's inner and inherent reason, one stays a longer and longer time in the realm of ultimate reality between the deaths and rebirths of a purifying process of reincarnation. This results in "recollection," the phenomenon in which people look at an imperfect circle, a shadow or semblance in the physical world, and somehow *know* that it is imperfect, implying they *know* of a perfect circle though they have never seen one. Through this process one còmes closer and closer to leading the perfect philosophic life each time one is reborn until finally one evolves to the point where upon death one's soul is freed from substance (the body, senses and phenomenal world) altogether, to directly experience the ultimate reality of eternal forms. While living one should try to assimilate this ideal immaterial state as much as possible, by withdrawing within oneself and using the mind to transcend the body.

In the *Phaedo*, which stands within Plato's corpus as the crucifixion stands within the *New Testament*, Plato writes:

> Surely the soul can reason best when it is free of all distractions such as hearing or sight or pain or pleasure of any kind — that is, when it leaves the body to its own devices, becomes as isolated as possible, and strives for reality while avoiding as much physical contact and association as it can....
>
> Don't you think that the person who is most likely to achieve [knowledge] flawlessly is the one who approaches each object, as far as possible, *with the unaided intellect, without taking account of any sense of sight in his thinking, or dragging any other sense into his reckoning* — the man who pursues the truth by applying his pure and unadulterated thought to the pure and unadulterated object, cutting himself off as much as possible from his eyes and ears and virtually all the rest of his body, as an impediment which, if present, prevents the soul from attaining to the truth and clear thinking? Is not this the person ... who will reach the goal of reality, if anybody can? [46]

In the drama of the *Phaedo*, Plato's Socrates welcomes his death because he claims to believe it is only in an ideal realm free of the mortal coil that true knowledge is possible:

> If no pure knowledge is possible in the company of the body, then either it is totally impossible to acquire knowledge, or it is only possible after death, because it is only then that the soul will be isolated and independent of the body.
>
> [H]e will never attain to wisdom worthy of the name elsewhere than in the next world.... [47]

Yet at the outset of the dialogue, when Phaedo is recounting all of those who were present at the execution he says the following:

> Echecrates: Who were actually there, Phaedo?
>
> Phaedo: Why, of the Athenians there were this man Apollodorus, and Critobulus and his father, and then there were Hermogenes and Epigenes

---

46 Ibid., *Phaedo*: 65c–66a

and Aeschines and Antisthenes. Oh yes, and Ctesipus of Paeanis, and Menexenus, and some other local people. I believe that Plato was ill.[48]

"...I believe that Plato was ill." It is likely that no author has ever written, nor ever will write, with such outstanding wit and such masterfully subtle irony. Unless Plato was on his own deathbed, nothing would have stopped him from attending the execution of his teacher, the teacher of whom he was the brightest and most beloved disciple. Nor is Plato merely saying this to write himself out of a scene that he is expected to have been present at in order to preserve his distance from his dialogues. Except for the case in the *Apology*, where establishing his presence is key to lending credibility to his "transcript" of the trial proceedings that led up to the death sentence, Plato never mentions his presence or absence in any of Socrates' conversations. He allows it to be tacitly assumed that he was there while at the same time excusing himself from being responsible for giving a literal account. Yet here he goes to the extent of naming all those who were present and explicitly excluding himself. Oh and by the way "...I believe that Plato was ill." What an outrageously nonchalant and matter-of-fact tone! Plato is bending over backwards to get us to read those preposterous words over and over again, because he knows that we know damn well that he was there. Those words *must mean something else — they must constitute some tremendous hint.* I believe that Plato means to say that he was *nauseated.*

Why? Because here is Socrates, Plato's beloved teacher, on the verge of a tragically unjust death and he is surrounded by his disciples as if by frightened children. Cebes himself says to Socrates: "Probably even in us there is a little boy who has these childish terrors. Try to persuade him not to be afraid of death as though it were a bogey."[49] Like a father who must force a smile and cheer up in the face of adversity so as to allay the fear of his children, Socrates tells his disciples:

---

48 Ibid.

If I did not expect to enter the company, first, of other wise and good gods, and secondly of men now dead who are better than those who are in this world now, it is true that it would be unjust for me not to grieve at death. As it is, *you can be assured* that I expect to find myself among good men; *while I would not particularly insist on this, I assure you* that I *could* commit myself upon [this] point *if I could upon anything…*[50]

…This makes Plato sick. Whereas Socrates clearly states that if pure intellection in the absence of embodiment and sensory mediation is not possible after death then rational knowledge is not possible at all, here he is contradictorily describing the state after death as one experienced by means of what the Greeks called a *soma pneumatikon* or spectral body — which is a "sensory" medium of experience even if not a material one. Very tangible agonies and mundane pleasures are experienced by means of it, so that pure intellection appears elusive even after death and before rebirth. In the *Republic* Plato elaborates on this view, which he inherited from the esoteric Pythagorean Order of which he was a member. Although Plato's belief in reincarnation is set forth in several other texts as well, it is in the story of Er the son of Armenius from 614b–621d of the *Republic* that we are presented with his most extensive treatment of the subject. In fact, its importance cannot be overemphasized since Plato chooses to bring the entire text of the *Republic* to its culmination and closure with this very tale.

Er is a soldier to whom it is given to have a Near Death Experience, with total recall, so that he may inform the living of what transpires after death. He bears witness to the process that finds its Eastern analogue in the *bardo* state described most famously in the *Tibetan Book of the Dead*.[51] As in the Eastern version, there are heavenly realms where souls enjoy extraordinarily pleasant experiences and hellish underworld realms where they are subjected to all manner of terrifying visions and torturous trials, but neither of these states

---

50 Ibid., 63c, my emphasis.

51 W.Y. Evans-Wentz, *The Tibetan Book of the Dead* (New York: Oxford University

is permanent. The souls of the deceased ultimately choose their next lives, and whether these are honorable and rewarding lives or whether they are miserable and violent ones is determined on the basis of how consciously and deliberatively they are able to make their choice.

It sometimes happens that those who have spent a long time in the heaven realms on account of having lived a good previous life become complacent and unconsciously choose a terrible subsequent life. They fail to look deeply enough into a vision of it so as to see beyond the thrills that shimmer on its surface. Sometimes those who have just come from tribulations in the hellish underworld have had the awareness to choose more soberly beaten into them. The extent to which a soul's awareness has been cultivated correlates to how much of its previous lives will be forgotten and how much it will be able to instructively remember so as not to repeat prior mistakes. Each must drink a measure from the river *Lethe* while in the netherworld, but those who are undisciplined find it sweet and gulp down a great deal more. In other words, the cycle of experiences that progressively purifies the soul until it becomes that of a philosopher is a very long one, and there may be many regresses where what appear to be good men suffer a great fall, perhaps even to the level of being reborn as an animal, and have to work their way up again. So, while Socrates might be somewhat confident that he will fare well after drinking the hemlock, the reassurances that he gives to his fearful disciples in *Phaedo* are most certainly soothing lies. Consider the implications of this realization given that Socrates seals this consolation with the claim that he is as sure of it as he is or ever was of anything. The full import of these words will be drawn out only as I conclude this essay.

Finally, it is worth noting that Plato's views on the equality of women to men may be bound up with the fact that, as Er recounts, not only can women choose rebirth as men but the souls of eminent men sometimes reincarnate as women. This would, in fact, have to be the case for there to be female philosophers, since the philosophic soul is the most perfected and it could have freely chosen its sex. The soul still has a sex and indeed may have hellish or heavenly sexual experiences by means of the *soma pneumatikon*, both in the state between lives and even once it is perfected and chooses the life of a philosopher whose highest calling is to serve as a republican Guardian. This further emphasizes how profoundly Plato's whole afterlife scheme undermines the idea of the kind of enduring airtight intellectual isolation from sensory experience that Socrates claims would be required to definitively demonstrate the possibility of perfectly rational knowledge.

The tale of Er is not the only part of *Republic* that undermines this core tenant of exoteric academic Platonism. The following passages of the *Republic*[52] on the idea of the Good — the form of forms — are also relevant, so much so that they deserve to be quoted at length; they are perhaps the key to unlocking Plato's unwritten doctrine:

> The good, then, is the end of all endeavor, the object on which every heart is set, whose existence it divines, though it finds it difficult to grasp just what it is. …

> 'We shall be quite satisfied if you give an account of the good similar to that you gave of justice and self-control and the rest.'

> 'And so shall I too, my dear chap,' I replied, 'but I'm afraid it's beyond me, and if I try I shall only make a fool of myself and be laughed at. So please let us give up asking for the present what the good is in itself; I'm afraid that to reach what I think would be a satisfactory answer is beyond the range of our present inquiry. But I will tell you, if you like, about something which seems to me to be a child of the good, and to resemble it very closely — or would you rather I didn't?'

> 'Tell us about the child and you can owe us your account of the parent,' he said.

'It's a debt I wish I could pay back to you in full, instead of only paying interest on the loan,' I replied. 'But for the present you must accept my description of the child of the good as interest. ...

[T]hough the sun is not itself sight, it is the cause of sight and is seen by the sight it causes. ... 'Well, that is what I called the child of the good,' I said. 'The good has begotten it in its own likeness, and it bears the same relation to sight and visible objects in the visible realm that the good bears to intelligence and intelligible objects in the intelligible realm.'

...'Then what gives the objects of knowledge their truth and the knower's mind the power of knowing is the form of the good. It is the cause of knowledge and truth, and you will be right to think of it as being itself known, and yet as being something other than, and even more splendid than, knowledge and truth, splendid as they are. And just as it was right to think of light and sight as being like the sun, but wrong to think of them as being the sun itself, so here again it is right to think of knowledge and truth as being like the good, but wrong to think of either of them as being the good, whose position must be ranked still higher.'

...'The sun, I think you will agree, not only makes the things we see visible, but causes the processes of generation, growth and nourishment, without itself being such a process.' 'True.' 'The good therefore may be said to be source not only of the intelligibility of the objects of knowledge, but also of their being and reality; yet it is not itself that reality, but is beyond it, and superior to it in dignity and power.' 'It really must be miraculously transcendent,' remarked Glaucon...

Taken together these passages suggest the following. The "form of the good" is the Sun in light of which all of the other forms are illuminated. Yet it must in some way be fundamentally different from the other forms, because while Plato's Socrates can explain "justice," "beauty," etc... he *cannot* explain the "form of forms." While at first he feigns that this is simply due to lack of skill, he ultimately admits that an explanation of *the Good in-itself* will never be forthcoming because it is inherently impossible. We are told to content ourselves with the simile of the Sun, which suggests that the form of the Good is to the other forms in the intelligible realm as the Sun is to the objects of perception in the sensuous realm.

So far this is no great revelation — *but* let us now recall how the mixture of the forms and matter, Being and Non-Being, in the receptacle which gives rise to becoming, compromises the transcendent sanctity of the forms. If the division between the ideal and sensuous worlds collapses according to the logic of Plato's metaphysics, then the form of the Good becomes Heraclitus' never-setting Sun. Is it really an accident that this Heraclitean symbol lies at the heart of Plato's philosophy? Or does Plato choose to place it there as a sign that in him the Heraclitean vision of his youth has surreptitiously assimilated, encompassed and triumphed over Parmenides' idealist revolt? Let us read on from where we left off in the *Republic*:

> I think you know that students of geometry and calculation and the like begin by assuming there are odd and even numbers, geometrical figures and the three forms of angle, and other kindred items in their respective subjects; these they regard as known, having put them forward as basic assumptions which it is quite unnecessary to explain to themselves or anyone else on the grounds that they are obvious to everyone. Starting from them, they proceed through a series of consistent steps to the conclusion which they set out to find. ...

> You know too that they make use of and argue about visible figures, though they are not really thinking about them, but about the originals which they resemble; it is *not* about the square or diagonal which they have drawn that they are arguing, but about the square itself or diagonal itself, or whatever the figure may be. The actual figures they draw or model, which themselves cast their shadows and reflections in water — these they treat as images only, the real objects of their investigation being invisible except to the eye of reason. ...

> This type of thing I called intelligible, but said that the mind was forced to use assumptions in investigating it, and did not proceed to a first principle, being unable to depart from and rise above its assumptions; but it used as illustrations the very things which in turn have their images and shadows

on the lower level, in comparison with which they are themselves respected and valued for their clarity. ...

Then when I speak of the other sub-section of the intelligible part of the line you will understand that I mean that which the very process of argument grasps by the power of dialectic; it treats assumptions not as principles, but as assumptions in the true sense, that is, as starting points and steps in the ascent to something which involves no assumption and is the first principle of everything...[53]

In this analogy to geometry Plato equates physically drawn triangles or circles with the objects of the sensuous world, and the ideal geometric ratios and axioms upon which they are based with the ideal forms that together in-form sensuous objects. What is striking is that he calls even these unseen axioms and, by analogy, the ideal forms "assumptions." He criticizes geometers for not questioning these assumptions and contrasts them with the guardians who will use the forms to ascend to "the first principle of everything" — i.e. the form of the Good — *in light of which all of the other forms will be revealed as mere assumptions*, as so many "steps" in a ladder which can be thrown away once one has ascended by means of it — in a word: necessary *constructs*. Furthermore, knowledge of the "form of the Good" is not attained by accumulation — i.e. it is not a sum total of the knowledge of other forms. It is not the last step in a causal progression. It "involves no assumption," i.e. it is not constituted by the forms and thus is not located within their ideal realm. "Assumption" is intended negatively here, thus the forms are also. Only through their *negation* is the ineffable vision of the *Good* attained.

Plato's method of dialectic does not "produce" the truth as a proof. Rather, the clash of contrary reasons leads to an insight beyond them all — just as rocks or dry sticks rubbed together produce a spark and then a fire. Plato evokes this image in the *Seventh Letter*, where he writes:

> It is only when all these things, names and definitions, visual and other sensations are rubbed together and subjected to tests in which questions and answers are exchanged in good faith and without malice that finally, when human capacity is stretched to its limit, a spark of understanding and intelligence flashes out and illuminates the subject at issue...

> ...It ['the first principle of everything'] is not something that can be put into words like other branches of learning; only after long partnership in a common life [with others] devoted to this very thing does truth flash upon the soul, like a flame kindled by a leaping spark, and once it is born there it nourishes itself thereafter.[54]

Dialectic is a means of stretching reason to its limits, of straining and then breaking the mind open so that the truth can "flash upon the soul" like sparks from the Heraclitean cosmic fire. The forms are constructs employed to attain this peak experience. Yet it is not only the mind that requires attunement. The body and its "visual and other sensations" must also be "rubbed together" and "subjected to tests in which... in good faith and without malice... it is stretched to its limit" in "a common life [with others] devoted to this very [same] thing." This is why, from a young age, men and women who are to be Guardians must train together to become excellent artists,[55] great athletes, brave warriors, and above all, divine lovers.

4. *EROSOPHIA* AND THE BIRTH OF A NEW *ART*

For Plato, a philosopher must always be a lover, not only in the abstract sense implied by the word *philosophia*, but in a thoroughly erotic sense. In the *Phaedrus*, we see why to be a lover must be an even more important prerequisite for philosophy than to be an artist, athlete or warrior. Socrates explains to Phaedrus that because "sight is the keenest of our physical senses" Beauty is the best form to seek

---

54   Ibid., *Seventh Letter*: 344; 341.

in order to attain the entire realm of forms, since it is the most seduc-
tive. The reflection of Beauty in the sensuous realm leads to its ideal
form more surely than that of any other form.[56] Plato's Socrates goes
on to equate this erotic seduction to transcendence with a kind of
divine madness, without which complete understanding can never be
attained. Reproaching Phaedrus for having condemned the lover for
being mad, Socrates says:

> If it were true without qualification that madness is an evil, that would be
> all very well, but in fact madness, provided it comes as the gift of heaven,
> is the channel by which we receive the greatest blessings. ... [M]adness
> comes from God, whereas sober sense is merely human.[57]

In the Greek society of Plato's time erotic madness was epitomized
by the cult of Dionysus. Opposed to this stood Apollo, the shining
god of reason and order, whose Delphic injunction Socrates evokes
on many occasions. In *The Birth of Tragedy*, Friedrich Nietzsche sees
the Apollonian as a lucid dream-like rational simplicity of crystalline forms that abides by logic and is the sustainer of individuation.[58]
Nietzsche takes the Olympian pantheon as a whole to be a manifestation of this essence of the god Apollo, while the god excluded from
membership to this pantheon, Dionysus, is the symbol through which
the Greeks comprehended the true nature of the world. Nietzsche
sees the Apollonian as a veil of illusion that guards the ego against the
chaos of reality as it is glimpsed in Dionysian intoxication.

Nietzsche argues that great art and culture are dependent upon
the continual strife and subtle interdependence of the Apollonian
and Dionysian. He sees Homeric epic and the classical sculpture
that embodied its scenes as Apollonian art, and lyric poetry and the
music that inspired it as Dionysian art. The strife between these two

---

56 Ibid., *Phaedrus*: 250.

57 Ibid., 244.

58 Nietzsche, Friedrich (1995) *The Birth of Tragedy* (New York: Dover

was reconciled into a tense and sublime harmony in the tragedies of Aeschylus and Sophocles, as well as the early Pre-Platonic philosophers such as Heraclitus who sought to evoke a life-affirming Dionysian vision through Apollonian forms and imagery. Yet Nietzsche sees philosophy from Parmenides onwards, and drama in the wake of the tragic playwright Euripides, as a progressive suppression of Dionysian vitality in favor of purely Apollonian rationalism. Most importantly, *Nietzsche identifies "Socrates" as the culmination of the decay of the Greek spirit due to a withering of the Dionysian.* The interpretation of Plato being forwarded here challenges this Nietzschean interpretation of Plato as valuing Apollonian rationalism over Dionysian erotic madness.

At first glance it seems that in the dialogue *Alcibiades* we find a confirmation of Nietzsche's interpretation. It is in this dialogue that Socrates refers explicitly to the Delphic injunction of the god Apollo: "Know Thyself," the injunction of the divinity whose oracle Socrates devotes his life to proving true and the god associated with the demonic voice that keeps him on the straight and narrow path. On the surface it also seems that we are presented with a fine example of Plato's quintessentially Apollonian method of dialectic (questions and answers which seek to expose contradictions and arrive at logical definitions of the terms involved in a given question). However, the same Alcibiades who is mercilessly subjected to this rational method in the dialogue by his name goes on to ecstatically describe Socrates and his philosophy in the most vividly Dionysian terms throughout his eulogy in the dialogue *Symposium.*

Alcibiades tells us how Socrates is like certain statues of sileni with pipes and such, with doors that open at the stomach and have miniature statuettes of the Olympian gods inside.[59] Socrates not only literally bears a physical resemblance to these figures but, according to Alcibiades, he also has the same spirit as them. Just as all who learn the satyr Marsyas' flute tunes and repeat them have a magical effect on their listeners, so also not only do those who listen directly to Socrates experience a Dionysian madness but even those who listen to second-hand accounts of his discourses. These discourses have a profound ability to move listeners to tears, and they even make the toughest-skinned or thickest-skulled people, like Alcibiades himself, feel ashamed. Thus Alcibiades spends his life running away from Socrates, so that he can carry on with the politics of pandering to the mob, only to feel heart-rending shame when he once again happens to come face to face with the master. This makes Alcibiades wish Socrates dead and yet at the same time he realizes that if his wish came true, he would really be devastated. In the course of his eulogy, Alcibiades utters these extraordinary words, in which he compares being passionately seized by Socrates' philosophy to being bitten by a poisonous snake and suffering from a kind of Dionysian madness:

> [W]hen a man's been bitten by a *snake* he won't tell anybody what it feels like except a fellow sufferer, because no one else would sympathize with him if the pain drove him into making a *fool* of himself. ... I've been bitten by something much more *poisonous* ... bitten in the heart, or the mind, or whatever you like to call it, by Socrates' philosophy, which clings like an adder to any young and gifted mind it can get hold of, and does exactly what it likes with it. ... [E]very one of you has had his taste of this *philosophical frenzy*, this *sacred rage*...[60]

The sileni and the satyr Marsyas were bearded, half-human, half-goatlike beings with huge phalluses and tails, who on the one hand acted like fools, and on the other like sages pronouncing dark oracular sayings. They formed one of two groups of Dionysus' companions. Members of the other group were the maenads, women who held serpents and staffs entwined with poison ivy in their hands and wore wreath-crowns. Both maenads and sileni played enchanting flute melodies. Nietzsche sees them as a symbol of what is still animal in man, a primal and erotic nature masked by reason and wrought through and through with contradiction. In the mystery rites of the Dionysian cults, by means of intoxication male and female initiates were to be transfigured into dancing Maenads and sileni/satyrs, and thereby symbolically enter into the company of their god. This "companionship" would mean a painfully blissful vision of the chaotic oneness of reality beyond the illusory individuation of beings. From the moment that Plato has Alcibiades enter the symposium, with flute girls and a train of revelers, the dialogue abounds in Dionysian imagery. The latter is not contrasted with Socrates, as one might expect. Rather, through Alcibiades' eulogy, Plato turns Socrates into the Dionysian divinity which the Maenad (flute girl), sileni (the revelers) and the satyr (Alcibiades) have come to dance around, crown with a wreath, and reverently praise.

Toward the end of his eulogy Alcibiades goes so far as to explain how Socrates' arguments also resemble the statues of sileni. On the outside they seem gaudy and ridiculous, encased in the language of horse trainers, blacksmiths and so on, and they all also seem the same to careless observers. However, when one "opens them up" one sees brilliant divinities inside — which Alcibiades is probably using as a metaphor for the Platonic "forms" "that help the seeker on his way to the goal of true nobility." Bearing this in mind, let us look back at Socrates' argument about the "just" and "advantageous" in *Alcibiades*.

At the beginning of the dialogue Socrates argues that if Alcibiades intends to convince many people in the assembly of his position then he should be just as able to persuade each of them individually, and Alcibiades agrees. Thus Socrates tells him to think of the proof of his claim that sometimes the "just" is not "advantageous" as an exercise to prepare him for convincing assembly members. After some reluctance, Alcibiades finally agrees to proceed by answering Socrates' questions. Beneath the surface of this seemingly benign encouragement, Socrates is actually mocking Alcibiades. Socrates probably believes that dazzling and swaying a mob into supporting one's position involves, or should involve, very different means than convincing an individual — unless the given individual has a mob-mentality and cannot use a one-on-one encounter to rationally question and examine the orator. Yet never in the course of the entire dialogue does Socrates point this error out to Alcibiades. It remains an inside joke. In *Symposium* Alcibiades takes irony of this kind as a hint of Socrates' insincerity — it is his way of condescendingly laughing at the whole world like a satyr.[61]

We have a much more serious example of trickery when Socrates asks whether Alcibiades would say that some just things are "admirable" while others are not, and has Alcibiades agree to this by defining the admirable as the opposite of what is "contemptible." It is only because Socrates demands that just things either be totally admirable or really contemptible that Alcibiades goes along with him on this point. This polar division is quite superficial and artificial, even on Plato's terms. Socrates now asks whether all admirable things are "good" and Alcibiades responds that some are "bad." He asks Alcibiades whether in making this assertion, he has in mind a case where, for example, someone does the admirable deed of trying to rescue friends or relatives in a battle but this has the bad result that the rescuer is wounded or killed. Once Alcibiades accepts that this is an appropriate example, Socrates has him agree that cowardice is as bad or worse than death, while living a courageous life is its opposite. These opposites cannot logically "touch" and so something admirable can only be good in so far as it is admirable and bad in so far as it is contemptible. This point, as it stands, seems to be logically flawed on Plato's own terms. If opposites really cannot come into contact with each other, then a just action cannot be both admirable and good in one sense and contemptible and bad in another completely distinct sense.

Socrates now finishes off Alcibiades by asking whether people who do what is admirable do things "well" and consequently live successful lives in the sense that they receive good "things" for their proper behavior. Needless to say, just because an action is admirable, perhaps for its intention, it certainly does not always follow that it is executed "well." Furthermore even well-executed actions of this kind are often (even *usually*) admired but not rewarded with "good things." Nonetheless, Alcibiades agrees that good conduct is both admirable and advantageous. Socrates then states that all "just things are advantageous" and it would be laughable to try and persuade an assembly otherwise. This last conclusion rests on the assumption that all just things are "good," a point that is never explicitly proven or even discussed in the dialogue. Nonetheless, Alcibiades agrees with Socrates' conclusion and exclaims in exasperation and bewilderment:

> I swear by the gods, Socrates, I have no idea what I mean—I must be in some absolutely bizarre condition! When you ask me questions, first I think one thing and then I think something else.[62]

This is just the kind of "acting like a *fool*" that Alcibiades retrospectively describes as the first symptom of being poisonously intoxicated by Socrates' philosophy.

The point is that the flaws of logic in Socrates' "argument" in *Alcibiades* are so serious and so numerous that when we consider them in light of Alcibiades' eulogy in *Symposium* it is grounds for the suspicion that Plato did actually intend Socrates to be some sort of satyr who intoxicates with his flute tunes rather than soberly convincing people with benignly rational arguments. In this case the flaws in the dialogue *Alcibiades,* as well as its dramatic linkage to the latter's eulogy of Socrates in *Symposium*, would be intentional devices employed by Plato as a means of providing a key to unlock the innermost chamber of his philosophy.

The Dionysian is an erotic energy or vision and in *Symposium* Socrates claims that "*eros* is the one thing in the world I understand"[63] and "*eros* will help our mortal nature more than all the world ... this is why I cultivate and worship ... [it] ... and bid others do the same."[64] Alcibiades says that only drunkards tell the truth.[65] We could take this as a hint from Plato that only in the Dionysian intoxication of the dialogue *Symposium*, particularly in Alcibiades' eulogy, will the whole truth about his philosophy be revealed. In light of this hint, and Socrates' own admission that *eros* is all he understands and teaches, we might reasonably assume that the wisdom unveiled by the enchanting lady Diotima is the closest we come to a revelation of Plato's own esoteric understanding.

She teaches Socrates that one must fall in love with the beauty of one body, then compare it to others and see that, as the love is for the bodily form, one should love *all* people with beautiful bodies and account any given one of little importance. This should ultimately lead to one being drawn to the beauty of a soul, even if in an ugly body — perhaps because the fascination with physical beauty is satiated through one's abandonment to all its abundance. This love will foster nobility in one's thoughts and words, provoking contemplation of the beauty of abstractions like laws and institutions. From here one will go on to love the beauty of knowledge and the sciences that lead to it and from this perspective one will see the narrowness of all other beauties, especially bodily love of one person. Then one stands on the threshold of ultimate Beauty-in-itself:

> [A]n everlasting loveliness which neither comes nor goes, which neither flowers nor fades, for such beauty is the same on every hand, the same then as now, here as there, this way as that way, the same to every worshipper as it is to every other. Nor will his vision of the beautiful take the form

---

63 Ibid., 177e.
64 Ibid., 212 b–c.

of a face, or of hands, or of anything that is of the flesh. It will be neither words, nor knowledge, nor something that exists in something else, such as a living creature, or the earth, or the heavens, or anything that is — but subsisting of itself and by itself in an eternal oneness, while every lovely thing partakes of it in such sort that, however much the parts may wax and wane, it will be neither more nor less, but still the same inviolable whole.[66]

I believe that Plato intends Alcibiades' description of Socrates as a garishly erotic silenus that opens up to reveal images of the gods inside as a symbol for the relation between the Apollonian and Dionysian in his doctrine. It is strongly implied that before one realizes the beauty of the soul one must have sexual relations with many beautiful people at the same time. In other words one must thoroughly indulge in physical love in order to see that it does not ultimately suffice to satiate the deepest (erotic) desires of one's soul. This orgiastic imagery of lady Diotima's "final mystery" is Dionysian not only on the surface, but also in that the orgy is supposed to result in some kind of ecstatic transcendence to an appreciation of divine oneness. While the pre-Platonic Dionysian vision only comes about occasionally, when one is driven into ecstasy by intoxication, music and erotic revelry, once attained, Plato's vision of oneness is permanent and ever-present. According to Plato's Diotima, the love of Wisdom — i.e. *philosophia* — is this deeper and more rapturous eroticism. Perhaps this is why Socrates, who is its perfect embodiment, drives Alcibiades "mad" like a "fool" to strip and embrace Socrates.

The erotic dynamic between male and female Guardians in the *Republic* reiterates the alchemically transformative potential of sexual energy that Diotima teaches in *Symposium* — especially in its insistence on the fact that as lovers, men and women philosophers will never *possess* each other, just as they will not possess any other forms of private property: "[A]ll the women should be common to all the men…" This frees *eros* from the chains of jealousy, envy, emulation, greed and violence and allows it to become a powerful means of transcendental seduction to wisdom. Here is the key passage, which we should read in light of that from *The Seventh Letter* quoted above — about wisdom flashing forth only amidst the intimacy of a communal life of intense seekers:

> Then the women guardians must strip, since they'll clothe themselves in virtue instead of robes, and they must take common part in war and the rest of the city's guarding, and must not do other things. ... And the man who laughs at naked women practicing gymnastic for the sake of the best, 'plucks from his wisdom an unripe fruit for ridicule' and doesn't know — as it seems — at what he laughs or what he does. ... [A]ll the women should be common to all the men. ... They will live and feed together, and have no private home or property. They will mix freely in their physical exercises [for which the Greeks always stripped naked] and the rest of their training, and [so] they'll be led by an inner natural necessity to sexual mixing with one another. ... [P]ossessing nothing private but the body...they will then be free from faction.[67]

Through the pure *eros* inherently involved in "the pursuit of wisdom" lovers become to each other symbols of Beauty-in-itself. Instead of dissipating in the flesh of the other, erotic desire is directed towards this form by its attraction to the beloved, and transcends to this form *through* the (earthly) beloved. Yet the form of Beauty is itself a mere construct used to attain the discipline and attunement that allows one to have a vision of the "first principle." Plato says the latter is beyond "reality," thus it is not only beyond Becoming but also beyond Being. It is the *why* or the *Good* for-the-sake-of-which there is a mixture of Being and Non-Being in the receptacle to produce the Becoming of the world.

What defines a *caress* — as opposed to touching, grasping, holding and taking — is an absorbed languor that almost forgets itself. It abandons the intellect's intentional deliberation and delivers itself over to the *presence* of the other's body as experienced through one's own. The seat of consciousness moves from the mind to stomach, and one feels compromised and vulnerable amidst the world. The "shiver of pleasure" brings forth embodiment, but if one becomes reflexively conscious of it and begins to seek it as a goal one loses sight of the Being of the other, who instead becomes an object of one's subjectivity. If this occurs, *eros* is defeated for one can never possess the transcendent Beauty of the other as "object." All of one's grasping and penetrating, and ultimately even one's climax of pleasure, become pervaded by the torturous refusal of surfaces.

The analogy is that the body, like the world itself, is a phenomenon in which Being shines forth and is sheltered *as* a Becoming — where form *limits* a Being which would otherwise be so blinding that it would escape us altogether, and thereby allows it to scintillate in its coming to presence. Heraclitus recounts how, while we go about lost in our worldly business everyday, the world itself escapes us. Like a fish that does not see the water it is swimming in, we fail to recognize that we *are*, and marvel *that* we are. He says, so poetically:

> Men forget where *the way* leads. … And they are at odds with that with which they most constantly associate. And what they meet with every day seems strange to them. … We should not act and speak like men asleep.[68]

The *forms* are Plato's answer to Heraclitus' exasperated and paradoxical question: "How can one hide from that [Sun] which never sets?!" Only through rigorous abstraction can we gain enough distance from the world which we "meet with every day" that we can then *look back* at the world in wonder, look at the phenomenon of existence in which Being and becoming are necessarily reciprocal manifestations of each other. This looking back is the Platonic reversal, which takes place once the philosopher has attained to the form of forms. In the *Phaedo*, Plato writes:

I thought that ... in the contemplation of true existence, I ought to be careful that I did not lose the eye of my soul; as people may injure their bodily eye by observing and gazing on the sun during an eclipse, unless they take the precaution of only looking at the image reflected in the water, or in some analogous medium ... I was afraid that my soul might be blinded altogether if I looked at things with my eyes ... and I thought that I had better have recourse to the world of *idea* and seek there the truth of things...[69]

Nietzsche argued that Greek tragedy originated in the chorus (not the dramatic action) and it was in its most ancient form nothing but the chorus. People of Dionysian spirit desire the truth of nature in its most unforgiving reality and when they achieve this through intoxication they are transformed into satyr-like beings that speak with an oracular wisdom, which flows from comprehending the heart of existence through union with it. This is the chorus in its most ancient form. In tragedy it becomes a realized projection of the desire of the civilized mass of spectators to regain this primordial state. The action is in turn a "vision" of the chorus. Originally the only subject of drama was the suffering and redemption of Dionysus. Moreover, this drama was not actually present but was *imagined*, literally as a *vision* of the chorus who in their intoxication were the servants of Dionysus. In music, dance, and words they conveyed this invisible epiphany of their god. The introduction of actors and drama is an Apollonian objectivization — in dreamlike epic imagery — of the Dionysian state of the chorus.

Nietzsche goes on to explain that all of the heroes of tragedy are masks of what was originally none other than Dionysus. The simplicity and clarity of their lines and characters are merely the glimmers of an Apollonian surface of light behind which there looms an infinite background of darkness from out of which they arise (as consolations). In tragedy, the hero's suffering or demise (originally the dismemberment of Dionysus) is dramatized in order to show that it is a mere phenomenon and the eternal life behind it remains untouched and persists (originally, Dionysus' rebirth). This suffering and redemption, dismemberment and rebirth, is an expression of the truth of the Dionysian mysteries: *that individuation is the source of all suffering and redemption is to be found in the intoxication that allows one to plunge into the primordial unity of all* (Dionysus returning to the womb for rebirth).

Plato ends the *Symposium* with the image of two dramatists, Agathon the tragedian and Aristophanes the comedian, discussing their art forms with Socrates. Plato tells us that Socrates was arguing that the same person should be able to write both tragedy and comedy. In *The Birth of Tragedy* Nietzsche argues that Apollonian-Dionysian tragedy suffered its demise at the hands of the purely Apollonian "Socratism" of Euripidean "comedy." Could it be that Plato, who began his life as a tragic poet like Agathon, is actually inventing a new artistic genre that seeks to rejuvenate the tense balance of *both* the Apollonian and Dionysian? This may be why the conversation is metaphorically set just before dawn, as if to anticipate the birth of something new. Agathon and Aristophanes, Tragedy and Comedy, both fall asleep and after respectfully covering them, Socrates gets up and leaves the symposium to start a new day.

Perhaps the archetypal "forms" or "ideas" are to Plato's new art of Philosophy what (according to Nietzsche) the Apollonian imagery of tragedy is to its dark, hidden and primal Dionysian background? In this one and only dialogue of intoxicated honesty, are we being told to look at the forms like the little statuettes of gods against the background of the silenus that envelops them? We again come face to face with the Platonic reversal. Let us look back at Socrates' first discussion with Alcibiades in which he evokes the injunction of the God Apollo. "…Trust in me and in the Delphic inscription and 'know thyself'" he says, and then continues:

> Now, how can we get the clearest knowledge of our soul? If we knew that, we'd probably know ourselves as well. … If the inscription…advised… 'See

noticed that when a man looks into an eye his face appears in it, like in a mirror. ... So if an eye is to see itself, it must look at an eye. ... Then if the soul, Alcibiades, is to know itself, it must look at a soul... [70]

In light of the development of Socrates' relationship with Alcibiades in *Symposium* as one of erotic seduction, and in light of the passages in *Phaedrus* and *Republic*, we see how this Apollonian commandment is written in the blood of Dionysian rites. Philosophical knowledge is *only* possible through dialogue because, as Plato says, the form of forms "is not knowledge" but lies beyond it. It is ultimately unknowable by the intellect, and thus unknowable in isolation. This is why Plato does not write his secret doctrine. It can only be discovered through "the skill in the science of love which thou hast given me... philosophical discussion directed towards love in singleness of heart." The philosophical dialogue with the other on the same quest for wisdom, when at its peak of intensity, is inherently erotic in its maddening Dionysian transcendence of subjectivity and attainment of union. We can only find ourselves inside the other. The Soul, Plato tells Alcibiades, is in the eye of the other. The orgiastic erotic ascension towards the form of the Beautiful in *Symposium*, and the common marriage of the Guardians in pursuit of the form of Justice in *Republic*, is like the flirtatious dance of Maenads around their vision of the god whose dismemberment is a symbol of the illusion of individuation, and whose rebirth symbolizes the death of the Self who finds itself inside the other. "Know Thyself!" whispers Apollo, through the lips of Dionysus... "Make Music Socrates!" whispers Dionysus, through the lips of Apollo.

5. THE *PHARMAKON* OF OCCIDENTAL RATIONALISM

If there is anything to the interpretation that I have been forwarding, and which now draws to its close, then Plato remains the most deceptively complex thinker in the history of Philosophy. We should expect as much from the philosopher who proposed to rebuild society on the foundation of a "noble lie." In "Plato's Pharmacy" Derrida focuses his study on Plato's use of the ambiguous Greek word *pharmakon*, which can mean drug in the sense of "poison" *or* in the sense of "medicine." He argues that when Plato condemns writing in the *Phaedrus*, he attempts to deny the positive meaning of the word. However, he notes that in other dialogues such as *Statesman*, Plato does acknowledge the double meaning of *pharmakon*, though for Plato, even in its "positive" sense, a *pharmakon* is only a medicine to be employed when all else fails and the stakes are life or death. Most interestingly, Derrida notes how, though Plato seems to insist on taking *pharmakon* negatively, he often describes Socrates as a *pharmakeus* or "sorcerer," one who administers the *pharmakon*. Derrida quotes one such instance as follows:

> Cebes: Probably even in us there is a little boy who has these childish terrors. Try to persuade him not to be afraid of death as though it were a bogey. —What you should do, said Socrates, is to say a magic spell over him every day until you have charmed his fears away. —But, Socrates, said Simmias, where shall we find a magician who understands these spells now that you are leaving us?[71]

It is very significant that this quote comes from *Phaedo*. For, as Derrida notes, the supposed "hemlock" that Socrates drinks in the death scene is referred to by Plato in only general terms—as a *"pharmakon."* Derrida does not clearly draw out the implications of all of this, limiting himself instead to subtle suggestions. As the conclusion of my interpretation, I dare to suggest that the dramatic character Socrates, as he appears in the dialogues, was indeed conceived by Plato as a kind of *pharmakeus*, a "witch doctor" or black magician, who administers the *pharmakon* of Platonic idealism — the wellspring of the entire history of occidental rationalism with all of its consequences.

Plato removes himself from this shady figure because he knows that in one sense he is poisoning people, but only in order to cure them from a far greater evil: the blinding epidemic of Homeric myth. In his study *Preface to Plato*, Erick Havelock interprets the *Republic* as an attack by Plato on the poetic experience of his time as *mimesis* (imitation or simulation [of reality]).[72] Plato is obsessed with the psychology of the audience's response to the arts and he uses the word *mimesis* to describe the *entire* "poetic experience," thereby refusing to differentiate between different genres or the role of creator (poet), actor (reciter), and audience (listener-viewer). In his time, poetry was something very different from what it is today. Fifth-century Greece was a "semi-literate" society. The new technology of writing had been invented for some time. However, only certain elites were literate. Even this limited literacy was not universalized. There were different styles of writing, and spelling and mechanics were somewhat arbitrary. Though the new technology had already been conceived, the people of an essentially tribal society were still in the unreflective mind-set of the oral tradition — one that had been ingrained in the cultural consciousness for thousands of years.

Amidst this setting, poetry was not the thought-provoking *art* that we know it as today. More practical than aesthetic, it acted as a means to preserve and pass on cultural and moral authority and as a giant encyclopedia and history, when no other means existed. Havelock sees the passages in the *Iliad* and *Odyssey* that descriptively enact practical tasks such as shipbuilding, the historical documentation of the "catalogue of ships," or the behavioral paradigms exemplified by

Greek heroes as the primary content of those works, with the epic narrative as a secondary means of delivering the former into the consciousness of society. This means of deliverance is particularly potent when one considers how in the enactment of epic poetry, the message is literally embodied in the dramatic physical movements of the bard who recites and its paradigms are thereby hardwired into the physiology of the audience, thus literally composing the social fabric. Contemporary rap music of the "gangsta" variety might not be a bad analogy.

A long treatment was needed, as long as Western history itself, and for this a very potent *pharmakon* was required. While Heraclitus and Parmenides understood the truth for themselves and condemned the Homeric tradition, they were not concerned about freeing masses of people from it. Their cryptic styles of writing make it clear enough that they in fact intended to conceal their pearls of wisdom from the sight of swine. The historical Socrates, Plato's teacher, did try to shake Athens out of Homer's spell and was swatted dead as a gadfly. The stakes were indeed life or death, and so the administration of the *pharmakon* seemed to Plato to be justified. He intended the exoteric content of his texts to be directly engaged by the intellectuals of his and following ages, while at the same time he hid an esoteric teaching between the lines more thoroughly than Heraclitus ever did — dropping a hint here and there for those initiated.

In conclusion I will consider one final hint, the only other one that belongs in the same class as "…I believe Plato was ill." It is also from the *Phaedo*, when after a lifetime of condemning art as mimetic, in his last days Socrates has taken to writing *poetry*, because as he explains to Cebes:

> I did not compose [the poetry] to rival either [Evenus] or his poetry. … I did it in the attempt to discover the meaning of certain dreams, and to clear my conscience, in case this was the art which I had been told to practice. It's like this, you see. In the course of my life I have often had the same dream appearing in different forms at different times, but always saying

the same thing: 'Socrates, practice and cultivate the arts [*musike*].' In the past I used to think that it was impelling and exhorting me to do what I was actually doing; I mean that the dream, like a spectator encouraging a runner in a race, was urging me on to do what I was doing already, that is, practicing the arts; because philosophy is the greatest of the arts, and I was practicing it. But when my trial had taken place, and this god's festival was delaying my execution, I decided that, in case it should be this popular form of art that the dream intended me to practice, I ought to compose and not disobey. … I reflected that a poet… ought to work on stories, not discourses; and I was no story-writer. So it was the stories that I knew and had handy which I versified — Aesop's, the first ones that occurred to me.[73]

Like the "…I believe Plato was ill" comment, we find the same juxtaposition of an earthshaking revelation delivered in an "Oh and by the way…" tone. Socrates, the paragon of Philosophy's rationalistic opposition to artistic mimesis is on the verge of death, *and what!? — he doubts whether his entire life has been a betrayal of his calling?!?!* And he's going to make up for it — *how?! — by versifying a few of Aesop's fables?!?!*

The keen reader should pause here with the same heart-sinking feeling as Plato's other billion-dollar clue demands. Something is very wrong with this picture. It is a terribly tragic image, precisely because of the benign tone with which Plato presents it. It is a sad, even miserably forlorn scene. The "philosophy of Socrates" is a *lie* that he has been living from one dialogue to the next… a noble lie, but a lie nonetheless. His calling was to be a great artist; Plato *is* one. His metaphysics is a *pharmakon*, one whose side effects have only just begun to wear off… but from the beginning, the poison hid the cure within itself. Plato's metaphysics does not need to be deconstructed, for it has in the course of history always already been working itself as its own dialectical reversal.

BUILDING THE
THEATER OF BEING

According to the well-established scholastic tradition, Aristotle views the human being as one type of being among others — a rational species of animal — and he thinks that merely human affairs, such as Politics, are neither first in the order of being nor first in the order of knowledge. In the context of the *Nicomachean Ethics*, this view is strongly supported by two passages in Book VI, Chapter 7. The first one reads: "[I]t is absurd for anyone to believe that politics or practical judgment is the most serious kind of knowledge, if a human being is not the highest thing in the cosmos."[1] Closely following it is this passage, which explicitly asserts that a human is *not* the "highest" being: "And if it is the case that a human being is the best in comparison to the other animals, that makes no difference, for there are also other things that are much more divine in their nature than a human being, such as, most visibly, the things out of which the cosmos is composed."[2] These passages suggest that Aristotle failed to recognize

---

1   Jonathan Barnes, *Early Greek Philosophy* (New York: Penguin Books, 1971), 1141a21–23.

any fundamental ontological difference between the being of humans and that of other beings, no matter how celestially rarefied.

Nevertheless, in what follows, I argue that Aristotle already had the intellectual resources to conceive of humans not as beings alongside other non-human beings within the world, but as beings whose socio-political existence is constitutive of a "God" that is not only the sustainer (as is usually thought), but also the creator of the world (in the sense of perpetual creation). In fact, whether he realizes it or not, at times Aristotle seems to be doing just that; and such a reading is required in order to resolve the basic contradiction in his system.

Aristotle's metaphysics is riddled with a deep internal contradiction. A God whose nature is pure *thinking on thinking* has no place in a world constituted by beings defined as substances that are each a particular *this*. God cannot be a unique *this* on account of his thinking for two reasons. First, man also has thinking as his essence. Aristotle proposes two distinct conceptions of human thinking. One of them, which more ordinarily characterizes human intellectual activity, seems wed to biological structure in a functionalist manner. While in this respect human thinking is different from that of God, we will see that Aristotle has another conception of human thinking that mirrors divine contemplation, and it is the latter faculty that Aristotle takes to be essential for human beings as such — even though it is rarely exercised. Second, since Matter is merely the potentiality for a specific form — and a substance is specifically formed matter — if God is pure Actuality then God is *all* forms and not any given specific form. This would mean that God, as thinking on thinking, is not a substance (at least in the same sense as other substances), and thus is not subject to the four causes of substances. This raises the further problem of how an immortal human soul whose essence mirrors that of God as eternal thinking, and thus by definition is not subject to the four causes of substance, can be co-mingled with a body that is substantially defined by these causes.

Aristotle needs two premises in order to restore coherence to his Metaphysics. These two premises are: 1) God is identical to the essence of Man; 2) God is not only the sustainer, but also the creator, of all beings. This would resolve the metaphysical contradictions discussed above. God and man could share the same essence, and yet man would have a substantial form whereas God would not, because God would simply be the essence of Man or an "interiority" (conceived non-spatially) of Man — a level of being more fundamental than that of the human substantial form. God could be conceived of within a world-picture of substances, since God is beyond the four causes defining Being (*ousia*) only in that (as the essence of Man) He grounds the four causes defining each and every substance as a particular *this*.

Even Aristotle's conception of "the gods" does not compromise this interpretation. This hierarchical view of degrees of being "human" — culminating in "god-like" philosophers — does, however, establish a radical inequality between citizens in respect to their relationship to civil law. Certain of Aristotle's remarks on *techne* qua art and scientific craft suggest that these "god-like" thinkers whose task it is to set the tone of the *polis*, to establish its architectonic, are the master craftsmen responsible for building something like a "theater of Being." Their exercise of the active intellect may be seen as a condition for the possibility of pure potentialities in Nature manifesting as the beings that we encounter in our world.

1. "GOD" AS THE CREATIVE INTELLECT OF MAN

Before going on to specifically treat God and the essence of Man, let us review Aristotle's notion of how substance is defined in terms of the four causes, and in terms of potentiality and actuality. Aristotle's metaphysics is a teleological one. It attempts to understand Being by discerning the *causes* of beings. By "cause" (*aition*) Aristotle actually means the "explainer," "why" or "because" of substances. The word should not be confused with its meaning in the modern conception of chains of material causes and effects manifesting as point-events. At 1013a24–1013b29 in his *Metaphysics* and 194b16–195a27 in his *Physics*, Aristotle defines the four causes of a substance as: 1) the "form" (*eidos*) of the thing, which is not simply its shape but also its essence, its capacity for the use for which it was designed; 2) the "final cause" (*telos*) or the actual usage that is the end or "that-for-the-sake-of-which" (*to hou heneka*) it was designed and which is beyond the choice of even an intelligent organism (we can however choose to improperly fulfill our ends); 3) the "efficient cause" (*arche tes kineseos*), that which is responsible for the movement of a substance, either from place to place or its movement in place (i.e. change, for example, the turning color of leaves); 4) the "matter" (*hule*) that has the capacity to receive form, that cannot exist apart from some form because it is merely a potentiality for a certain form.

In Book 7 (*Zeta*) of his *Metaphysics*, considered by many to be the core of Aristotle's thought, Aristotle argues that substance is what is ontologically basic or "most real." He categorizes four different candidates that claim to be "substantial," finding that the essence, the universal and the genus of beings all satisfy its "whatness" and can be collectively referred to as Form, while its aspect as a subject captures its "thisness" and can be referred to as its Matter. Finally, he unifies these aspects of substance by equating Matter with "Potentiality" and Form with "Actuality." Both are further divisible into two types: Matter is a first potentiality (this would be the clay of a bowl); Form is the first actuality (the bowl being appropriately shaped by a potter) and also the second potentiality (for use); the End or For-Which is a second actuality (the bowl actually being used). In sum, a "substance" is now defined as: matter that has a certain form or end that gives it the cohesiveness that is so important for it being a *this*. There are two types of substances: 1) those made by nature (*phusis*), which each have their own inner teleology, and those made by craft (*techne*), which require human initiative

Now, bearing the terms of the Aristotelian definition of substance in mind, let us turn to examine God in its light. Aristotle's idea of "God" appears to differ radically from the way we ordinarily conceive of God. He is the ultimate sustainer *and* ultimate good, but on most interpretations he does not seem to create the world as a product of *techne* (craft). God seems to explain the world *not* as an efficient cause, but as its final cause. It is what the whole world is towards or "for the sake of." God does not act on the world. Rather, he only thinks and his thinking is not even about the world but about himself. He thinks on his thinking. We see this in 1074b34 of the *Metaphysics*. Thus Aristotle's Prime Mover imparts end-directedness unto beings in the sense that they strive to partake in the eternity of his self-contemplation. In 415a27 of *On the Soul* we see how the *threptic* or "nutritive" soul reproduces to partake in the eternal and divine. The notion of reproduction as a means to the eternity of a species composed of perishable individuals is also seen at 731b18 of the *Generation of Animals*. In 279a25 of *On the Heavens* Aristotle claims that all things *are* for the sake of the eternity of God; we also see this at *On the Soul* 415a28. God himself is eternal on account of being completely actualized *energeia*, without any unfulfilled potential. Aristotle clearly states this in two vital passages at *Metaphysics* 1050b1–5,15–20 and 1071b20:

> [I]t is obvious that actuality is prior in substance to potentiality; and as we have said, one actuality always precedes another in time right back to the actuality of the eternal prime mover. ... Nothing, then, which is without qualification imperishable is without qualification potentially. ... [I]mperishable things, then, exist actually. Nor can anything which is of *necessity* be potential; yet these things are primary; for if it did not exist, nothing would exist. Nor does eternal movement, if there be such, exist potentially; and, if there is an eternal mover, it is not potentially in motion. ... [T]his will not be enough, if its substance is potentially; for there will not be *eternal* movement; for that which is potentially may possibly not be. There must, then, be such a principle, whose very substance is actuality.

If, as we have seen in our review of the definition of substance, Matter as such is strictly speaking a mere potentiality for a given form, and if God is fully actualized potentiality, then, as Aristotle wishes to maintain in *Metaphysics* 1071b21–22, one might assume that God has no "matter." However, for Aristotle, we have seen that any substance is defined as formed matter. The only logical conclusion that can be drawn here is that God is not a substance on the same level as other substances. This means that if He is to exist at all, within a world-view comprehensively defined by substances that are each a particular *this*, then God must be a substance-defining principle. This would not mean that God is *in* all things, or that God *occupies* the same space as all things. Rather it would mean that God *is* all things even though they are manifold and diverse whereas he is one. This is analogous to the way that an "Organism" is not something that pervades organs or exists inside organs. Rather, it is the coherently functional whole of all of the individual organs taken together in their relations to each other.

While there may be no explicit textual evidence for this "organic" conception of God, it seems an appropriate analogy in light of the central role of biology in Aristotle's thinking. His father was the doctor (*aescleipid*) of the king of Macedon, and Aristotle himself was trained in his father's profession. Aristotle spent eight years of his life, between the end of his studies at Plato's academy and his tutorship of Alexander the Great, studying sea organisms. He continued this in his own school, the Lyceum, including dissections with a staff of assistants. He also consulted a wide range of people for expert biological knowledge (fisherman, beekeepers, etc.). *History of Animals, Parts of Animals*, and *Generation of Animals* are all major works of Aristotle concerned with biology. As such it is his foremost subject matter and his biological thinking extends into the rest of his thinking. Most importantly, it is on the basis of having primarily taken organisms as "substances" that Aristotle derives his metaphysics of Being in general.

Bearing this in mind, we should now recall that Aristotle defines God as no more than a *thinking on thinking*. We see this in

Nicomachean Ethics 1177b1, where Aristotle states that divine thought "alone would seem to be loved for its own sake; for nothing arises from it apart from the contemplating," as well as in *Metaphysics* 1074b15–34, where Aristotle writes: "The nature of divine thought…must be itself that thought thinks (since it is the most excellent of things), and its thinking is a thinking on thinking." Taken together with the above, this would mean that the thinking of God is one with the forms of the world (which I am viewing as analogous to the organs of a body). In a way analogous to the fact that the matter of a body cannot be conceived but through the forms of its organs (and limbs), God's thinking may be a means by which prime matter is rendered conceivable to Himself, through human *aisthesis* and *noesis*. Such a notion is the only metaphysically sound basis for drawing the conclusion, as Aristotle does, that man has an essential nature separate from all that which he shares with other life. This nature not only mirrors the essential nature of God, but would have to be actualized *through* the essential nature of God. Otherwise, Aristotle's claim that Man and God share the same essential nature, without also having the same substantial form, would be metaphysically incoherent.

In most respects Aristotle shares with his fellow Greeks the belief that life and soul are co-extensive, that anything "alive" has a soul. Soul cannot be the body itself, which body is the potentiality of its "first actuality." This means that for Aristotle, in one sense, the soul is the hierarchic functionality of body, its capacity to engage in nutritive, reproductive, perceptive and other activities. However, Aristotle clearly states that a part of the soul is not a fact about the body but an "active intellect," which is potentially separable from it and immortal. This is unique to human beings. We see him make this claim at *On the Soul* 430a25: "When separated [the active intellect] is alone just what it is, and this alone is immortal and eternal." The souls of all other beings perish with their bodies, or even before death if the body of an organism loses its capacities (for example, in a coma).

Aristotle also explains how we share the *aisthetic* powers of perception proper, imagination, and movement together with animals. We see this in the following passages of *On the Soul*: 425b11 and 429b9; 428b10 and 429a1; 433a22. The case is somewhat more complex with the power of desire. For Aristotle, Desire has two types, "appetite" and "wish." Aristotle says that the former is possessed by both humans and animals, while the latter is possessed only by rational beings (i.e. humans). The former is irrational and seeks immediate pleasure, while the latter is rational and directed at a long-term good. In *On the Soul* 433b5 we see that wish is only possible for beings with a sense of time and thought that can resist the attraction of some present pleasure. Desire essentially takes the content of Imagination and wants or wills it. To do so requires a *noetic* soul whose essence is "thinking," just as the essence of God is thinking. At least for man, the *aisthetic* soul depends on the *noetic* soul, the latter is more essential. All beings with *threptic* and *aisthetic* souls are substances defined by the four causes. However, the same cannot be said of human beings, an aspect of whose *noesis* is pure actuality without a specific "form." For this aspect of man to interact in a non-contradictory and holistic manner with the *threptic* and *aisthetic* natures that he shares with other living beings, Aristotle must assume that this more fundamental and form-less *noesis* is not itself subject to the four causes but grounds them.

Likewise, a more coherent version of Aristotle's God would *not* be merely the final cause of the world (as is commonly assumed), rather, it would exist as *all four* causes of the world by always already establishing the four causes as such. Aristotle does give us some, albeit scant, textual resources for developing this actively creative conception of God. In *On the Heavens* 271a33, Aristotle writes: "God and nature create nothing that is pointless." This blatantly states that God creates the world and also implies God's identity with Nature, which in this context is not likely to be referring to living beings alone, but to *physis* naturally generating all beings through the four causes. In 336b27 of *Generation and Corruption*, Aristotle writes:

Coming-to-be and passing-away will, as we have said, always be continuous, and will never fail owing to the cause we stated. And this continuity has a sufficient reason. For in all things, as we affirm, nature always strikes after the better. Now being... is better than not-being; but not all things can possess being, since they are too far removed from the principle. God therefore adopted the remaining alternative, and fulfilled the perfection of the universe by making coming-to-be uninterrupted; for the greatest possible coherence would thus be secured to existence, because that coming-to-be should itself come-to-be perpetually is the closest approximation to eternal being.

This passage seems to establish God as both transcending and accommodating a necessitating reason, beyond which there is no more fundamental reason, of the becoming of all beings as determined by the four causes of substance. Thus, in reference to the passage from *Nicomachean Ethics* quoted at the outset of this paper, "the things out of which the cosmos is composed" may be "more divine in their nature than *a* human being," but they are *not* more divine or fundamental in nature than that immortal essence of Man which sustains them. Such ontology could explain in what sense the active intellect of the human soul "makes" the object of thought that the passive intellect becomes. In *On the Soul* 430a10–25, Aristotle writes:

...[T]hought, as we have described it, is what it is by virtue of becoming all things, while there is another [aspect of *noesis*] which is what it is by virtue of making all things: this is a sort of positive state like light; for in a sense light makes potential colors into actual colors. Thought in this sense of it is separable, impassable, unmixed, since it is in its essential nature activity ... It does not sometimes think and sometimes not think. When separated it is alone just what it is, and this alone is immortal and eternal...

In this passage, as elsewhere, we have seen that the essence of Man is perpetual contemplation, like God "it does not sometimes think and sometimes not think." In this context, it does not seem unreasonable to interpret the analogy of the active intellect "making all things" the way that "light makes potential colors into actual colors" as indicating the essence or "inner light" of Man as that which renders an otherwise unthinkable prime matter conceivable, through the de-limitation of substantial forms of living and non-living beings. On this reading, Aristotle's words "when separated," in the last line of this passage, would be taken to mean "when considered in-itself" — or in its persistence through all that is perishable — the soul of Man actualizes pure potentialities in Nature.

2. THE *POLIS* AS THE THEATER OF BEING

What complicates this view is that Aristotle clearly did not view human "individuals" as self-standing beings. In Book 1, Chapter 2 of the *Politics*, Aristotle claims that the *polis* is not only (temporally) the crowning achievement and fulfillment of man's natural potential, but that (ontologically) "the state is by nature clearly prior to the family and to the individual."[3] "Man is by nature a political animal,"[4] and individuals (and their families) are like limbs that would be unable to carry out their proper function, or fulfill their purpose, without being members of the *polis*-body and the Justice which organically regulates it.[5] Aristotle takes the laws of a political community to aim at the happiness of its citizens [1], and he believes that this *eudaimonia* can only be achieved through the virtuous life [2]. From these two premises it follows that it is the task of the laws to enjoin citizens to behave according to the virtues of character. Aristotle lays this out at 1129b20–26 in Book V, Chapter 1 of the *Nicomachean Ethics*.

For Aristotle, virtuous conduct is self-reinforcing habit. In order to become a virtuous person one must act as *if* one is a virtuous person, until this manner of acting becomes "second nature," so that it feels "wrong" or out of place *not* to act virtuously.[6] Those who have

---

3   Ibid., 1253a19–20.

4   Ibid., 1253a3.

5   Ibid., 1253a21–22.

not been "beautifully brought up by means of habits" will have little if any capacity to improve themselves ethically.[7] In this sense, virtue is an "active condition" that has no meaning abstracted from the practical judgment exercised in concrete situations.[8] "Active conditions" involve a feedback loop, wherein "on account of themselves they make one apt to do those things by which they come about"[9] and "it is from one's being at work involved in each way of acting that one's active conditions come about."[10] Acting according to vice is also self-reinforcing. Aristotle believes that after initially making a few decisions to do things which one knows are wrong, one may "get in a rut," so to speak, of performing vicious actions from which it is eventually as impossible to extricate oneself as it is for a sick man to simply *wish* himself well.[11]

Whether or not one is virtuous is not a matter of natural predisposition for Aristotle,[12] but the socio-economic conditions of one's birth and early upbringing can drastically restrict or expand the scope of one's potential to become a virtuous person. Aristotle goes so far as to say that being habituated from childhood makes "all the difference" in whether or not one is virtuous.[13] Note the following key passage(s):

> [W]e learn by doing. ... [W]e become just by doing things that are just. ... [L]awmakers make the citizens good by habituating them, and since this is the intention of every lawmaker, those that do not do it well are failures, and one regime differs from another in this respect as a good one from a worthless one. ... [I]n the case of the virtues... by acting... and getting habituated... active states come into being from being at work. ... Hence it is necessary to make our ways of being at work be of

---

7   Ibid., 1095b1–10.

8   Ibid., 1107a.

9   Ibid., 1114b25–30.

10   Ibid., 1114a10.

11   Ibid., 1114a10–25.

12   Ibid., 1106a5–15.

certain sorts. ... It makes no small difference, then to be habituated in this way straight from childhood, but an enormous difference, or rather all the difference.[14]

Indeed, Aristotle claims that "it is necessary to be brought up in some way straight from childhood" to feel pleasure and pain at the right things, at the right time, and in the right measure.[15] The text is rife with the formulation "what one ought... as one ought, when one ought" (one instance of which is at 1115b18–19). Those who have not been "beautifully brought up by means of habits" will have little if any capacity to improve themselves ethically.[16] Moreover, Aristotle recognizes that a certain degree of material prosperity is a necessary but not a sufficient condition for the exercise of *arête*.[17]

Of course, this material prosperity cannot be achieved without distributive justice at work in the *polis*, and particular justice (both distributive and corrective), is subsumed by Universal Justice. In a passage at 1134a24–30, Aristotle describes Universal Justice both as lawfulness and as the whole of virtue. The passage begins with "what we are seeking is also unqualifiedly just action and politically just action." In this statement, "unqualifiedly just action" and "politically just action" should be interpreted as two names for the same thing, rather than as two separate items named in succession. We can take as evidence for this the fact that nowhere does Aristotle explicitly define "unqualifiedly just action." The implication being that the definition of politically just action as that which concerns "people who share in a life aimed at self-sufficiency" (through trade of diverse goods by people of different crafts) and "who are free and either proportionately or arithmetically equal" is also meant to be the definition of unqualifiedly just action. So, for example, the relations between master and

---

14   Ibid., 1103a29–1103b26.

15   Ibid., 1104b10–15, 1105a1–15.

16   Ibid., 1095b1–10.

slave, father and child, or husband and wife only involve something "similar" to justice.[18] Support for this interpretation can also be drawn from 1134a24, where Aristotle defines non-politically just action as "something just in virtue of a similarity," i.e. *qualifiedly* just action. This directly implies that politically just action *is* one and the same as *unqualifiedly* just action. Finally, there is a passage near the end of *Politics* III.6 that explicitly refers to political justice, which manifests solely in cities with good rulers, as the only unconditional justice: "It is clear that those *political* arrangements that aim at the common interest are correct in conforming to what is *unqualifiedly just*, while those that aim at the interest of their rulers alone are all mistaken and are perversions of the correct political arrangements."[19]

Not only does Aristotle equate unqualified justice with lawfulness, but to have particular justice as a character virtue means to assume the perspective of a good *citizen*. Particular justice, whether distributive or corrective in kind, is concerned with external goods of fortune,[20] especially those of which one could want and take more of than one's fair share: honor, wealth, and safety.[21] In the *Nicomachean Ethics*, there is an overlap between Aristotle's discussion of particular justice (or injustice) with respect to honor, wealth, and safety, and his treatment of the virtues of magnanimity[22] and proper pride,[23] which are concerned with honor; liberality[24] and magnificence,[25] which are relevant to wealth; and courage,[26] which deals with safety. If there is to be a clear distinction between (particular) justice and these other

---

18 Ibid., 1134b8–18.

19 Ibid., 1279a17–20, my emphasis.

20 Ibid., 1129b1–3.

21 Ibid., 1130b2.

22 Ibid., *Nicomachean Ethics*, IV. 3.

23 Ibid., *Nicomachean Ethics*, IV. 4.

24 Ibid., *Nicomachean Ethics*, IV. 1.

25 Ibid., *Nicomachean Ethics*, IV. 2.

particular virtues, it is that the latter concern honor, wealth, and safety *as such* in their significance for oneself, whereas the particular virtue of justice is concerned with them in respect to one's attitude towards other citizens who are also more or less entitled to them.

In other words, Universal justice encompasses particular justice (as one virtue among others) and is in turn the socio-political condition for the possibility of all of the other particular virtues whose practice alone allows human beings to fulfill their purpose. If having been properly habituated from childhood counts for *everything* in virtue, and each virtuous person was at one point a child who needed to be raised by already virtuous parents who also were once children in need of proper habituation, then where does the chain of responsibility end? It cannot be traced in a linear manner back to a particular person or group of persons — even to a sagacious lawgiver of the past, such as Solon. Rather, for Aristotle, its "end" must lie in the circular structure of the self-perpetuating *polis*: the abode of the eternal essence of Man. This turns the *polis* into both the creative matrix through which all beings come to be, and the crowning accomplishment whose excellence is that for-the-sake-of-which all things, artificial *and natural*, have their being.

To be sure, Aristotle never explicitly sets forth this view. Nevertheless, it is a legitimate development from out of the tensions in Aristotle's thinking, and something like it is in order if he is to justify the following statement in his *Politics*, which contradicts the quotations from *Nicomachean Ethics* that open this paper: "*we set down that the highest good is the end of politics. …* [I]t takes the greatest part of its pains to produce citizens of a certain sort, namely, ones that are good and inclined to perform beautiful actions."[27] If Man — taken not as an individual, but collectively in the *polis* — were essentially one with Nature's God, then the highest good would indeed be the end of politics. Political activity, which opens the space for all other uses of the *logos* definitive of being human, would be the "divine" final cause even of "the things out of which the cosmos is composed."[28] Indeed, the political subordinates all theoretical understanding of Nature. The word "theory" stems from the Greek verb *theorein*, the noun belonging to which is *theoria*; these words involve a conflation of two more basic ones, *thea* and *horao* — which taken together mean to attentively see to the appearance or manifestation of things in an engaged and absorbed manner that abides with them. This root *thea* is also the basis of the Greek word *theatron* or "place" (*-tron*) of "viewing," from which we have derived "theater." The active intellect does not creatively actualize phenomena in isolation, but by building the viewing-place of the *polis*.

3. THE MASTER CRAFTSMEN

It might seem that Aristotle's notion of *the gods* in certain passages in the *Nicomachean Ethics*[29] violates the essential identity of the singular divine Being and collective socio-political human existence, for which I have been arguing. First of all, at least in certain passages, the gods seem to be a *finite* multiplicity of beings above human beings, and *their* distinctive essence is also thinking. Aristotle contrasts changing social conventions and standards of justice in the human realm with unchanging laws of nature, and then implies that the "customs" of the gods would be as unchanging as the latter: "among the gods, no doubt, nothing changes at all."[30] A similar passage at 1154b25–33 in the *Nicomachean Ethics* states that only a bad-natured, or deficient, being needs change and finds it sweet, because the transition from pain to pleasure is pleasurable, whereas gods enjoy an enduring and single pleasure that is greater on account of its motionlessness. We find out that this single, continuous pure pleasure is that of intellectual

---

28 Ibid., 1141b2.

29 Ibid., 1134b28; 1154b25–33; 1177b25–1178b25.

contemplation, which Aristotle distinguishes at length from the other merely human virtues.[31] Intellectual virtue is radically unlike and separate from distributive justice, courage, generosity, and other virtues that require other people in order to be practiced, and also from virtues like temperance or self-restraint, which are contingently dependent on our composite nature as desiring beings subject to pain. Intellectual virtue is unconditioned, and it is the sole "virtue" of the gods.

Aristotle claims that no one would (or should) deny that the gods are really alive, and therefore at-work in some way. However, he maintains that it is also absurd to imagine them making contracts with one another, or showing bravery in the face of death during war, or being generous to others, and so forth. Thus, the only way they are at-work is in their continuous contemplation, and they seem not to need anything or anyone else, even other gods, in order to experience this singularly blessed pleasure. This seems especially problematic for the interpretation that I have been developing when we consider that the gods have no political community. In addition to the implication of this in the passages referred to above, at 1145a10–11 in the *Nicomachean Ethics* Aristotle explicitly states that Politics, which orders human cities, does *not* rule the gods.

There are, however, some passages that blur the categorical distinction between humans and gods in such a way as to allow us to take Aristotle's "gods" as symbolic of the divine element in man, which transcends his composite animal nature. In the course of laying out the opposites of three types of character flaws — namely vice, lack of self-restraint, and an animal-like state — Aristotle notes that the opposite of the animal-like state is not obvious like the other two, and he goes on to identify it as becoming "godlike." Just as an animal-like state is something different from vice, the state belonging to a god "is something more honorable than virtue" and is "a virtue that transcends us." He seems to affirm the view that "people are turned from humans into gods by a surpassing degree of virtue." Aristotle concludes these remarks[32] with the observation that both the animal-like man and the godlike man are rare, which of course implies that, however rare, he takes godlike men to actually exist. Aristotle compares the gods to the highest goods, claiming that they are above praise, since they cannot be measured by any human standard.[33] Yet, in the same passage he implies that there is nothing wrong with measuring the other way, since he holds humans up to the standard of gods, calling them "the most godlike among men, blessed and happy." It is also the case that at the end of the discussion of the uniqueness of intellectual virtue (referenced above), Aristotle says that we humans should not rest content with our mortal nature. We should, rather, strive to be as much like the immortals as possible.[34]

These passages certainly allow for a reading of "the gods" not as a finite class of existing beings separate from humans, but as a foil or counter-point for all that is *animal* in man. They would hypostatize *what*, in the finite multiplicity of human being, *exists* beyond the four causes, as the in-forming principle of all substances. It would be in this sense, then, that "those who are completely base… do ungodly things."[35] In other words, vicious persons "can do ten thousand times as much evil as an animal"[36] because they are also something far more than "a rational species of animal," and so to betray this is to be worse than an animal without such a potentiality. It is to fail to realize the ontological difference that there is between beings and our Being.

However, the view that I have been developing here of the *polis* as the theater of Being is further complicated by Aristotle's implicit

---

32   Ibid., 1145a20–35.

33   Ibid., 1101b18–25.

34   Ibid., 1178b9–25.

35   Ibid., 1166b5–6.

establishment of a hierarchy of *humanness* that begins with a natural slave, goes on to a "merely human" being, and then to a "most human" being that is *god-like*. Rational judgment involves clearly and distinctly delineating things, and "making distinctions is not something most people do."[37] Rather, *most* people are natural slaves, no better than "fatted cattle" or other "beasts of burden"; they are incapable of living their own lives properly and need political slave drivers to beat them into obedience or banish them if they prove "incurable."[38] Aristotle's analogy between the relation of a master to his slave and the relationship between the rational part of the soul and the irrational part that is commanded by it strongly implies that a slave is not a rational being.[39] Therefore, a slave is also incapable of virtue, since "there is no virtue without wise judgment."[40] People who *are* capable of practicing all of the other virtues except the intellectual one are described by Aristotle as "merely human," whereas the intellectual virtue is something "separate" and "most human"; it is the divine nature within humanity.[41] Unlike other virtues, such as courage or charitableness (which require someone to be courageous or generous to), contemplation can be pursued without reliance on anything external; it also does not aim at any greater good or profit for which it may become merely a useful means.[42] It is divine in that it approximates the self-sufficiency of the gods.[43]

This calls into question the socio-political status of god-like humans with intellectual virtue. Just as it undermines the reading of virtue as always already socio-politically conditioned and contextual, the "god-like" ideal of fully actualized human potential calls

37 Ibid., 1172b3–4.

38 Ibid., 1095b19–22; 1180a1–13.

39 Ibid., 1138b8–10.

40 Ibid., 1144b21–22.

41 Ibid., 1177b25–1178a25.

42 Ibid., 1177a20–1177b5; 1178a29–35.

for a reinterpretation of Aristotle's conception of friendship (*philia*) — which he takes to be the binding force of the *polis*. Friendships usually break up because one or the other of the partners mistakes the type of *philia* upon which their relationship is based.[44] These breakups are so distressing that they become cause for questioning oneself. This follows from the fact that the intimacy of friendship, extended over a long span of time, is necessary in order to secure justified belief concerning our own moral character.[45] We come closest to objective knowledge of our own actions only in the "mirror" of character friendship, and this means that we may be faced with redefining ourselves or losing our virtuous friends — possibly because we cannot tolerate the way in which they make us aware of our own failings. According to Aristotle, virtue friendships are the only ones inherently resistant to slander and other violations of trust, and it is on this account that they should be enduring.[46] This, however, presumes that *we* are capable of *enduring* them.

Is it possible for anyone who is not a "god-like" philosopher to endure a virtue friendship with someone who is one? This is as much as to question whether a virtue friendship is genuinely possible between non-philosophers. Aristotle is aware of this difficulty. One is supposed to wish the best for one's friends, but no one who is not a philosopher would wish that one's best friends become god-like, otherwise one would no longer be fit to be their friend. Note this passage at 1158b29–1159b15:

> But what is equal in matters of justice does not seem to work the same way as what is equal in friendship. ... [T]his is clear if the divergence becomes great... for no longer are they friends, nor do they deserve to be. This is most manifest in the case of the gods. ... In such cases there is no precise boundary up to which they are friends, for when many things have been taken away the friendship still remains, but when they are separated

---

44 Ibid., *Nicomachean Ethics*, 9.3.

45 Ibid., 9.9 1169b28–1170a4; see also: *Magna Moralia* 1213a10–26.

greatly, as from a god, it no longer does. From this an impasse is raised, that perhaps friends do not wish for the greatest goods for their friends, such as that they be gods; for then they would no longer have friends. ... [For a person like this to wish] for good things for a friend for that friend's own sake, that friend would need to remain whatever he is...

Here self-love and the supposed altruism of the truest friendship seem to collide. If we are to maintain that Aristotle's ethics is not egoistic, then we must draw the conclusion that character friendship is only possible between genuine philosophers. Only those with the ruthless aspiration to become "god-like" would be unafraid of constantly drawing each other ever further beyond the "merely human." This is in line with two passages where Aristotle describes the highest type of friendship as consisting of the dynamically transformational contemplative dialogue exemplified by Plato's Socrates.[47] Aristotle's use of the phrase "going hunting" in the latter of these two passages is a metaphor for the love of wisdom. Aristotle also refers to this proverbial "fellowship of eagles" at 1177a27–1177b3 (my emphasis): "the wise person is able to contemplate even when he is by himself, and more so to the extent he is more wise. *He will contemplate better, no doubt, when he has people to work with*, but he is still the most self-sufficient person." To conclude, the only enduring *philia* is one wherein friends are bound together not by "need" of any kind, but by *philo-Sophia* — their hopelessly falling for the same beloved, namely Wisdom. Philosophical friendship is always at least a *ménage a trois*.

This *esoteric* reading requires taking Aristotle's pronouncements on the virtues as *exoteric*. He deliberately concealed his radical view that, inwardly, the free circle of god-like friends lives beyond society and above its laws. For such a person the plurality of socially conditioned, public virtues are merely something to be tolerated in order to keep from arousing suspicion and meddling that would interfere with contemplation:

But for someone who contemplates there is no need of such things for his being-at-work; rather, one might say they get in the way of his contemplating. But insofar as he is a human being and lives in company with a number of people, he chooses to do the things that have to do with virtue, and thus will have need of such things in order to live a human life.[48]

In this sense only, are the virtues of character a precondition for the true *eudaimonia* of contemplation. The philosopher must be *able* to practice them, and to do so perfectly, but he must also live beyond the need for them and the social order that they structure and sustain. "Man *is* by nature a political animal,"[49] but Aristotle's most provocative idea is the overcoming of the "merely human" *animal* in the philosophic life. Those who have attained to such a state of being, do however retain a responsibility to craft the context for human flourishing, and consequently, for the actualization of natural potentialities. This is the aim of the art (*techne*) of Politics, which Aristotle sees as the master craft.

Aristotle explains how the ends pursued in various arts (some of which we would refer to as *crafts*) are subordinated to the ends of master arts, and then he describes ethics or knowledge of the "good" as "*the* master art." He goes on to equate this "most authoritative art… which is most truly the master art" with Politics. His rationale for this is that this art determines who, in a properly ordered state, ought to learn all of the other arts and sciences, and to what extent they should do so. But who makes this determination? Aristotle's equation of the other arts subordinate to Politics with "sciences" is also noteworthy. Even the mathematical sciences say a great deal about the beautiful, which is also found in motionless things.[50] The Greek word here is *techne* — which is the root of both technology and craft in the sense of "arts and crafts." Its root is the verb *tikto*, which means "to bring forth

---

48   Ibid., 1178b3–8.

49   Ibid., *Politics* 1253a3.

or to produce." Statecraft is, then, according to Aristotle, the Master Craft that fosters mankind's collective fulfillment of its end or goal and employs all of the other arts and sciences as means towards this end. If this were not so, Aristotle claims, there would be an infinite regress of ends-for-the-sake-of-which various crafts are practiced.[51] Who could the master craftsmen (*technites*) be other than the "god-like" thinkers whose creative intellect first shapes the bare potentialities of Nature into the beings that we encounter in our world?

Understanding the role of chance in art is indispensable to properly conceiving of human activity. Art is concerned with those things that could be otherwise, that may come into being through our producing or building them, but that would not be but for us. The conception of "chance" at work here is not at all synonymous with "blind chance" in the sense of random effects of an ever-receding causal chain. Furthermore, Aristotle defines the building activity characteristic of art as "a reasoned state of capacity to make" and he claims that not only is it the case that there is not "any art that is not such a state," it is also the case that there is not "any such state that is not an art." In other words: "*art* is identical with a state of capacity to make, involving a true course of reasoning... i.e. with contriving and considering how something may come into being which is capable of either being or not being, and whose origin is in the maker and not in the thing made... for art is concerned neither with things that are, or come into being, by necessity, nor with things that do so in accordance with nature." Aristotle also defines a lack of art, or artlessness, as "a state concerned with making, involving a false course of reasoning."[52] What these statements amount to, is a claim that *any* human reasoning that is concerned with bringing into being that which is not bound to be by necessity or by nature, is the exercise of an aesthetic faculty. This is as much as to say that purely logical or analytical reasoning, which are

---

51   Ibid., 1094a1–1094b10.

fit to describe structures of necessity, are *artlessly* inadequate when it comes to deliberative production. The grandest project of deliberative production, which establishes the context for all others, is the regulation of the *polis*. Through the exercise of statecraft, the "god-like" master builders first make both theoretical research and ethical action possible.

The master builders are the supreme artists. Such a view allows us to make more sense of Aristotle's repeated use of the term *kalon* — which means not just "fine" or "fitting," but "beautiful" — as the descriptor for ethical action and the manifestation of Justice. According to Aristotle "it is for the sake of the beautiful that the courageous person endures"[53] and he chooses to die a beautiful death in war, amidst the "most beautiful sort of danger."[54] In his *Poetics*,[55] Aristotle defines Tragedy as a serious imitation of action that has a magnitude complete in itself, with an integral beginning, middle, and end (and that is aimed at the arousing of fear and pity towards the end of catharsis). This suggests that the life of excellence (of which Tragedy is a serious imitation) ought to also be ordered by a project, which has an internal structure with an inception and culmination, and wherein any given moment is deeply interrelated to others. At 1115b15 in the *Nicomachean Ethics*, Aristotle straight out defines "the beautiful" as "the end that belongs to virtue." This is repeated even more elegantly at 1120a25: "Actions in accord with virtue are beautiful and are for the sake of the beautiful." It appears in yet a third formulation, in the context of the discussion of friendship, at 1168a28–29: "a decent person acts on account of what is beautiful, and the better a person he is, the more on account of the beautiful, and for the sake of a friend, while he disregards his own interest." A little further down in the same discussion, we have this striking passage where a beautiful

53   Ibid., 1115b 24–25.
54   Ibid., 1115a30–1115b5.

life is contrasted with a "random" one — which is to say a life lived by someone without purpose, someone without a project, a drifter who is "all over the place":

> [A] person of serious worth... will give up... all the goods people fight over, to gain what is beautiful. ... [H]e would choose to... live in a beautiful way for a year rather than in a random way for many years, and to perform one great and beautiful action rather than many small ones. ... [H]e seems appropriately to be someone of serious stature, since he prefers the beautiful above all things.[56]

Failure in virtue is more often characterized as something shameful, i.e. being malformed or misshapen, than it is in terms of wickedness or what we commonly think of as moral "evil."[57] Taking pleasure in what one ought and as one ought, is also described by Aristotle as desiring only that which is "not contrary to what is beautiful."[58] Aristotle writes that: "anything that has a lot of growth while stretching out toward ugly things needs to be kept back," and he claims that "the aim to which both [the desiring part of the soul and its right reason] look is the beautiful."[59]

Even when the language of virtue *and* vice is employed, Aristotle draws on analogies to aesthetic harmony: "a person of serious stature... enjoys actions in accord with virtue and distains those that result from vice, just as a musical person is pleased by beautiful melodies and pained by bad ones."[60] Finally, the "complete virtue" of Universal Justice — which encompasses the "proportion"[61] or proper measure of particular justice — is also described in aesthetic terms, namely as

---

56 Ibid., 1169a19–35.

57 Ibid., 1115a13–14; 1116a14–15; 1117a17; 1144a25–27.

58 Ibid., 1119a15–22.

59 Ibid., 1119b5–15.

60 Ibid., 1170a9–11.

a beauty surpassing that of the sunrise or sunset.[62] What it is in the human soul that is capable of *living beautifully* is the very same informing principle at work in the beautiful natural order of things. The latter does not stand in a hierarchical relationship to the immortal Soul of Man (which ontologically transcends any given individual), because the immortal Soul of Man is identical to the in-forming principle at work in natural beings in the way that an organism is identical to the organs that constitute it and the processes that sustain it.

AGAINST PERENNIAL PHILOSOPHY

"Perennial Philosophy" is not Philosophy at all. In fact, it is fundamentally anti-philosophical. In particular, the attempt on the part of traditionalist thinkers such as Julius Evola to claim that there is an Islamic Philosophy that is one expression of the *Sophia Perennis* is neither historically grounded nor conceptually sound. To the extent that there was ever anything approaching Philosophy within an Islamic context, its epicenter would have been Greater Iran. Although principle texts were forcibly written in Arabic, under the dominion of the Caliphate, nearly all of the thinkers of this so-called "Golden Age" were Persians — in other words, ethnic Aryans. What becomes clear when you take a closer look at this period is the extent to which the Islamic conquest straightjacketed the once promising Indo-European genius of Iran.

Although Christianity was overall destructive of European civilization, and cause for a major retardation of European science and culture, there are two major structural factors that make Christianity different from Islam in a way that allowed for a kind of Reformation that created the atmosphere where a Hegel and Nietzsche were possible, a kind of Reformation that did not and cannot ever take place

First, there is the internal incoherence of the Gospels and their incompatibility with key parts of the Old Testament. These books were written over the course of hundreds of years by tens of different authors, and the resulting contradictions in turn required an even larger group of people to constantly engage in different interpretations of the scripture in an effort to make some sense out of it. This makes Christianity much more flexible than Islam, the scripture of which was composed by only one man, is relatively more internally consistent, and claims not to be amenable to any change whatsoever.

Second, this man, namely Muhammad, was also the founder of a political state and the Quran is in essence a legal constitution. By comparison, in the Gospels we see an emphasis on the separation of Church and State as well as the rejection of the use of force to propagate the message of Christ. Of course, in actual fact many Christians did subsequently use force to spread their faith, but at least those in the Reformation who insisted on personal conscience had both Christ's pacifism and his secularism to lean on in order to oppose the politics of the Catholic Church.

The fact that Islamic scripture is relatively internally consistent, at least with respect to law, that it is repeatedly and explicitly made clear nothing in the Quran can change, that the Quran establishes a form of government and renders separation of religion from state impossible, that the Quran justifies Jihad and that Muhammad himself used force to spread the religion — all of these factors make a Reformation of the kind that took place in Europe impossible within a Muslim country.

Let me give you two examples of the straightjacket that Islam put on Iranian thinkers in the period of the so-called "Islamic Golden Age." The first is the duplicitous relationship that Abu Rayhan Biruni (973–1048) had to the culture of India, and the second is the way in which Islam forced Abu Ali Sina to waste his tremendous intellect with his hypocrisy.

Biruni's most famous work, more renowned than any of his scientific writings, is his book *Tahqiq ma li'l-hind* (Researches on India).[1] This work offers us a masterful exposition of Indian thought on the nature of the cosmos and the human psyche, for example Patanjali, which Biruni takes pains to distinguish from crass popular forms of the Hindu religion. He discusses in detail, and with an objective scholarly attitude, subjects that would be considered heretical from an Islamic standpoint, such as the theory of reincarnation. He even explicitly targets bigoted Muslim misconceptions about the Sanskrit spiritual and intellectual tradition. When he engages in a comparison of the Hindu and ancient Greek worldviews, it becomes clear that this man whose native language is Persian, and who is writing in Arabic, is capable of carefully reading texts in ancient Greek as well as Sanskrit. We are looking at an Indo-European savant who could in principle have resumed the historic role of the Persians in drawing from both Western and Eastern ways of thinking to arrive at new insights that would broaden the intellectual horizon of all of humanity. If the Renaissance and Enlightenment had happened in Iran, it would truly have resulted in a universal civilization rather than a modern Western civilization dominating the rest of the planet.

But Biruni could not have helped to bring that about. Why? Because his researches on India and much of the rest of his work was done under the patronage of the Turkic-Mongol Sultan Mahmud of Ghaznah (971–1030), a genocidal Islamic fundamentalist who invaded India in order to destroy Hindu temples and impose Islam by force on that territory that we now know as Pakistan. Biruni essentially got away with doing some good research on India in the course of Sultan Mahmud's campaign of conquest, which had exactly the opposite aim as the one that we can discern in between the lines of *Tahqiq ma li'l-hind*.

---

1   Seyyed Hossein Nasr and Mehdi Aminrazavi (Eds.), *An Anthology of Philosophy*

Abu Ali Sina (born 370 Hijri, 980 Miladi) was an extraordinarily energetic polymath who produced more than two hundred works before his death at the age of fifty-seven. Most of these were written during a fifteen-year period of rare peace and quiet in Isfahan, which was an exception in his otherwise troubled life of perpetual persecution and dislocation. Interestingly, with respect to what I just remarked about Biruni, Ibn Sina's productive Isfahan period was brought to an end by an attack on the city by Mahmud of Ghaznah's son, Masud. It is quite possible that if Ibn Sina had been able to think freely the quantity of his writings would have been matched by a quality and caliber of thought equal to that of the greatest European philosophers.

Unfortunately, instead, Islamic oppression turns him into a consummate hypocrite. Towards the end of his life Sina writes a book called *Mantiq al-mashriqiyyin* where he disowns all of his earlier philosophical work (all of his thought that goes beyond the scope of practically oriented science and technology). He claims that the peripatetic outlook of his philosophical writings were an exoteric façade that he was forced to erect in order to protect himself from "people devoid of understanding who considered the depth of thought as innovation (bid'ah) and the opposition to common opinion as sin..."[2] Presumably such people included some of the Muslim potentates who withdrew their patronage once they discovered his true views, forcing him to spend much of his life as a refugee.

What is even worse is that the one final work in which Sina exposes his true philosophy, meant only for a spiritual elite, wound up being almost completely destroyed. We do not have a single intact copy of the book. What few tantalizing fragments remain from the Introduction to *Mantiq al-mashriqiyyin* include Sina's claim that the views he sets forth in this work are based on his study of ancient Persian philosophy.[3] In other words, he is Shahab al-din Suhrawardi's

---

2   Ibid., 269.

direct predecessor in the attempt to somehow resurrect the pre-Islamic wisdom religion of Iran in the form of a *Hekmat al-Eshraq*. Of course, Suhrawardi was executed as a heretic by the Muslim authorities.

In light of the fact that we have almost nothing left of *Mantiq al-mashriqiyyin*, Sina's confession that what is written in, for example, *Kitab al-shifa* consists of Aristotelian or Neo-Platonic platitudes meant for "commoners" is really a disaster. It makes it impossible to estimate the strength of Sina's thought by comparison to a mind like that of Hegel. In the *Kitab al-shifa* Sina claims that evil is always only a privation, that there is no positive force of evil, and that necessary evils are incidental to the overall rational design of the almighty creator of man and the Cosmos. This argument, which is too twisted to rehash in detail for our purposes here, runs counter to the very core of ancient Iranian thought, and it is also illogical on its own terms.

It does not help Sina that at the end of his life he admits that this was one of the many lies out of which he wove his philosophy, because without the *Mantiq al-mashriqiyyin* we do not know what he truly thought about such matters. In *Fi Maqaamaat al-aarifin* Sina destroys any hope we have of attributing a serious political philosophy to him, because he claims that the legitimacy of the legislator whose law and order are needed for social stability comes from divine signs that the Lord gives in order to manifest his power and demand our obedience to his prophet and vice-regent.[4] Sina legitimates the very Islamic rule that he, in the end, admits oppressed and victimized him.

Of the major thinkers from the period of the zenith of science and knowledge in Iran after the Islamic conquest, Zakariya Razi and Omar Khayyam are the two who rejected Islam. Consequently, one might be inclined to see them as the true "philosophers" of the period. However, Razi and Khayyam do not develop any new philosophical concepts or express any unprecedented insights into the nature of reality or the structure of society. Their philosophical thought is on the level of followers of the Stoic or Epicurean schools in the Roman Empire, both in terms of form and in terms of content. It is true that both men contributed significantly to the advancement of scientific knowledge, but this is not the same thing as being a philosopher. Most of the work produced by professional so-called "philosophers" in academia today is not philosophy at all. Philosophy is a kind of thinking that upholds the unity of the sciences, including political science and aesthetics. Scientific theories and discoveries may be the product of philosophical thought, insofar as that thought establishes new fundamental frameworks for seeking and organizing knowledge, but the philosopher must question basic assumptions in a way that is not necessary for scientists and inventors. Philosophy is fundamental thinking on the nature of Truth, Beauty, and Justice.

The person who actually comes closest to being a genuine philosopher in Iran during the period in question is Abu Nasr Farabi (257 Hejri, 870 Miladi). Like Plato and Aristotle, and also like Hegel, Farabi's thought extends from ontology and epistemology to ethics, political theory, and aesthetics. However, the work of Farabi also clearly demonstrates how far Iran remained from producing a thinker like Hegel, and why that is the case. In his *Kitab al-burhan* (a commentary on Aristotle's *Analytica Posteriora*) we see that Farabi has a first-rate logical mind, capable of the most hair-splitting analysis and careful reasoning.[5] Yet in his *Kitab al-jam 'bayn ra'yay al-hakimayn, Aflatun al-ilahi wa Aristu* he tries to assert that there are no significant differences between Plato and Aristotle, and that any merely apparent differences in their thinking have to do with their different ways of life and styles of writing.[6] I do not say he makes an argument for this because no argument can ever be made for such a preposterous position. Then in *Mabadi' ara' ahl al-madinat al-fadilah*, which I believe was Ayatollah Khomeini's favorite book, Farabi adopts the political theory

5   Ibid., 93–110.

of the ideal state from Plato's *Republic* and has the audacity to claim that Muhammad and the Imams are essentially what Plato meant by the ideal philosopher-kings.[7] The same problem lies at the basis of these two very embarrassing expositions. Farabi cannot tolerate intellectual tension on fundamental questions. For him, if Plato and Aristotle did not think the same things on the same matters of ultimate importance, this would be an indictment of human reason as such. The reality is that not only does Aristotle argue against Plato repeatedly, on matters both metaphysical and political, but Plato uses the method of his dramatic dialogues to constantly argue against himself. He chooses Socrates as a mouthpiece because he understands that the philosophical life is a life of fundamental questioning, and only on account of this can it lead to discoveries. The most famous saying of Socrates is "Wisdom begins in wonder," whereas regarding the attainment of knowledge Farabi says, "If he encounters this meaning, he rests at it, feels peace with it, and enjoys the removal in him of the harm of wonder and ignorance."[8]

Someone who considers wonder a harm does not understand the first thing about Philosophy. For Farabi knowledge is cumulative. Plato and Aristotle together attained it, and so they cannot be in any fundamental disagreement. If they were, it would mean that both ignorance and wonder persist in even the most powerful minds precisely because knowledge is not cumulative and discovery is an ongoing process. Since Farabi is well aware of the essential connection between ontology or epistemology and political theory, this incompleteness and mutability of knowledge would mean not only intellectual unrest but also a threat to the long-term peace and stability of society. Someone might arrive at a different understanding of nature, including human nature, that could for example be reflected in a new political theory that produces something like the French Revolution.

---

7   Ibid., 119–133.

That possibility unconsciously terrifies Farabi, whereas it was very clear to Plato (whom Farabi claims to revere so much). Socrates was martyred as a revolutionary political dissident, and Plato is almost killed himself for experimenting with an ideal state in Syracuse. Even Aristotle, who is relatively more conservative, had to exile himself from Athens because as he put it, he did not want to make the Athenians responsible for murdering two philosophers. Aristotle ran a think tank that would experiment with different constitutions for different city-states whose leaders would privately come to him for advisement. By contrast, Farabi has a mind like that of a Chinese Confucian. He treats Plato and Aristotle as if they are Confucius. This is also why he can so perversely equate the philosopher-king with an Imam.

For Farabi knowledge is fixed and handed-down all tidied-up, like a divine revelation. As far as I am concerned, there is no native Chinese philosophy. There might be some Buddhist philosophy which took place in China after Iranian missionaries such as Bodhidharma brought Mahayana Buddhism there through the Silk Route. But neither the Confucian nor even the Taoist sages or wise men can be considered philosophers. The Chinese have this saying, "May you live in interesting times," which they consider a curse. It is for this reason that I worry if the Chinese are left as the only bulwark against Islam, the Caliphate may dominate the world because the Asian mentality — which the Turks and Mongols shared — is actually very much in accord with Islam. Farabi has this mentality. He wants to sit at the foot of silk-robed sages and receive Wisdom. This is also similar to the mentality of guru-worship in India, but the analogy to Confucianism is more appropriate because Hindu gurus usually did not speak on politics.

The precondition for producing a Hegel or Nietzsche is centuries of dialectical tension, a conflict of fundamental standpoints that plays itself out in both scientific and political revolutions that are as productive as they are destructive. The closest conditions approximating this in the history of Iran were during the Sassanian period, where we witnessed a conflict between at least four different worldviews: Manichaeism, Orthodox Zoroastrianism, Mazdakism, and Sassanian Court Platonism (which had Zurvanite elements). I have noticed that the tendency in the Iranian Renaissance movement is to conflate the court Platonism of Khosrow Anushirawan with orthodox Zoroastrianism and then dismiss Mani and Mazdak's revolutionary doctrines as totally degenerate. I imagine that if European thinkers of the New Right were to advance their own interpretation of Sassanian Iran they would arrive at the same conclusion, especially those who are Traditionalist rather than Archeo-Futurist. But it is important to remember that Mani was endorsed by Shapur the Great and that Mazdak received the support of Kavad I.

We know that each of these movements had extensive scriptures produced over a very long period of time. Mazdakism survived past the Islamic conquest in the form of the Khorramdin and Qarmatian. Manichaeism spread all the way from northwestern China to Bulgaria and the South of France. In Europe, in its Bogomil and Cathar forms it was such a potent social force that it catalyzed the Holy Inquisition of the Catholic Church in response to it. If we were to charitably suppose that the fragments of these movements that survived both Sassanian state persecution and the Islamic and Mongol conquests are a pale shadow of what they were in terms of their sophistication and depth of reflection, then we can postulate that if the culture of Sassanian Iran had continued for another century or two, it might have yielded a thinker like Hegel.

Such a man could have analyzed the dynamics of the evolution of consciousness, in hindsight, understanding the Mazdakite revolution as a stage in the self-correcting development of reason, and he could have reflected on the metaphysical shift from Zoroastrian cosmology to a Manichean or Neo-Platonist cosmology. As far as I am aware, no other non-Western culture besides Iran ever had the kind of open conflict between fundamental intellectual and spiritual standpoints that we see in the late Sassanian period. These were the birth pangs of an Enlightenment.

When one dismisses Mani and Mazdak as aberrations from some falsely idealized *Khosravani* wisdom and virtue, and then attributes Shapur and Khosrow's eclectic interest in Neo-Platonism to the orthodox Zoroastrian Mobeds who were probably nervous on account of it, one is tidying up the intellectual, spiritual, and social conditions of the Sassanian period in a way that denies that an Iranian Hegel was ever even a possibility. An example of this kind of tidying up is the reconstruction of Sassanian so-called "Philosophy" that we see in two works by Ibn Miskawayh, a thinker from Rayy who was born in 320 Hijri or 932 Miladi into a family that had only recently converted from Zoroastrianism to Islam. His book *Jawidan-Kherad* or "The Perennial Philosophy" claims to preserve a Sassanian book of wise sayings and judgments by Hushang Shah, as well as the sayings of Kasra Qobad, a letter from Bozorgmehr to Kasra, and "words of wisdom" from Anushiravan.[9]

Indeed, there are many fine (*nikou*) words of wisdom here, in the sense of sayings of a sage that the Chinese might neatly wrap up inside a fortune cookie. Some of them are more insightful than others that must be considered platitudes of the kind you would find in a 19th century European handbook on morals and proper etiquette. Even the most profound and penetrating of these sayings are not connected to each other by any systematic thought process that could, on account of its principles and logical structure, enter into a fundamental conflict with a rival system. One would be hard-pressed to find anything in here that a person might die for or that might drive him to kill another. Compare this to the zeal of the Manicheans and the martyrdom of around a hundred thousand Mazdakites at the hands of Khosrow I. Whoever that Khosrow was, or for that matter whoever Kavad was that he had the audacity to back a revolutionary as radical as Mazdak, the intellectual force of these Sassanian period personages is not captured by *Javidan Kherad*.

Actually, the problem is not any specific error on the part of Ibn Miskawayh but the very idea of *Javidan Kherad* or "Perennial Philosophy," which Mohammad Reza Shah resurrected and institutionalized in the Imperial Academy of Philosophy. This was the institute in Pahlavi period Iran where Henry Corbin collaborated with the likes of Seyyed Hossein Nasr. Its pariah was Peter Lamborn Wilson (a.k.a. Hakim Bey). If a society believes that there is an eternal, unchanging Wisdom that can be definitively attained by a person living within the present time, and that another intelligent person need only to study under such a sage to have this knowledge imparted to him, then that society will never see the kind of scientific and political revolutions that are catalyzed by genuine philosophers and that are also preconditions for a Hegel who tries to understand what is at work in these revolutions. If I were to believe that Ibn Miskawayh's *Javidan Kherad* adequately represents the intellectual life of Sassanian Iran, then an Iranian Hegel was never possible and I would even have to wonder whether the reason that Heraclitus did not accept Darius' invitation to become the Court Philosopher of Iran is not for the reason I have repeatedly suggested in interviews with Iranian Renaissance leaders, but rather because Heraclitus knew that in the Court of Iran he would have to become Confucius.

That is the last thing he could ever have become, since dialectical opposition and generative conflict is the very heart and soul of Heraclitus' thought. Nietzsche and Heidegger idolize him for this, and without this mode of thinking on his part, there would never have been a Plato. Aristotle tells us that Plato belonged to the school of Heraclitus in his youth and that what he learned there remained the foundation for all of his future work. What he learned was not some piece of information, it was not a cumulative addition to his knowledge. He learned how to think beneath and beyond any assumptions, whether cosmological or sociopolitical. This is extremely dangerous not only because you might be killed for expressing what emerges from such thinking, but even more so because it brings you face to face with an abyss both within yourself and around you. The revolutionary transition from one framework of knowledge to another, and the revaluation of fundamental principles, requires an intellectual equivalent of *Pahlavani* (Heroism) and *Javanmardi* (Chivalry) that began with Zarathustra and that you do not see outside of the Aryan world.

I have noticed that even within the Iranian Renaissance movement there are people who try to read the *Gathas* of Zarathustra as if they are the *Analects* of Confucius. This is to completely miss what it is about Zarathustra that makes him totally incomparable to Confucius. Nietzsche does far more justice to Zarathustra than those who try to use the *Gathas* to increase their knowledge, as if by increments. He fundamentally grasps the spirit of the man and claims that were that man alive today he would teach almost exactly the opposite of everything that he taught in his own time and place. This is an exaggeration on Nietzsche's part, but his essential insight is absolutely right. Nietzsche grasps the form of Zarathustra's thought and the ethos of this personality, an epitome of the "Promethean" or "Faustian" spirit characteristic of the Aryan genius long before Aeschylus' Prometheus or Goethe's Faust.

Yet I do not mean to suggest in any way that Iran's greatness lies only in the past. Islam is according to its own claim the third and final of the Abrahamic revelations. So if the fact that it cannot be reformed also means that once Iranians are fed up with it they will reject the religion in its entirety, then in a sense Iran has the potential to suddenly leap ahead of Europe. The Abrahamic religions are a three-stage project and Europe is only now being prepared to move from stage two to stage three. The prospect of an Islamic conquest of Europe over the next twenty years is very real and it would destroy what is left of the West. Iran, on the other hand, has been almost completely immunized against Islam. Indeed unlike in the case of a post-Reformation European thinker like Hegel, for there to be a figure comparable to Hegel in Iran, that person would have to unequivocally reject Islam, and preferably not by ignoring it but by intellectually destroying it. Otherwise the person cannot really even be considered a "philosopher."

The Iranian Renaissance will only succeed, for the benefit of both Iran and Europe, if it can produce thinkers that make revolutionary scientific and sociopolitical breakthroughs. That is not going to happen with Confucian-style readings of the *Gathas* of Zarathustra or the *Shahnameh* of Ferdowsi. We have to think from out of the heroic Aryan spirit of Zarathustra and produce a future history that will be more mythic than anything in the *Shahnameh* or anything that Ferdowsi could have conceived. Our greatest enemy in this venture is not Islam, but the Traditionalist mentality of *Javidan Kherad* or "Perennial Philosophy" that cannot tolerate fundamental uncertainty and honest intellectual conflict. This *Javidan Kherad*, which Leibniz imported into the West and Guénon later elaborated and used to legitimate Islam, has its origins in a false reconstruction of Sassanian culture on the basis of an Islamic-Mongol mentality that is truly going to be the death of both Iran and the West if we do not have the courage to free ourselves from it. If there is going to be an Iranian Hegel, first we need another Mani, we need another Mazdak, even if we also need another Khosrow, and we need this violently productive intellectual conflict within a few years from now. How is that possible? If even one man has the courage to be all three, to divide himself and think against himself, as Plato did, beginning from out of a wondrous recognition of radical incompleteness.

VERSE 4:34

Men have authority over women because God has made the one superior to the other, and because they spend their wealth to maintain them. Good women are obedient. They guard their unseen parts because God has guarded them. As for those from whom you fear disobedience, admonish them and send them to beds apart and beat them. Then if they obey you, take no further action against them. Surely, God is high, supreme.

— *The Quran*, N.J. Dawood translation

In their struggle for women's equality in Islam, the contemporary Muslim women and scholars Amina Wadud and Asma Barlas have had to face up to this most notoriously challenging verse of the *Quran* for an endeavor such as theirs. Their interpretations depart both from classical *tafsir* of this verse, as exemplified by Ibn Kathir (14ᵗʰ century), and traditional *tafsir* of the modern era such as that of Abdul A'la Maududi (mid 20ᵗʰ century). I hope to demonstrate that Ibn Kathir and Maududi's interpretations of this verse are far more true to the place of women in the greater context of the *Quran* than the forced and floundering readings of Wadud and Barlas.

In his reading of verse 4:34 Ibn Kathir employs two methods typical of classical *tafsir*: he proceeds forward line by line, and he offers *hadith* and views of previous scholars rather than explicitly stating his own view. However in grasping his essential interpretation of the verse I will treat his *tafsir* thematically (not line by line) and will assume that Ibn Kathir cites certain authorities (out of many others in a vast corpus) because they do in fact speak for him on a given point. Ibn Kathir explains that men are responsible for women's material sustenance and welfare and are to guard them from harm.[1] He quotes a *hadith* to the effect that men must feed and clothe women when they themselves eat or buy clothes, and must guard them by never abandoning them (leaving them at the mercy of others) in public.[2] This responsibility, he explains, is not only given to men on account of their being endowed with greater material wealth (and thus with the burden of being the provider), but because God has made men inherently superior to women in all tasks that involve leadership (including prophethood and judgeship). He cites a *hadith* of Bukhari to the effect that female leadership is detrimental to society.[3]

The righteous wife, according to Ibn Kathir, appreciates the guardianship and sustenance granted by her husband by protecting "her honor," i.e. her chastity, and his property while he is absent and obeying him and sexually pleasing him whenever he wishes while he is present. Ibn Kathir even cites a *hadith* to the effect that if Muhammad had allowed any humans to prostrate before other mere humans (rather than before God alone) it would have been a wife bowing-down before her husband to acknowledge his enormous rights over her. He also cites a *hadith* from Bukhari about how angels curse a woman all night long if she refuses her husband sex for some reason or another.[4] So long as a wife fulfills her obligations, her husband must not harass her in any way for fear of God's power to punish his injustice.[5]

---

1   Ibn Kathir, *Tafsir* (Dar-us-Salam Publications, 2000), 442.

2   Ibid., 445.

3   Ibid., 442–443.

4   Ibid., 444–445.

However, if a wife is disobedient—which Ibn Kathir interprets as her being not subordinate to her husband, ignoring her husband or disliking him—then the husband should verbally rebuke her, reminding her of the wrath of God. He should refrain from cursing her in the process of doing this. If such a rebuke does not persuade her to change he should deny her sex (by sleeping with his back to her) or possibly shun her (within his own house) in general.[6] Finally, if neither of these measures work, a man should beat his disobedient wife, but—according to *hadith* and various authoritative interpreters—he should do so only lightly and should not strike her face.[7]

Maududi's reading of 4:34 is very concise. He interprets men's guardianship of women in accordance with the full range of meaning of the Arabic word *qawwam* as: "governor, director, protector, and manager" of their affairs. He explains that men are given this role in respect to their wives (and families) because men are naturally endowed with "qualities and powers" that women have only to a lesser degree or lack altogether. Thus women are the dependents of men for their own good, so that being the weaker of the two sexes they may enjoy the protection of the stronger.

Wives have certain obligations to the men who protect and provide for them, and Maududi summarizes these by quoting a *hadith* also cited by Ibn Kathir, who claims that it was a comment made by Muhammad immediately before reciting verse 4:34: "The best wife is the one who pleases you when you see her; who obeys your orders and who guards your property and her own honor when you are not at home." However, unlike Ibn Kathir, Maududi goes beyond the lines of verse 4:34 itself and in fact puts a check on the verse's authority by sternly warning that a wife is obliged to *not* obey any command or wish of her husband that goes against the obligatory "commandment(s) of

---

6   Ibid., 444–445.

Allah." A wife (or any woman's) obedience is first and foremost to God, and only then to her husband, argues Maududi.

If a wife disobeys her husband he must try admonishing persuasion (verbal rebuke and sexual abandonment) *first, before* moving on to the last resort of beating her. Maududi agrees with Ibn Kathir that this beating was not to be severe. He says (without providing *hadith*) that Muhammad disliked it and forbade that it be administered on the face or with any implement or force that could bruise or mark the wife's body.

Wadud begins her *tafsir* of verse 4:34 by arguing that *fadl* (preference, superiority) is a relative term in the *Quran*, as evidenced by the fact that some prophets are "preferred" over others in certain verses and yet at the same time other verses say that God makes no distinction between any of them. She acknowledges that *fadl* is god-given and cannot be earned through one's effort.[8]

Wadud then turns her focus to the preposition *bi*, which appears between *qawwamun 'ala* and *fadl*, etc… which she claims suggests that men are only guardians of women when the conditions are met that they are preferred *and* they in fact support women from their means.[9] This if-then clause reading is based on the translation of *bi(ma)* as "on the basis of (what)…." Based on my very limited knowledge of Arabic, it seems this is a mistranslation of *bi(ma)*, which actually is "through (what)" or "by means of (what)" as in "I go to work (*bi-sayyara*) by means of car" or "I study Arabic (*bi-alqra'a*) through reading books." In this case there is no conditional doubt expressed as to the divine preference and financial support that follow the preposition.

Her argument is furthered by the assertion that the only specified preference or thing that God has given a greater portion of to men than to women in the *Quran* is inheritance. This is not true. The verses on women's testimony in court say that the need for *two* female witnesses

---

8   Amina Wadud, *Qur'an and Woman: Rereading the Sacred Text from a Woman's Perspective* (New York: Oxford University Press, 1999), 69.

to make up for the lack of only *one* of the two legally required male witnesses is due to the feeblemindedness of women.[10] Women are also clearly allotted a lesser portion in polygyny laws, which assume that women are not as sexual as men and should be satisfied with only one man.[11] Wadud's argument, elsewhere, that polygyny was not established to cater to the desires of men but to suit the socio-economic situation of the time does not hold given that the many "temporary wives" or "slave-concubines" which men are allowed are not provided guardianship by them in any meaningful sense, yet women are not allowed to sleep with male slaves whom they may desire.[12]

Nonetheless, Wadud supports this connection to the verse on inheritance by translating *amoulhm* as "their (m.) *property*" rather than "their wealth" or "their means" as most translators do. She then uses this to make a circular argument justifying why women only inherit half of the property that men do, so that that man who gets double a woman's share will be responsible for her welfare.[13]

Wadud argues that the ambiguous usage "*some* of them over *others*" suggests that men as a class and on the whole are not superior to all women. Some women may be superior to some men.[14] Even if this is the case (which based on the intellectual inferiority seen in the verse on legal testimony, and other examples, is not true) these women would still be exceptions to the generality that men are superior; otherwise this sentence in 4:34 would make no sense at all in the context of explaining men's guardianship of women.

Ultimately, Wadud views men's *qiwammah* or guardianship over women as something meant to protect them from the oppressive situation of having to both bear and care for children *and* to provide

10   Nessim Dawood (Trans.), *The Koran* (New York: Penguin Classics, 1995), 2:282.

11   Ibid., 23:1–6; 4:16.

12   Ibid., 23:1–6.

13   Wadud, *Qur'an and Woman*, 70–71.

for themselves by their own labor or effort. It is a biological necessity of the family structure that women must bear the children in their wombs and nurse them in their infancy. Men are thus obliged to provide everything a woman needs both to sustain herself and to devote herself to properly performing the function of mother. The man also thereby takes part in child rearing himself.[15]

Wadud argues that 4:34 does not enjoin women to obey their husbands but that in the phrase "good women are *qanitat*," the Arabic word refers to a submission to God that is also desired of men. She extends this by arguing that in "those from whom you fear *nushuz*" the Arabic word means something causing marital discord and not "disobedience." She then cites the preliminary means of settling a dispute before moving on to "beating." Wadud tries to argue that *daraba* does not only mean "to strike" in the sense of using force but can also mean to set an example or "strike out on a journey."[16] Neither the word "example" nor "journey" follows *daraba* here such that it may alter its usual meaning, but it refers instead to the wife and so such a suggestion is ridiculous. Even Wadud seems to recognize this half consciously as she continues to squirm around the word by arguing that the injunction was not an allowance but was intended to severely curb existing marital violence against women. This is an untenable claim in light of sparse and unreliably contradictory historical accounts of seventh-century Arabian society.

Finally, Wadud ends by considering the line "if they obey (*ta'a*) you do not seek a way against them."[17] Here she admits that obedience to the husband (not God) *is* intended by *ta'a*, a word she contrasted to the earlier words in the verse whose usual translation as "obedient" or "disobedient" she contested. This contradicts her claim that these other words (namely *qanitat* and *nushuz*) are referring to submission

---

15 Ibid., 73.
16 Ibid., 74–76.

to God alone. In light of this last phrase, the preceding remarks "good women are obedient [*qanitat*]" and "those from whom you fear disobedience [*nushuz*]" are more probably (though not definitely) referring to the husband as the recipient of wifely obedience.

Wadud tries to contextualize this one admitted usage of obedience to the husband by again appealing to a mythical seventh-century Arabia. She baselessly asserts that this phrase was acknowledging the kind of marital relation then prevalent, but since the *Quran* is divine, it must also "present a compatible model to the changing needs and requirements of developing civilizations worldwide." This is really the crux of her "argument," which is not an argument at all. In the last analysis she does in fact admit that verse 4:34 is concerned with wives' obedience to their husbands as a condition for husbands not to harass their wives. Yet she *asserts* that this statement is historically conditioned and no longer applies in the modern context, even though this contradicts the *Quran*'s claims regarding the eternal validity of its specific decrees and the worthlessness of human social conventions (see below).

Barlas' *tafsir* of verse 4:34 refers to Wadud's repeatedly and draws on it heavily for support. Like Wadud, she interprets the advantage of men over women as purely financial and in this context interprets their guardianship as merely being the "breadwinner" of the family. Also, like Wadud, she argues that the phrase "more on some of them than on the others" means that some women are more financially endowed than some men, and thus men of lesser means cannot be the guardians of these women.[18]

Barlas quotes Wadud's interpretation of "obedience" verbatim and at length, arguing like Wadud, that obedience to God is intended. However, unlike Wadud, Barlas completely shies away from the use of *ta'a* in the phrase "if they *obey* you do not seek a way against them." As we saw above, the admission that obedience to husbands is clearly

---

18   Asma Barlas, *"Believing Women" in Islam*, (Austin: University of Texas Press,

intended here, and Wadud's failure to effectively qualify or excuse it,
is what ultimately unravels her interpretation of the verse. That Barlas
treats every line of verse 4:34 except this line at its conclusion not only
makes her *tafsir* incomplete and out of context, but also (given her
obviously close reading of Wadud) suggests overt deception or at least
her own repression and denial in confronting the text.

Unlike Wadud, who clearly believes that women are naturally
meant to be mothers within a family, Barlas cites other modern authors to the effect that a self-supporting woman does not live under
the guardianship of a given man.[19] While it is true that the *Quran*
never explicitly says that a woman cannot support herself financially
or otherwise, the vision of marital relationship in verse 4:34, where
men and women have different but reciprocal obligations in respect to
each other, is clearly set forth as the Islamic ideal. It is a precept of the
Quran, a guidance in life, and the *Quran* says that these are eternally
valid, inscribed as they are on an imperishable heavenly tablet and
merely translated into Arabic (see below).

Barlas quotes and refers to Wadud's most ridiculous assertion that
daraba in this verse may not refer to hitting a wife at all. She cites several other possible meanings given by other, no doubt contemporary,
interpreters. Her aim in doing so is to be able to conclude her interpretation of 4:34 by suggesting that the verse should be de-emphasized
in a reading of the *Quran* due to its murky ambiguity, as testified by a
variety of divergent readings. In fact, the "different" views on *daraba*
she offers are not many, and they all actually boil down to the same
alternative translation of the word as "confinement."[20] Unbeknown
to Barlas, this actually runs counter to her aim in making the verse
sound more lenient. Logically, a man cannot subject his wife to house
arrest without using physical force. If a wife, so unruly that reasoning
with her and shunning her has no effect, wishes to leave her house she

---

19 Ibid., 187.

can, and probably would, simply walk out no matter what her husband tells her. For house-*arrest* to really work under these circumstances, a man would have to apply much more physical force against his wife than if he were merely "to hit" her along the line of the traditional interpretation of *daraba*.

Finally, because even Barlas realizes that *daraba* in verse 4:34 probably does mean "to hit" (though much more grudgingly than Wadud) she says without any citation that "tradition holds" that it is not suppose to inflict pain and is thus only symbolic. Her appeal to tradition here, when she wholly rejects the "traditional" interpretation of this verse as well as traditional methods of interpretation altogether, is hypocritical.

Like Wadud, she also argues that it was a restriction on already severe and liberal battery of women by their husbands and could not have been permission, given the socio-historical context of seventh-century Arabia. She claims that it was an injunction aimed at a less civilized society and that we who are "more civilized" should not use it as an allowance.[21] As we stated above, seventh-century Arabia can be used as a straw-man to prop up many different and contradictory arguments, since there is little objective social history of the pre-Islamic era. Also, the concept of a historical progression in "civilization" is one born of the Western Enlightenment and is not only absent from the Quranic world-view, but profoundly contradicts it.

As we have seen, Wadud and Barlas' interpretations are very unsound. Their reinterpretations of specific words like *qanitat, nushuz* and *bi*, to which they devote much attention, are questionable from a linguistic point of view given the context of the passage as a whole — a context which Barlas explicitly ignores by refusing to treat a whole and important phrase in the verse that would compromise her argument. Beyond these details, Wadud and Barlas share two major biases in common that prevent them from engaging in viable *tafsir*.

The first of these is that as a matter of principle God, being "God" (whatever that means), inherently *cannot* subordinate women in human society. We see this when Wadud explains that she is "calling for a reading that regards [the] reforms [of the *Quran*] as establishing precedent for continual development toward a just social order," and then adds "[a] comprehensive just social order not only emphasizes fair treatment of women, but also includes women as agents, responsible for contributing to all matters of relevance to human society."[22] Barlas writes, even more strikingly, in a phrase that discredits her entire endeavor at its outset: "*At the very least*, we should be willing to agree that 'theologically speaking, whatever diminishes and denies the full humanity of women must be *presumed* not to reflect the divine or an authentic relation to the divine.'"[23] These statements show that Wadud and Barlas are approaching the *Quran* with the preconceived *demand* that it *must* accommodate the equality of women, because only that would be fitting of a religious message from God. Of course, this also involves a notion of God and Divine Justice that is not drawn from the *Quran* but is preconceived by these two women who are, admittedly, not even open to the possibility of finding that the Muslim divinity, Allah, could be otherwise than they wish him to be.

In fact a very strong case can be made that Allah does view the subordination of women to men as Just and Natural. There are many verses other than 4:34 that suggest this. In 4:11 a woman is given the right to only half of the inheritance entitled to a man. In 2:223 men are told that they may sleep with their women whenever it pleases *them* to do so. In 43:15–18 and 53:27 the notion of female divinity is ridiculed and in the same breath the idea that male heirs are more desirable than female children is sanctioned. Verses 78:31–33; 55:54–66; 56:35–38; 52:19–20; and 37:40 all objectify women as sexual playthings for men in paradise, while there is never any mention in the *Quran* of

22 Wadud, *Qur'an and Woman*, xiii.

heavenly sexual consorts for women. 2:282 requires two female witnesses to compensate for the lack of only one of two prescribed male witnesses at a legal proceeding, on account of the feeblemindedness of women. 23:1–6 allows a man to have sexual relations with as many slave women as he has seized in battle (in addition to his legal wives), whereas a woman is the sole sexual possession of her lawful husband. Verse 2:222 burdens women with the stigma of being ritually unclean during their monthly menstrual cycle, which, given Islam's code of ritual purity, prevents them from religious leadership. Verse 4:16 enjoins men to confine women convicted of adultery to their houses until death overtakes them, but the same verse says that adulterous men (which interestingly is only homosexually conceived) should be let alone if they repent after a corrective punishment.

Wadud and Barlas would attempt to explain away as many of these incidents as they could by claiming that the *Quran* was in each case intending to ameliorate an already deplorable social situation in pre-Islamic Arabia. The argument is that the *Quran* showed restraint in the degree of its "progressive" reforms so that they would not be rejected altogether by such a society. Wadud writes: "With regard to some practices, the *Quran* seems to have remained neutral: social patriarchy, marital patriarchy, economic hierarchy, the division of labour between males and females within a particular family."²⁴ She goes on to explain that women activists who question this neutrality basically do not realize that while the *Quran* is concerned with "consciousness raising with regard to women" this is only one of its concerns, and some other ones are more important.

This claim does not hold at all. The *Quran's* message does not simply involve an evolutionary "consciousness raising." It *did* confront seventh-century Arabia with impossibly sudden and radical demands for social change. These include the total eradication of the society's centuries-old religious polytheism by the sword, the dismantling of

tribal order and relationships in favor of a universal Muslim brotherhood, the restructuring of the Arabian peninsula's economic system,
and the demand to accept dogmas that were totally ridiculous to most
pre-Islamic Arabs, such as the Day of Judgment and the resurrection
of the dead. Any God that would consider these priorities above the
total liberation of women from subordination to men, *is* in effect
sanctioning their subordination.

The second bias that Wadud and Barlas share in common is this:
as a matter of principle, the *Quran* being a "divine" text (whatever that
means), must be "culturally and historically transcendent" in such a
way that it accommodates the progressively "changing needs and requirements of developing civilizations worldwide."[25] Barlas echoes this
statement by Wadud when she defines her opponents as believing that
"the Quran's meanings have been fixed once and for all as immutably
patriarchal and ...one cannot develop a new way of reading it that incorporates theories and insights that have matured twelve or so centuries after its own advent." She then defines her own task as finding out
"how the Quran's teachings address or accommodate ideas we find to
be true or compelling today."[26] As believing Muslims, neither Wadud
nor Barlas, deny that there are eternal verities in the *Quran* and that it
is historically transcendent. However they believe that eternal verities
are to be found by *subtracting* any perceived reflection of the historical
context in which an injunction was revealed from the essence of the
injunction itself. For them the text transcends history by allowing one
to implement this extracted essence in a radically different cultural
and historical context where it would concretely manifest itself as a
different practice, but supposedly one "with the same spirit."

In fact, the claim Barlas cites as the position of her opponents,
namely, that of the eternal validity of Quranic decrees in their specificity, is emphatically and repeatedly declared by the *Quran* itself. Wadud

---

25 Ibid., 77–78.

and Barlas do not realize that "historical transcendence" does not
mean "historical adaptability"; in fact it means its opposite. According
to the *Quran* itself this "transcendence" means that human society, at
all times in history, and irrespective of different pre-Islamic or non-
Islamic cultures, must accommodate the divinely ordained culture of
the *Quran* — not the other way around.

The *Quran* takes great pains to make clear that its injunctions are
perfect, eternally valid, and are to be followed without any alteration.
Verses 6:114–116 depict the *Quran* as a perfect and complete guide
to life that should be followed over the opinions of the majority of
people in the world: "Should I seek a judge other than God when it is
he who has revealed the Book for you with all its precepts? Those to
whom we gave the scriptures know that it is the truth revealed by your
Lord. Therefore have no doubts. Perfected are the words of your Lord
in truth and justice. None can change his words. If you obeyed the
greater part of those on earth, they would lead you away from God's
path." Verses 43:2 and 85:21–22 both clearly state that the *Quran* is a
literal transcript of an "eternal book" inscribed on an "imperishable
tablet" in God's keeping: "We have revealed the Koran in the Arabic
tongue that you may understand its meaning. It is a transcript of the
eternal book in Our keeping, sublime, full of wisdom";[27] "Surely this is
a glorious Koran, inscribed on an imperishable tablet."[28] The description of the revealed *Quran* as a "transcript" of the imperishable *Quran*
and of its translation into Arabic (from some verses in another, perhaps universal, language) makes clear that the eternal *Quran* includes
the specific injunctions of the revealed text in a more or less verbatim
manner and not simply some abstract "essential spirit" or "vision of
justice." If one has any remaining doubt as to the eternal validity of
the verses of this book inscribed on the heavenly tablet and merely
translated for Muhammad, verses 86:12–14 are sure to eradicate that

---

27 Dawood, *The Koran*, 43:2.

doubt: "By the sky that thunders, by the earth that splits, this [*Quran*] is a word once and for all, not meant lightly." Verse 2:85 insists that the *Quran* must be followed in the entirety of its injunctions: "Can you believe in one part of the Scriptures and deny another? Those of you that act thus shall be rewarded with disgrace in this world and with grievous punishment on the Day of Resurrection." This condemnation for heresy by selective belief is echoed by verses 2:174–177: "Those that suppress any part of the Scriptures which God has revealed in order to gain some paltry end shall swallow nothing but fire into their bellies. ... That is because God has revealed the Book with the truth; those that disagree about it are in extreme schism."

Finally, Muhammad's last revelation in verse 5:3: "This day I have perfected your religion for you and completed My favour to you," means that Islam, as defined by the content of the *Quran*, was perfected at that time in such a way that any historical evolution in Muslim practices along the lines desired by Wadud and Barlas is ruled out. When Muhammad addressed his followers in 632 CE at Ghadir Khumm with this final *ayeh*, the "spirit of Islam" was already completely embodied by the *Quran*'s injunctions on the just life and the practice of piety. To suggest otherwise is blasphemous "innovation" (*bida'*). In this light we see that the lines along which Ibn Kathir and Maududi interpret verse 4:34 are much more sound than the approach of Wadud and Barlas. I have not critiqued their readings because I find them both in harmony with each other and with the Quranic text. Ibn Kathir and Maudidi both claim that 4:34 involves the ideas that: *a) women are subordinate to men; b) men are therefore responsible for being their protectors and sustainers; c) women in turn owe their male guardians obedience; d) disobedient women are to be first rebuked, then shunned and finally beaten, but only lightly; e) if they return to obedience, or are obedient, women should never be harassed by their husbands.*

Given the many verses of the *Quran* cited above as support for
women's subordination by God and the non-evolutionary nature of

Islam evidenced by many other verse citations above, I believe that this is the most convincing reading of verse 4:34. Moreover, both Ibn Kathir (and surprisingly) Maududi use *hadith* material not only to support the subordination of women, which is not necessary in light of the Quranic material I have cited, but also to make clear that the "beating" referred to by the verse should be mild and avoid the face. This is not a conclusion that can be drawn from the verse itself or the greater context of the *Quran*. Thus, when Wadud and Barlas reject the use of *hadith*, they are compromising the little possibility that exists for lessening the plight of Muslim women — especially given that their alternative readings and methods are an embarrassing failure if not a self-conviction of blasphemy.

A CRITIQUE OF SHIITE ESOTERICISM

In the very words of its title, Mahmoud Ayoub's essay "the Speaking Qur'an and the Silent Qur'an" sums up the basic principle of Shiite *tafsir* (interpretation) of the *Quran*. Shiites believe that their holy book possesses an esoteric inner dimension beyond its exoteric dogmas and decrees, a dimension whose interpretation is entrusted to infallible spiritual leaders known as the *Imams*. I do not believe that this esotericism withstands an examination in light of the *Quran's* own claims concerning its nature and its relationship with those to whom it was revealed.

Ayoub begins by discussing the Shiite belief that when the *Quran* was revealed to Muhammad, so too was its proper exegesis (*tafsir*). While Muhammad openly taught the *Quran* itself to the masses, he secretly taught its exegesis to his son-in-law and cousin 'Ali.[1] Some even believe that 'Ali literally wrote down this secret commentary along with the text of the *Quran*, and passed this work down to his successors, the Imams. The supposed "complete *Quran*" is now in hiding

1   Mahmoud Ayoub, "The Speaking Qur'an and the Silent Qur'an" in *Approaches to the History of the Interpretation of the Quran*, Andrew Rippin Ed. (New York:

with the Twelfth Imam.[2] According to Shiites, 'Ali was chosen for the
role of successor by God, and Muhammad was initially informed of
this during his *miraj* to heaven by a voice from beneath God's throne.[3]
However, Muhammad feared his companions' reaction to 'Ali being
appointed as his successor, so he suppressed this divine command,
until these verses descended amidst the final revelation: "O Apostle,
convey that which was sent down to you from your Lord; for if you
do not, you will not have conveyed his message. God will protect you
from the people; surely God guides not the rejecters of faith."[4] Shiites
believe that Muhammad heeded this decree by declaring 'Ali as his
successor before a mass of followers at the spring of Ghadir Khumm,
on the way back from his final pilgrimage. From the start there was
dissent and some even plotted to kill the prophet.[5]

Aside from verse 5:67, Shiites ground their esotericism in verses
3:6–7 of the *Quran*, where the Book declares concerning itself:

> It is He who has revealed to you the Book. Some of its verses are precise in
> meaning — they are the foundation of the Book — and others are ambigu-
> ous. Those whose hearts are infected with disbelief follow the ambiguous
> part, so as to create dissension by seeking to explain it. But no one knows
> its meaning except God. [And those] who are well-grounded in knowledge
> say: 'We believe in it; it is all from our Lord.'

In the original Arabic the text lacks punctuation, and so while Sunni's
see a break between "except God" and "[T]hose who are firmly
grounded in knowledge...," Shiites read them as a single sentence.
Two completely contradictory meanings emerge. On the one hand,
Sunnis (unless they also happen to be Sufis) insist that the verse is a
command by God forbidding all human beings from interpreting the
mysterious verses of the *Quran*, whose meanings are known to God

---

2   Ibid., 182.

3   Ibid., 193.

4   N.J. Dawood (Trans.) *The Koran* (New York: Penguin Classics, 1995), 5:67.

alone, and instead adhere to the legal and ethical precepts of the clear verses. On the other hand, Shiites (as well as Sufi Sunnis) interpret the verse as meaning that there is an esoteric mystical dimension of the *Quran* which is hidden from ordinary people, but is understood by "those firmly rooted in knowledge" whom God has made "pure" in the sense of being infallible. These chosen ones, argue the Shiites, are the twelve Imams. Ayoub explains how Shiites see them as vice-regents that rein after every messenger of God, serving as intermediaries between the message entrusted to the Prophet and the people to receive it.

According to Shiites the interpretive medium of the Imams is necessary for people to understand and properly follow the *Quran*.[6] This is because, as Ayoub writes, "the *Quran* has many levels or dimensions of meaning. The most important principle of Shi'i *tafsir* therefore is that 'the *Quran* has an outer dimension (*zahir*) and an inner dimension (*batin*); its inner dimension has yet another dimension, up to seven inner dimensions.'"[7]

While previous religions have also had Imams, the latter are accorded an unprecedented place in Islam. This is on account of Muhammad being the "seal of the prophets," which means that in the wake of his death there will not be another messenger, and so the message of God is entrusted to the Imams until the end of Time. These Imams were so persecuted that the twelfth of them, son of Hassan Al-Asghari, was forced into hiding during childhood in the year 874 AD. He communicated with his followers indirectly, issuing decrees through a few messengers until the time of what should be his natural death. Thereafter, Shiites believe, he enters "greater occultation" (a mystical veiled presence in the world), from which he will return as the Messiah at the end of Time. He will then judge Muslims according

---

6   Ibid., 182–183; 186–187.

to the true exegesis of the *Quran* and establish a millennial kingdom of righteousness on Earth preceding Judgment Day.

Ayoub admits that Shiites believe that the Imams are the very purpose of God's creation, their luminous bodies being born, and their authority being decreed, before all else.[8] He quotes Imam Ja'far saying: "God made our authority the pole of the *Quran* and the pole of all scriptures. Around it the clear verses of the *Quran* revolve; through it scriptures were elucidated and through it faith becomes manifest."[9] In fact, being created neither in the manner nor at the same time as human beings, the Imams do not even seem to be "human" but rather arch-principles on the basis of which God creates the world of time and space: "[the Imams] are the purpose of the creation, and the purpose of their creation is the purpose of the Truth [that is, God]."[10]

A close reading of the *Quran* poses serious problems for this scheme of Shiite (and Sufi) esotericism. The idea of Imams introduces a hierarchy of believers into Islam that is fundamentally against the spirit of the *Quran*. Adam's (read humanity's) covenant with God is marked by his recognition of servitude,[11] and God repeatedly reminds Muslims that even the most exalted messengers are not beyond his wrathful reproach.[12] Prophets are different from their fellow human beings only in their perfect submission to God. Furthermore, with an eye to the idolatrous sin committed by Christians who "associated" the prophet Jesus with God, Muhammad time and again explicitly forbid praise and worship of himself, especially by forbidding all forms of religious imagery including portraits of himself. While Shiites claim that the Imams are infallible, we clearly see Muhammad's fallibility in verse 80:1 of a Surrah that takes its theme from God's chastisement of

---

8   Ibid., 180.

9   Ibid., 181.

10 Ibid., 180.

11 Dawood, *The Koran*, 7:172.

the Prophet for having turned a deaf ear to a sincere believer while seeking to persuade wealthy hypocrites. The *Quran* also explicitly claims that Muhammad did not have any secret knowledge of the kind Shiites impute to him. In verse 6:50 God commands Muhammad: "Say: I do not tell you that I possess God's treasures or know what is hidden. ... I follow only that which is revealed to me." Of course, aside from the ambiguous verses 3:6–7 and 5:67 cited above, the *Quran* makes no mention of the Imams whatsoever. Rather, it repeatedly announces itself to be addressed to the soul of each and every believer, on behalf of which no one can mediate or intercede on the Day of Judgment.

It is noteworthy that the passage 3:6–7 cited above from the *Quran* speaks of the clear and ambiguous verses of the book as two distinct kinds of verses, and exhorts the believers to follow the former without a doubt. The context of verses 3:6–7 of the *Quran* make it clear that the foundation of the text is actually what Shiites claim to be the "exoteric," and what they claim to be "esoteric" is merely peripheral: "[S]ome of the verses are precise in meaning — they are the foundation of the book — others are ambiguous." Yet Imam Ja'far says that the entire *Quran* enfolds a mysterious dimension that lies beyond the literal meaning of its verses. He says: "We possess such knowledge of God's sanctions and prohibitions as would oblige us to keep its secret, not telling anyone about it."[13] If by this mysterious pronouncement the Sixth Imam means to at all suggest that knowledge of the interior dimension of the *Quran* would challenge the ordinary believer's adherence to exoteric dogmas and decrees, there is no basis for this in the *Quran* whatsoever.

Genuinely mysterious passages (*mutashabih*) in the *Quran* are rare and they are clearly different in tone from its straightforward precepts (*muhkam*). One example is the evocation of God's omnipresent Light, lit by a metaphorical olive tree, in verse 24:35 : "God is the light of the heavens and the earth. His light may be compared to a niche that enshrines a lamp, the lamp within a crystal of star-like brilliance. It is lit from a blessed olive tree neither eastern nor western. Its very oil would almost shine forth, though no fire touched it. Light upon light; God guides to His light whom He will." Another example is verse 18:109, which may suggest that God's Word extends beyond the portion of it that has been recorded in the *Quran* revealed to Muhammad: "Say, if every sea became ink for the words of my Lord, surely, the sea would be exhausted before the words of my Lord were exhausted, even if a similar amount is brought as additional supply."

However, these passages are "mysterious" precisely because we who are fallible would only be guessing at their meanings, and thus running the risk of heretical "innovation" (*bidah*). This would be especially heretical if we were to suggest that whatever inner meaning they possessed were to call into question the clear precepts of the faith. Even if the mysterious image of verse 24:35 ends with the phrase "God speaks in metaphors to men / God has knowledge of all things," it is emphatically clear from verses 3:6–7 that this does *not* mean that all of the verses and precepts of the *Quran* are metaphorical, only a few, while the others are explicitly clear (*muhkam*) and it these latter verses that constitute the foundation of the faith to be followed by all believers. Likewise, if 18:109 implies that God's word extends to other precepts not encompassed by the *Quran* revealed to Muhammad, this can only mean that God did not wish the Islamic *'umma* to live by these precepts but rather by those which were indeed revealed.

To be sure, there are certain statements in the *Quran* that imply there is an essence of the faith that underlies its rituals. However, there is nothing mystical about this; rather it concerns an almost perpetual dread of the judgment and a profound hope for God's mercy. In 25:63–64 we hear: "True servants of the Merciful are those who walk humbly on the earth and say: 'Peace!' to the ignorant who accost them; who pass the night standing and on their knees in adoration of their Lord; who say: 'Lord, ward off from us the punishment of Hell for its punishment is everlasting: an evil dwelling and an evil resting place." Verse 32:15–16 echoes the suggestion that only believers of this kind are "true" servants of God, and Verse 76:25–27 again evokes the all-night vigil of sincere prayer as well as perpetual remembrance of the Lord: "Remember the name of your Lord morning and evening; in the night-time worship Him: praise Him all night long."

It may be the case that if one's faith is this profound and essential certain infractions of *sharia* will be overlooked because one's *nafs* is generally mortified by the dread of God (in a sense somewhat similar to Pauline Christian "mortification" rendering one "sinless"). In respect to dietary restrictions, verse 5:93 declares: "No blame shall be attached to those that have embraced the Faith and done good works in regard to any food they may have eaten, so long as they fear God and believe in Him and do good works. ... God loves the charitable." In respect to ritual prayer verse 29:45 declares: "Prayer fends off indecency and evil. But your foremost duty is to remember God. God has knowledge of all your actions." Verses 5:44–45 offer forgiving non-retaliation as a way to expiate one's sins. This offer is made in the context of citing the *Torah*'s law of commensurate punishment, and this would imply that similar laws in the *Quran* that decree certain proper recompense for certain wrongs done to individuals can be discarded by the wronged individuals themselves in favor of forgiveness. However, the verse ends by clearly making the point that this does not mean one can invent other (harsher or more lenient) laws dealing with punishment for transgressions against oneself or others. The verse only gives the choice between total forgiveness, by which some of one's sins may be expiated, or complete adherence to the letter of the *Quran*'s own code of justice: "We have revealed the Torah, in which there is a guidance and a light. ... We decreed [therein] for them a life for a life, an eye for eye, a nose for a nose, an ear for an ear, a tooth for a tooth, and a wound for a wound. But if a man charitably forbears from retaliation, his remission shall atone for him. Transgressors are those that do not judge according to God's revelations."

Thus we see that the pardons explicitly mentioned by the *Quran* are restricted to infractions concerning dietary restrictions and perhaps also the performance of the daily prayers (on account of a spontaneously perpetual remembrance of God), but certainly not the legal precepts of the *Quran*. Moreover the infractions remain as such, i.e. as "sins" against real prohibitions, but they are outweighed by the believer's righteousness: "As for those that have faith and do good works, We shall cleanse them of their sins and reward them according to their noblest deeds."[14]

This notion of essential verses, superficial belief and practice is supported by the *Quran*'s use of the two terms *mu'minin* and *muslimin* to refer to believers. The former simply means "believer," while the latter means "submitter." Every Muslim, with a capital "M," is a "believer" in the dogma of the Quran, but only certain believers truly live in submission to God with their whole heart, soul and will. These two stages of belief are most clearly contrasted in verse 3:102 of the *Quran*: "O believers (*mu'minin*), fear God as He ought to be feared, and become true submitters (*muslimin*) before you die." Here those who have already accepted the Islamic religion are being addressed, not unbelievers, and so there is the implication that adherence to dogma does not necessitate the heartfelt or sincere faith upon which salvation depends.

In addition to verses 3:6–7 discussed above, the *Quran* takes great pains to make clear that its injunctions are perfect, eternally valid, and are to be followed without any alteration. Verses 6:114–116 depict the *Quran* as a perfect and complete guide to life that should be followed over the opinions of the majority of people in the world: "Should I seek a judge other than God when it is he who has revealed the Book for you with all its precepts? Those to whom we gave the scriptures know that it is the truth revealed by your Lord. Therefore have no doubts. Perfected are the words of your Lord in truth and justice.

None can change his words. If you obeyed the greater part of those on earth, they would lead you away from God's path." Verses 43:2 and 85:21–22 both clearly state that the *Quran* is a literal transcript of an "eternal book" inscribed on an "imperishable tablet" in God's keeping: "We have revealed the Koran in the Arabic tongue that you may understand its meaning. It is a transcript of the eternal book in Our keeping, sublime, full of wisdom";[15] "Surely this is a glorious Koran, inscribed on an imperishable tablet."[16]

If one has any remaining doubt as to the eternal validity of the verses of this book inscribed on the heavenly tablet and merely translated for Muhammad, verses 86:12–14 leave us with no doubt: "By the sky that thunders, by the earth that splits, this [Qur'an] is a word once and for all, not meant lightly." Verse 2:85 insists that the *Quran* must be followed in the entirety of its injunctions, which means that whether or not one has a more profound inner faith one is still bound by its legal precepts: "Can you believe in one part of the Scriptures and deny another? Those of you that act thus shall be rewarded with disgrace in this world and with grievous punishment on the Day of Resurrection." This condemnation for heresy on account of selective belief is echoed by verses 2:174–177: "Those that suppress any part of the Scriptures which God has revealed in order to gain some paltry end shall swallow nothing but fire into their bellies…That is because God has revealed the Book with the truth; those that disagree about it are in extreme schism."

In light of these passages, verses 3:6–7, which are used by Shiites as evidence of an esoteric dimension of the *Quran* and of the authority of the Imams to interpret it, cannot mean that the gnosis of this "esoteric" dimension would in any way invalidate the *Quran*'s "exoteric" *sharia*. This is clear enough from the passage's own exhortation to follow all of the foundational "clear verses" rather than being perversely driven

---

to obscure interpretation based on the mysterious ones. In conclusion, we see that there is no "true and limitless meaning of the Quran" to be fathomed by Muslims, as Ayoub describes the Shiite *batin*.[17] If there is an "essence" of Islam at all, it is concerned with a profound inner faith characterized by holy dread of Judgment and perpetual remembrance of God, one that does not challenge the exoteric dogmas or laws of the *Quran* but underlies their sincere observance. There is no evidence for any other kind of esoteric understanding of Islam in the *Quran* revealed through Muhammad.

Now let us lay to rest the belief that Muhammad secretly initiated his cousin and son-in-law Ali ibn Abu Talib (4th Caliph) into a gnostic wisdom that is passed on in a *silsila* or "chain" from Imam to Imam and down on to the Sufi masters and founders of orders. The only way, if any, that this belief would be verified is if the vast corpus of sermons of Ali testified to his mystical understanding. Quite to the contrary, Ali's *Nahjul Balagha* shows just how literally he subscribes to all of the most ridiculous and barbaric dogmas of the *Quran*.

In *Sermon 1* Ali describes how Allah kneaded and molded Adam from different kinds of clay, dried him and blew into him to animate his mind and limbs. He then describes how all of the angels bowed to Adam at Allah's command, except for Iblis (Satan) — at which point he explicitly quotes the *Quran*. Ali then continues to describe Adam's temptation by Iblis and his fall from Paradise, in which Allah "sent him down to the place of trial and procreation of progeny" and promised him an ultimate return to the garden by way of pious action. There is nothing mystical about this at all. Neither is there anything mystical about Ali's literal belief in the Quranic vision of Judgment Day and the resurrection. In *Sermon 82* he says that "Allah would bring them [people] out from the corners of the graves," whereupon the resurrected will "run towards the place fixed for their final return, group by group, quiet, standing and arrayed in rows." Finally their "ears would resound with the thundering voice of the announcer calling towards the final judgment, award of recompense, striking of punishment and paying of reward." Later in the same sermon Ali emphasizes perpetual fear of God (rather than divine love) as the proper state of the true believer: "O creatures of Allah, fear Allah, like the fearing of the wise man whom the thought (of the next world) has turned away from other matters, fear (of Allah) has afflicted his body with trouble and pain, his engagement in the night prayer has turned even his short sleep into awakening, hope of eternal recompense keeps him thirsty in the day..." Ali adds: "Certainly paradise is the best reward and achievement, and hell is appropriate punishment and suffering."

Hope of paradise and detailed descriptions of it that seduce the believer into earthly piety are just as much part and parcel of Ali's teaching as of Muhammad's. In *Sermon 164* Ali says in light of the beauty of paradise this world and its desires and pleasures should seem cheap to the believer, whereupon he describes in detail "the rustling of the trees whose roots lie hidden in the mounds of musk on the banks of the rivers in Paradise and in the attraction of the bunches of fresh pearls in the twigs and branches of those trees, and in the appearance of different fruits from under the cover of their leaves. These fruits can be picked without difficulty as they come down at the desire of their pickers. Pure honey and fermented wine will be handed round to those who settle down in the courtyards of its palaces."

Ali concludes with a statement that betrays the basis of Muslim piety is striving for the above described delights of paradise, a desire so intense that it makes one long to leave this world and go straight to the next: "O listener! If you busy yourself in advancing towards these wonderful scenes which will rush towards you, then your heart will certainly die due to eagerness for them, and you will be prepared to seek the company of those in the graves straight away from my audience here and hasten towards them." In reading such passages we can easily understand the psychology of Muslim martyrdom, it being the only means to in fact go straight from this cheap world into the delights of the heavenly garden.

Ali's views on half of humanity are most un-mystical and in line with the barbarity of the *Quran*'s dark Surah on women. In *Sermon 152* Ali speaks contemptuously of beasts, carnivores and women in the same breath when he says: "Beasts are concerned with their bellies. Carnivores are concerned with assaulting others. Women are concerned with the adornments of this ignoble life and the creation of mischief herein. On the other hand believers are humble, believers are admonishers and believers are afraid of Allah." The last part of this statement takes the degradation of women even further than the *Quran* by shockingly suggesting that only men are spiritually and intellectually fit to be "believers." Like a beast, a woman is also incapable of true faith. In *Sermon 79* Ali employs a ridiculously circular argument that condemns women for the very strictures that the *Quran* binds them with in the first place: "O ye peoples! Women are deficient in Faith, deficient in shares and deficient in intelligence. As regards the deficiency in their Faith, it is their abstention from prayers and fasting during their menstrual period. As regards deficiency in their intelligence it is because the evidence of two women is equal to that of one man. As for the deficiency of their shares that is because of their share in inheritance being half of men." Ali concludes this statement with a warning to believers never to listen to a woman or heed to her wishes, even if it seems that she is right. This verse offers the perfect compliment to the *Quran*'s infamous verse (quoted above) concerning women's duty to obey men because of the latter's superiority: "So beware of the evils of women. Be on your guard even from those of them who are (reportedly) good. Do not obey them even in good things so that they may not attract you to evils."

Not only does Ali literally reiterate and uphold every major dogma of the *Quran*, he also believes that the *Quran* is such a perfect and complete guide that any and every bit of "innovation" outside of its *sharia* is heresy and blasphemy. In *Sermon 175* he writes:

[K]now that this *Quran* is an adviser who never deceives, a leader who never misleads and a narrator who never speaks a lie. ... You should also know that no one will need anything after (guidance from) the *Quran*. ... Know, O creatures of Allah, that a believer should regard lawful this year what he regarded lawful in the previous year and should consider unlawful this year what he considered unlawful in the previous year. Certainly people's innovation cannot make lawful for you what has been declared unlawful; rather, lawful is that which Allah has made lawful and unlawful is that which Allah has made unlawful. ... People are of two categories—the follower of the *shariah* (religious laws), and the follower of the innovations to whom Allah has not given any testimony by way of *sunnah* or the light of any plea.

Therefore the notion that the *Quran* was an exoteric message of discipline for the ignorant rabble and that there is an esoteric mystical Islam for a spiritual elite, would have been considered totally heretical by Ali himself—never mind the preposterous and totally unsubstantiated claim that he himself was the first initiate of this mystical tradition! After thoroughly examining the sermons of Ali we see that beyond a shadow of a doubt he *was* no mystic at all. Not only did he subscribe completely to the dogma of Muhammad's Quranic revelation, he also fervently reaffirmed the eternal validity of all its decrees. Thus the *silsilat al-Irfan* (chain of gnosis) breaks at its very first link, and the tradition of "Islamic Mysticism" is severed from Muhammad and his *Quran*, in other words, from Islam itself.

SPINOZA, THE
UNTIMELY ONE

As noted in the previous chapter, verses 86:12–14 of the *Quran* are clearer still: "By the sky that thunders, by the earth that splits, this [*Quran*] is a word once and for all, not meant lightly." Together with verses 2:85 and 2:174–177, also cited in Chapter 5 of this book, there can be no doubt about the *Quran*'s intentions.

More than any other philosopher before him, Friedrich Nietzsche considered himself a visionary and revolutionary thinker, a man born outside of time, an "untimely one." In the last half-century, much scholarship has questioned this Promethean image of Nietzsche. His debts to Schopenhauer were well known even in his own time, and the influence of such figures as Dostoyevsky and Emerson have since been discerned. By comparison, the affinity of Nietzsche's thought with the much earlier work of Baruch Spinoza has been neglected. This despite a number of strong indications, in Nietzsche's published works and private notebooks,[1] that Spinoza is the one figure who by far holds the greatest title to being Nietzsche's predecessor.

---

1   Friedrich Nietzsche, *Writings from the Late Notebooks* (New York: Cambridge

In section 475 of *Human, All-too-Human*, Nietzsche is arguing against anti-Semitism.[2] He claims that it is the Jews "to whom we owe the noblest human being (Christ), the purest philosopher (Spinoza), the mightiest book, and the most effective moral code in the world." This is all the more remarkable because the Jews are "a people which, not without guilt on all our parts, has had the most sorrowful history of all people," persecuted by all nations on account of their being perceived as threatening because of "their energy and higher intelligence, their capital of spirit and will."

In section 408 of *Mixed Opinions and Maxims*, Nietzsche lists Spinoza as one of eight thinkers in terms of which his own thinking unfolds and who have the right to judge his work from beyond the grave. He writes: "With these I must come to terms when I have long wandered alone; they may call me right and wrong; to them will I listen when in the process they call each other right and wrong. Whatsoever I say, resolve, or think up for myself and others—on these eight I fix my eyes and see their eyes fixed on me. May the living forgive me that occasionally *they* appear to me as shades, so pale and somber, so restless and, alas, so lusting for life—while those men then seem so alive to me..."

In a later notebook entry Nietzsche revises the list, writing: "My ancestors: Heraclitus, Empedocles, Spinoza, Goethe."[3] Heraclitus and Schopenhauer are usually cited as the two philosophers who had the greatest impact on Nietzsche, and who might be considered his predecessors. Interestingly, Heraclitus fails to appear on the first list, while Schopenhauer, who does appear on the first list, is dropped in the second. Nietzsche never seriously engages with Epicurus, Montaigne or Pascal (from the first list), nor with Empedocles (from the second), and his extensive comments about Plato and Rousseau (cited in the

2   Friedrich Nietzsche, *Human, All Too Human* (University of Nebraska Press, 1984).

3   Friedrich Nietzsche, *Basic Works of Friedrich Nietzsche* (New York: The Modern

first list) are almost completely critical and negative. The only two thinkers present in *both* lists are Spinoza and Goethe. Goethe is not a philosopher in the strictest sense, so this leaves us with Nietzsche suggesting that, of all philosophers, Spinoza is the most intimately related to him.

In a third list of greatest thinkers and kindred spirits, which appears in Nietzsche's notebooks from the period of the *Gay Science*, Spinoza alone appears of the figures from the first and second lists and is now equated with the likes of the founders of the world-religions (and of Nietzsche himself!): "In that which moved Zarathustra, Moses, Mohammed, Jesus, Plato, Brutus, Spinoza, Mirabeau — I live too."[4]

A letter of July 30, 1881, written by Nietzsche to Franz Overbeck, may be the clearest single piece of evidence for his debt to Spinoza, or at least proof of a strong affinity with this predecessor. Here Nietzsche clearly states that he and Spinoza are in agreement on five main points, *the denial of*: 1) free-will; 2) purpose; 3) the moral world order; 4); the un-egoistic; and 5) the existence of evil. Nietzsche writes:

> I am really amazed, really delighted! I have a precursor! I hardly knew Spinoza: what brought me to him now was the guidance of instinct. Not only is his whole tendency like my own…in five main points of his doctrine I find myself; this most abnormal and lonely thinker is the closest to me in these points precisely: he denies free will, purposes, the moral world order, the nonegoistical, evil; of course the differences are enormous, but they are differences more of period, culture, field of knowledge.

As we shall see, this is no exaggeration. Spinoza anticipates nearly every major aspect of Nietzsche's thought. There are more than twenty-five significant references to Spinoza in the course of Nietzsche's published works and private notes. I will focus on those of them that underline the affinity of Nietzsche and Spinoza, as the majority of critical remarks on Spinoza antedate Nietzsche's own claim (in 1881) that the differences between the two thinkers are superficial and are far outweighed by the fundamental similarities.

Let us begin with a comparison of the respective views of Spinoza and Nietzsche on the relationship between the Mind and Body. Spinoza believes that the Mind is an idea of the Body.[5] It is not a simple idea representing a coherently unified body, but a complex of ideas whose "objects" (*ideatum*) are diverse bodily processes.[6] Thus the relationship between Mind and Body is more intimate than a mere causality, wherein either the movements of the Body would depend on the ideas of the Mind, or bodily processes would determine these mental ideas. Instead, forging beyond both idealist and materialist reductionism, while at the same time avoiding Cartesian dualism, Spinoza holds that: "the mind and the body are one and the same thing, which is conceived now under the attribute of thought, now under the attribute of extension."[7]

This is essentially the same way that Nietzsche conceives of the relationship between mind and body, though in very different language. It is often assumed that Nietzsche reduced the Mind to an effect of bodily drives. This is the sense that we get from passages like the following, from sections 489 and 491 of the *Will to Power*: "Thinking is for us a means not of 'knowing' but of describing an event, ordering it, making it available *for our use*... [and] belief in the *body* is more fundamental than belief in the *soul*. ... [T]he body is the richer, clearer, more comprehensible phenomenon: to be placed first methodologically."[8] Such passages can be very deceptive, because Nietzsche's use of the language of the body is polemical and is not

---

5   Benedict de Spinoza, *A Spinoza Reader: The Ethics and Other Works* (Princeton, NJ: Princeton University Press), *Ethics* 2:13.

6   Ibid., *Ethics* 2:15.

7   Ibid., *Ethics* 2:21, Scholium.

8   Friedrich Nietzsche, *The Will to Power* (New York: Random House, 1968).

indicative of biological reductionism. This becomes clear in the following passage from section 552 in the *Will to Power*:

> There are no opposites: only from those of logic do we derive the concept of opposites — and falsely transfer it to things. ... If we give up the concept 'subject' and 'object,' then also the concept 'substance' — and as a consequence also the various modifications of it, e.g., 'matter,' 'spirit,' and other hypothetical entities, 'the eternity and immutability of matter,' etc. 'We have got rid of *materiality*.'

Here we see Nietzsche reject both a spiritual *and a materialistic* interpretation of the world, going beyond both idealism and materialism, as Spinoza had before him. Still, Nietzsche does not believe that Spinoza has gone far enough to overcome the idealist scorn for the body, though he has gone further than most thinkers. In section 372 of the *Gay Science*, Nietzsche critically calls "even Spinoza" an idealist, afflicted with a vampirism that sucks everything dry of the "blood" of the senses — leaving us the clattering bones of mere words, like Spinoza's "amor intellectualis Dei." This is noteworthy because Nietzsche ultimately views *every* philosopher since Socrates as an idealist of some sort, so that "*even* Spinoza" should be read as a qualifier that almost elevates Spinoza above the whole history of philosophy and brings him nearest to Nietzsche's own overcoming of the tradition.

Nietzsche's views on selfhood and self-preservation are remarkably similar to those of Spinoza in every way. Even though Spinoza conceives of beings as finite modes of a single substance, he does believe that these modes enjoy a relative independence on account of possessing an individual essence or *conatus*. Reflecting on Descartes' demonstration with the molten wax (intended to show that only the properties of size, shape and motion are definitively real), Spinoza notes that many beings do not behave in the same manner as the wax. Instead, they resist damage; they seem to strive to persist in their own being and can even restore themselves if injured. This suggests that an individual essence defines a given being, such that if it were removed that being would no longer be itself.[9] Given that every bodily process also has a mental aspect, this endeavor of self-preservation is what we conceive of as will (*voluntas*). When we become self-conscious of the "appetites" of our conatus, we experience willful "desire" (*cupiditas*).[10] Nevertheless, though our "individual essence" strives for its own preservation through various desires, this endeavor itself is not something that we can will, rather our apparent will is itself a function of it. For those phenomena which, when considered under the attribute of thought, we call the decisions of the mind and acts of the will, are the very same phenomena that, if considered under the attribute of extension, would be seen as the biological appetites of bodily processes governed by the physical laws of motion and rest.[11]

According to Spinoza, in so far as we do not have an adequate idea of these causes we are governed by unconscious forces. Furthermore, the self-as-agent is an illusion brought about by the mind's ideas of its ideas, which in turn are bodily processes conceived intellectually.[12] Thus, while our emotions seem to be outwardly focused on certain objects or persons, they are actually confused conceptions of affectations of the body at the hands of uncontrollable external causes that are caused by other causes, in an untraceable recession *ad infinitum*.[13]

It is widely believed that Nietzsche is the supreme philosopher of a social-Darwinist will to self-preservation. Instead, the truth is that like Spinoza, and though he thought that beings are characterized by self-preservation, Nietzsche paradoxically recognized that the same beings lack an agency to preserve, or by means of which they might seek self-preservation, so that self-preservation is only a function of a

---

9   Spinoza, *Ethics* 3:6; 2: Definition 2.

10 Ibid., 3:9.

11 Ibid., 3:2, Scholium.

12 Ibid., 2:21.

greater will of life acting through beings. In section 490 of *The Will to Power,* Nietzsche views "the subject as [a] multiplicity," wherein "the important main activity is unconscious and... consciousness is the effect of forces whose essence, ways and modalities are not peculiar to it." Nietzsche, like Spinoza, believes that the ultimate causes of this greater will of life are not discernable to the beings affected by them.

In Section 13 of *Beyond Good and Evil,* Nietzsche is arguing against the Darwinist claim that self-preservation is "the cardinal instinct of an organic being." He praises Spinoza and says that "we" owe it to him that we do not make this mistake because Spinoza realized the apparently inconsistent truth that beings seek "self-preservation" (paradoxically) not for their own sake, but to serve a greater will to power of "life itself." Self-preservation is only a result of this. Oddly enough, in section 349 of the *Gay Science,* Nietzsche criticizes Spinoza and the Darwinists for holding self-preservation as a prime principle. He claims that they made the mistake of abstracting their own down-trodden struggle for *mere* existence under conditions of distress and imposing it on a world truly characterized by the squandering and overabundance of the will to power, i.e. the will to superiority and dominance (not mere "survival"). He goes so far as to call the will to self-preservation a "Spinozistic dogma."

The *Gay Science* was written in two installments. Parts one through four were written before *Beyond Good and Evil,* while part five was written immediately after it. The critical comments in Section 349 were thus written after Nietzsche's commending of Spinoza for understanding self-preservation more clearly than Darwinists. Since the words of praise in Section 13 of *Beyond Good and Evil* show a more subtle understanding of Spinoza as well as deeper thinking in general, the latter charge in the *Gay Science* must be viewed not only as polemical, but as a knowing distortion of Spinoza's doctrine so as to make it fit a certain stereotype or caricature. It is a commonly employed tactic in Nietzsche's writings to take people and turn them into symbols of an idea, often to dramatize some polemic

Nietzsche's views on agency and causality are substantially similar to those of Spinoza. In Section 5 of Chapter 3 in *Twilight of the Idols*, Nietzsche writes that the grammatical discourse of language, which defines thought, erroneously

> sees everywhere deed and doer...believes in will as cause in general...believes in the 'ego,' in the ego as being, in the ego as substance, and...*projects* its belief in the ego-substance on to all things — only thus does it *create* the concept 'thing.' ...Being is everywhere thought in, *foisted on*, as cause; it is only from the conception 'ego' that there follows, derivatively, the concept 'being.' ...At the beginning stands the great fateful error that the will is something which *produces an effect*— that will is a *faculty*...Today we know it is merely a word.[14]

In Section 3 of Chapter 6, Nietzsche adds: "the will no longer moves anything, consequently no longer explains anything — it merely accompanies events, it can also be absent." In sections 633–634 of the *Will to Power*, Nietzsche writes: "Two successive states, the one 'cause,' the other 'effect': this is false. The first has *nothing* to effect, the second has been effected by *nothing*." It might come as a surprise to those who know Nietzsche as the philosopher of "will" to power that Nietzsche, like Spinoza, is an ardent fatalist and views "free will" as a fiction.

Even though Spinoza proposes three stages of knowledge, so as to make it appear that there is a spectrum of degrees in the adequacy of ideas, underlying this theory is a simpler and more fundamental conception of knowledge. Imaginative and scientific knowledge both conceive of things "in relation to a certain time and place," while intuitive knowledge conceives of things "as contained in God, and following from the necessity of the divine nature."[15] From the perspective *sub specie durationis* ("under the aspect of time"), we identify ourselves with the apparently free and autonomous will of our individual

14 Friedrich Nietzsche, *Twilight of the Idols & the Anti-Christ* (New York: Penguin Books, 1990).

conatus. However, when we transcend to the perspective *sub specie aeternitatis* ("under the aspect of eternity"), by the use of our reason, we understand that free will is an illusion following from our inability to trace the causes of all our actions back to the dictates of divine Necessity.[16] In fact, all of our endeavors are no more contingent than the movements of a stone rolling down a hill, which stone, ignorantly absorbed in itself, might believe itself to be freely pursuing its desire. Contingency and possibilities are not real qualities of the world but defects of our intellect.[17]

Nietzsche's great doctrine is that of "will to power." Yet in section 8 of chapter 6 of *Twilight of the Idols,* which Nietzsche himself frames with the title "what alone can our teaching be," he does not use the misleading words "will to power" at all. Instead he states that in the absence of causality and substance: "*No one* is accountable for existing at all, or for being constituted as he is, or for living in the circumstances and surroundings in which he lives. The fatality of his nature cannot be disentangled from the fatality of all that which has been and will be…" In respect to Necessity and free will, Nietzsche disagrees with Spinoza only on the relationship between "God" and Fate. In entry 18 of Notebook 36 (June–July 1885), Nietzsche claims that Spinoza's desire for infinite creative novelty from his "Deus sive Natura," betrays the persistence of a traditional religious sentiment and is hypocritical in light of Spinoza's own claim to affirm the purposelessness of existence. Spinoza insisted on infinite novelty because he did not want to equate "Deus sive Natura" with *fate,* as Nietzsche seems to do at times. However, two years later in Section 15 of Essay II in *On the Genealogy of Morals,* Nietzsche praises Spinoza for having "wrathfully defended the honor of his 'free' God against those blasphemers who asserted that God effected things *sub ratione boni.*" Nietzsche says that this

---

16 Ibid., 2:35, Scholium.

freed God from fate and restored the innocence of the world as it was before the rise of bad conscience. These apparently contradictory passages can be reconciled in the following way. Though he often props himself up as the greatest enemy of God or as the proclaimer of the "death of God," Nietzsche does sometimes describe his own vision of a divinity in positive terms. In Section 16 of the *Birth of Tragedy*, Nietzsche, like Spinoza, equates God with the incomprehensible and terrible power of "the eternally creative primordial mother" that is *Nature*. In Section 797 of the *Will to Power*, he affirmatively refers to Heraclitus' vision of God as the eternal child playing games of chance: "Play, the useless — as the ideal of him who is overfull of strength, as 'childlike.' The 'childlikeness' of God: *pais paizon* [a child playing]." In Section 381 of the *Gay Science*, as elsewhere, he evokes the image of God as the 'Lord of the Dance,' and of the philosopher as a master of dance: "I would not know what the spirit of a philosopher might wish more to be than a good dancer. For the dance is his ideal, also his art, and finally also his only piety, his 'service to God.'" When we view these passages in the light of Nietzsche's comments on the nature of *fate*, we are left with the sense that Nietzsche's God is not equal to fate, nor is his divinity free from fate. Metaphorically, it could be said that Nietzsche's fate is not mechanistic, it is a dance, or a game of chance — which remains engrossing as a game despite having only a certain vast but limited number of possible outcomes.

It is unclear how different Spinoza's view of the relationship between God and Fate really is from that of Nietzsche. After all, though Spinoza views God as free from fate, he also views God's instantiation of fate as not bound by the requirement of having a sufficient reason. Though Spinoza's entire moral doctrine is based on seeking knowledge of reasons, Spinoza, like Nietzsche following after him, views the foundation of the world as without reason, irrational, *insane*. Of course, Spinoza would not have admitted the latter so bluntly. It is on account of this hypocritical failure to realize just how radically his own thinking has departed from tradition, that Nietzsche finds fault with Spinoza while at the same time echoing Spinoza's revolutionary thoughts in a purified form.

According to Spinoza, ironically, it is the illusion of free will born of the imagination that renders us most passive and powerless in respect to our fate and prevents us from claiming it as our own. "Free will" is responsible for a reactive type of morality. A person who comprehends and reaffirms Necessity is freed from the negative passions of hatred, contempt, envy, vengeance, pity, humility and weakness in respect to others.[18] Nietzsche wholeheartedly agrees.

In *On the Genealogy of Morals*, Nietzsche argues that the weak mass of humanity needs something *more* than life in order to be able to bear the suffering of its existence. However, it has turned out that "the characteristics which have been assigned to the 'real being' of things are the characteristics of non-being, of *nothingness*—the 'real world' has been constructed out of the contradiction to the actual world…"[19] Thus the will to truth that has undergone so many transformations throughout the course of history, must ultimately reveal itself as "a will to nothingness, an aversion to life" — an *attitude towards life*, towards a "riddle of existence" to which we are *fated*. In a passage from Chapter 20 of Book 2 of *Thus Spoke Zarathustra*, "On Redemption," Nietzsche writes:

> All 'it was' is a fragment, a riddle, a dreadful accident—until the creative will says to it, 'But thus I willed it.' Until the creative will says to it, 'But thus I will it, thus shall I will it.'
>
> But has the will yet spoken thus? And when will that happen? Has the will been unharnessed yet from his own folly? Has the will yet become his own redeemer and joy-bringer? Has he unlearned the spirit of revenge and all gnashing of teeth? And who taught him *reconciliation with time* and something higher than reconciliation? For *that will which is will to power must*

18   Ibid., 5:50, 53.

will something higher than any reconciliation; but how shall this be brought about? *Who could teach him also to will backwards?*[20]

Certainly, an effective "will" as we traditionally conceive of it, or a will that could at once command and actualize its desire amidst the world of men by virtue of its power, could not do the same to *what has already passed in time.* We can only have an *attitude* towards the past, how it has brought us to our present and burdens our future. To nonetheless wish to go back and change the past is to be dominated by the "spirit of revenge," revenge against time, against one's fate. If one believes that there remains the consolation that, burned by the past, one can at least seize the present furiously in one's claws and mold it with meticulous precision then one is "harnessed" by the "folly" of belief in the effective will, which does not exist.

The future is as fated as the past and this is just what defines the nature of fate. According to Nietzsche, if any final state of the world could come to be in the future, it would have to be infinite and eternal and thus be manifest in the present as well as in the past. Since we experience finitude and time this cannot be so. Yet if the world is *open* in its ceaseless becoming *and closed* in its finitude, then there are a finite number of possible states of affairs. Thus every moment of every life is bound to repeat itself over again in another life after an ever-withdrawing "end of the world." Nietzsche calls this most burden-some thought "the Eternal Recurrence of the Same." It would appear that in light of this eternal recurrence the only choice one has is to express "good will" or "aversion" towards one's fated life. Nietzsche's Zarathustra tells us that the "will" of *will to power* is an attitude to-wards the fated past, present and future which says "*...thus I willed it...thus I will it, thus shall I will it.*"

In Entry 6 of Notebook 5 (summer 1886–autumn 1887), Nietzsche is contemplating the eternal recurrence of the same as if for the first

---

20 Friedrich Nietzsche, *Thus Spoke Zarathustra* (New York: The Modern Library,

time. Interestingly, he concludes by calling it "the most extreme form
of nihilism" and a "European form of Buddhism." It is against this
background that in Entry 7 of the same notebook, he wonders whether pantheistic affirmation is possible in the face of eternal recurrence.
He asks himself whether it is still possible to affirm life once it has
been revealed to be purposeless and amoral. He concludes that: "This
would be the case if something within that process were *achieved* at
every moment of it—and always the same thing. Spinoza attained
an affirmative stance like this insofar as every moment has a *logical*
necessity: and with his fundamental instinct for logic he felt a sense of
triumph about the world's being constituted *thus*." It seems from these
notebook entries that Nietzsche might have first gained the courage
for the ultimate affirmation of fate, or *amor fati*, that stands at the
heart of his later philosophy, by means of Spinoza.

Attacking Judeo-Christian morality, Spinoza argues that "we do
not strive towards, desire or long for a thing because we deem it to be
good; but on the contrary, we deem a thing good because we strive,
desire or long for it."[21] A morality of "good and bad" is not metaphysically rooted in the nature of the world, but is wholly relative to individual subjects and their particular desires and aims. For Spinoza,
the only "good" is that which is *useful*, while the only "bad" is that
which is disadvantageous.[22] Nietzsche's vision of an ethic of "will to
power" is well known. In Section 149 of the *Will to Power*, Nietzsche
writes: "*Justification,* as function of a perspicacious power which looks
beyond the narrow perspectives of good and evil, thus has a wider
horizon of *advantage*—the intention of preserving something that is
more than any given person."

For Spinoza, the idea that God engages in punishment and
reward is absurdly ridiculous; He neither hates nor loves anyone in

---

21   Spinoza, *Ethics* 3:9.

particular.[23] Rather, we punish ourselves with despair when we act in a way that is not true to our own nature. Nietzsche, the great "immoralist" also believes in an ethics of conscience or the instinct to adhere to one's own nature. In Section 270 of the *Gay Science*, Nietzsche writes: "What does your conscience say? — 'You shall become the person you are.'" He continues in section 275: "What is the seal of liberation? — No longer being ashamed in front of oneself." In Section 7 of Chapter 12 of Book 3 of *Thus Spoke Zarathustra*, Nietzsche contrasts moral ethics with his ethics of conscience: "To be true — only a few are *able*! And those who are still lack the will. But the 'good' have this ability least of all. Oh, these good men! *Good men never speak the truth*; for the spirit, to be good in this way is a disease. They give in, these good men, they give themselves up; their heart repeats and their ground obeys: but whoever heeds commands does not heed *himself*." Finally, in Section 906 of the *Will to Power*, Nietzsche describes the "strong man" as one who "is led by a faultless and severe instinct into doing nothing that disagrees with him."

In Entry 131 of Notebook 2, Nietzsche discusses Spinoza in the course of an outline for his never-to-be-realized magnum opus, *The Will to Power*. Nietzsche deems "Spinozism extremely influential" in "the devaluation of all values up to now." He praises Spinoza for an attempt to accept the world as it is, to "rid oneself of the moral order of the world," and to realize (perhaps for the first time) that "Good and evil are only interpretations, by no means facts or in-themselves." Nietzsche concludes by commenting that: "one can track down the origins of this kind of interpretation [so as to] slowly liberate oneself from the deep-rooted compulsion to interpret morally." This suggests that Nietzsche's characteristic method of the genealogy of morality proceeded from out of Spinoza's move beyond good and evil. In Section 15 of Essay II in *On the Genealogy of Morals*, Nietzsche says that Spinoza "banished good and evil to the realm of human

imagination." He praises Spinoza for viewing punishment as an unfortunate consequence of transgression, not as a sign that one should
have done differently or as a cause for guilt, but simply as something
having unexpectedly gone wrong, leading to an emotion that is the
opposite of joy. He quotes Spinoza on this, citing Ethics III, proposition XVIII, Schol. I.II. He favorably identifies this view of Spinoza
with the outlook of Pre-Christian societies who believed in corporal
punishments, having the dignity to discipline the criminal rather than
make him feel guilty.

For Spinoza, though human liberty is illusory, this does not mean
that human *freedom* is impossible. Spinoza claims that in so far as we
use our Reason to comprehend what is necessary and then consciously
affirm this in action, we are acting freely. The degree of our freedom
depends on the degree to which we rationally comprehend the necessary causes of our actions, so that our act is free in consciously following from the truly free will of God. In this sense Spinoza's *amor
intellectualis Dei* ("intellectual love of God"), is an *amor fati* ("love of
[one's own] fate"), which fills one with joy.[24] By affirming Necessity we
cease to be passive and we gain power over that which affects us, not
"power" in the sense of "force," but power as *elevation* or *perspective*.[25]
Spinoza equates "virtue" and "perfection" with *power* in this sense.[26]
He argues that the source of our pleasure is to constantly increase
our power, while true pain is a lapse into the weakness of negative
passions born of "narrow-mindedness."[27] Mental states are an expression of a degree of power, wherein a greater or lesser awareness and
affirmation of one's bodily processes is present. In this sense in which
Power *actualizes* one's "bodying-forth" in the world, Spinoza equates

---

24   Ibid., 5:15.

25   Ibid., 5:6.

26   Ibid., 4: Definition 8.

it with "Reality." Degrees of power are degrees of reality and of the enhancement of one's *conatus*.[28]

If by *Wille zur Macht*, Nietzsche means a (free) will to empowerment, then the similarity with Spinoza's metaphysics and ethics of power would be merely superficial. However, as suggested above, Nietzsche does not believe in an effective and free will. If he also does not believe in a positive definition of *power*, we are forced to completely reevaluate what he means by "the will to power." In sections 633–634 of *The Will to Power*, Nietzsche writes:

> Two successive states, the one 'cause,' the other 'effect': this is false. The first has *nothing* to effect, the second has been effected by *nothing*. It is a question of a struggle between two elements of unequal power: a new arrangement of forces is achieved according to the measure of power of each of them. The second condition is something *fundamentally different* from the first (not its effect): the essential thing is that the factions in struggle emerge with different quanta of power. ... *A quantum of power is designated by the effect it produces and that which it resists. The adiaphorous state is missing, though it is thinkable.*

The "adiaphorous state" which is missing, though readily conceivable as an intellectual abstraction, is the positive quality of "power." Nietzsche explicitly defines this "power" as *nothing* but the *difference* of power between two states of two or more entities in respect to each other. If he then also defines the essence of these entities or "beings" as "power" — he is implicitly stating that every "being" defers its being to the others in terms of which it exists at all and also defers its present to its past conditions of existence. To speak of the difference of two quanta of power is redundant, for it is to speak of the difference of difference. This differentiation is the structure of the creative matrix.

In German, *Wille* ("will") is derived from the verb *wollen*, meaning "to want," even in the sense of "to be lacking" in such and such. Furthermore, *Macht* ("power") is derived from the verb *machen*, "to make" or "to render," in the sense of dynamic creation rather than a static locus of "power-in-itself." Finally, *zur* is a contraction of *zu der*, which means "towards the...." So that *wille zur macht*, suggests perpetually moving "towards," but never arriving at "the making" or the creation of the world. As Nietzsche writes in section 796 of the *Will to Power*: "the world as a work of art that gives birth to itself." This is not very different from Spinoza's idea that to say we aim at the increase of power is to say that we strive to understand and knowingly affirm the will of *Deus sive Natura*.

According to Spinoza, the execution of mathematical or logical proofs is the only activity in which we are likely to be able to attain the comprehensive knowledge of necessary causes required for total freedom. However, in this light, Spinoza believes that we can increasingly bring our hitherto unconscious emotions within the grasp of our conscious power by treating them "geometrically," that is, by analyzing them (and their effect on us) in a cold, almost mathematically rigorous calculus.[29] By means of this "emendation of the passions," emotions cease to be something in respect to which we are *passive*.[30] Thus the love of knowledge and the pursuit of understanding is the path to the serene blessedness of freedom, and Spinoza equates following this path with the realization of our essential "human nature" (that which differentiates us from other beings).[31]

All of these notions are basically present in Nietzsche's thinking as well, even if they are not related in the same way as they are for Spinoza. In section 490 of the *Will to Power*, Nietzsche writes that: "the important main activity [of the human mental and emotional life] is unconscious and... consciousness is the effect of forces whose essence, ways, and modalities are not peculiar to it." Though Nietzsche does not insist that these unconscious drives be rendered conscious,

---

29   Ibid., 3: Preface.

30   Ibid., 5:3, Corollary.

he does speak of taming the chaos of human affects or emotions into something obeying cold mathematical and logical necessities. In Section 530 of the *Will to Power*, Nietzsche writes: "All human knowledge is either experience or mathematics." In Section 842, he elaborates: "To become master of the chaos that one is; to compel one's chaos to become form: logical, simple, unequivocal; to become mathematics, *law* — that is the grand ambition here." Superficial readers of Nietzsche would be surprised to learn that, like Spinoza, he values the quest for knowledge above all else. In his July 30th 1881 letter concerning Spinoza, he writes, "[H]is whole tendency [is] like my own — to make knowledge the most *powerful passion*..." These few lines make a subtle but very important point. Nietzsche interprets Spinoza's view of knowledge as something that conquers the passions, *not* by neutralizing them (as is commonly supposed), but by dominating them as the strongest *passion*. For lack of agency, in both Spinoza and Nietzsche's systems, there is no way that the passions could be neutralized because they can never become the object of action for a non-existent subject.

In Section 2 of Book 1 of the *Gay Science*, entitled "The Intellectual Conscience," Nietzsche praises the conscientious pursuit of certainty as "that which separates higher human beings from the lower." He writes, "[W]hat is good-heartedness, refinement, or genius to me, when the person who has these virtues tolerates slack feelings in his faith and judgments and when he does not account *the desire for certainty* as his inmost craving and deepest distress..." This "desire for certainty" is the essence of Spinoza's quest for knowledge as a means to affirm necessity. While Nietzsche values it as much or more than Spinoza does, he realizes that it is ultimately no more than another affect without a traceable cause, as Spinoza does not, but should realize, given the implications of his metaphysics.

Finally, Nietzsche, like Spinoza, equates this transformation of consciousness both with a sense of serene blessedness and with the re-alization of an essential humanity. In section 700 of *The Will to Power*

Nietzsche describes "the highest feeling of power" as "calm, simpli-
fication, abbreviation, concentration. ... To react slowly; a great consciousness; no feeling of struggle." In section 337 of *The Gay Science*,
Nietzsche describes the realization of our *true nature* (by affirming the
will of "the whole"), as the "divine feeling" of "humanity":

> He who knows how to regard the history of man in its entirety as *his own*
> *history* feels in this immense generalization all the grief of the invalid who
> thinks of health, of the old man who thinks of the dream of his youth, of the
> lover who is robbed of his beloved, of the martyr whose ideal is destroyed,
> of the hero on the evening of the indecisive battle which has brought him
> wounds and the loss of a friend. But to bear this immense sum of grief of
> all kinds, to be able to bear it, and yet still be the hero who at the com-
> mencement of a second day of battle greets the dawn and his happiness as
> the one who has a horizon of centuries before and behind him...to take all
> this upon his soul, the oldest, the newest, the losses, hopes, conquests, and
> victories of mankind: to have all this at last in one's soul, and to comprise
> it in one feeling: — this would necessarily furnish a happiness which man
> has not hitherto known — a God's happiness, full of power and love, full
> of tears and laughter, a happiness which, like the sun in the evening, con-
> tinually gives of its inexhaustible riches and empties into the sea — and like
> the sun, too, feels itself richest when even the poorest fisherman rows with
> golden oars! This divine feeling might then be called — humanity.

We have seen how almost every major "innovation" of Nietzsche's
doctrine is already to be found in Spinoza's thought, more than two
hundred years earlier. We have also seen evidence that, at least in some
instances, Nietzsche probably inherited these uniquely paradoxical
and iconoclastic ideas from Spinoza. Nietzsche follows Spinoza in
abolishing the materialist/idealist division between mind and body, in
denying agency while discerning a will to self-preservation as characteristic of beings, in finding an ecstatic freedom or realization of the
human potential in the denial of free will and the affirmation of fate,
and finally, Nietzsche, the self proclaimed "first immoralist," follows
Spinoza in opposing the reactive moral opposition of "good" and

"evil" with a positive ethics based on the enhancement of perspectival power. Where do the two thinkers really diverge? It may be that Nietzsche's most serious departure from Spinoza is not in his doctrine, but in his *attitude*. In Section 157 of *Human, All-too-Human*, Nietzsche speaks of Spinoza, together with Kepler, as a "learned genius," contrasting him with the type of the artistic genius. The latter type, which Nietzsche sees as characterizing himself, laments of his greater sorrows and privations (in proportion to other men), whereas a learned genius like Spinoza does not, because "he can count with greater certainty on posterity and dismiss the present." In Section 37 of the *Gay Science*, Nietzsche calls Spinoza's faith in the benign nature of Science and the "unselfish, harmless, self-sufficient, and truly innocent" character of genuine scientific inquiry, one of the three errors on account of which science has been promoted over the last several centuries.

In Section 5 of *Beyond Good and Evil*, Nietzsche criticizes Spinoza for having clad his philosophy in a "mail and mask" of "hocus-pocus of mathematical form" in order to intimidate those who would challenge it, to scare them off from defiling it, as if his doctrine were the goddess Athena protected by her armor. Spinoza is not singled out for this, but cited as an example of philosophers in general, who are dishonest in pretending that their wisdom is the product of cold, pure and unconcerned logical argumentation, whereas the latter are usually marshaled after the fact in order to give form to a mystical inspiration or filter and make abstract "a desire of the heart." Nietzsche is not denying that he and Spinoza might share an essentially similar "desire of the heart," he is simply criticizing Spinoza for demanding that *everyone* should recognize the "truth" of his values. To the contrary, on the grounds of the metaphysics of power (first proposed by Spinoza), Nietzsche believes that his values are *his own*, even though they are also the *highest*. Spinoza does not have the strength for this. However, in addition to accusing Spinoza of "personal timidity and vulnerability," Nietzsche ends by calling him a "sick hermit." An interesting accusation, given that Nietzsche spent most of his own life ill and in profound solitude.

In Section 25 of *Beyond Good and Evil*, in addition to reiterating his description of Spinoza as one of "the compulsory recluses," he levels a more serious accusation against Spinoza, namely that the latter had become one of the "sophisticated vengeance-seekers and poison-brewers," calling on us to "lay bare the foundation of Spinoza's ethics and theology." The comments come in the course of a warning to philosophers not to be deluded into believing that their struggles and persecution in the world are sacrifices in the name of defending truth. Their inability to openly and forcefully confront and defeat their enemies breeds a poisonous craftiness in them and robs them of the playful innocence and good humor that characterizes a truly free spirit. If they ultimately go from being outcasts to being "martyrs," then they have ceased to be tragic philosophers and have instead become farcical "stage-and platform-bawlers." In the following section, Nietzsche elaborates on this idea in a way that makes clearer his criticism of Spinoza in particular. Nietzsche acknowledges that choice human beings strive to create "a citadel and a secrecy" of solitude that saves them from the disgusting masses. Spinoza, the recluse, is certainly the kind of figure that he has in mind here. However, Nietzsche claims that it is even more exceptional to "go down" and live amongst men, to study them, but also to test oneself and become a more inward (more "spiritual") person, for the lack of an external fortress. Those who lack the strength for this, such as Spinoza, were "not made… not predestined, for knowledge."

It should be noted that in his preface to *Human, All-too-Human*, Nietzsche describes a "great separation" as the most decisive event in the life of a man who is to one day become a genuinely free spirit. He describes this need to "go off into some desert" as symptomatic of spiritual illness. Here, as in many other passages throughout his works, Nietzsche speaks of the uncanny state of mind brought about by such an illness as a womb of creativity and a path to liberation. An especially vivid example of this is in *Thus Spoke Zarathustra*, when after returning to his hermetic solitude, Zarathustra falls ill only to realize that the common man or "last man" must also be affirmed as necessary and that he must descend once again amongst men to learn from them. Thus it is clear that Nietzsche suffered from the same hermetic illness that he identifies in Spinoza, so that even Nietzsche's most vitriolic criticisms of Spinoza appear on closer examination to be another example of Nietzsche's painfully intimate relationship to his predecessor. He chastises himself by way of chastising Spinoza, because he suffers from the same wounds, from having followed the same perilous and solitary mountain path to spiritual freedom. Nietzsche concludes his July 30th, 1881 letter describing his "discovery of Spinoza" with these telling words: "*In summa*: my solitariness which, as on very high mountains, has often made me gasp for breath and lose blood, is now at least a solitude for two. Strange!"

ALIENS AND THE MORAL LAW

Beginning in the *Groundwork of the Metaphysics of Morals*, Immanuel Kant attempts to fashion a genuinely *universal* ethics — a moral law which would apply to all the types of alien intelligence that he was convinced fill the heavens. To this end, namely in order to ground a moral law relevant to all rational beings, Kant needs to first define what it is that all and only rational beings share in common. He claims that this is the *existence* of a rational being as "an end in itself." However, in the relevant passages it is unclear who or what *is* the "end in itself." Is it the rational being(s) as entities that Nature ultimately aims to produce, or the "own" *existence* of each and every rational being? The first section sets out this problem and ventures a provisional solution to it.

However, in order to address this question in the most interpretively charitable way, the second section considers innovations of Kant's later moral philosophy, in the *Critique of Practical Reason* and the *Metaphysics of Morals*, which affect the meaning of key concepts in the *Groundwork* and modify certain of its central claims. Among these is the transformation that Kant's concept of "will" (*Wille*) undergoes with the later development of the concept of the "power of choice" (*willküre*). Such a transformation of the concept of will has significant consequences for the *Groundwork*'s notion of freedom, a notion which Kant claims is somehow inseparably connected with his definition of a rational being as a being whose existence is an end in itself. There is also a related change in Kant's view of whether the moral law can allow for (or indeed, requires) the happiness of others and one's own perfection to be objects of the faculty of desire and material determining grounds of the will.

In the third and final section, after having ascertained how we are to understand an end in itself with respect to the existence of beings, its relationship to Kant's single innate Right of *freedom* is determined. An attempt is made to draw out the empirical claims about the nature of extraterrestrial intelligence that are implicated by Kant's *a priori* attempt to develop a universal moral philosophy — both an ethics *and political principle of Natural Right* that would apply to any and all non-human rational beings. To this end the reader is asked to patiently immerse himself for a time in a world of truly alien intelligence, without which it is not possible to be struck by the boldness of Kant's claim that all extraterrestrials would be *persons* whose power of free choice renders them individually responsible to one another under *the* moral law.

I.

Kant refers to non-human intelligence no less than eleven times in the *Groundwork of the Metaphysics of Morals*, and he draws an explicit distinction between human beings and rational beings in general on six of these occasions (see 4:389, 4:408, 4:425, 4:428–4:29, 4:447–448, and 4:449). When we view these references through the lens of the third part of Kant's 1755 astronomical work *Universal Natural History and Theory of the Heavens*, it begins to become clear that applicability to extraterrestrial intelligence was the key motivation behind Kant's attempt to develop an *a priori* moral philosophy.

Kant's *Universal Natural History* is famous for two novel astronomical theories that more or less proved to be true: the disc shape
of the Milky Way and the idea that distant nebula are actually other
"universes" (really, other galaxies). However, in the long-suppressed
third section of this work, Kant develops a theory of aliens of varying degrees of rationality, depending on the empirical conditions of
their development (with distance from the sun being the key factor).
There are some beings so perfect in their physical and spiritual constitution that they adhere to the moral law virtually flawlessly, while
there are others so malformed and pathologically driven that they are
incapable of sin only because they lack the capacity for responsible
actions. Between these extremes, there are beings out there like ourselves — fallible, but capable of resisting our sensuous inclinations and
obeying the single moral law within us all.[1]

This core insight remains a background for the development of
Kant's moral philosophy, even if he eventually dismissed the specifici-
ties of his theory of extraterrestrial intelligence in the third part of this
speculative work and consented to its suppression within his own
lifetime. In the *Critique of Pure Reason*, Kant writes:

> I should not hesitate to stake my all on the truth of the proposition — that,
> at least, some one of the planets, which we see, is inhabited. Hence I say
> that I have not merely the opinion, but the strong belief, on the correctness
> of which I would stake even many of the advantages of life, that there are
> inhabitants in other worlds.[2]

We also have a passage towards the end of the *Critique of Practical
Reason*, where Kant suggests that were it not for the moral law within
each man, his perishable physical being as an animal creature alone
would render him insignificant in the face of the vastness of the

---

1   Michael J. Crowe, *The Extraterrestrial Life Debate: Antiquity to 1915* (University
     of Notre Dame, 2009), 149.

2   Immanuel Kant, *Critique of Pure Reason* (New York: Cambridge University

cosmos. It is the fact that the heavens are populated by beings capable of acting on the moral law that renders contemplation of the vastness of the heavens edifying, rather than cause for a sense of terrifying absurdity. Significantly, the first lines of this passage from the Second Critique are quoted on Kant's tombstone:[3]

> Two things fill the mind with ever new and increasing admiration and awe, the oftener and more steadily they are reflected on: the starry heavens above me and the moral law within me. ... The former... broadens the connection in which I stand into an unbounded magnitude of worlds beyond worlds and systems of systems. ... The former view of a countless multitude of worlds annihilates, as it were, my importance as an animal creature, which must give back to the planet (a mere speck in the universe) the matter from which it came.[4]

Now, bearing in mind Kant's firm belief in a plurality of worlds, let us return to the *Groundwork of the Metaphysics of Morals* and trace the line of argument that leads to his definition of rational beings as beings the existence of which is in an end in itself. Kant begins by arguing that it is inherent to the idea of duty, and of moral law, that it holds not only for human beings, but for all rational beings. Consequently, whatever the ground of ethical obligation may be, it cannot be sought in empirically conditioned human nature. Anthropology is only useful in humans' application of moral rules effectively in the conduct of their daily lives.[5] Thus an action from duty must set aside or even run against all inclinations, or habitual sensual desires. The will of rational beings must be able to be determined objectively solely by the law and subjectively by pure respect for the law.[6] This law must not be derived from any special tendency of human reason. This point is emphasized

---

3   Crowe, *The Extraterrestrial Life Debate*, 151.

4   Immanuel Kant, *Groundwork of the Metaphysics of Morals* in *Practical Philosophy* (New York: Cambridge University Press, 2006), 5:161.

5   Ibid., 4:389.

by characterizing it as an objective principle on which we would be directed to act *even if* it went against the grain of "every propensity, inclination, and natural tendency *of ours* (i.e. of we *Homo sapiens*)."[7] For it to do so would only render the command in a duty more sublime and dignified, according to Kant, while taking nothing away from its validity. After having stripped away all inclinations and or motives relevant only to human sensibility, nothing can be left other than action in conformity with universal law itself—a law whose representation must determine the will without regard for any *effect* that could be the *object* of desire.[8] It is at this point that Kant first introduces the Categorical Imperative: *I ought never to act except in such a way that I could also will that my maxim should become a universal law.*

Kant goes on to claim that this requires us to accept that no possible experience could be grounds for inferring an apodictic, universal law of this kind. Given his reiteration that such a law must hold for all rational beings, the implication here is probably that the conditions for subjective experience could be radically different for non-human rational beings. Kant also makes reference to a passage from the Gospels, Matthew 9:17, in which Jesus asserts that even the example of his life is not sufficient for inferring the goodness of God. Kant claims that reason frames *a priori* the idea of God as the supreme good, and that it is really an idea of moral perfection.[9]

All moral concepts grounded in reason *a priori* are as present in the most common reason as they are in the highest degree of speculative reason.[10] This further circumscribes the idea of a rational being as such, by asserting that one cannot be a rational being by degrees. One either is or is not a rational being capable of adhering to the moral law. This prepares us for the following claim, namely that, not only

---

7   Ibid., 4:425, my emphasis.

8   Ibid., 4:402.

9   Ibid., 4:408–409.

is the moral law unconditioned by any human sensibilities, but in order to hold for all rational beings, moral laws must not be derived from any empirically contingent cognitions pertaining to the special nature of *human* reason. Whether by the latter Kant means a generic rational faculty geared to function in the context of human sensibilities, or some distinctly human cognitive faculty that is a variation on the theme of rational faculties in general, either way this further criterion requires Kant to seek "the universal concept of a rational being as such."[11] Only then can we really understand what a Categorical Imperative is, or wherein its ground lies.

Everything in nature works according to laws. What is unique about those beings that are rational, is that they have the capacity to act in accordance with their representation of these laws. If the will of a rational being were perfectly determined by reason, then that being would have a perfectly good — or "holy" — will. However, in a being whose will is not perfectly determined by reason, actions that are cognized as objectively necessary are *imperatives*, or commands of reason — they indicate an "ought."[12] Imperatives are either hypothetical or categorical. Hypothetical imperatives are those that command actions undertaken toward some other end, actions which are *means* toward some end beyond themselves, whereas *the* Categorical Imperative would be an action represented as objectively necessary in-itself.[13] We cannot know in advance what the content of a hypothetical imperative may be, but we always already know what a Categorical Imperative will contain; since it cannot be limited by any empirical condition, the maxim of action under the Categorical Imperative conforms solely to the universality of law as such. This universal lawgiving is what the Categorical Imperative represents as necessary. Kant argues that this means that there is, strictly speaking, only *a single* Categorical

---

11   Ibid., 4:412.

12   There would be no "ought" for a "holy" being.

Imperative: *act only in accordance with that maxim through which you can also will that it become a universal law.*[14]

Now we are very close to Kant's definition of a rational being as a being the existence of which is an end in itself. The move towards that definition comes through consideration of the type of *ends* at which the two kinds of imperative aim. Subjective *ends* rest on incentives. They are material ends in the sense that they can be effects of one's actions. These are consequently only the grounds of *hypothetical* imperatives. All of these are only relative. On the other hand, objective ends hold for every rational being. It is at this point that, in order to define an objective end, Kant rhetorically asks whether there could be something "the *existence of which in itself* has an absolute worth, something which as *an end in itself* could be a ground of determinate laws."[15] He claims that the ground of a possible Categorical Imperative or practical law, referring to no end beyond itself, would lie in this alone. What is more, without an "end in itself," there would be nothing of absolute worth that could serve as a standard for something like a Categorical Imperative. From this we see that the "end in itself" is an objective principle that grounds the Categorical Imperative.

Interpretation of the following key passages in the *Groundwork of the Metaphysics of Morals*, from 4:428 through 4:429 are the core concern to which I will repeatedly return. For now, it should suffice to point out that in these passages Kant offers four or five distinct reformulations of the idea of "beings the existence of which is an end in itself." He defines such beings, which may not be used merely as a means, as "persons," distinguishing them from natural beings that may be used merely as means on account of their being "things" without reason. The two most significant among these key passages (for our purposes here) come immediately after Kant draws the

---

14   Ibid., 4:420–21.

distinction between "persons" and "things." Their relevant sections
read as follows:

> [Rational beings are] beings the existence of which is in itself an end, and
> indeed one such that no other end, to which they would serve *merely* as a
> means, can be put in its place, since without it nothing of *absolute worth*
> would be found anywhere; but if all worth were conditional and therefore
> contingent, then no supreme practical principle for reason could be found
> anywhere.
>
> If, then, there is to be a… Categorical Imperative, it must be one such that,
> from the representation of what is necessarily an end for everyone… it
> constitutes an *objective* principle of the will and thus can serve as a univer-
> sal practical law. The ground of this principle is: *rational nature exists as an
> end in itself.* The human being necessarily represents his own existence in
> this way; so far it is thus a *subjective* principle of human actions. But every
> other rational being also represents his existence in this way. … [T]hus…
> it must be possible to derive… [t]he practical imperative… *So act that you
> use humanity, whether in your own person or in the person of any other,
> always at the same time as an end, never merely as a means.*[16]

The claim that "every other rational being necessarily represents his
own existence" the same way that the "human being" does, makes
it clear that in the last line above, stating the practical imperative,
"humanity" refers not to human beings in the sense of *Homo sapiens*
as in the preceding sentences, but to *humanitas* as rational nature in
general — a philosophical usage common since Stoic cosmopolitan-
ism. These passages suggest that what is shared by all rational beings — namely, their *humanitas* of them — consists of the manner in
which they are able to represent their "*own* existence" to themselves.
In other words, to be an "end in itself" is to be a being conscious of
one's own existence. The use of "his own" by Kant as a qualification
of the manner of the representation of existence strongly supports
this reading. Non-rational beings are "things" in the sense that their

manner of being is that of an entity within the natural world; they are for the sake of nature, and are not their "own." Nature, on the other hand, *is* for the sake of rational beings. Two passages taken together make this controversial claim:

> [T]he human being… is subject *only to laws given by himself but still universal* and… he is bound only to act in conformity with his own will, which, however, in accordance with nature's end is a will giving universal law.[17]

> A kingdom of ends is possible only by analogy with a kingdom of nature; the former, however, is possible only through maxims, that is, rules imposed upon oneself, the latter only through laws of externally necessitated efficient causes. Despite this, *nature as a whole*, even though it is regarded as a machine, is still given the name 'a kingdom of nature' insofar as and because it *has* reference to *rational beings as its ends*.[18]

This claim that "nature as a whole…has…rational beings as its ends" does, however, pose a further problem for our interpretation of what it means to be "an end in itself." Are rational beings end*s* in themselves in the sense that their coming-to-be as entities is the supreme end of Nature? In other words, are rational beings only qualitatively unique among entities, and not categorically distinct from them?

The question may be decided by a passage in which Kant claims that "Rational nature is distinguished from the rest of nature by this, that it sets itself an end," and he very significantly adds that "the end must here be thought not as an end to be effected but as an *independently existing* end, and hence thought only negatively, that is, as that which must never be acted against and which must therefore in every volition be estimated… the subject of all possible ends itself…"[19] If the being of a rational being, qua entity, were "an end in itself," then it could presumably be an end—or rather, *the* most important end "to

---

17 Ibid., 4:432.
18 Ibid., 4:438, my emphasis.

be effected" by Nature. Yet, as we have seen, Kant states that "an end in itself" is one that cannot be effected by anything, in other words, cannot be brought into being through any apparent natural process. Their independent existence is itself "the subject of all possible ends" in that they do not exist as actors in the world, as it were, amidst or alongside other things. All of their ends are pursued through their *own* existence, which means that for each rational being, her existence encompasses her world of practical activity.

In every activity her existence "reaches consciousness immediately," not as the discursive thought "I exist," but in the sense that every aim of activity is grounded in, and bounded by, this existence and repeats a representation of this existence within itself.[20] In sum: rational beings *are* an end in themselves in the sense that they are not within the world, they *are* the existence of their world. Whatever is to prevent this from collapsing into solipsistic idealism is somehow connected to the concept of a "kingdom of ends," which, as Kant claims is the archetype *and end* of the merely so-called "kingdom" of nature. The world becomes "a world of rational beings (*mundus intelligibilis*) … a kingdom of ends… [with] all persons as members."[21]

What is it that allows a rational being to gain the vantage point over and above nature that non-rational animals do not have? What is it that gives him "consciousness of himself" and accounts for *the ontological difference between him and other beings* brought about by this self-consciousness?[22] Freedom. It is not incidental that the next major discussion in the *Groundwork* is an understanding of the moral law in terms of free will. In depth consideration of this is deferred to the second section's examination of Kant's redefining of "will" in his later moral philosophy, and the effect it has on our understanding of the problem of the "end in itself" with which we are engaged in the

20 Ibid., 4:451.

21 Ibid., 4:438.

Groundwork. For now, suffice it to say that Kant makes the following very elegant set of three claims, inferring each from the previous one in accordance with what he takes himself to have already established in the *Groundwork*: 1) Every*thing* in nature is necessitated by a heteronomy of causes; in other words, no *thing* in nature is an end in itself because it is the effect of "some*thing*" else, which is again only derivatively a "cause"; 2) As opposed to this heteronomy of efficient "causes," the voluntary actions of a rational being have an altogether different kind of causality, one whose unified and non-derivative nature can be characterized as "autonomy" — or *freedom* of the will; 3) For the will of any being to be in all actions a law unto itself, means for it to act on no maxim other than that which can have as its object itself as a universal law, in other words, the Categorical Imperative.[23] Therefore, a "free will" is not a "lawless" will; it is in fact nothing other than a will under moral law. Kant claims thereby to have "traced the determinate concept of morality back to the idea of freedom."[24]

Since Kant has already established, at the outset of the *Groundwork*, that the very idea of morality is nonsense unless it applies not only to human beings but to all rational beings, and since it has now been shown that morality "must be derived solely from... freedom," it follows that *all* and *only* rational beings are free beings.[25] A being that is an end in herself, is one whose *existence* makes it so that she "cannot act otherwise than *under the idea of freedom*."[26] An "end in itself" is existentially condemned to freedom, in other words to self-consciousness and responsibility for her own actions, "cognizant of [the moral 'ought'] even while he transgresses it."[27]

---

23   Ibid., 4:446–47.
24   Ibid., 4:449.
25   Ibid., 4:447–48.
26   Ibid., 4:448.

II.

The problems raised by Kant's claim that the rational subject has "free will," insofar as he is conscious of his own causality, are notorious. Kant attempts to resolve the contradiction between "free will" and natural determinism by setting up a parallelism of two "different standpoints."[28] From the standpoint of speculative reason all phenomenal "mere appearances," including that of the subject as an object, are determined by laws of nature. From the standpoint of practical reason, the subject is immediately conscious of his own causal autonomy or freedom of will.[29] Scandalously, this requires positing things-in-themselves in an "intelligible world" beyond mere appearances, which cannot be the object of any intuition, and of which nothing further than its existence can be cognized.[30]

At times Kant writes dismissively of the subject as thing-in-itself conscious of its freedom as "*only* a standpoint that reason sees itself constrained to take,"[31] a merely "useful and permitted idea,"[32] "the objective reality of which is in itself doubtful."[33] At other times, he claims that in respect to the distinction between the "world of sense" and the "world of understanding," the former can be very different depending on the diverse sensory faculties (sensibilities) of various rational beings, whereas the world of understanding is the same for all of them and "is its basis" — in other words, the world of understanding is not parallel to the merely apparent world of sense, but grounds it.[34] It is not an alternative standpoint, but *the* fundamental and inescapable existential standpoint of rational beings. The following key passage

---

28   Ibid., 4:450.
29   Ibid., 4:451.
30   Ibid., 4:451–52.
31   Ibid., 4:458.
32   Ibid., 4:463.
33   Ibid., 4:455.

in the *Critique of Practical Reason* lends strong support to the latter
position:

> [I]n the union of pure speculative with pure practical reason in one cogni-
> tion, the latter has primacy. ... [T]his union is not *contingent* and discre-
> tionary but... *necessary*. For, without this subordination a conflict of reason
> with itself would arise. ... [I]f they were merely juxtaposed (coordinate)...
> one cannot require pure practical reason to be subordinate to speculative
> reason and so reverse the order, since all interest is ultimately practical
> and even that of speculative reason is only conditional and is complete in
> practical use alone.[35]

There is, however, a change in the concept of "will" in the *Metaphysics
of Morals*, and we should take this into account before arriving at a definitive interpretation of what it means that existential Freedom (with
its inescapable ethical responsibility) is the "end in itself" which rational beings are. In two key passages, from 6:213–14 and at 6:226, Kant
modifies his concept of will and he introduces the concept of "the
power (or faculty) of choice" (*Willküre*), in such a way as to replace
the concept of "free will" with a concept of a "free choice." The will
becomes nothing other than "law itself," directed with absolute necessity, so that it "cannot be called either free or unfree."[36] What is "free"
is only the rational being's power of choosing to accept the directive
of the will, by acting on a maxim fit for universal law-giving — as
opposed to exercising arbitrary "animal choice" (*arbitrium brutum*).
This does not mean, for Kant, that freedom of choice lies in the ability
to *either* accept or to choose *not* to accept the directive of the will.
Rather, freedom of choice *is* being independent of determination by
sensible impulses.[37] This negative concept of freedom is complement-
ed by a positive concept of freedom as "subjection of the maxim of
every action to the condition of its qualifying as universal law," which

35   Kant, *Critique of Practical Reason* in *Practical Philosophy*, 5:121.

36   Kant, *Metaphysics of Morals* in *Practical Philosophy*, 6:226.

Kant claims is the same as "the ability of pure reason to be of itself practical."[38] Clearly, this latter formulation harks back to the key passage from the *Critique of Practical Reason* cited above. Consequently, through the primacy of practical reason established by that passage in the Second Critique, we may reinterpret the "free will" at issue in the *Groundwork*'s idea of "an end in itself" as the power of rational beings to select which actions they perform.

Does this replacement of "free will" with "free choice" clarify matters? Not yet. If the will is merely universal law, then each of us cannot have *a* will. There is only Will. Furthermore, if the power of "free choice" is not a power to choose *against* Will/Law, and is naturalistically determined *arbitrium brutum* when it does not so "choose," then on what grounds can it ever be said to "choose" anything at all? Will either moves me, or "I" am as naturalistically determined as brutes are. In order to avoid this collapse into absurdity, the power of *choice* needs some content that is sensibly conditioned, that is an object of the faculty of desire, and yet which does not reduce it to mere "animal choice." Indeed, Kant says that this is exactly what is required if we are to be able to think of Will as *our own will* — in other words, to make Will ours.[39]

The universal law as Will cannot simply determine our actions, we need a maxim with content that allows us to link up with the universal law of our own accord, as it were, in a self-motivated manner. Kant identifies the happiness of others and one's own perfection as objects of the faculty of desire, or material determining grounds of Will for each subject, that are nonetheless "ends in themselves."[40] For Kant, pursuit of one's own perfection means cultivation of physical and mental faculties, including one's moral cast of mind.[41] By "happiness"

---

38 Ibid., 6:214.

39 Ibid., 6:389.

40 Ibid., 6:385–88.

Kant means "satisfaction with one's state, so long as it is assured of lasting,"[42] and so pursuit of the happiness of others as an end means seeing to their physical well-being, including the external goods necessary for this, as well as their ability to pursue their own moral perfection.[43] They are distinct as duties just in so far as each rational being is solely capable of making his *own* perfection his end, and can only aid others in perfecting themselves by making their happiness his end.[44]

This innovation abrogates a strong line of argument in the *Groundwork* and the *Critique of Practical Reason* against the possibility of any object of the faculty of desire being fit to furnish practical laws consistent with the Categorical Imperative. In the *Groundwork* Kant argues that happiness cannot be the end in itself, because it is such an indeterminate concept that, although every human being wishes to attain it, not only do different human beings have a different conception of happiness, but even any one human being is not really consistent with himself in what he wills or wishes for in "happiness." All of the elements that belong to the concept of happiness are empirical and derived from experience. Kant claims that "for the idea of happiness there is required an absolute whole, a maximum of well being in my present condition and in every future condition."[45] He argues that nothing short of an omniscient and omnipotent being could form a determinate concept of what he really wills here. He criticizes various ideas of happiness, showing why each of them is subject to unintended negative consequences that would call into question whether to will *this* would be to will true happiness. Kant goes on to assert that "the human being claims for himself a will" *only* in so far as he disregards

---

42 Ibid., 6:387.

43 Ibid., 6:394.

44 Ibid., 6:386.

all desires and sensible incitements.[46] The rest of this passage makes a thoroughly confused argument, which lapses into something close to antinomian Gnostic dualism:

> [R]eason alone, and indeed pure reason independent of sensibility, gives the law, and, in addition... since it is... as intelligence only, that [the rational being] is his proper self (as a human being he is only the appearance of himself), those laws apply to him immediately and categorically, so that what inclinations and impulses (hence the whole nature of the world of sense) incite him to cannot infringe upon the laws of his volition as intelligence; indeed, he does not hold himself accountable for the former or ascribe them to his proper self, that is, to his will, though he does ascribe to it the indulgence he would show them if he allowed them to influence his maxims to the detriment of the rational laws of his will.

If the "will" is nothing other than law-giving reason itself — which, as we can see, Kant is *already* tacitly asserting at least in *this* passage of the *Groundwork* — then based on what grounds can the rational subject show indulgence to sensible inclinations and impulses? The problem is that, in the *Groundwork*, Kant also wants to maintain that this will is "his," i.e. the rational subject's, whereas it is in fact a generic Will and not one that can be the causal source of actions for which persons may be held individually responsible. Although Kant claims that "freedom... signifies only a 'something' that is left over when I have excluded from the determining grounds of my will everything belonging to the world of sense," the preceding passage demonstrates that this exclusion leaves the subject with no grounds to be responsible for his failure to adhere to the moral law.[47]

In the *Critique of Practical Reason* Kant maintains this opposition to any object of the faculty of desire, and its attendant "intervening feeling of pleasure or displeasure," as mediating reason's lawgiving.[48]

---

46 Ibid., 4:457.
47 Ibid., 4:462.

Reason, which is to say Will, gives the law directly. Of course, as we have seen, this is incoherent, because there would be no way to hold a person responsible for not abiding by the moral law, since Will/ Law either determines his action or brute sensible inclinations do. Nevertheless, not realizing this, and continuing to refer to action determined directly by Will as "free will,"[49] Kant makes an argument that a principle, any principle, in which one may take "pleasure or displeasure (which can always be cognized only empirically and cannot be valid in the same way for all rational beings)" cannot serve as a practical law, but only as a subjective maxim.[50] (In the language of the *Groundwork*, it is fit for a hypothetical but not a Categorical Imperative.) He further claims that all material practical principles of this kind are really variations on the general principle of self-love or concern with one's own happiness — which is obviously not fit for universal law-giving, because the "own happiness" of each person can only ever be his own.[51] Most significantly, according to the Kant of the Second Critique, this includes the desire for "*universal* happiness."[52] Although "the happiness of other beings" can be the object of the will of a rational being following the moral law, and although "every volition must also have an object and hence a matter," even universal happiness cannot act "as a condition of its possibility" — in other words as what furnishes a maxim fit for universal law-giving.[53]

What seems to change in the *Metaphysics of Morals*, is that the matter of the desire for the happiness of others (and for one's own perfection) is no longer only allowed to be added to the mere form of law, but *is* in fact *presupposed* in any ethical action of a rational being adhering to moral law. What allows for this change is Kant's

---

49   Ibid., 5:29.

50   Ibid., 5:21–22.

51   Ibid., 5:22.

52   Ibid., 5:26.

realization that unlike other objects of the faculty of desire, the ends of the happiness of others and one's own perfection are not incentives to some other end, they are incentives to their pursuit as ends in themselves shared by all and only rational beings.[54] These ends that are in themselves duties[55] and that provide a matter of the power of choice[56] fit for universal law-giving because they are shared by everyone,[57] are another instance of "an end in itself" of rational beings that we encounter in Kant. Are the happiness of others and one's own perfection different ends in themselves, or are they somehow the same as the *Groundwork* idea of "an end in itself" with respect to the existence of beings? How is it that what, in the *Groundwork*, would have been a "subjective end" that is merely a means to be used by a rational being as a matter of preference[58] has now become an — or *the* — "objective end"? In the *Groundwork*, the only "objective ends" are rational beings themselves, qua their *existence*.[59] Kant was emphatic there that no other end, to which they would serve merely as a *means*, could ever be put in their place. So have the happiness of others and one's own perfection replaced rational beings as *the* ends in themselves?

There is a passage at 4:430 in the *Groundwork* that suggests that Kant conceived of the pursuit of one's own perfection and the happiness of others (which in turn allows them to pursue *their* own perfection) as already inherent in his original concept of the rational being *existing* as an end in itself. In this passage, Kant claims that there is a predisposition towards attainment of greater perfection in humanity (by which he means universal *humanitas*, not *Homo sapiens*), and that while humanity would be preserved if this were neglected, adherence

---

54   Kant, *Metaphysics of Morals* in *Practical Philosophy*, 6:222.

55   Ibid., 6:381.

56   Ibid., 6:380–81; 6:389.

57   Ibid., 6:395.

58   Kant, *Groundwork of the Metaphysics of Morals* in *Practical Philosophy*, 4:427–28.

to the Categorical Imperative respecting rational beings (including oneself) as ends in themselves requires one to actively further one's own perfection. He also claims that, while humanity would subsist if no one sought the happiness of others, but did not intentionally compromise their happiness, treating others as ends in themselves demands also furthering the ends of others to the extent possible. The problem is that the universal law formula, as it appears in the *Groundwork*, is insufficient for this *ethical* acceptance of the well being of others as one's own end. It would allow for no distinction between juridical duties enforced through state coercion and ethical duties that ought not to be coerced and that are *ethical* only insofar as one performs them for their own sake.[60] Distinguishing the will from the power of choice and allowing for one's own perfection and the happiness of others to be a material determining ground, not of the will, but of the power of choice, allows for this distinction to be drawn between *ius* and *ethica*.

III.

Kant's jurisprudential Doctrine of Right may consist almost entirely of acquired rights, but it is nonetheless grounded on a single inherent Natural Right: "the sum of the conditions under which the choice of one can be united with the choice of another in accordance with a universal law of freedom."[61] Or put otherwise: "Any action is *right* if... on its maxim the freedom of choice of each can coexist with everyone's freedom in accordance with a universal law."[62] On this definition of the Natural Right to reciprocally respected Freedom, coercion is justified if it aims to prevent one person from coercing another person who is not doing anything that would interfere with his own freedom:

---

60   Kant, *Metaphysics of Morals* in *Practical Philosophy*, 6:220.

61   Ibid., 6:230.

If then my action or condition generally can coexist with the freedom of everyone in accordance with a universal law, whoever hinders me in it does me *wrong*. ... [I]f a certain use of freedom is itself a hindrance to freedom in accordance with universal laws, coercion that is opposed to this (as a *hindering of a hindrance of freedom*) is... right.[63]

Note the word "coexist" here. A case could be made that it is referring to the same "existence" at issue in rational beings existing as ends in themselves, that it is their coexistence *as* a "kingdom of ends." The Natural Right to Freedom, as an inherent right, should apply to the coexistence of all rational beings. In other words, it is the basis of a political system that could rightly govern both terrestrial humans and any possible types of extraterrestrial intelligence.

What is more significant though, is the following. We have just established that allowance of furthering the happiness of others and, by this means (indirectly), their perfection as well as one's own, as objects of the faculty of desire, is necessary in order to prevent a political system from being a totalitarian one that would destroy ethical duties by making all of them legal obligations to the state. The reason that Kant did not originally want to allow for this is because he believed that any material objects of the faculty of desire, such as desiring the happiness of others, presumed certain sympathetic sensibilities that not all rational beings may share with humans.[64] He was concerned that "a principle that is based on the subjective condition of receptivity to a pleasure or displeasure...can always be cognized only empirically and cannot be valid in the same way for all rational beings."[65] Kant comes around to asserting that it would indeed be valid in the same way for all rational beings. In order for extraterrestrials to be able to have my happiness as their end, and indirectly to further my perfection while directly furthering their own, we have to presume an *empirical*

---

63 Ibid.

64 Kant, *Critique of Practical Reason* in *Practical Philosophy*, 5:26.

commonality of sensory capabilities and physical and mental faculties capable of infinitely approximating themselves to, or converging on, some common standard of perfection. In fact, this is exactly what Kant does presume in the theory of extraterrestrial intelligence that he sets forth in the third part of his *Universal Natural History and Theory of the Heavens*, discussed at the outset. In sum, Kant's *a priori* universal ethics requires that there be an empirical convergent evolution of intelligent life, not only in this universe, but in all logically possible universes that could have been. The world of understanding does not just ground the world of sense,[66] it is an attractor that draws rational beings initially differentiated by their contingent encumbrances in the world of sense towards an increasingly refined realization of an underlying archetype.

Suppose a person is born so severely handicapped and mentally retarded that he will never be able to use any rational faculty; i.e. physically speaking, he has none. According to Kant, this unfortunate creature would still be a "person," with an innate Natural Right (although perhaps with no duties obligating him). This cannot be because certain instrumental interventions, surgery or technological augmentation, could provide such a being with the capacities that he presently lacks. For if this were to be Kant's response, he would have to admit that the same would hold true for chimpanzees, so that *prior* to such augmentation a chimpanzee would have rights in the same measure as a human born severely retarded. We must therefore conclude that this retarded "person," is a "person" to be treated in accordance with the Categorical Imperative, because his biological formation was unsuccessfully aiming at realization of some archetype. This *telos* cannot be a species-specific "human" one either, since, as the entire line of Kant's argument demonstrates, ethical and juridical obligations are grounded in a Categorical Imperative common to all rational beings. That the severely retarded person is a *person*, means that all intelligent extraterrestrials must also be individuated *persons*; that the retarded human has rights means that he shares with all intelligent aliens an archetype guiding their physical evolution towards a common structural goal determined *a priori*.

Kant's divine "model to which all finite rational beings can only approximate without end"[67] can no longer be thought of as purely abstract, if common sensibilities are required insofar as we, together with all intelligent extraterrestrials, make each other's happiness and perfection objects of our faculty of desire. A concrete discussion of the evolutionary biology of possible intelligent life forms will help clarify the enormity of the claim implicit in Kant's attempt to construct a universal ethics. Imagine a fictitious, although plausible, natural history of an intelligent life form radically different from mankind. What we are trying to imagine are intelligent beings whose distinction from *Homo sapiens* would be of a different order than the variation between human cultures. Any primate-like life form would be too similar to offer an instructive contrast, since according to Kantian anthropology any hominids that behave largely as we do would qualify as "human" (in the narrow sense) even if they were the products of convergent evolution halfway across the galaxy and we could not actually interbreed with them (even if we were sexually attracted to them).

While dolphins, whales, and even octopuses have been proven to be strikingly intelligent (and in the case of bottlenose dolphins, more intelligent than chimpanzees), their viscous undersea environment is prohibitive of the development of technology. The size of the avian brain is constrained by the need to maintain a lightweight frame for flying. Even on a planet with lower gravity, there would still presumably be a local economy of weight distribution. So we need a land-based life form capable of manipulating its natural environment. Reptiles have neither the requisite intelligence nor the proper bodily structure for tool use. Moreover, they do not seem to compensate for their dull-wittedness by forming any kind of aggregate intelligence with other members of the same species; even canine packs are more coordinated. On Earth, social insects are the one type of land-based non-simian life form that is well built for manipulating the environment and that does act as a highly coordinated group to accomplish feats utterly impossible to its individual members. Incredibly rapid and astonishingly complex collective activities have been observed in ant colonies, beehives, and hornet nests. Members of these species act as if they were parts of a single organism. Their group intelligence is *qualitatively* far greater than that of any of its components. (The opposite seems true of human beings. While there are some highly intelligent human individuals, large human groups are by comparison stupid to the point of being self-destructive.)

To object that such creatures have *not* in fact developed a technological society is to lose sight of the fact that for hundreds of millions of years, the only mammals on Earth were scurrying little rodent-like critters that were in constant danger of being eaten by dinosaurs and birds. It is not beyond the pale to imagine that if we were to cause a mass extinction of ourselves and other large species, it would open an evolutionary niche to be filled by ever larger, more complex insects to dominate the Earth and build their cities high upon the ruins of ours. A similar course of events may have taken place on other planets, or there may be planets where asteroid impacts or any one of a million other environmental conditions favored the rise of social insects rather than of reptilian or hominid life forms.

Even now, here on Earth, the social structure of insects is such that their collective problem solving capacity is second only to that of human beings, although each individual ant or termite is far less intelligent than an individual chimp or dolphin.[68] In the following I will draw from Simon Conway Morris' extended discussion of the collective intelligence of insects in his book on convergent evolution, entitled *Life's Solution*.[69] Morris, a professor of evolutionary paleobiology at Cambridge University, believes that life forms similar to these insects may, on other planets, have evolved to be as intelligent and industrious as humans.[70] He notes that, for example, the *Acromyrmex* and *Atta* ants of Central Asia and South America engage in every essential aspect of the activity that we call "agriculture." They maintain gardens, transport plant material, weed their crop, apply herbicides extracted from plant material, deliberately fertilize their crops with manure, and exchange crop cultures.

The often-observed leaf-cutting procedures carried out above ground by these ants is impressive enough, but the highly complex farming techniques take place in underground chambers where the attine ants harvest mushrooms. The ants clear and pave roads that run from the sites where they cut leaves to their underground chambers, and they set up a complex division of labor between leaf cutters, secondary leaf cutters who bring the plant material to the road, and road travelers who carry the material back to a further series of specialized workers underground. Aside from three distinct castes, there are also miniaturized versions of these attine ants called "minims." These minims ride on the larger ants to groom and clean them, they patrol the edges of trails to warn of approaching dangers, and finally, they are also found riding on top of the transported leaf fragments in order to defend the leaf-carriers from attack by parasitoid flies. Upon arrival within the entryway to the nest itself, one finds the soldier caste on guard against foreign invasions by other insects.

Within the fungus farm the leaves are first licked clean of their waxy film, so as to prevent infection of the crop by associated microorganisms. Then the ants shred the leaf to a pulp and apply it to the fungus, which breaks down the plant material and releases the cellulose into fungus, turning it into a crop that can be eaten by the

---

69 Ibid., 197–229.

ants. Infected parts of the crop are weeded, first being loosened by the minima and then moved away by the larger ants. The minima are also tasked with removing alien spores. The ants move the fungi around their underground enclosure based on small changes in temperature and humidity that might inhibit growth at one location but not another. Knob-like ends of the fungus, which are rich in proteins and sugars, are specifically removed from the crop for separate consumption. The ants prevent pathogens from invading the crop by applying something like an herbicide to the crop, one that derives from bacteria that grows on their own bodies and acts like an antibiotic.[71] These ants also use their excrement as fertilizer, and they do this deliberately. Only some of their waste is used as fertilizer for the crop, and at that in a carefully measured manner. We know this because they also build vast waste management pits that are manned by older workers who are nearing the end of their functionality and are not allowed to leave the nest.[72]

The constant food supply provided by the agricultural activities of these ants allows each colony to grow to include seven million members.[73] This size is, however, exceeded by more aggressive army ant colonies, where the population of a single colony can reach twenty million. These army ants are as collectively intelligent in waging war as the attine ants are in farming. Their relentless mobile columns can extend tens of meters in length, and they may defy terrain obstacles to the advancing front by building bridges using their own bodies. Their coordinated action allows them to attack and dismember comparatively large prey and carry its pieces back to the nest, prey so large that it would be utterly impossible for one or a few ants to dismember and transport.[74]

---

71   Ibid., 198–200.

72   Ibid., 205–206.

73   Ibid., 207.

The industrious capabilities of termites exceed even those of these attine ants. Outside of human engineering, termite nests are the most impressive artificial constructions on Earth. Temporary and comparatively shoddily built access tunnels from the surface lead down into a maze of very carefully constructed branching tunnels with few crossroads. The walls of these tunnels are smoothly modeled and curve upwards in the middle at sharp bends, as if to form archways. The deep tunnels can run for several kilometers in length, with 50 meter tunnels extending up to the surface as access routes to foraging areas. The termites apparently cultivate fungus, but not to eat it as the attine ants do. Rather, they allow the fungus to break down foraged food into a more digestible form.[75] Experimental set-ups have also noticed the construction of latrines for waste disposal.[76]

The termites construct a complex system of ventilated passages that cleanse the mound of excess carbon dioxide and waste gases and allow the circulation of fresh oxygen. The size and shape of these passages is precisely corrected by worker termites, in order to carefully calibrate oxygen levels. Temperature inside the hive is also collectively regulated by the termites, who despite being cold-blooded, collaborate to regulate their body temperatures to provide just the right amount of ambient heat for the good of the group. These termite cities can be up to eighteen feet in height. If a termite were the size of a human — as a termite-like creature might evolve to be on a planet with a lower gravity — such structures would be 4,000 feet in height, some three times taller than the Empire State Building.[77] Termites do not use tools, other than their limbs, to help them excavate their hills into these complex structures. However, if larger termite-like creatures were to evolve on another planet, their size would permit them to use tools and possibly to develop advanced tool-making techniques that

---

75   Ibid., 209.

76   Ibid., 208.

77   Clifford Pickover, *The Science of Aliens* (New York: Basic Books / Perseus, 1998),

require mining, iron forging and smelting. Empowered by technology, an industrious termite-like group mind could produce veritable cities of such scale and complexity that our metropolises on Earth would look like shantytowns by comparison.

Whereas collectively, this alien intelligence may far exceed that of *Homo sapiens*, on an individual level, such beings might be far inferior to the average human — both mentally and physically. For example, each ant hardly has any directional sense of its own. Its directional preferences are conditioned by tactile signals and trail pheromones collated and amplified across an ant swarm.[78] A human being, once raised to adulthood, can do a fair job of surviving on her own, but ant-like or termite-like alien intelligence in isolation from its Collective may only be capable of unreflectively carrying out a limited range of stereotyped actions.[79] It might even be helpless in reacting to its environment if deprived of the "eyes" and "ears" of other members. Given that ants have only vestigial eyes and are effectively blind, it has been surmised that an ant colony perceives its environment through its member units. The whole swarm of ants forms a single compound "eye" with hundreds of thousands of facets, each ant contributing two lenses to form the swarm's ten to twenty meter wide field of vision.[80]

If an intelligent, technologically advanced, hive mind were to evolve out of a species like Earth's social insects, we could expect its sense of morality to be entirely different from ours. In fact, in the absence of a conflict of interest between *individual persons* there might be no need for social negotiation, so such a species may lack morality altogether. In his layman's guide to astrobiology, entitled *The Science of Aliens*, Clifford Pickover surmises that if insect behavior on Earth is to be any guide, the form of life of such an alien technological society ("civilization" is the wrong word here) would deeply offend even the

78   Morris, *Life's Solution*, 204.

79   Pickover, *The Science of Aliens*, 37.

most broadly shared human sentiments of what constitutes ethical conduct.[81]

Collective insect intelligences are often divided into castes, with each caste having a specialized function. The worker drones among the bees or the soldiers among attine ants have no choice whatsoever as to the function that they perform. Unlike humans oppressed by a caste ideology that need not constrain their life possibilities, the intelligent insects' caste status would indeed be a fact of nature for them. They could not even conceive of the "heretical" mixing of castes and lament its allegedly "degenerative" social consequences. The brahmanical Hindu might be persuaded to come over to a different view of the possibilities for his *human* life, but no ground whatsoever would give in the case of alien intelligences similar to the denizens of perfectly ordered beehives or ant colonies.

What of the equal rights of the sexes? Females might eat their mates during sexual intercourse, as in the case of the praying mantis that can continue to copulate with the female of his species even after his head has been adoringly eaten away by her. The fly *Serromiya femorata* mates belly-to-belly and mouth-to-mouth with its partner, until at the end of the mating, the female literally consumes the male, sucking out the entire contents of his body into her mouth. Certain insect species feature a huge size difference between female and male members of the species, with the males sometimes more than eight times smaller than the females.[82] Beehives have long been taken as a model for science-fictional societies of intelligent extraterrestrials. The complexity of behavior and cognitive processing abilities of bees, with memory that is sustained by periods of sleep, is comparable only to that of vertebrate animals.[83] However, the male bee's penis always

---

81   Pickover, *The Science of Aliens*, 123–124.

82   Ibid., 35.

breaks off once it is inserted into the queen, so that he bleeds to death as a result of copulation.

Orthodox Muslims might strongly reject the idea that women can enjoy the same rights and responsibilities as men, but any given *person* holding this view could potentially be persuaded to abandon it by changing his or her environment. A Muslim woman might renounce this dogma, inculcated in her from childhood, once she has been given the space and encouragement to act as freely and responsibly as she had once thought impossible. Similarly, a slave owner can come to appreciate the oppression and constraint on human potential that slavery represents, perhaps if he himself is bound up in chains and subjected to the whip for a sufficient period of time. But try telling some intelligent tool-using analog of a queen bee that the males of her hive have a right to be "loved" without being killed, or that the worker drones have a right to periods of rest and leisure and are entitled to due compensation for their labor. Could the technologically advanced equivalent of attine ants be made to understand that it is ungracious to condemn their elderly to waste disposal management simply because they are too weak and slow to continue performing other tasks?

Laws against murder, torture, sexism, rape, and slavery mean different things to different human societies. However, we can debate them at all because they do *mean* something. To such species, they would be nonsense. *Who* would we hold responsible for adherence to these standards anyhow? Some intelligent species with a group mind might not even have something like a queen that oversees and directs the behavior of the hive. They might be more like termites than bees, where no one unit is in itself cognizant of the behavior of the whole group, and consequently where no one unit is *responsible* even for its "own" behavior, which is after all determined by the group mind. It may be that only the entire ensemble is, distributively, self-aware of its behavioral patterns in response to its environment.[84] How this could possibly function is hard to imagine, but that is exactly the point. Nevertheless, it does function in social insects on Earth, and some quadrant of the galaxy may already be colonized by more intelligent versions of such creatures.

Clearly such beings would not be capable of even conceiving of the happiness of others or their own perfection as individuals, let alone holding these as objects of the faculty of desire so that the attendant sentiments of doing so could provide a mediating incentive for making the moral law one's own. Kant's allegedly *a priori* universal ethics would seem to be invalidated by the *empirical* possibility of encountering even one species of alien intelligence of this type. Kant would protest that acting *as if* one belonged to a Kingdom of Ends cannot be based on the expectation of the empirical realization of such a Kingdom of Ends.[85]

In other words, within Kant's theoretical framework, it is always possible that such a species could continue to evolve, or in his language, further its perfection, along lines that would eventually allow its members to be sufficiently individuated so that they co-exist with us as responsible members of a Kingdom of Ends. However, practically speaking, it utterly strains credulity to believe that an alien intelligence of the type evoked above, with a level of technical development hundreds of thousands or millions of years beyond our own, should be expected to take some radically different evolutionary turn — and at that, in our direction — upon encountering us. Kant could perhaps also assert that such beings, although "intelligent" in the sense of being capable of technological manipulation of the environment, are not "rational" beings. Such a desperate distinction between "intelligence" and "rationality" is vacuous and would only deepen his anthropomorphic prejudices. This does not mean that Kant's universal ethics is a failure, only that it implicates a theory of the convergent evolution of all intelligent beings towards self-consciously individuated and responsible *personhood*.

Now we can definitely answer the core question posed at the outset. We are to understand "an end in itself" with respect to the *existence* of beings, as a claim that the world of sense exists only through and towards rational beings. They are the only ends in themselves insofar as they are the ends of everything that *is*. This is why Kant assumes that natural processes must *always already end* in *persons*, regardless of the great differences in the empirical conditions of diverse worlds throughout the cosmos. His claim, in *Universal Natural History and Theory of the Heavens*, that it would be absurd if the universe were not filled with intelligent life, is rooted in this. It is not a question of a waste of space, but of the fact that without rational beings to be conscious of their existence in it, there could be no universe — because nothing else in the universe properly *exists* ("properly" meaning exists for its own sake, as its *own end*). This is why, as we have seen, in the *Critique of Pure Reason* Kant was willing to stake his entire reputation on the existence of *humanitas* elsewhere in the Cosmos.

SERPENT POWER OF
THE SUPERMAN

In *The Anti-Christ*, Friedrich Nietzsche recognizes the spirit of Science as the antithesis of the Christian mentality. Christianity, in Nietzsche's view, extols foolish ignorance and condemns the "wisdom of this world" as sinful. In fact, as Nietzsche recognizes, the Bible begins with the story of a jealous god who is terrified at the human attainment of knowledge of life, of Nature, as symbolized by the Serpent and by the serpentine woman, Eve (*Hava*), whose Hebrew name means "life." The advocate of Science strives in the spirit of the Antichrist as the mortal enemy of God:

> A religion like Christianity, which is at no point in contact with actuality, which crumbles away as soon as actuality comes into its own at any point whatever, must naturally be a mortal enemy of the 'wisdom of the world,' that is to say of science...

> Paul wants to confound the 'wisdom of the world': his enemies are the good philologists and physicians of the Alexandrian school — upon them he makes war. In fact, one is not philologist and physician without also being at the same time anti-Christian. ...

Has the famous story which stands at the beginning of the Bible really been understood — the story of God's mortal terror of science? …God had created for himself a rival, science makes equal to God… Moral: science is forbidden in itself — it alone is forbidden. Science is the first sin, the germ of all sins, original sin. This alone constitutes morality. — 'Thou shalt not know' — the rest follows. … [A]ll thoughts are bad thoughts. Man shall not think. … Distress does not allow man to think. … And none the less! Oh horror! The structure of knowledge towers up, heaven-storming, reaching for the divine — what to do! — The old God invents war, he divides the peoples, he makes men destroy one another… War — among other things a great mischief-maker in science! — Incredible! Knowledge, emancipation from the priest, increases in spite of wars. — And the old God comes to a final decision: 'Man has become scientific — there is nothing for it, he will have to be drowned!'[1]

In *The Anti-Christ* Nietzsche identifies the Jewish mentality as an epitome of the falsification of life that one sees in the conception of the Fall as a rightful punishment for the sin of knowledge-seeking that was committed in Eden. This is reiterated in *The Birth of Tragedy*. Given that the *Promethea* trilogy of Aeschylus was a supreme work of the tragic age of the Greeks that Nietzsche so admired, and given that it becomes the subject of *The Birth of Tragedy*, it ought to be no surprise that we find his most extended meditation on Prometheus there. He contrasts the Prometheus mythos of the Aryans with Semitic religiosity in the most striking terms. The passages deserve quoting at length:

Let me now contrast the glory of activity, which illuminates Aeschylus' Prometheus, with the glory of passivity… Man, rising to Titanic stature, gains culture by his own efforts and forces the gods to enter into an alliance with him because in his very own wisdom he holds their existence and their limitations in his hands. But what is most wonderful in this Promethean poem, which in its basic idea is the veritable hymn of impiety, is the profoundly Aeschylean demand for justice. The immeasurable

---

1   Friedrich Nietzsche, *Twilight of the Idols / The Anti-Christ* (New York: Penguin

suffering of the bold 'individual' on the one hand and the divine predicament and intimation of a twilight of the gods on the other...

In view of the astonishing audacity with which Aeschylus places the Olympian world on the scales of his justice, we must call to mind that the profound Greek possessed an immovably firm foundation for metaphysical thought in his mysteries, and all his skeptical moods could be vented against the Olympians. The Greek artist in particular had an obscure feeling of mutual dependence when it came to the gods; and precisely in the Prometheus of Aeschylus this feeling is symbolized. In himself the Titanic artist found the defiant faith that he had the ability to create men and at least destroy Olympian gods, by means of his superior wisdom which, to be sure, he had to atone for with eternal suffering. The splendid 'ability' of the great genius for which even eternal suffering is a slight price, the stern pride of the artist — that is the content and soul of Aeschylus' poem...

But Aeschylus' interpretation of the myth does not exhaust the astounding depth of its terror. Rather the artist's delight in what becomes, the cheerfulness of artistic creation that defies all misfortune, is merely a bright image of clouds and sky mirrored in a black lake of sadness. The Prometheus story is an original possession of the entire Aryan community of peoples and evidences their gift for the profoundly tragic. Indeed, it does not seem improbable that this myth has the same characteristic significance for the Aryan character which the myth of the fall has for the Semitic character, and that these two myths are related to each other like brother and sister. The presupposition of the Prometheus myth is to be found in the extravagant value which a naïve humanity attached to fire as the true palladium of every ascending culture. But that man should freely dispose of fire without receiving it as a present from heaven, either as a lightning bolt or as the warming rays of the sun, struck these reflective primitive men as sacrilege, as a robbery of divine nature. Thus the very first philosophical problem immediately produces a painful and irresolvable contradiction between man and god and moves it before the gate of every culture, like a huge boulder. The best and highest possession mankind can acquire is obtained by sacrilege and must be paid for with consequences which involve the whole flood of sufferings and sorrows with which the offended divinities have to afflict the nobly aspiring race of men. This is a harsh idea which, by the dignity it confers on sacrilege, contrasts strangely with the Semitic myth of the fall in which curiosity, mendacious deception, susceptibility to seduction, lust — in short, a series of pre-eminently feminine affects was considered the origin of evil. What distinguishes the Aryan notion is the sublime view of active sin as the characteristically Promethean virtue. With that, the ethical basis for pessimistic tragedy has been found: the justification of human evil, meaning both human guilt and the human suffering it entails. ...

Whoever understands this innermost kernel of the Prometheus story — namely, the necessity of sacrilege imposed upon the titanically striving individual... [who, like] the swelling... tide... takes the separate little wave-mountains of individuals on its back, even as Prometheus' brother, the Titan Atlas, does with the earth. This Titanic impulse to become, as it were, the Atlas for all individuals, carrying them on a broad back, higher and higher, farther and farther, is what the Promethean and the Dionysian have in common.[2]

Returning to *The Anti-Christ*, there Nietzsche observes how the Church links the Christian embrace of ignorance as bliss with an affirmation of submissive weakness. As a world-historical force, Christianity has made war on the rare and higher type of person who seeks knowledge and worldly wisdom above all else. Nietzsche, who was by profession a classicist, sees the classical world as having, after centuries of struggle, established a foundation for the flourishing of this type in Alexandrian Rome.[3] Here all of the key elements of the scientific orientation towards life were already developed.

Of course, this was in the context of an aristocratic society more closely aligned with the natural distinction between three types of "human" being: 1) a miniscule elite who lives for knowledge; 2) a small but significant minority who are the guardians of knowledge insofar as they recognize the superiority of the first type and have the physical strength and spiritual discipline to serve them as a knightly class;

---

2   Friedrich Nietzsche, *The Basic Writings of Nietzsche* (New York: Random House, 2000), 71–73.

3) the vast mediocre majority who, unless they are riled up by rabble rousers that instill false expectations in them, are ready, willing, and able to function as "intelligent machines." With respect to the first two of these castes, Nietzsche observes that Jesus as "the redeemer" is the antithesis of the type of the genius and hero. In Nietzsche's view these three castes of soul ought to be arranged in a pyramidal structure. While this was not exactly the case in the actual society of the classical world, the ideal of a scientific society—as most famously exemplified by Plato's Republic—was at least recognized by many of the thinkers of the classical world, going all the way back to the Pythagorean Order. These men and women were amassing institutional power in cities such as Alexandria.

Since the destruction of the classical academies, scientific geniuses and heroic spirits have been viciously persecuted and inquisitorially tortured as if they were something intolerably lower than what the Hindus call Chandala—those that they tolerate as "untouchables." The harbingers of the Superman have been associated with everything Evil. In Nietzsche's view, it is now time for a reversal of this grotesque Christian inversion of a rightful ethical order wherein those with the strength to boldly seek wisdom and knowledge are recognized as sovereign. He intends for the true Chandala to retake their rightful place as robots that build a broad foundation for the self-directed evolution of the intellectual elite beyond the merely "human" and into a superhuman condition. Whoever said that interdependence entailed equality had no sense of relations in nature or the evolutionary force of life.

In *The Gay Science* and *The Will to Power*, Nietzsche elaborates on this interdependence of the "last man" and the Promethean "masters of the earth." There he sees the transformation of the teeming rabble into a machine as a platform on which a new nobility of renaissance men erect a new world order unifying Science, Art, and Politics:

So many things have to come together for scientific thinking to originate. … Their effect was that of poisons. … Many hecatombs of human
beings were sacrificed before these impulses learned to comprehend
their coexistence and to feel they were all functions of one organizing
force. … [A]rtistic energies and the practical wisdom of life will join with
scientific thinking to form a higher organic system in relation to which
scholars, physicians, artists, and legislators — as we know them at present — would have to look like paltry relics of ancient times.[4]

Inexorably, hesitantly, terrible as fate, the great task and question is approaching: how shall the earth as a whole be governed? And to what end
shall 'man' as a whole — and no longer as a people, a race — be raised and
trained?[5]

[A]s the consumption of man and mankind becomes more and more
economical and the 'machinery' of interests and services is integrated ever
more intricately, a counter-movement is inevitable. … [T]he production of
a synthetic, summarizing, justifying man for whose existence this transformation of mankind into a machine is a precondition, as a base on which
he can invent… this higher form of aristocracy… that of the future… a
hothouse for strange and choice plants.[6]

Despite the brilliant insight and evocative imagery of such passages, Nietzsche fails to live up to his own-most insights regarding
the primacy of the dynamic force of becoming. The doctrine of
eternal recurrence, if interpreted ontologically as Nietzsche himself
interprets it when he occasionally denies free will despite the essential
thrust of his thinking, is a doctrine developed under the influence
of Spinoza — one wherein it is still possible to take a view *sub specie
aeternitatis* in light of which what appears as a becoming driven by
desire is *really* a bounded nexus of possibilities always already inherent in Being and, consequently, one that is fated to repeat itself in its
actualization within the frame of finite Time.

---

4   Friedrich Nietzsche, *The Gay Science* (New York: Vintage Books, 1974), 173.

5   Friedrich Nietzsche, *The Will to Power* (New York: Random House, 1968), 501.

The north Indian Tantric understanding of *Shakti* or "Power," if taken radically and without compromise with traditional forms of Hindu thought, is more Nietzschean than Nietzsche in the sense that it adheres to his insight that "Reality" is perspectival through and through so that it is impossible to gain a vantage-point on the creative force of becoming. We are presented with a view of the world as the will to power or of Reality as *Wirklichkeit* — in just the sense that Nietzsche meant this: that power is not a positive state but a dynamic relationship defined in terms of otherness and self-transcending desire, and that the "truth" is what *works* within this deferent and differentiating play of forces.[7] For Tantric devotees of Shakti, just as for Nietzsche, the human condition is something to be overcome — it is a transitional state between the bestial and a form of life beyond the gods who no longer deserve to be set up as something above ourselves.[8] Yet, even in terms of this convergence, the Tantric conception of the Superman is more faithful to Nietzsche's deepest insights than he is.

Nietzsche goes on at great length, especially in *The Will to Power*, regarding the undemocratic and radically aristocratic character of the Supermen and their coming world order. He sees technological development as transforming the majority of mere humanity into a machinery whose productive power will serve as a foundation upon which those artist-philosophers who have cultivated themselves in a superior fashion will be able to erect a higher culture devoted to bold exploration and discovery.[9] Nietzsche no doubt sees Eugenics as a means of discipline and breeding that has a different effect from merely instrumental leveling technologies, but is this — when taken together with the cultivation of intellect, valor, and taste — sufficient

---

7   Julius Evola, *The Yoga of Power: Tantra, Shakti, and the Secret Way* (Rochester, VT: Inner Traditions International, 1992), 20, 22.

8   Ibid., 16.

9   Friedrich Nietzsche, *The Will to Power* (New York: Random House, 1968),

to define a class of beings that act as a countercurrent to the historical unfolding of nihilism at its culmination?

Modern technology, based as it is on a mechanistic metaphysics of Nature grasped in terms of equations that equalize all things as variables, is inherently democratic: anyone can use a telephone or ride a train in order to collapse distances and the medium or the conveyance is neutral with respect to what is being conveyed.[10] Even Eugenics could be used by a so-called Social Democracy to "enhance" an entire population. As Julius Evola recognizes in *The Yoga of Power*, the same cannot be said of the *siddhis* or superpowers cultivated by the Tantric practitioner. Materialistic modern science prides itself on the power of the mechanistic technology supposedly engineered on the basis of its theoretical discoveries, and takes these feats of engineering to be the ultimate validation of its theoretical models — to such an extent that these are viewed as a mirror of structures inherent in Nature.[11] However, if modern man were to be stripped of his technology on account of some natural catastrophe — or perhaps through a catastrophe attendant to his own supposed technological empowerment, for example, a nuclear war — he would be reduced to a condition more desperate, feeble, and helpless than that of any of the great predators in the wilderness.[12]

From this it can be gleaned that machine technology has atrophied the human being rather than catalyzed an overcoming of the merely human condition. But there is a *techne* — a craft, technique, or technology (in the classical sense) — that can place any mechanical contrivance at its mercy and that cannot be democratized. Psychical superpowers such as clairvoyance, telepathy, and telekinesis accrue only to those individuals who have cultivated such *siddhis* for and by

---

10   Evola, *The Yoga of Power*, 16.

11   Ibid., 14.

themselves.[13] Moreover, an attempt to universalize these abilities so that they would extend to the majority of predominately bestial men would be utterly ruinous to *any* form of social order.

The utmost discipline of the will and cultivation of the mind, including and especially a contemplative engagement with the subconscious mind, is a prerequisite not only for the attainment of such abilities but also for wielding them in a way that does not threaten to unweave the fabric of the cosmos itself—let alone the tapestry of norms necessary for the survival of human societies. Supermen are exceptional; they presuppose the stability of the human condition as a launch platform for projects exploring inner and outer space.

When viewed in terms of their significance to the human psyche and its need for socio-politically stabilizing beliefs or tacit assumptions, the paranormal power unleashed by practice of the Left Hand Path can be instructively compared to the maelstrom surrounding the event horizon of a black hole. The first known theoretical postulation of a black hole, or "dark star" as it was then called, is in a 1783 letter written by geologist John Michell to Henry Cavendish of the Royal Society. In 1915, the German physicist Karl Schwarzschild developed the idea into a testable hypothesis and devised a metric for calculating the size of an event horizon. It has since been discovered that as much as 96 percent of the universe consists of dark matter that is only obliquely detectable. Furthermore, millions of the 80 billion or so galaxies in our universe may contain a super-massive black sun that gives birth to stars, planets, and ultimately to life itself, by churning the gasses in its environs. Such super-massive black holes appear to be the efficient agency for the creation of galaxies.

Buddhism and Hinduism both understand the ultimate nature of reality as a void rather than a plenum of Being. The *swastika* is a Hindu and Buddhist symbol for "well being" or *su asti* in Sanskrit. In this connection, it faces to the right and is ubiquitous at holy sites in India, Tibet, and Japan. When the Atlantis Society designed the talismanic standard of the Nazi Party that it established as its political front, several years after Schwarzschild's elaboration of the black hole theory, this occultist organization that included numerous scientists among its membership seems to have employed the Swastika as a symbol with a dual meaning. The left-facing Swastika signifies the Left Hand Path. That it has been depicted in a spinning fashion suggests a rotating vortex that collapses into a point. This black symbol is set within a white Sun on a red field. I suggest that the red field not only connotes the fiery light of the white Sun, but also the bloody maelstrom wrought by the invisible and collapsed black Sun that tears everything around its vortex into pieces.

Although the *Schwarze Sonne* (Black Sun) that became a prominent Nazi occult symbol — especially among the SS — was usually a more elaborate twelve-armed wheel most infamously incorporated into the floor of the central chamber at Wewelsburg Castle, it was known to have variant simplified iconographic representations. The two suns, the white and black, can be interpreted as references to the visible physical Sun and the occulted dancing Star, as well as to the orthodox Dharma and the Left-Hand Path. The centrality of the black Sun, set within the white one, bespeaks a recognition that the terrifyingly groundless Void is the ultimate "truth" that lies behind or beyond an apparently purifying Orthodoxy in Science and Spirituality.

Whereas the right-facing Swastika is associated with the creator god Brahma or with the Buddha, the left-facing one is associated with Kali and the cosmic destroyer, Shiva — who, not incidentally, are lovers. The destructive force of Kali and Shiva is a purgative or *creative* destruction. The left-handed Swastika highlights the amorality of the abyssal heart of darkness, the Black Sun whose confounding signature can be seen in phenomena that we call "paranormal" because they defy our expectation that *arche* of some kind allow us to abide in a rational *cosmos* rather than face absurd *chaos*. At the same time, such phenomena indicate the possibility of genuine creation — since in a materially finite cosmos bound together by a crystalline structure of unchanging fundamental principles, subject only to material iterations over measurable Time, there would be no genuine possibility for unforeseeable creative acts.

Orthodox Hinduism and Buddhism have always been uncomfortable with the cultivation of superpowers and the exploration of the occult corporeity inextricable from them. Contrary to what has often been supposed the reasons for this run deeper than any moral concerns about the abuse of a power that could potentially be wielded with impunity, from beyond the reach of the law of any traditional society—ancient or modern. It is a question of metaphysics, bearing on the ultimate nature of "Reality."

There are two predominant polarities in Indian Philosophy. One is dualistic and is epitomized by the Samkhya school; the other is monistic and is most broadly represented by Advaita Vedanta. Orthodox Buddhism has its roots in an internal critique of Samkhya metaphysics and while it thereby opposes Brahmanical Vedic religion by radicalizing the Samkhya divergence from it, with the rise of Mahayana, Buddhist thought and mysticism essentially takes a position largely overlapping that of Advaita Vedanta, which has imploded Samkhya dualism and gone beyond Vedic orthodoxy on what can be conceived as a parallel track. (In other words, historically speaking, the greatest divergence between Hindu and Buddhist religion is at that point when the Buddha Dharma remains close to its origins in Samkhya, a time before the rise of Advaita Vedanta on the one hand and Mahayana on the other.) In any case, the basic structure of the two polarities of Indian Philosophy can be sketched out in the following terms.

In the Samkhya dualism, whose crystalline expression may perhaps be found in the *Yoga Sutras of Patanjali*, there are two primary principles in the cosmos: *Purusha* and *Prakriti*.[14] The former is the eternal, immutably still, immaterial, and supremely self-conscious, absolute Being. The latter is the blind and restless activity of apparently differentiated beings, as seemingly manifested in the sequential chains of cause and effect, action and consequence. *Prakriti* is *maya* or deceptive "illusion."

Maya not only deceives one into mistaking an illusory and ephemeral world for a reality in which one ought to invest oneself, but a person who suffers terribly on account of this misidentification is also thereby prevented from recognizing that his own deepest and truest Self (*atman*) is the Absolute Being (*brahman*). Consequently, the means to this transcendent insight is to purify oneself from identification with any phenomena belonging to *Prakriti*—all of which have the nature of *maya*—and to become increasingly unmoved by them, just as *Purusha*. The complex physical postures (*asana*), breathing exercises (*pranayama*), and mental disciplines of concentration (*darana*) belonging to classical *yoga* (literally "union," i.e. with *Purusha*) have this as their primary aim.[15]

The *asanas*, for example, are meant to discipline one's bodily disposition to a wide range of carefully determined postures so as to avoid disorderly and unconscious movement, with the eventual outcome of attaining what can be compared to an Egyptian degree of poise characteristic of the sublime detachment and immovability of the Pharaoh.[16] It is not incidental that Patanjali calls this form of Yoga *raja-yoga* or "kingly" union, for it aims at sovereignty over *maya* by identification with the *Purusha*. While Patanjali and others of the Samkhya school—including the young Siddhartha Gautama—do acknowledge and enumerate occult abilities, they see these as powers that spontaneously arise on the path of purifying withdrawal from *Prakriti*.[17] As "powers" (*siddhis*) they still belong to the sphere

---

15   Ibid., 79–92.

16   Ibid., 90–92.

17   I.K. Taimni, *The Science of Yoga: The Yoga Sutras of Patanjali in Sanskrit with Transliteration in Roman, Translation and Commentary in English* (Wheaton,

of *Prakriti* and are not one's "own" insofar as one comes to increasingly renounce any self other than *Purusha* — who has no will, strictly
speaking — and so willful pursuit or purposive development of them
is considered a snare and temptation of *maya*.

Advaita Vedanta begins in the intellectual recognition of the
logical incoherence of Samkhya dualism and it expresses a more life-
affirming ethos intent on seeing the world of everyday experience as
something more than a deceptive illusion. Instead of seeing *maya* as
a merely occluding force, the cosmic illusion is conceived of in theatrical terms as a magic show or illusionist's performance, whereby
the timeless Ultimate Reality comes to self-consciousness through a
process of internal differentiation.[18] *Maya* becomes *maya-shakti*. The
word *shak* means to be able to work, to be able to do, or to have an
effect, and so what for Samkhya is *Prakriti* becomes the *Shakti* or active power of an Ultimate Reality that Samkhya sees as *Purusha* by
too narrowly identifying it only with its passive and abidingly eternal
Being.[19] For beings such as ourselves to come to know that we are
being acted by Being, ascetic practices of isolation and disciplined
dispassion will not do.

Three qualities, moods, or modalities of being (*gunas*) are inter-
woven in life: *tamas*, *rajas*, and *sattva*.[20] Tamasic being is blind, dark,
and obtuse; it characterizes the craving of beasts and of crass and
undisciplined men and women. On a cosmic level, it is responsible for
that concretization of unconsciousness into what appears to be matter — especially inorganic matter. Sattvic being has the luminous and
pure qualities that Samkhya wants to attribute to the Ultimate Reality;
it is, however, associated not simply with pure Being in itself but also
with the manner of being of the gods, whom one may suppose to
be abiding in *yoga* or "communion" with Being. Rajasic being is the

---

18 Julius Evola, *The Yoga of Power*, 27.

19 Ibid., 5–6.

dynamic and vital force that drives all heroic and creative activity; it is
found in the hero or titan. Cosmically, it is the intermediary between
the Ultimate Reality and *maya-shakti*—a dynamic centrifugal and
centripetal oscillation through which Being becomes its own other
only to recognize itself.

When conceived of in terms of the Hindu pantheon, Advaita
Vedanta associates these three modalities of being with the Trinity
(*trimurti*) of Brahma the Creator, Vishnu the Preserver, and Shiva
the Destroyer or Transformer.[21] It is a complex question how exactly
Brahma and Vishnu relate to the Sattvic and Tamasic modalities of
Being, other than to say that, however heretical associating Vishnu
with the sway of *tamas* may be, the most dense and occluding materiality is a precondition of preservation. *Maya-shakti* is more definitely
associated with Shiva and often pictured as his female consort, his
power that he *has* while remaining impassive qua male divinity and
manifestation of the godhead. How then is Brahma a Creator in any
real sense?

Advaita Vedanta is beset with an even more troubling question
attendant to its attempt to preserve Vedantic or Vedic-rooted religion
in the face of a transformation that is ultimately destructive for it,
the transformation of *maya* conceived in a negative and life-negating
manner into the life-affirming *maya-shakti*. If the Ultimate Reality
understood as *Purusha* by Samkhya is truly ultimate and perfect,
why does it fall into life under the Rajasic and Tamasic condition?
Moreover, if gods enjoy the Sattvic state of mind why do they fall into
incarnations or rebirths characterized by a Rajasic if not a Tamasic
mentality? What are the metaphysical implications of the doctrine of
the declining ages (*yugas*) in Advaita Vedanata and Indian thought
more generally? Vedantic thinkers wanted to see the concupiscence
of *maya-shakti* as responsible for the godhead's alienation from itself,
in the form of the fall of Eternal Being into the finitude of becoming

under the increasingly degenerate conditions of a successive series of world ages (*yugas*) ending with the Kali Yuga—which corresponds roughly to the Iron Age of the Greco-Romans or the Age of the Wolf for the Nordic peoples.[22] Is this not a retreat into dualistic thinking? And why is *maya-shakti* quite clearly associated with Kali now, rather than being sanctified as an aspect of Shiva and thus of the Vedantic Trinity?

It is widely believed that Tantric yoga, as opposed to the classical yoga of Samkhya sages such as Patanjali, is an accommodation appropriate to our degenerate epoch. In the Kali Yuga, we are told, *pashus* or bestial men—literally those who are "bound"—predominate and *divyas* or godly men are virtually non-existent.[23] Consequently, *viras* or heroic natures must use any and all means to tap the destructive forces of the time as transformative ones capable of violently wresting breakthroughs to a higher state of being.[24] This is to turn the poison, the snake venom, into the cure—or, as a Chinese expression puts it, to "ride the tiger."[25]

To take this view is to suppress the fundamental metaphysical reorientation that has taken place. Among the many clues to this reorientation is the Tantric view, which already has roots in Samkhya, that the gods are deluded and seek to block one's path towards ultimate realization.[26] More significant still is the insistence that *maya-shakti* is not only driven by desire, but that she is totally free in her creative impulse.[27] Hers is a creative desire that cannot ever be encompassed by a comprehensive knowledge, not even the self-knowledge of Brahman. She is the Mistress who delights in cosmic play (*lila*) not subject to

22   Ibid., 2, 39.
23   Ibid., 53–54.
24   Ibid., 54–55.
25   Ibid., 2–4.
26   Ibid., 58–59.

any law for which she cannot make an exception.[28] The free-creative impulse or *spanda* of *Shakti* cannot even be properly conceived of as *maya* or "illusion" once the meaning of this new Tantric metaphysics is fathomed. As compared to what self-consistent Reality would *Shakti* be illusory? She is no longer the power *of* Shiva.

The archetypal Tantric image of the terrifyingly armed Kali dancing seductively over the corpse of Shiva and yet somehow sexually arousing that corpse — or the various images of her Mahavidya forms astride Shiva in a sexually dominant position — can be most honestly interpreted as a psychological recognition of *Shakti* as the ultimate "Reality." Albeit, a dynamic reality of Power that never endures as a pure positivity but that seduces the aspirant from out of a living void and forces him to dismember what he was. When it is honest to its essential insight into the non-essentiality of creative energy, Tantra — whether in Hindu form or as Vajrayana so-called "Buddhism" — is inevitably synonymous with the most radically heterodox Shaktism.

This conclusion requires us to reconsider why mainline Hindu and Buddhist schools are so uncomfortable with occult power and subtle corporeity. The subtle body is supposed to occupy an intermediate position between two other types of body, a pure causal body and a gross material body.[29] This, however, presumes, as its metaphysical background, the scheme of three domains of being: the formless domain of pure principles or final causes; the domain of subtle forms — where the subtle body is, so to speak, in its element; and, finally, the gross material realm wherein the subtle body and its extrasensory powers can manifest but where it is, to put it crudely, something like a fish out of water.[30] The basic metaphysical position of Shaktism demolishes the distinction between three realms or, rather, collapses them into

---

28   Ibid., 57.
29   Ibid., 48.

the spectrality of the "intermediate" one. As the Vajrayana Buddhists put it, there is no Nirvana distinct from Samsara and so every samsaric condition conceptualized as intermediate between Samsara and Nirvana — from the highest heavens to the bleakest hells — is marked by the same inessentiality.[31]

Adharma (chaos, immortality) only leads you to hell if you sow *karma* without recognizing that all *dharmas* (natures, paths) are empty of any inherent essence and that the hero's liberation may take place anywhere, under any existential condition.[32] There is naught but intermediacy in life, and what the mind hopes to grasp in terms of matter or to escape to in terms of (relative) formlessness is nothing but the greater or lesser stability of one or another degree of the life force's concrescence. Despite the widely held Western view that, as compared to modern European materialism, the *spectral* is more at home in the East, the *spectrality* of existence or — if you prefer, the finitude of being — has always haunted orthodox Indian thought as what is neither Being nor Nothingness and what has never yet been but may become so through creative activity: the simulacrum without an original; *maya* as *Shakti*. Such is the radical Tantra of a serpentine feminine energy that both poisons the human condition and is the cure to it. It is She who possesses one with a vital force that carries one above the gods. As the Tantric texts put it, this *daimonically* inspiring creative force is bound to supersede the gods to whom She gives birth:

> Shakti is the root of every finite existence. ... She is the mother of all the gods. She supports them and one day they will be reabsorbed into her. ... It is by Thy [Shakti's] power only that Brahma creates, Vishnu maintains, and, at the end of things, Shiva destroys the universe. Powerless are they for this but by Thy help. Therefore it is that Thou alone are the Creator, Maintainer, and Destroyer of the world.[33]

31 Ibid., 32.
32 Ibid., 58.

This is a radically empirical, ruthlessly pragmatic view of life. In the vast expanse of Indian mysticism and religious thought it has never been the view of anything but an extreme minority of dangerous rogues. The mainstream of even the more liberal and lenient Hindu and Buddhist sects have equated this antinomian gnosis with an *asuric* or "titanic" view of life.[34] When I use the Western terms "empirical" and "pragmatic" one should not think of the empiricism of Hume or of the common sense of so many eighteenth-century European and American gentlemen. I mean these terms as William James did. In Tantra *sadhana* or "practice" takes precedence over theory.[35] The Greek word *theoria* shares a common root with theater and involves assuming the position of a spectator with respect to the cosmos. Much of Western science, even when its content is materialist, has understood itself in these idealist terms. The form of Western science has been predominately idealist in its self-image and understanding of the primacy of theory.

Of course, in actual fact scientists are practitioners and elaborating theoretical frameworks is really a kind of practical work. The English word *id*ea shares a root with the Sanskrit *Veda*, namely *vid* — which we also find in *vid*eo and evi*d*ence.[36] In a sense, the Vedas are texts of a theoretical nature produced by visionary intellection. Within the worldview where *atman* must wake up to the fact that he is really *Brahman* by liberating himself from this illusory world — including his embodied existence — *practice*, which not incidentally shares an Indo-European root with *Prakriti*, can only be conceived negatively, in terms of self-destructive acts of erasure.[37] How, then, could Yoga *work*?

---

34   Ibid., 75.
35   Ibid., 11.
36   Ibid., 10–11.

The fundamental incoherence of this cannot be exorcised by means of any mystical mumbo-jumbo concerning the ineffable and paradoxical character of the sacred path. Those who recognize that the ultimate reality is Power (*Shakti*) or the will to a power never positively possessed also understand that life *is* praxis. Theoria is only *about* life, and its worth—not its objective "truth" or "falsity"—lies in what it empowers one to accomplish. The *siddhis* or superpowers are, literally, "accomplishments." There is no one and nothing above or beyond those who have refined their embodiment to one or another degree of subtlety and enhanced their capacities as compared to those lacking in the superhuman desire for exploratory evolution without a predetermined end. This means seeing dark ignorance (*avidya*) and the passionate unconscious as a necessary limiting condition that sheathes the sword of Wisdom.[38]

Insight is lightning. The radically empirical and ruthlessly pragmatic attitude towards life is precisely the opposite of sensibleness. It is the very uncommon sense of the hero (*vira*) who braves danger and risks damnation, to test head on every claim that something is "impossible." Its history is a saga of accomplishing the Impossible. "Wisdom is a woman," said Nietzsche, "and she always only loves a warrior." This could just as well be an aphorism from the Tantric Way of the Thunderbolt Scepter (*Vajrayana*). God is dead, we have killed him, and only the dance of the sky-clad *Vajra Yogini* can rouse us to a life greater than that of gods. "One must still have chaos inside, in order to give birth to a dancing star."[39]

---

38 Ibid., 29, 41–42, 45.

39 Friedrich Nietzsche, *Thus Spoke Zarathustra* (New York: The Modern Library,

PARANORMAL PHENOMENOLOGY

In his book *UFOs: Myths, Conspiracies, and Realities*, Dr. John Alexander uses the term "phenomenology" to refer to paranormal manifestations in general.[1] There have been objections to this usage on the part of persons trained in academic philosophy, where the term "phenomenology" has a clearly defined meaning and refers to a particular school of thought that begins with George Wilhelm Friedrich Hegel and continues through such figures as Edmund Husserl, Martin Heidegger, and Maurice Merleau-Ponty. Yet two of these phenomenologists, Hegel and Merleau-Ponty, wrote fairly extensively on the paranormal. Moreover, their having done so is not at all incidental to the basic character of the phenomenological method. The latter involves a bracketing of specific theoretical knowledge and a suspension of commitment to potentially conflicting frameworks for the acquisition of such knowledge. This is done not only with a view to understanding the cultural-historical construction of such frameworks, but with the aim of delineating basic structures of our experience, perception, and understanding that are more fundamental and stable

---

1   John B. Alexander, *UFOs: Myths, Conspiracies, and Realities* (New York: St.

than any particular scientific theories or their broader paradigmatic structures.

Consequently, Colonel Alexander's use of the term "phenomenology" is apt insofar as he insists on engaging with the data of UFOs, or perhaps more accurately, Unidentified Aerial Phenomena, without being prejudiced by any unexamined assumptions, for example the materialist assumption that these "phenomena" are objects rather than, say, psychic or psychokinetic manifestations of some kind.[2] This adoption of the discourse of "phenomenology" should be generalized within the field of exploratory scientific research on the paranormal, but in a way that explicitly acknowledges, appropriates, and furthers the insights of thinkers such as Hegel and Merleau-Ponty. To this end, I intend to examine the most significant point of contention between Hegel and Merleau-Ponty on the question of the implications of paranormal phenomena for the enterprise of scientific exploration in general.

Hegel's repeated affirmation of the veracity of psychic phenomena and his sketch of a paranormal phenomenology takes place in § 379, § 393, §§ 405–406 of his *Philosophy of Mind*, together with their *Züsatze* or addenda. The *Züsatze* to § 406 of the *Philosophy of Mind* is shockingly revealing. There, Hegel claims that "the occurrence of very marvelous premonitions and visions of this kind which have actually come to pass can certainly not be denied."[3] He also says, of paranormal phenomena more generally: "Whatever charlatanism there may be in accounts of such happenings, some of the cases mentioned seem worthy of credence…"[4] Hegel discusses numerous types of psychic phenomena in the *Züsatze*, giving examples from what he takes to be credible case histories.

---

2   Ibid, 227–230.

3   A.V. Miller and N.J. Findlay, *Hegel's Philosophy of Mind* (New York: Oxford University Press, 1971), 113.

The basic thesis of Hegel's treatment of psychic phenomena can be found in § 379 and §§ 405–406 of the *Philosophy of Mind*, without even considering their *Züsatze*. In § 379 Hegel notes that we have an experiential sense of the unity of our mind, and yet in our desire to comprehend that unity we are tempted — for example, in neurology — to analyze the mind in such a way as to break it up into an aggregate of independent forces and active faculties. These tendencies, at odds with one another, ultimately culminate in apparent contradictions such as the antithesis between the freedom of psychical agency and the determinism of the presumed corporeal substrate of mind. Hegel believes that in "modern times" psychic phenomena have provided us with an especially "lively and visible confirmation of the underlying unity of soul, and of the power of its 'ideality.'"[5]

However, he goes on to add that while these phenomena are "facts," it remains the case that "the rigid distinctions of practical common sense are struck with confusion" in the face of them. In § 405 psychokinetic maternal impressions on the fetus, as well as telepathy between persons close to one another, are mentioned as examples of the "magic tie."[6] In § 406 Hegel once again refers to phenomena such as clairvoyance,[7] telepathy,[8] and other forms of extrasensory perception[9] as *factual*, and he elaborates on the inability of the practical intellect to accept them as such.[10]

The reason that the practical intellect cannot comprehend these phenomena is that they violate the chains of mediate causality and thus cannot be conceived in terms of what Hegel calls "the laws and relations of the intellect."[11] We will not be able to understand psychic

---

5   Ibid., 4.
6   Ibid., 94–95.
7   Ibid., 103.
8   Ibid., 104.
9   Ibid., 105.
10   Ibid., 101.

phenomena "so long as we assume the absolute spatial and material externality of one part of being to another."[12] The philosophical significance of these phenomena is that they are phenomenological evidence for the lack of any fundamental ontological "distinctions between subjective and objective" or "between intelligent personality and objective world"; they show us that we need to give up the assumption of "personalities, independent one of another and of the objective world which is their content."[13]

This does *not* mean that we should give up these distinctions for practical purposes, only that we should not conceive of them as ontologically grounded. Hegel believes that exceptionally strong psychic ability is a "morbid" or "degraded" state that threatens the freedom and responsibility of the individuated intellect.[14] The garbled information attained by means of it, which is so often "at the mercy of every private contingency of feeling and fancy" as well as to "foreign *suggestions*," is certainly no substitute for rationally ascertainable general truths.[15] Nevertheless, *denial* of the existence of paranormal phenomena, and of their ontological significance, is unscientific (in the broad sense of "Science" as *Wissenschaft*) and such a denial clearly indicates that Absolute Knowing has not been attained.

Before phenomenology can guide the sciences into Science, into Absolute Knowing, these "phenomena, so complex in their nature and so very different one from another, would have first of all to be brought under their general points of view."[16] This would seem to play a significant role in Science's being able to overcome, and not simply dodge, the last of the three slave ideologies, namely the Unhappy Consciousness of Religion. Hegel claims that the "miraculous cures

---

12   Ibid.
13   Ibid.
14   Ibid., 102–103.
15   Ibid., 103–104.

said to have been effected in various epochs by priests" that fill the "old chronicles" and "which are not to be too hastily charged with error and falsehood" are actually cases of psychic phenomena that can be understood in their ontological significance rather than marveled at in blind faith.[17]

In other words, Hegel's overarching view of the paranormal is that, although these phenomena are evidence for a pre-rational and primordial dimension of experience, they can and should be surmounted and circumscribed by scientific thinking. In fact, such a development of human reason will take the ground out from under religious doctrines that are legitimated, above all, by holy terror in the face of paranormal phenomena. But if the roots of rational thought extend deep down into the occulted soil of an essentially irrational Nature, and of an intuitive power capable of engaging it pre-rationally, then why would we see the edifice of scientific rationality as anything more than a construct consisting of useful abstractions rather than abstract but objective truths?

Maurice Merleau-Ponty takes just such a view when he examines the structure and function of Science against the background of what cannot be comprehended by its rationality. Like Hegel, Merleau-Ponty sees paranormal phenomena as a clue to recognizing the superficial and reciprocally reinforced distinction between the objective and the subjective, but unlike Hegel, he is more consistent in following this insight through to the conclusion that the structures of scientific thought and practice are basically totemic.

In *The Visible and the Invisible*, Merleau-Ponty sees the scientist assuming the position of a spectator above all things, so that taken together these things grasped as objects turn the world into a Great Object — what I would call an *atlas* of the world.[18] For example, when different real-world astronomical perspectives of those who observe

---

17   Ibid., 111; 117.

18   Maurice Merleau-Ponty, *The Visible and the Invisible* (Evanston: Northwestern

the starry heavens are rendered commensurate with one another it is not in terms of a universal world but as the function of a methodology grounded in the assumption of the position of the great spectator.[19] Whereas for a while this methodology seems to effect breakthroughs that allow us to observe both microphysical and astronomical realms closed to our immediate perception, as Physics advances on these dimensions it is forced to confront the limit of its assumed objectivity by admitting the interdependence of the praxis of the observer and the observed phenomena. Insofar as the physicist attempts, on the basis of a philosophical ontology of materialism, to explain away these empirical discoveries by treating as objective realities quantum "entities" that well up from the flux of nature for milliards of a second and that are dependent for their manifestation on carefully controlled conditions of observation, the physicist is translating these intangible and elusive phenomena into localizable classical entities just of a much smaller scale and in terms of a much shorter interval of time.[20]

This projective transformation really entails assuming the aspect of a giant or Promethean titan with respect to the microphysical world.[21] Similarly, when, as in the case of Einstein's theory of relativity, the presumed possibility of the integration of the perspectives of two observers traveling over vast astronomical distances at different speeds — which is a precondition of concluding that time flows at a different rate for them — is dismissed as "merely psychological," the approximation of the entire cosmos *qua Object* is being dwarfed by a gigantic observer that stands over it as if it were a scale model.[22] Losing sight of *"that upon which we have an openness"* only *"that upon which we can operate*" is taken to be Real.[23] Merleau-Ponty goes on to refer to the "sovereign gaze" that seems to find "the things each in its own time, in its own place, as absolute individuals in a unique local and temporal disposition" as that of a giant or titan that he calls the *kosmotheoros* or cosmic theoretical observer.[24]

In *The Visible and the Invisible*, Merleau-Ponty claims to be making his way toward "the *problem of the world*."[25] He elaborates on this by restating it as an attempt to understand how what is not nature is a "world," and how a visible and an invisible world can be formed as well as what the relationship between them may be.[26] It is a question of how we have an openness to the world that does not preclude occultation, of how occultation can take place amidst the illumination of the world *as such*.[27] Upon reflection, the perception of things and the phantasms of imagination can be understood as two modes of "the ideality of the world."[28] A reflection or meditation that understands the "world" as an ideality "liberates us from the false problems posed by bastard and unthinkable experiences" in accounting for these phantoms as apparitions of what objectifying thought marginally excludes; that which is so excluded haunts what is taken as "objective reality" by returning from its fringe.[29]

The imaginary is framed as un-real and as consisting only of things "half-thought, half-objects, or phantoms... disappearing before the sun of thought like the mists of dawn" when "the real becomes the correlative of thought... [and] the narrow circle of objects of thought..."[30] Our "power to re-enter ourselves" and our "power to

---

23   Ibid., 18.
24   Ibid., 113.
25   Ibid., 6.
26   Ibid., 27.
27   Ibid., 28.
28   Ibid., 29, 31, 47.
29   Ibid., 31.

leave ourselves" is intrinsic to the possibility of a world of lived experience—a "possibility of a wholly different type" than those framed in
advance by objective thought, and one that maintains "a secret and
constant appeal" to what is objectively taken to be "impossible" but
remains integral to the world of lived experience.[31] Merleau-Ponty
elaborates: "It is not because the world called 'objective' has such or
such properties that we will be authorized to consider them established for the life world. ... And, conversely, it is not because in the
'objective' world such or such a phenomenon is without visible index
that we must forego making it figure in the life world."[32] This is relevant to all paranormal phenomena, what Merleau-Ponty refers to as
"bastard and unthinkable experiences" when they happen spontaneously rather than being elicited in a laboratory where they are liable to
pose "false problems."

The "seat of truth within us" is this "unjustifiable certitude of a
sensible world common to us."[33] Prior to being convinced by Descartes
that thought is our reality, "our assurance of being in the truth is one
with our assurance of being in the world."[34] Our experience of "the
true"—in distinction to error and falsehood—is primarily bound up
with the tensions between our perspective on things and those of others.[35] The consciousness of "truth"—of a perspective over something
that others ought to be in agreement with—presupposes an intelligible world of a kind that connects the perspectives of our private
worlds and allows a transition between them, as in those instances
when I enter the perspective of an other to offer him a response to
a question that he has not yet voiced or a rejoinder to a thought to
which he has not yet given voice.[36]

---

31 Ibid., 34.
32 Ibid., 157.
33 Ibid., 11.
34 Ibid., 12.
35 Ibid., 12.

This unjustifiable certitude of a sensible world that we have in common that is not any of our perceptible worlds and is thus in a sense an "intelligible" world — but not in an abstract sense — is what Merleau-Ponty refers to as "the perceptual faith," a faith which science presupposes but does not elucidate.[37] The objectivism of science excludes just those phenomena that clue us in to the common world that abides as the grounding for all "truths." Insofar as the scientist attempts to secure all things — including persons taken as things — in an "objective" manner, that is, as entities that are variables with algorithmically functional relationships to one another, he strips away as "phantasms" everything about beings as we encounter them.[38]

In Merleau-Ponty's view this objectification of beings involves a reciprocal subjectification of those phenomena that, from its perspective, remain invisible as if they were also things hidden behind certain of the objects and as if one could see through to them by gaining a certain angle on them.[39] These are "psychological" phenomena when they are framed in terms of objectively conceived physical phenomena.[40]

Merleau-Ponty notes that just as in the case of physicists, the psychologists can only circumscribe the irrational in an eliminative manner, in other words, *limit* it.[41] They cannot exorcise it, as they wish to. This is because the "irrational" is itself constructed as the excluded remainder of both the objective and subjective modeling of nature. This *normalization* defines the "para*normal*" as such.

The task is not to affirm experiences of the irrational that break through this framing or "escape" it as another anti-scientific "psychical" order of facts in the manner that Spiritualism does when it opposes itself to the materialism that has become prevalent in the wake

---

37   Ibid., 14.

38   Ibid., 14–15.

39   Ibid., 19.

40   Ibid., 19–20.

of Descartes.[42] Rather, one must deconstruct the "objective" and the "subjective" idealizations together by demonstrating the manner in which they are constructed—rather than *given*—from out of the "life world."[43] This "life world" is that lived experience that we have through our field of embodiment—but *not* our bodies conceived of as "objects" that house "subjects."[44] The biologists are now more materialist than the physicists, who for their part have had to come to terms with the psychological dimensions of their work.[45]

The basic concepts at work in Psychology remain essentially as mythical as the governing ideas of archaic societies.[46] In their quest to grasp laws of subjective experience or the function of mental acts in terms analogous to physical laws, psychologists not only fail to recognize the mythic or totemic structures enduring in their methodology, they also render themselves incapable of forwarding an adequate social psychology of archaic cultures.[47] Laboring under the assumption that the "magical" experiences of primitive peoples or their account of a primordial temporality very different from our own chronological projection of time are merely "subjective" and a function of relative ignorance is going to foreclose an understanding of those cultures. It also precludes an insight into the way that magic and mythical time are still at work, albeit in an occulted fashion, in contemporary modes of thinking, above all in Science.[48]

So it is fair to say that Hegel views psychic phenomena and uncanny abilities as a holdover from pre-rational, and predominately unconscious, human cognitive functioning. In fact, he sees an inverse relationship between psychic ability and the analytical intellect. Adept

---

42   Ibid., 22.

43   Ibid., 18, 26.

44   Ibid., 18, 27.

45   Ibid., 26.

46   Ibid., 18.

47   Ibid., 23–24.

psychics are atavisms and their abilities should in no way be seen as an alternative to much more reliable modern scientific or technological means of acquiring the same information or accomplishing the same aims with which such individuals were once tasked. Nevertheless, pretending that such paranormal phenomena are merely hallucinations or delusions is unscientific and, in Hegel's view, the progressive and phased evolution of human understanding toward the perfection of Science qua "Absolute Knowing" with its attendant utopian sociopolitical implications, cannot come about until and unless there is a scientific recognition and contextualization of these increasingly anomalous phenomena.

By contrast with this progressive exorcism of the paranormal by Science on the part of an arch-rationalist, Merleau-Ponty looks at scientific research against the backdrop of an inherently irrational life-world that is "wild" in nature before being tamed by any culturally and historically conditioned system of belief and practice. Paranormal phenomena, or what Merleau-Ponty calls "bastard and untameable experiences," can never be objectively comprehended by scientific theorization. Consequently, Science does not afford us a mirror of objectively existent structures in Nature. In fact, the form of subjectivity characteristic of the theoretical observer of the cosmos is itself a god-like archetypal projection, similar to the gods of less sophisticated tribal societies but infinitely more powerful in its world-conquering and world-forming capacity. The *kosmotheoros* is a gigantic modern totem.

While this seems terribly abstract, Merleau-Ponty attempts to elucidate this idea with reference to the experience of artists. This is not only helpful in itself, it also affords us an opportunity to draw a sharper contrast with Hegel's paranormal phenomenology by comparing Merleau-Ponty's understanding of art to Hegel's theory concerning the epochal evolution of consciousness and the end of art.

Merleau-Ponty compares the spectrality of the kind of idea he is attempting to evoke to musical ideas that we do not possess but that possess us in the way that the virtuoso musician experiences possession when he "is no longer producing or reproducing the sonata: he feels himself, and the others feel him to be at the service of the sonata; the sonata sings through him or cries out so suddenly that he must 'dash on his bow' to follow it."[49] The cohesion of the idea is "a cohesion without concept" of the kind that we find in "the moments of the sonata."[50] This is also the nature of the cohesion of my body with the world. It is "an ideality that is not alien to the flesh, that gives it its axes, its depth, its dimensions."[51] This element brings a "style" of being with it that makes facts have a meaning and be "true" about something in a certain way. He also evocatively describes it as a "rarefied flesh" and a "glorified body" that come together with "the massive flesh" and the "momentary body" that we ordinarily experience.[52]

The "primordial property" that belongs to the flesh "of radiating everywhere and forever," which effects "the reversibility of the visible and the tangible" is also what allows me to have a relationship to the other as if he were my *alter ego* because "it is not *I* who sees, not *he* who sees, because an anonymous visibility inhabits both of us… which extends further than the things I touch and see at present."[53] It is what makes it possible for us "to be open to visions other than our own."[54] This reversibility is also that of "sound and meaning," or "speech and what it means to say," so that if I am close enough to the other I can hear his meaning even if he has not spoken it in words and the "sayable" has metamorphosed into "a gaze of the mind, *intuitus mentis*."[55] Even the possibility of psychokinesis seems to be implied by this understanding of worldly embodiment as "the flesh," when

---

49 Ibid., 151.

50 Ibid., 152.

51 Ibid., 152.

52 Ibid., 148.

53 Ibid., 142–143.

54 Ibid., 143.

Merleau-Ponty adds that: "there is even an inscription of the touching in the visible, of the seeing in the tangible [that] founds transitivity from one body to another."[56] Finally, recognizing the folding of the "actual, empirical ontic visible" back on itself into an invisible that is not its shadow but what principally renders it possible, takes us beyond the duality of thought and extension just as it deconstructs the dualist distinction between the visible and the invisible, revealing them to be the obverse of one another.[57]

Merleau-Ponty observes that when I think of a certain place un-reflectively and in an absorbed manner, I am not *in* my thoughts but at the place even if my body is sitting at this table and my gaze ought to terminate at the density of its surface.[58] The horizon of all such "visions or quasi-visions," among which clairvoyance or "remote viewing" ought to be counted, is still the natural and historical world that I inhabit.[59] That the observable world can withdraw in visions that allow us to be present at places other than those wherein a scientist would locate our measurable bodies, so that we lose our spatiotemporal reference markers in such a way as to wonder whether we have ever really had them in the sense that we thought we did, brings us to ask whether any sharp distinction ought to be legitimately drawn between the world of perception and the fabric of dreams.[60] Even dreams have a certain logic, or at least a finite and bounded structure.

The purest ideality is still not free from horizon structures: "It is as though the visibility that animates the sensible world were to emigrate, not outside of every body, but into another less heavy, more transparent body, as though it were to change flesh, abandoning the flesh of the body for a new flesh — that of language, and thereby would be

56   Ibid., 143.

57   Ibid., 152.

58   Ibid., 5.

59   Ibid., 5.

emancipated and longer-lived, but not freed from every condition."[61] Merleau-Ponty recognizes that "there is no essence (*Wesen*), no idea, that does not adhere to a domain of history and of geography."[62] This does not mean that ideas so situated are therefore inaccessible to those in other domains than the ones relevant for these essences, but that in view of the fact that "the space or time of culture is not survey-able from above," any more than that of "nature" is, it remains the case that "communication from one constituted culture to another occurs through the wild region wherein they all have originated."[63] This wilderness is the preserve of artists, not the domain of allegedly "ob-jective" or object*ifying* scientists who tacitly presuppose a materialist ontology.

My relationship with the world is not a relationship with an object. It involves, as an ever-present possibility, "a sort of dehiscence" that "opens my body in two" so that it becomes not only my body look-ing and touching, but my body looked at and my body touched. In this intuitive "reflection" there is a leaving oneself and retiring into oneself, a kind of lived distance with respect to oneself.[64] The body sentient and body sensed are two phases of a single movement that incorporates into itself the whole of the sensible, in other words the "flesh of the world."[65] My body is no more an object than the world is.[66] Merleau-Ponty notes how painters sometimes remark on the way in which they feel looked at by the things that they observe so intently as if to capture their essence.[67]

One group of artists that would certainly have been familiar with this uncanny experience are the Surrealists. The origins of Surrealism

61 Ibid., 153.

62 Ibid., 115.

63 Ibid., 115.

64 Ibid., 124.

65 Ibid., 138.

66 Ibid., 141.

in Paris are as dingy as the story of any occult movement could ever be.[68] Adrienne Monnier, the woman who introduced the principal founders of Surrealism to one another, namely André Breton, Louis Aragon, Philippe Soupault, and Paul Eluard in the Spring of 1919, was an occultist well versed in Hermeticism who conducted palm readings at her bookshop. Max Ernst joined them when he arrived in Paris in the fall of 1922, and shortly thereafter these men, together with René Crevel, Max Morise, Robert Desnos, and Simone Breton began to hold séances and experiment with automatic writing or "magic dictation." These séances were held at Breton's small studio at 42, rue Fontaine. Sometimes the proceedings got out of hand. When the participants collectively entered an unconscious state, the symptoms of tuberculosis that one of them had been suffering began to manifest itself in several others for days after the conclusion of the séance. Some participants even seemed to be possessed. At one point Desnos attacked Eluard with a kitchen knife, and was restrained with difficulty by Ernst and Breton. He could remember nothing of what he had done when he was brought out of the magnetic trance.

This period was known as the "époque des sommeils" and its tumultuous experiences were summarized in Breton's article "Entrée des medium," which he published in the November 1922 issue of *Littérature* — the magazine he had founded with Breton, Aragon, and Soupault. It is in this article on his experience of paranormal phenomena with his fellow artists that, as a reference to the process and character of psychic automatism, the founder of Surrealism actually used the word *surréalisme* for the first time. It was in their attempt at creatively channeling information from the "subliminal self," then being studied by psychical researchers such as Frederic Myers, that the artists who became the surrealists first decisively broke with deliberately nonsensical Dada activities. Although they used some of the same techniques as mediums in the business of prophecy and

68   M.E. Warlick, *Max Ernst and Alchemy: A Magician in Search of Myth* (Austin,

contacting the dead, what the surrealists were really after in these psychic workshops was a creative breakthrough brought about by reaching into a genuinely irrational depth of the unconscious mind. Moreover, they saw in these parlor evenings the potential for a communal creativity, one that proceeded to some degree from out of a collective unconscious being collectively drawn towards self-consciousness. They occasionally reported having telepathic communication with one another. Max Ernst swore that back in Cologne, he had experienced a phenomenon of levitation, wherein some hats and overcoats had spontaneously relocated to a distant rack without any apparent human intervention, and on his suggestion experiments in telekinesis were also pursued.

Max Ernst's 1922 painting *Rendezvous of Friends* employs numerous symbolic and stylistic references to alchemy and Hermeticism in its depiction of the early surrealists involved in these occult pursuits. He appears in this painting seated on the lap of the departed spirit of Dostoevsky. In particular, the painting has strong affinities to the old drawings and paintings of "The Children of Mercury," where artists, painters, writers, architects, and sculptors are seated together at work around a table with the planetary influence of Mercury or Hermes depicted above them. In Ernst's painting, the black sky above the artists features an illustration of a solar eclipse and its halo, which appeared in the week of his first birthday; it is reproduced turned on its side, in such a manner that it resembles the astrological glyph for the planet Mercury. Ernst also reaches beyond these old drawings and paintings, to affirm the connection between the alchemical Mercury and the Egyptian Hermes Trismegistus of classical Hermeticism, by rendering the gestures of his associates in a geometric and hypnotic manner suggestive of ancient Egyptian art.

The erotic and esoteric were often mingled in the course of these surrealist explorations of the outer limits of human experience. The early male surrealists believed that women had a greater capacity for accessing the unconscious mind and significantly involved them in

their evenings of séances and other types of psychic experimentation. Some of the men even claimed to be in contact with succubus
demons — not quite human females who would materialize in their
bedrooms at night, and who bore certain signs of having just crossed
over from hell, for example the smell of Sulfur, which calls to mind
the alchemical mixture of Sulfur and Mercury.

Max Ernst painted many versions of the fusion of male and female
figures to create the alchemical Androgyne. A number of Ernst's
paintings of this period feature the athanor, a cylindrical furnace
containing the alembic vessel in which King and Queen are united.
The sexual imagery of alchemical union between the solar King and
the lunar Queen, mirrored "as above, so below" by an astronomical
conjunction, is at the core of Ernst's 1923 painting, *Men Shall Know
Nothing of This*. It also features a whistle that is a stand-in for the alchemist's bellows, which blows the air fanning the spiritual fire that
allows the chemicals to fuse. Nadja, a female clairvoyant involved with
Breton, offered an esoteric analysis of this painting, whose accuracy
Ernst confirmed. However, since another medium, Madame Sacco,
had once predicted that Ernst would meet a woman named Nadia
or Natasha who would harm someone he loved, he refused to have
Breton introduce him to Nadja.

As the Surrealist movement crystallized over the course of the
1920s in Paris, it ever more explicitly affirmed its occult character.
A special October 1923 issue of *Littérature*, includes a list of the surrealists' favorite artists, writers, philosophers, and poets of the past
that features occultists quite prominently, including the legendary
Hermès Trismégiste, Nicolas Flamel, and Cornelius Agrippa. This
same issue featured rather explicitly hermetic line drawings by Max
Ernst as accompaniments to its poetry, for example *The Cold Throats*
where two disconnected alchemical vessels that ought to be connected are next to a headless woman lying on the floor like a manikin
with a chastity belt. In October 1924, Breton issued the first *Surrealist
Manifesto*, which unambiguously defined surrealism as "pure psychic

automatism."[69] He praises Desnos' trances, despite their volatility, and he refers to automatic writing as among the "Secrets of the Magical Surrealist Art." In a 1925 "Letter to Seers," Breton commends psychics for their perseverance in important work despite relative impoverishment on account of the unwillingness of academic scientists to recognize the validity of their experiences. He compares their patience to that of the alchemist Nicolas Flamel—who, being dismissed by man as materialistic, scornfully retorted that had he discovered a way to transmute base metals into gold, he would be "richer" than he was. In point of fact, unlike many other alchemists, Flamel was quite wealthy; had he been any wealthier he might have attracted a great deal more unwanted attention.

The publication of Fulcanelli's *Mystères des cathédrals*[70] in 1926, with its elucidation of alchemical symbolism in Parisian cathedrals and other medieval buildings, inspired the surrealists to take walking tours of mysterious passageways in Notre Dame cathedral and other sites mentioned, especially the Les Halles neighborhood of Flamel, the rue Saint-Martin, the rue des Escrivains, and the Tour Saint Jacques. They would haunt these places into the twilight hours and the night, and some of the surrealists were quite convinced of having met phantoms at certain of these sites, including the ghost of the infamous murderer Liabeuf and that of the poet Gérard de Nerval. Around 1928, the surrealists began actively investigating occult manuscripts from the magical traditions of Alchemy, Hermeticism, and Kabbalah; symbols and diagrams from these illuminated manuscripts would often be reproduced in the movement's periodicals.

In the *Second Manifesto* of Surrealism[71] that Breton put out in 1929, as a definitive statement of the now mature artistic movement, signed and endorsed by his colleagues, he takes an even more radical

---

69 André Breton, *Manifestoes of Surrealism* (Ann Arbor, MI: University of Michigan Press, 1972), 1–48.

70 Fulcanelli, *The Dwellings of the Philosophers* (Boulder, CO: Archive Press, 1999).

stance on the occult than in the first manifesto. He identifies a kabbalistic concern with the power of language in the poetry of Arthur
Rimbaud, but then criticizes Rimbaud for not going far enough — for
not recognizing that the world is constituted by poetic *logos*, in other
words that poetry literally has the power to transform the world. The
alchemical Philosopher's Stone becomes, for him, that which allows
the "imagination to take a stunning revenge on all things," to re-
imagine the human reality. Breton called for a "derangement of all the
senses" directed toward this end, and for a revolt against centuries of
"domestication" and "insane resignation" to an all-too-unimaginative
conception of "reality." He also suggested that a "veritable occultation
of surrealism" should take place, by which he meant not only that the
movement should explicitly concern itself with the occult, but also
that it should conceal its investigations in this area and their outcome
from the general public just as the alchemists had guarded their own
secrets.

Breton explicitly lays out the means toward such "occultation": a
"serious investigation into those sciences which for various reasons
are today completely discredited," among which he includes astrology,
extrasensory perception, telekinesis, and so forth. He has no problem
with experiments in these areas being carried out in the stimulat-
ing manner of "parlor games," so long as a modicum of "necessary
mistrust" is maintained to eschew blatant fraud and make genuine
discoveries. The inscription on Breton's tombstone, "Je cherche l'or
du temps" ("I seek the gold of Time") is clearly a reference to the
Philosopher's Stone that he spent his life seeking.

Jackson Pollock's early paintings are an evolution directly out of
Surrealism, and they continue the surrealist concern with alchemical
or occult themes and motifs. If the later were not obvious from the
content of the paintings themselves, the titles he chose for them make
this explicitly clear. Here are some of my personal favorites from this
period: *Male and Female* (1942–43); *Guardians of the Secret* (1943);
Troubled Queen (1945); *Alchemy* (1947). There is also a related totemic

quality and shamanic trend in this early work, for example: *Bird* (1941); *Birth* (1941); *The She-Wolf* (1943); *Totem Lesson 2* (1945). Yet once he makes the transition to his fully abstract expressionist style, somehow the magical dimension is still there and in a few pieces it appears to be working its effect on the viewer at an ever deeper level; again, the titles that Pollock chose reflect his awareness of this: *Lucifer* (1947); *Full Fathom Five* (1947); *One* (1948). Pollock made a similar transition as Max Ernst did when he went from painting overtly alchemical pieces to creating paintings alchemically — even if they do not feature any explicitly discernable esoteric symbols. The nature of the magic at work in Pollock's paintings has now been discovered, and it is far from any trickery unless real conjuring of the kind practiced by a sorcerer is to be considered trickery.

Richard P. Taylor, a physicist at the University of New South Wales, who is also an abstract painter, discovered that there are fractals in Jackson Pollock's abstract paintings at many different levels of magnification.[72] Taylor happened upon this discovery during a break from his work at the university to go on a retreat organized by the Manchester School of Art. However, a storm struck the Yorkshire moors in northern England and instead of simply being holed up indoors, Taylor recruited some fellow artists to build a contraption made of fallen branches with paint buckets attached to them that would harness the wind pattern and direct the paint onto an appropriately positioned canvas. What they found after the windstorm was astonishing: a Jackson Pollock painting. Taylor had an insight and went back to test it at the University, working with a group of experts in respective fields from mathematics and computer science to perceptual psychology.

It turns out that if quintessential Jackson Pollock paintings are scanned into a computer and then overlaid with a grid that can be loosened or tightened in its level of magnification, a mathematical

---

72   Richard P. Taylor, "Order in Pollock's Chaos" in *Scientific American* (December,

analysis of the drips on the canvas reveals that they conform precisely to the kind of fractals that are found in nature: in sea shells, in sunflowers, in tree branches, in weather patterns, and so forth. The difference between these fractals and those mechanically produced by a computer are that they display only a probabilistic statistical self-similarity that has an organic feel to it, rather than an exact self-similarity where the pattern breaks and repeats the same way at regular intervals. Moreover, these natural fractal patterns are discovered in Pollock's paintings at many different levels of magnification, in other words — there are fractals within fractals within fractals. The smallest fractals found are 1,000 times smaller than the largest.

There is no way that Pollock could have planned this kind of painting, at that in the 1950s — decades before the scientific study of the fractals discovered by Benoit Mandelbrot. It is absolutely impossible for the rational mind and lies completely beyond the conscious or analytical perceptual capacity of human beings. Yet, Pollock once chose to epitomize his artwork with this statement: "My concern is with the rhythms of nature." There is documentary evidence that he would dance around his canvas with movements that very closely resemble the ritual dances of Native American Shamanism, except more fluid and dynamic. He would also paint in bursts, over a long period of time — sometimes months. This would account for the many different layers of fractals. He would lay down only so many as he could while an unconscious force was still moving his body, then he would stop.

The best evidence that such an extraordinary process was at work is that *only* Jackson Pollock's abstract paintings have these fractals in them. When other drip paintings in "the Pollock style," including clever forgeries that might even fool some art critics, are scanned into the same computer program, they fail to yield the fractals in a genuine Pollock. Taylor theorized that the unique aesthetic experience of Pollock paintings, the reason why they are more widely appreciated than other works of abstract expressionism by people with a well-developed aesthetic intuition, is that the human mind is naturally keyed to respond to the beauty of fractals in nature.

Pollock's paintings pose a serious problem for Hegel's understanding of paranormal phenomena in their relationship to the development and perfection of scientific rationality. They are the most abstract expression of artistic creativity, as Hegel would put it, the form of art that has most freed itself from its content, but these artworks are even more clearly produced by psychic automatism than the occult art of the surrealists. Even the latter, coming as it did after Impressionism, would leave Hegel at a loss to account for why these successive — and thus presumably progressive — art forms were not expressive of an increasingly rational and self-conscious mind.

You see, Hegel thinks that art passes through a series of successive stages: the symbolic or naturalistic, the classical, and the romantic. In the first of these periods nature itself was regarded as divine, and what he calls "natural meanings" were expressed in vegetable, human and animal symbolism, which presumably adorned the *architecture* which Hegel views as the quintessential art form of this period. In the second of these periods, *sculpture* is the quintessential art form and it celebrates the divinity of human individuality, but only in a corporeal form whose nature it is to be bound by fate. Finally, the third stage sees the realization of the subjective inner depth of human individuality and emotions such as love, valor, fidelity, etc., in contrast to the merely corporeal and natural, which is deemphasized or even viewed negatively. Hegel acknowledges that these art forms do not strictly exclude each other, but that one or another of them is emphasized in a certain historical epoch and that borrowed elements of another or others are either superficial adornments or are anticipations of a transition.

According to Hegel each of these stages is not merely a "style" but a world-view that infuses every aspect of the culture of a people at a certain time and constitutes their religion, what he calls: "the substantial spirit of people and ages." It is merely the task of art to epitomize this spirit, in a radicalization of the way that any man should reflect in his works the spirit of his society and age.[73]

Hegel inquires into the need for art, wondering whether it is a mere fancy, if it is an extraneous means to ends best fulfilled in other ways, or whether there are not higher aims of man than those which can be fulfilled by art. He then goes on to explain that art is rooted in the unique nature of human ontology. Human beings exist as objects of the natural world, however, they are unique in that they also exist *for themselves*. In other words, they become conscious of their own existence. The striving to realize self-consciousness can be seen from the earliest childhood, in such behavior as a child's throwing of a rock into a pond in order to have the ripples formed on its surface reflect back to him, and to gain recognition from others like himself, the fact that he exists and has objective power in the world.

Humans alter objects of the natural environment in order to become conscious of themselves in the mirror of the altered objects. Hegel notes that this extends to the alteration of the human body itself, qua natural object, by means of cosmetics or disfigurement of various kinds. Thus art is the means of making the inner life of human consciousness explicitly aware of itself through outward manifestations that are apprehended by the intuition (*Anschauung*) and knowledge (*Erkenntnis*). However, according to Hegel this "free rationality of man in which all acting and knowing... have their basis and necessary origin," is not uniquely characteristic of art, as opposed to other types of action that are a means to self-consciousness, such as the "political and moral... religious representation and scientific knowledge."[74]

After announcing that art does not aim merely at arousing feelings, Hegel launches into a semi-historical critique of preceding aesthetic theories. He believes that most aestheticians worthy of the

---

73   G.W.F. Hegel, "Lectures on Fine Art" in *The Origins of Modern Critical Thought: German Aesthetics and Literary Criticism from Lessing to Hegel*. Edited by David Simpson. (New York: Cambridge University Press, 1988), 380; 383.

name realize that the study of works of art should not focus upon the vague and sometimes indistinguishable feelings to which they give rise in those who experience them, thereby losing sight of the art object itself. Aestheticians realized that art, if it is to be admitted as such, must more precisely be viewed as affecting the observer with a *feeling of the beautiful*. It was understood that such a feeling cannot be as natural or instinctual as others, but requires at least some degree of education (*Bildung*). Thus for a time aesthetics focused on imparting *taste* by means of education, as a means of understanding and hence evaluating the status of a given production as a work of art (or not).

However, according to Hegel, the mere combination of "sensing and abstract reflections" not only is incapable of plumbing the depths of the work of art, it is even offended and scared away by the force of true genius, since the latter's work often scorns learnable conventions and thus cannot be comfortably anticipated by one schooled in them. Thus the attempt to inculcate taste was replaced by connoisseurship, which sought to provide a better appreciation and understanding of the work of art through scholarship in respect to circumstances and conditions of its origins, such as its historical context and the biography and character of its creator, other individuals who might have influenced him, etc. Yet Hegel criticizes even mere connoisseurship for its tendency to avoid or even discourage engagement with the deeper aspects of an artwork, the essence that is more than the sum of the parts rendered comprehensible through scholarship.[75]

Hegel goes on to contrast our relation to the work of art with both our relation to natural objects of desire and our relation to objects of scientific inquiry. While the work of art is a sensuous object, it is unlike an object of desire in that it is not intended to be used or consumed. A mere sculpture of an animal will not satiate hunger and a picture of logs will not build a house. Consequently, what Hegel calls "practical desire" will view art as useless and of less value than "organic and inorganic individual things in nature," because it cannot "let the object persist in its freedom." For such desire, a thing is only real if it can be canceled out in its independence and thereby consumed. Indeed, the work of art *should be* useless, in the sense of being left to be appreciated just as it is in its completion. It should be sensuous only in the superficial sense of mere appearance, as it is essentially intended for *spiritual* apprehension.[76]

Scientific inquiry is also not concerned with the sensuous individuality or use of any given product of nature. Even if it can explain how a particular object took on a certain color or shape, in so doing it moves beyond the object and leaves it behind in the development or demonstration of a universal law. However, the Reason by means of which this theoretical understanding is exercised is a universal faculty and is not unique to any given individual. Consequently, it also attributes no value to the individuality of the sensuous objects of its theoretical studies. Hegel sees this as the key difference between science and art, which are similar in their transcendence of practical desire. Art, unlike science, depends on a free or uninterested spiritual relation to the sensuous appearances *in their individuality*. Hegel writes:

> From the practical interest of desire, the interest of art is distinguished by the fact that it lets its object persist freely and on its own account, while desire converts it to its own use by destroying it. On the other hand, the reflection on the work of art differs in an opposite way from theoretical consideration [Betrachtung] by scientific intelligence, since it cherishes an interest in the object in its individual existence and does not struggle to change it into its universal thought and concept.[77]

Hegel sees the work of art as lying between immediate sensuousness and pure thought. It transcends the former in that it addresses only the senses of sight and hearing, and not smell, taste, and touch — which concern themselves with the pure materiality of an object. Nor should

---

76 Ibid., 364–365.

one ascribe this limitation to "impotence" on behalf of the artist; rather it would be a failing of a work of art if it were to address the same senses as practical desire, which seeks only to manipulate or consume its object. Even the sensuous appearances (*Schein*) of a work of art are to become something ideal and transcendent of the material medium in which they are expressed.[78]

On the other hand, the artist must always express the universal in terms of some concrete situation or imagery drawn from a store of particular instances in lived experience. He is still incapable of drawing general conclusions or principles from the sum of these, though he intuitively understands the interrelationships between the imagery involved in various significant events and can reproduce them in novel combinations.[79] This is not to say that the artist comes up with a certain theme and then adorns it with poetic imagery, rhyme and meter, in such a way as the latter only serve as a means of expression for an otherwise "prosaic thought." Hegel says this is sure to produce only *bad poetry*, because the true artistic production requires a oneness of the sensuous and spiritual in *imagination* (*Phantasie*) from start to finish.[80]

In order for this to be the case the artist must be endowed with a natural talent that works in him *unconsciously,* as a force of "instinct-like productiveness" or "natural activity" belonging to "the natural side of man," so that the work of art is only partly the expression of conscious intent. While acknowledging that everyone is capable of some kind of artistic production, Hegel thinks that beyond a certain point, "an inborn, higher talent for art is necessary." He does not believe that any true talent of this kind exists in the sciences, which requires only the universal capacity for rational thought in order to abstract from all natural activity in an artificial manner. Furthermore, the intentional

---

78 Ibid., 366.
79 Ibid., 367–368.

or "spiritual" aspect of the artist must always be inclined to express itself in a sensuous medium. Someone with the inborn talent for art will consequently take hold of clay or paint, or make use of their voice melodiously, from the earliest years, in order to give form to and express, often with great effortlessness, "whatever rouses and moves them inwardly."[81] The work of art also eschews pure thought in that in its subject matter it is also derived from the sensuous realm of nature. Hegel writes, "even if the subject is of a spiritual kind, it can still be grasped only by displaying spiritual things, like human relationships, in the shape of phenomena possessed of external reality."[82]

Each of the stages of art is not merely a "style" but also a worldview that infuses every aspect of the culture of a people at a certain time and constitutes their religion, what Hegel calls: "the substantial spirit of people and ages." It is merely the task of art to epitomize this spirit, in a radicalization of the way that any man should reflect in his works the spirit of his society and age.[83] Hegel claims that the present inability of artists to continue to fulfill this role is not merely on account of the apathetic, uninspired or prosaic character of the times. (This is to view the situation backwards.) Instead, art itself must be held responsible for bringing its content before intuition as an object, in such a way that over a series of stages art frees itself from the content that it represents and becomes purely formal.[84] Hegel also more concretely attributes this to the rise of criticism (*die Kritik*) and free thought in European civilization. Even artists have come to be acquainted with Aesthetics in their critical reflection on what was the content of art from the symbolic to the romantic period, and have become conscious of art as changing over the course of periods of time,

---

81   Ibid., 368.

82   Ibid., 368.

83   Ibid., 380, 383.

which brings forth the realization that it is not atemporally wedded to any given content.

The profound significance of this stark contrast between, on the one hand, Hegel's theory of art history as an expression of the rationalization of consciousness and, on the other hand, Merleau-Ponty's claim that artists have an insight into a deeper dimension of nature and human experience that will forever be denied to objectifying scientists, can be brought to light by setting it within the context of Hegel's conception of humor as the final and most self-conscious stage of art in his Lectures on Aesthetics.

Hegel insists a work of art exists only to "set forth in an adequate sensuous present what is itself inherently rich in content."[85] Thus he believes that the divine remains the absolute subject matter of art, but now the divine content of art assumes the formless form of "the depths and heights of the human heart as such, universal humanity in its joys and sorrows, its strivings, its deeds...expressing the infinity of its feelings and situations."[86] This transformation is effected by none other than humor, which allows art to transcend itself. In its irreverent reflection on everything and anything that was formerly an absolutely determinative content, humor forces man within himself to the source of this content, to meditate on it in such a way that the artist *qua* human being becomes "self-determining and considering."[87] Hegel eloquently describes this effect of humor as "the liberation of subjectivity, in accordance with its inner contingency."[88]

In other words, humor irreverently engages emotional and intellectual constructions that, so long as they remained unapproachable due to their sanctity, were also imperative and thereby deprived us of genuinely free expression. The latter only becomes possible when

---

85   Ibid., 387.

86   Ibid., 384.

87   Ibid., 383–384.

these constructs are reevaluated as relative to the use they may have for us as objects of our subjective consciousness, which transcends them. Hegel reiterates this at the conclusion of his discussion of "the spiritual work of art" in sections 743 to 747 of his *Phenomenology of Spirit*, where he writes of Comedy in distinction from preceding art forms:

> [T]he religion of art is fulfilled and consummated. ... [T]he individual consciousness in its certainty of self...has lost the form of something...ideally separated from and alien to consciousness in general — as were the statue and also the living embodiment of beauty or the content of the Epic and the powers and persons of Tragedy. ... [R]ather the self proper of the actor coincides with the part he impersonates, just as the onlooker is perfectly at home in what is represented before him, and sees himself playing in the drama before him. What this self-consciousness beholds, is that whatever assumes the form of essentiality as against self-consciousness, is instead dissolved within it — within its thought, its existence and action, — and is quite at its mercy. It is the return of everything universal into certainty of self, a certainty which, in consequence, is this complete loss of fear of everything strange and alien, and complete loss of substantial reality on the part of what is alien and external. Such certainty is a state of spiritual good health and of self-abandonment thereto, on the part of consciousness, in a way that, outside this kind of comedy, is not to be found anywhere.[89]

But what if it were the case that the comedic overcomes the power of rational comprehension, and not the other way around? What if the ultimate paranormal phenomenon is the power of a diabolical trickster who appears to have a cosmic scope of influence and can act to undermine the authority of Science's totemic *kosmotheoros*?

As far as archetypes go, that of the Trickster is a cultural universal. In a sense this is paradoxical because the Trickster archetype appears to be a de-structuring force that undermines the binary oppositions defining the taboos of various cultures. George P. Hansen has shown

---

89   A.V. Miller, *Hegel's Phenomenology of Spirit* (New York: Oxford University

how this *spectral* force defies the distinctions between Life and Death, Spirit and Matter, Sacred and Profane, Male and Female, Clean and Unclean, King and Pauper.[90] In his study "On the Psychology of the Trickster Figure," Carl Jung notes how the alchemical figure of *Mercurius* or "Mercury," which evolved out of the Latin assimilation of Hermes, takes the archetype of the trickster back into primordial shamanic roots. The fondness for sly jokes and malicious pranks is there, as it is in Hermes, but there is also the power of shape-shifting between the animal and the divine, and his exposure to initiatory tortures that confer upon him salvific healing power.[91] Insofar as the tortures are concerned, the Spirit Mercurius occasionally allows others to outwit him so as to play the divine jester or fool toward a greater end — like an animal playing dead. Unlike Zeus, who is always concerned to defend his apparently very fragile honor, the god Hermes is willing to be made a fool of, but he uses his foolishness as another device for his machinations. What is so significant about The Cosmic Joker in his guise as arch-comedian is that he dynamites the Hegelian dialectical progression from the overcoming of the irrational in Art through its final stage of comedy, onward to the autonomy of rational Man over Nature in modern Science.

Carl Jung explicitly draws a connection between the Trickster archetype and the paranormal phenomena and psychic experiences studied by parapsychologists.[92] He sees the malicious tricks played by poltergeists as manifestations of the Trickster. He notes how these often take place in the ambience of pre-adolescent children. The deceptively stupid and inconsistent character of some "communications"

---

90 George P. Hansen, *The Trickster and the Paranormal* (Bloomington, IN: Xlibris Corporation, 2001).

91 Carl Jung, "On the Psychology of the Trickster Figure" in Paul Radin, *The Trickster: A Study in American Indian Mythology* (New York: Schocken Books, 1972), 195.

from spirit mediums is also the Trickster at work.[93] Jung understands the Trickster archetype to be a dissociated or split-off personality, not belonging exclusively to any one individual or another, but a personification that is produced by the totality of individuals in a society. Consequently, it can be perceived by individuals as if it were something external — in a way that they would not be able to recognize a dissociated aspect of their own personality.[94] This projection is a collective analog of the personal *shadow* side of the psyche, and it expresses itself whenever accidental circumstances convey the impression of jinxes, or again, in poltergeist activity or spiritualist séances. It has been well noted that "channeled" material often reflects the contents of the unconscious of all those present at a séance on any particular evening.[95]

The more the shadow of the irrational is found to be at odds with the conscious ego and is repressed in the individual, the more impressively it may be able to manifest as an antagonistic force on a collective level.[96] The Trickster figure gains even greater strength on account of the secret allure that its primal vitality has for a repressed psyche. In primitive cultures this collective projection had a kind of autonomy and was even capable of possessing certain individuals.[97] Suppressing this relative autonomy, as the rationalistic "scientific" mind has, is not going to cause the Trickster to disappear. Jung believes that on the contrary there will be an even more violent and destructive return of the repressed on a collective level, especially if conditions of sociopolitical uncertainty open an opportunity for its release from out of the unconscious.[98] When it seems that fate is playing tricks on us, or

---

93   Ibid., 196.
94   Ibid., 201.
95   Ibid., 202.
96   Ibid., 204.
97   Ibid., 205.

things appear to be bewitched, then the Trickster is breaking through the crust of civilization and making his way back into our world.

In his book on *Flying Saucers*, Carl Jung speculated that contemporary close encounters represent a reemergence of the Trickster from out of a collective unconscious rebelling against the overly mechanistic and materialist framework of modern science.[99] There is increasing clamor for UFO "Disclosure" but, if Jung was right, just what would it be a disclosure of? In his study of the UFO phenomenon, Colonel Alexander, whose use of the term "phenomenology" opened this chapter, comes to a very similar conclusion as Jung. Dr. Alexander and other researchers set up a laboratory of sorts at the Skinwalker Ranch to study the Trickster and its relationship to close encounters.[100] On the basis of a phenomenology of the occurrences that he and others witnessed on the ranch, he formulated the term "Precognitive Sentient Phenomena" (PSP) to refer to the form of intelligence behind close encounters and UFO phenomena. Here is how the Colonel explains his idea:

The issue of *The Trickster* is well established in paranormal research. That means that whatever is generating the incidents does so in a manner that does not remain consistent over time. What is being proposed is a derivation of that idea. The precognitive sentient phenomena concept suggests that there is some external controlling agent that initiates these events that are observed and reported. It appears as though that agent not only determines all factors of the event, but is already (i.e. precognitively) aware of how the observers or researchers will respond to any given stimuli. The agent can be considered like the Trickster that is always in control of the observations. Every time researchers get close to an understanding of the situation, the parameters are altered or new variables are entered into the equation.

The preface to John Alexander's book is written by Dr. Jacques Vallée. In his decades of research on the close encounter phenomenon,

---

99   Carl Gustav Jung, *Flying Saucers* (New York: Princeton University Press, 1979).

Jacques Vallée has demonstrated that the UFO phenomenon of the 20th century is on a continuum with the airship sightings of the 18th and 19th centuries, the Fairy aerial conveyances of the Medieval and Renaissance periods, and the chariots of the gods and heavenly armies of the Lord observed in antiquity.[101] Vallée has also noted the inextricability of UFOs from psychic phenomena and from a theatrical display of absurdity characteristic of the Trickster archetype. He characterizes "the mechanism by which UFO events are generated" as a "phenomenon whose manifestations border on both the physical and the mental… a medium in which human dreams can be implemented…"[102]

Vallée suggests that the human imagination may be behind close encounters, but in that event it is a far more powerful force than scientists in the grip of materialism believe it to be.[103] UFOs may be collective hallucinations of a kind, as Jung suspected, but if so they are what early psychical researchers called "veridical hallucinations" or apparitions, and moreover telekinetic apparitions that leave physical traces.[104] Vallée compares the quality of the disembodied voice "heard" by those who experience a close encounter with the characteristics of psychic automatism studied by the Society for Psychical Research, and interestingly he cites the work of Frederick Myers in particular.[105] This imaginative force may not be as entirely irrational as it seems; there may be purposeful patterns to discern beneath its outward aspect of patent absurdity.[106]

Vallée finds that one of the clearest overlaps between fairy folklore and close encounter experiences is time distortion. People who dimly hear the distant music of the fairies making merry and try to trace it, are sometimes drawn into the fairy rings or magic circles of the

---

101 Jacques Vallée, *Passport to Magonia* (Chicago: Contemporary Books, 1993).

102 Ibid., 153, 159–160.

103 Ibid., 49.

104 Ibid., 67, 94.

105 Ibid., 94.

Celts or the *elf-dans* of the Norse, which Vallée compares to the contemporary "crop circles," imprinted on wheat fields and hillsides so that the fairies or elves can dance at night.[107] These perfectly circular imprints or clearings, measuring two to ten yards, have been reported for centuries.[108] Mortals who dance with the ethereal beings in their circles, may even go away with them inside a round or conical object that stands on tripod-like legs inside the magic circle, for what they take to be a brief visit to the fairies' abodes. They return looking just as they were and thinking that they have only been away for a few hours, whereas in fact days, weeks, months or even years have elapsed from the perspective of ordinary folk, who have aged in the meantime.[109]

One particularly extraordinary case involved a bride who, on her wedding day wandered off for a little while in pursuit of the strains of a strange, ethereal music. She soon found a knoll "where the elves were making merry" around a large, flattened circular or disc shaped "magical object" that the woman later described as a round table. This "table" was standing on red pillars. After drinking a cup of wine offered to her by the "wee folk" and dancing with them for a round, she hastened to return home to her own wedding festivities. Her family was not there to greet her. Everything and everyone had changed in the village. Finally, upon hearing the panicked bride hysterically relate her story, a very old woman identified her as the wife-to-be of her grandfather's brother, who disappeared without a trace on his wedding day a hundred years ago. Hearing this unfathomable truth, the miserable young woman dropped dead of shock on the spot.[110]

On the basis of the significant time distortions implicit in the phenomenon, Vallée speculates that close encounters may represent some sort of window into the future — a window through which people who

107 Ibid., 32, 38.
108 Ibid., 38–39.
109 Ibid., 29.

have freed themselves from linear time are accessing various epochs of our history as it approaches the singularity of their own present:

> [S]hould we hypothesize that an advanced race… sometime in the future has been showing us three-dimensional space operas for… thousand[s of] years, in an attempt to guide our civilization? If so, they certainly do not deserve our congratulations! …Are the UFO's 'windows' [into the future] rather than 'objects'? [111]

In other words, Precognitive Sentient Phenomena or — the Trickster, who may or may not be traveling through space but is certainly working backwards through time and history. Vallée even describes the Trickster's creation as "a pure form of art." It may be that, "Like Picasso and his art, the great UFO Master shapes our culture, but most of us remain unaware of it." [112]

111 Ibid., 153.

TRIAL GODDESS

Joseph K. is "guilty" as charged by the mysterious "Law" that is brought to bear upon him. His crime is the failure to recognize and reconcile the strife between two aspects of his character — the possessive, conscious, rational self in pursuit of advantage, and the unconsciously reckless seeker of chaos and ecstatic transcendence of the ego. Fraulein Burstner, the Usher's wife, and above all Leni, are in some way involved with the mysterious "Law," and they invite Joseph K. to acknowledge the second of these two aspects. I will argue that these promiscuous women hold high unofficial positions in "the Court" and that they are emanations of the Triune Goddess of Witchcraft, Artemis-Hecate, whose image Titorelli paints above the High Seat of the Judges of the Court. Mythic imagery of esoteric significance associated with this goddess, pervades *The Trial*.

In his present life, Joseph K. fails to resolve the duality of his character into the spiritual harmony of a Trinity forged beyond judgments of "good" and "evil." He cannot overcome his rationalizing and possessive ego in order to understand the true nature of the Law presided over by the Goddess in Titorelli's painting. He forgoes the help of the three witches of the Law on account of his inability to transcend his desire to possess these wild and untamable maidens. Drawing from references to the subject in Franz Kafka's *Blue Octavo Notebooks*, I examine the possibility that reincarnation might allow Joseph K. a chance to learn from this shameful failure.

In this connection, I suggest that the "definite acquittal," "ostensible acquittal," and "indefinite postponement" explained by Titorelli, can be interpreted as metaphors for the transmigration of the soul. I reveal a connection between "indefinite postponement" and the imagery of the wise innocence of the children of the Court, and of the Court officials who have returned to the playfulness of childhood. Finally, in light of the above, I argue that the third interpretation of the parable "Before The Law," the one accepted by K., is more or less correct. In other words, the deception of the exoteric aspect of the Law and its scriptures is a necessary deception — a means of preserving the manifestation of a world of diverse beings, by concealing the devastating Oneness of Being itself.

1. EXTANT INTERPRETIVE FRAMEWORKS

Interpretation of Franz Kafka's masterwork, *The Trial*, has hitherto fallen into one of four basic categories: psychoanalytic, political, religious, and existential. So as to see more clearly how the reading to be developed here transgresses all of these superficial interpretive rubrics, it would be in order to briefly remind one of the broad strokes of these four positions. This should sharpen the contours of my own proposals, without compromising their clarity and directness by repeatedly interrupting my text to draw explicit contrasts with one or another of these interpretations.

The psychoanalytic interpretation is perhaps the most superficial of all, and the one that can be most easily dismissed — especially in light of Kafka's own view of psychoanalysis. Within a decade of Kafka's death Hellmuth Kaiser came forward as the first representative of this interpretation,[1] which has since been developed by many

---

1   Walter Benjamin, "Franz Kafka: On the Tenth Anniversary of His Death," in

others. According to this interpretation Kafka's writings, including and perhaps especially *The Trial*, are an attempt to rationalize his own psychological injuries. The conspiracy of the omnipresent court is ostensibly indicative of paranoid delusions and projections from out of a persecution complex, while the hierarchy of officials is taken to be an attempt at establishing mediate relationships to authority so as to temper the envy that would predominate in a direct encounter between persons with too great a social difference separating them.[2] Joseph's relationships with the women that are supposedly reified as sexual objects and connections, are seen as expressive of his own neurotic feelings of guilt over his sexuality, motivated in part by an obsessive concern with "purity."[3] A perversely enduring infantile sexuality is allegedly crafted into a sophisticated critique of accepted erotic norms.[4] As we shall see from entries in his notebooks, Kafka was a harsh critic of just such reductive psychobabble. He recognized that in its infinitely regressive manner of interpretation psychologism only pretends at "explaining" anything.[5]

Although they are also overly reductive, political interpretations of *The Trial* have a little more substance to them. These are often grounded in notes wherein Kafka makes fleeting references to anarchist figures such as Peter Kropotkin, Lily Braun, and Alexander Herzen.[6] One note of particular significance is a sketch of a "Propertyless Workingmen's Association," which seems to have been a suggestion for a Zionist commune.[7] In June of 1912 Kafka apparently attended an anarchist lecture on the class structure of America delivered by

2   Theodor Adorno, "Notes on Kafka" in *Prisms* (MA: MIT Press, 1983), 250.

3   Ibid., 263.

4   Ibid.

5   Ibid., 250, 270.

6   Bill Dodd, "The Case for a Political Reading" in *The Cambridge Companion to Kafka*, Julian Preece (Ed.), (Cambridge, UK: Cambridge University Press, 2003), 132.

Frantisek Soukup.[8] Michael Mares, who was a member of the anarchist *klub mladych* in Prague, claimed (perhaps falsely) that Kafka was
also in attendance there from 1909–1912.[9] With support from these
suggestive ties to radical leftists, some critics have read *The Trial* as
an argument that the Law is inherently hegemonic — that legal order
as such is a *Machtergreifung* or ethically unwarranted "seizure of
power."[10] (This presupposes some fundamental distinction between
the Ethical and the Political, with the latter understood juristically.)

Although the country that the narrator of *The Trial* lives in is
supposed to be in a state of universal peace on account of being well
governed through a legal constitution,[11] Klaus Mann and others in
his wake have suggested that it bears a nearly prophetic resemblance
to the Third Reich.[12] The radically anarchist implication is that any
legal order is as violently grounded on unjustifiable mob rule as the
worst of them. A sadistic band of criminals has installed itself as the
government. While putting great store by decorum and symbols of
officialdom, it is at the same time so corrupt that it amuses itself by
offering its victims a questionable chance to bribe and bargain their
way out of "arrests," which are really capricious assaults that could
come at any hour, and a means to avert "prosecutions," which are
grotesquely comical persecutions. The women in the service of court
officials have reminded certain readers of German ladies who, even if
married, were forbidden to refuse the advances of those officers who
had distinguished themselves heroically and went about in medal-
encrusted SS uniforms. There is a pervasive atmosphere of impending
death amidst life in the city that is the novel's setting, a city in which
many live in squalor and that, bit by bit, is revealed to be a thinly

---

8   Ibid., 134.

9   Ibid., 133.

10   Ibid., 145–146.

11   Franz Kafka. *The Trial*. Willa and Edwin Muir (Trans.) with an Introduction by
     Georg Steiner. (New York: Schocken Books, 1996), 4.

veiled slaughterhouse that so easily accommodates the execution of Joseph K. when it does finally fall upon him. This has seemed to some a prevision of concentration camp conditions, which are simply an extreme case of the inherent alienation and instrumentalization of man at the hands of arbitrary power and his annihilation through the same social forces that engender individuation.[13] On this reading, the socio-political forces that appear to be sustaining us (from birth) are devouring us parasitically.[14]

Religious interpretations of *The Trial* mostly consist of attempts to cast it as a modern Kabbalistic text, in other words as a work of Jewish mysticism. It had not been ten years since Kafka's death (and post-humous publication of *The Trial* by Max Brod) before H.J. Schoeps, Bernhard Rang, and Bernhard Groethuysen all advanced interpretations of this kind. Walter Benjamin reviews these in his memorial essay on Kafka, before going on to add his own layer to the messianic mystique through his correspondence with Gerhard Scholem.[15] There has more recently been a comprehensive book-length review of the subject by Karl Erich Grözinger.[16] The latter presents compelling evidence from Kafka's diaries to the effect that he was at the very least quite familiar with the folk Judaism of Eastern Europe,[17] that he had a source of information about the Hasidic wisdom tradition through his zealously observant friend Georg Langer,[18] and, perhaps most significantly, that he had an at times agonizingly self-conscious relationship with his Jewish heritage.[19]

Those who interpret Kafka kabbalistically all agree on the claim that *The Trial* is concerned with the relationship between *haggadah*

---

13   Ibid., 225, 256.

14   Benjamin, *Illuminations*, 114.

15   Ibid., 127–128, 141–144.

16   Karl Erich Grözinger, *Kafka and Kabbalah* (New York: Continuum, 1994).

17   Ibid., 18–26.

18   Ibid., 29–30.

and *halakhah* — between esoteric verbal tradition and the exoterically explicit letter of the Law. Kafka supposedly adopts themes that developed in Judaism only beginning with medieval Kabbalah, including the ideas that there is not a single judgment at the end of the world but that the divine court is always in session;[20] that there is an extensive divine hierarchy of bureaucratic complexity, in which one may get lost, mediating the relationship of the individual with the highest Judge;[21] that the lower levels of this hierarchy manifest an appearance that reflects the state of one's own consciousness (accounting for its filth and seedy disorderliness);[22] that the bureaucracy is corrupt, lecherous, and open to unorthodox means of influence;[23] that without recourse to such means there is no way to win one's case (i.e. attain salvation) since one is always in the wrong before the Court — especially for thinking that one's own justification of one's life would be sufficient for salvation;[24] and finally, that if one loses one's case in this lifetime it may be deferred to another (this is a late mystical Jewish conception of reincarnation known as *gilgul*).[25]

If Kafka is implicitly working within this tradition these interpreters fail to recognize how radically he innovates it. Benjamin has an inkling of this when he writes: "Kafka's real genius was that he tried something new: he sacrificed truth for... its haggadic element. Kafka's writings are... *more* than parables. They do not modestly lie at the feet of the doctrine, as the Haggadah lies at the feet of the Halakah. Though apparently reduced to submission, they unexpectedly raise a mighty paw against it."[26] Yet even Benjamin does not go far enough. It is mistaken to see the "man from the country" as a euphemism for

---

20 Ibid., 33, 61.

21 Ibid., 62–63.

22 Ibid., 64–68.

23 Ibid., 36–37.

24 Ibid., 38.

25 Ibid., 47–49.

someone not properly Jewish. He is rather one who is too grounded to suffer from "a seasickness on dry land."[27] The man is not shut out of the door to the Law (made only for him) because he is uninitiated into the *Torah* and fails to understand that divine "grace" is indispensible—as some kabbalistic readers would have it.[28] On the contrary, as we shall see, it is because he accords the Law with more authority and respect than it deserves, and his mistake is to have waited even for permission—let alone "grace." The women of *The Trial* are also far more than what the kabbalistic Jew can see them as: crafty "helpers" that play both sides as gossipy go-betweens in the relationship between an accused man and male officials.[29]

As I endeavor to make clear in what follows, in the parable "Before The Law" that stands at the heart of *The Trial*, Kafka diabolically aims at inciting a rebellion against divine order and natural law that is fundamentally anti-religious and at the same time positively supernatural. Although he does not go as far as Adorno—who tries to claim that Kafka's kabbalism is rationalistic (and that Kabbalah itself is a demythologizing proto-rationalism),[30] Benjamin also downplays Kafka's supernaturalism[31]—this, despite the fact that he is perhaps the first to connect the Law of *The Trial* to the quantum upheaval in the laws of Physics.[32] In my view, the greatest merit of the profoundly mistaken religious interpretation is that it alone takes seriously the supernatural element of *The Trial* (and of Kafka's writing in general), an element which is reductively exorcised by psychoanalytic interpreters and disregarded by political ones. *The Trial* is a transcription smuggled out of the same twilight zone that Serling later visited, and but for Max Brod it would have been left behind there together with Kafka.

---

27   Ibid., 130.

28   Grözinger, 53–54.

29   Ibid., 77–82.

30   Adorno, "Notes on Kafka," 268.

31   Ibid., 127.

This is something that so-called "existential" interpretations also fail to recognize, even in the case of the most "religious" existentialists — such as the followers of Kierkegaard and Dostoyevsky, on account of their tacit substance dualism. Existentialist thought, as epitomized by Jean-Paul Sartre, holds that the "human" being is the uniquely subjective being. Manufactured objects always have some predefined essence. There could be no such *thing* as a knife or a table without and apart from the purpose for which it is designed. For such objects, their essence precedes their existence.[33] Perhaps less evidently, this is also the case for any other beings who are not capable of individuated self-determination, and are consequently not "responsible" for their actions. Unlike various species of animals, human beings have no "nature" that *essentially* defines the range of behavior of all members of the species. The brute fact of the existence of each human being precedes her interpretation of her life and her definition of her individual character by means of her chosen actions. It is not of our own choosing that we are "thrown" into the world and always already find ourselves in it, and yet it is entirely of our choosing how we respond to our existential situation.[34] The only certainty is death. This translates into a reading of *The Trial* where the arrest is a metaphor for the moment of realization of being thrown into the world, which compels us to justify our own existence in the face of a certain and yet unjustifiable death sentence.

However many constraints of whatever kind there may be on our actions, insofar as we are intelligent conscious beings, we always have some margin of choice. Not to make any given decision, to defer it indefinitely, is also to make a choice — albeit an inauthentic one. In the eyes of an existentialist, consciousness always has latitude for action beyond the grip of passions with a material basis.[35] In the context

---

33 Jean-Paul Sartre, *Existentialism is a Humanism* (New Haven: Yale University Press, 2007), 20–21.

34 Ibid., 22–23.

of *The Trial*, one could see Joseph's evasive excuses as an expression of this inauthenticity. For Sartre, "man is condemned to be free" in so far as he did not choose to exist, and yet he does exist and he alone is free to choose the manner in which he exists.[36] We are only what we make of our own lives *in deed*, not what we hope for, or what we resentfully assert could have been if things out of our control had not conspired against us to prevent us from fulfilling our potential. In other words, Kafka's "man from the country" was free to walk through the door to the Law at any moment. Deference to the authority of the guard was a divestment of his responsibility to act decisively regarding his own case.

For the Sartrean existentialist there are no divine signs that reveal to us what we should do in a certain situation. Even if there were signs of some sort, each person would be left to interpret them as she sees fit.[37] This could not be truer of the various ambiguous, inconclusive, inscrutable, or deliberately misleading directives issued by the court and the advice of the extra-legal officials in *The Trial*. Furthermore, there are no ethical truths — no absolute and eternal values — because there is no absolute and eternal consciousness to conceive of them.[38] All mass ethics are an escape from personal responsibility and are in "bad faith." The person who understands her own existence realizes that "everything is permitted."[39] The doorway into the Law is always uniquely one's own, and it can only be entered by an act of violence. As Sartre infamously observed with respect to the Nazi occupation of France in a widely reproduced short essay entitled "The Republic of Silence," life under a dictatorship where power is absolute and unquestionable — as in *The Trial* — may force an individual to make more authentic and grave decisions from out of an understanding of

---

36 Ibid., 28–29.

37 Ibid., 26.

38 Ibid., 27–28.

her own total freedom than would be possible in a mass democracy, which allows for a "legitimate" legal tyranny of the majority of society over the individual. By offering an insight into the arbitrary nature of power, a dictatorship affords one that total freedom that one can have only over and against a legal order whose fundamentally unjustified character stands in stark relief.

At this point the existential interpretation begins to converge with the anarchistic political ones. If it were not for their tacit materialism, the existential interpretations might also run into the religious ones here. They would have to admit that unlike Sartre, for whom death was a finality that bounds the finitude of human existence, and unlike Kierkegaard and Dostoyevsky for whom there might be deliverance into some ineffably transcendent beyond — but only through an ungrounded "leap of faith," Kafka's thought effaces the distinction between the realm of the living and the underworld of the dead. What was only a colorful allegory for Sartre in "No Exit" is empirically real for Kafka. *The Trial* presents us with a living hell populated by "various shades of the departed." Unification of the existential and kabbalistic interpretations would also demand that the kabbalists, for their part, leave faith behind and recognize in Kafka an advocate of antinomian supernaturalism. That, however, is precisely what they are incapable of doing, and what I intend to do. As I develop my own interpretation of *The Trial*, anyone following along should now be primed to recognize both convergences and points of divergence from the four extant frameworks of interpretation laid out above.

2. TITORELLI'S PAINTING

We will begin with the image that stands at the heart of *The Trial*, the painting in progress encountered in Titorelli's office. Understanding the divinity that it depicts is key to appreciating what manner of "Justice" reigns in Joseph's ordeal. Here is the passage in full:

'It is Justice,' said the painter at last. 'Now I can recognize it,' said K. 'There's the bandage over the eyes, and here are the scales. But aren't there wings on the figure's heels, and isn't it flying?' 'Yes,' said the painter, 'my instructions were to paint it like that; actually it is Justice and the goddess of Victory in one.' 'Not a very good combination, surely,' said K., smiling. 'Justice must stand quite still, or else the scales will waver and a just verdict will become impossible.' 'I had to follow my client's instructions,' said the painter… The sight of the picture seemed to have roused his ardor, he rolled up his shirt-sleeves, took several crayons in his hand, and as K. watched the delicate crayon-strokes a reddish shadow began to grow round the head of the Judge, a shadow which tapered off in long rays as it approached the edge of the picture. This play of shadow bit by bit surrounded the head like a halo or a high mark of distinction. But the figure of Justice was left bright except for an almost imperceptible touch of shadow; that brightness brought the figure sweeping right into the foreground and it no longer *suggested* the goddess of Justice, or even the goddess of Victory, but looked *exactly like* a goddess of the Hunt in full cry.[40]

These might well be the most important lines in the whole of *The Trial*. There is nothing arbitrary about them, despite the casual tone of this conversation between K. and Titorelli. All of the images de-scribed have symbolic significance and are esoteric references to an-cient mythology and mysticism. Before unfolding these significations, it is worthwhile to note that Kafka could read Greek, and we know that he appreciated some classical literature in the original — such as Xenophon's story of "Heracles at the Crossroads."[41] Hartmut Binder suggests that Kafka took certain Greek models for his own writing, and Marthe Robert claimed to have discerned in his handling of ancient legends an underlying tension between classical Greek and Jewish religious beliefs.[42]

---

40 Kafka, *The Trial*, 146–147 (emphasis mine).

41 David Schur, *The Way of Oblivion: Heraclitus and Kafka* (Cambridge, MA: Harvard University Press, 1998), 189.

While at first there are suggestions that the painting depicts *Dike* combined with elements of *Nike*, there was a Greek goddess of the Hunt who was also an avenger against injustice and guarantor of victory at war: *Artemis*, whom the Romans knew as *Diana*. The wrathful and relentless divine vengeance of Artemis, which parallels that of *Nemesis*,[43] far more appropriately fits Titorelli's highly questionable Justice — which is always on the move and does not stand still — than *Dike* would. Winged depictions of goddesses were very rare in Greece, and were associated with the Near East. Artemis is often depicted as a winged goddess and (if we except Hecate) she shares this distinction only with *Nike*, the goddess of victory, and *Nemesis*, the goddess of vengeance.[44] Artemis was at times even equated with *Nemesis*, the virginal Avenger[45] driven by righteous anger.[46] This notion of "Justice" as cunningly unpredictable and relentless is closer to the spirit of the novel as a whole. As we are told repeatedly, this Court's type of prosecution allows for no successful defense. This should make us recall the original meaning of "the Trial" or *Der Prozeß* in German. In addition to the derivative meaning of a legal process, it can also mean an "ordeal" or simply "process" as such. A "process" is what is always in motion, never static. An attempt to defend oneself according to fixed legal principles, within the context of a perpetual flux, would certainly be an "ordeal."

In court proceedings such as these victory is more like a martial triumph than an impartial verdict. Artemis and *Ares* (the Roman *Mars*) were together the two patron deities of the Amazons, and the Amazon queen Otrera, who was a wife of Ares, is alleged to have been the founder of the great temple of Artemis at Ephesus (one of the seven

---

43   Sorita D'este, *Artemis: Virgin Goddess of the Sun & Moon — A Comprehensive Guide to the Greek Goddess of the Hunt* (London: Avalonia Press, 2005), 91–96.

44   Ibid., 11, 80.

45   Ibid., 113.

wonders of the ancient world).[47] Artemis shared a shrine together with Ares on Illissos.[48] She is also linked to Ares through the *pyrrichists* or "war dancers." Artemis is the goddess of dance, and these war dancers were (predominately) women who danced nude—wearing nothing but helmets and shin guards—bearing a shield and weapons such as a sword, spear, or javelin.[49] Attempts to abduct these fierce maidens, if only to ransom rather than rape them, did occasionally disrupt ceremonial performances of such dances at Ephesus and other temples of Artemis.[50] It was believed that the Amazons inaugurated these war dances,[51] and they were especially popular in Sparta, the most martial of the Greek cities, where there were more temples dedicated to Artemis than elsewhere.[52] The Spartans and other Greeks prayed to her for victory at war, with long lines of soldiers marching from their respective gymnasiums to deliver dedicatory wreaths to the temple of Artemis at Ephesus.[53] The divinity in Titorelli's painting, which is at once the Goddess of the Hunt and the Goddess of (martial) Victory, could only be Artemis.

What clinches this is the reference to her fiery halo. Artemis was known both as *Selasphoros* or "the light bearer"[54] and *Phosphorus* or "light-bringer."[55] Within the same spell of the *Greek Magical Papyri*, Artemis is referred to as both the "bringer of light" and the "crafty... infernal one."[56] The light-bearer that we all know from Greek mythology is, of course, Prometheus—who becomes the Roman *Lucifer*.

47   D'Este, *Artemis*, 105.

48   Ibid., 29.

49   Ibid., 85–86.

50   Ibid., 86.

51   Ibid., 90.

52   Ibid., 89.

53   Ibid.

54   Ibid., 55.

55   Ibid., 61.

Artemis persuaded Zeus to allow Heracles to release Prometheus.[57] In order to draw out the luciferian dimensions of infernal light surrounding the figure of the goddess in Titorelli's painting, it is imperative to recall how Artemis was conflated with Hecate. From the 5th century BC onwards, Artemis and Hecate were so closely associated with one another on account of common attributes that they were effectively fused into a single divinity.[58] The attributes that they had in common included both being maidens, light-bringers bearing torches, depicted as winged (like Near Eastern goddesses and unlike Greek ones), association with dogs, serpents, and *gorgons*, as well as the moon and saffron.[59] As with Artemis, it is said that Hecate is the only one to have been aware of the abduction of Persephone into the Underworld by Hades on account of being "the one who keeps in mind the vigor of nature."[60] Hecate was a companion to Persephone in her journey to and from the Underworld.[61]

The aura suggested by Kafka in the halo around the figure of the Goddess in Titorelli's painting is not a halo of light — but one of shadow — *shades* being the ancient name for "ghosts." Hecate was known as the "Queen of Ghosts." She controlled many shades and *daimones*.[62] Hecate was associated with the untimely dead, who might wander the Earth as ghosts.[63] These were considered to have more magical power than the living, and they could be summoned to one's aid.[64] Those who suffered a violent death, especially while young, were considered the

---

57 Ibid., 112.

58 D'Este, *Artemis*, 110; Sorita d'Este and David Rankine *Hekate: Liminal Rites: A study of the rituals, magic and symbols of the torch-bearing Triple Goddess of the Crossroads.* (London: Avalonia Press, 2009), 25, 169.

59 D'Este, *Artemis*, 88, 115.

60 D'Este, *Hekate*, 52.

61 Ibid., 86.

62 Ibid., 60.

63 Ibid., 84.

best assistants.[65] *Defixiones* or binding spells requesting such aid from the restless dead were thrown into a water source, such as a well or a lake.[66] One of the most popular *defixiones* of Hecate, were those for "judicial binding to win court cases," wherein "the person was bound, along with any legal advocates or witnesses for them."[67] Hecate was particularly relevant to summoning the spirits of those young persons who had done away with themselves by means of drowning.[68] She was involved with divining the future incarnation of these suicides.[69]

Like Artemis, Hecate was a lunar goddess.[70] Hecate also shared with Artemis an association with wolves, being called the "She-wolf" on certain protective charms.[71] Other charms even referred to her as "chief huntress," clearly a title of Artemis.[72] Hecate also shares with Artemis, the role of nurse goddess who presides over childbirth.[73] On account of all of these affinities, images of Artemis and Hecate are often indistinguishable.[74] In addition to both being the goddess of crossroads, they were both also known as the watcher over harbors.[75] In this connection, I suspect that the Statue of Liberty in New York harbor is actually Artemis-Hecate. As with Artemis, the priestesses of Hecate were torch bearing. The "running maiden" figure depicted on a vase bearing two torches has now been identified as Hecate[76] after long

---

65   Ibid., 85.

66   Ibid.

67   Ibid., 86.

68   Ibid., 148.

69   Ibid.

70   Ibid., 52.

71   Ibid., 66.

72   Ibid., 75.

73   Ibid., 169.

74   Ibid., 170.

75   D'Este, *Artemis*, 88, 115.

having been thought to be Artemis.[77] This bears directly on Titorelli's goddess always being in motion. Like Artemis, Hecate was not only known as *Phosphorus* or "light-bringer," but also as *Purphoros* or "fire bringer."[78] Her fire ultimately became the coiling stellar fire and intellectual fire described in the Chaldean Oracles.[79] Venus, the morning star — the last star seen in the sky before the dawn, was considered one of the torches of Hecate.[80] The morning star is, of course, also known as *Lucifer* — so that Artemis-Hecate, the goddess haloed by infernal light in Titorelli's painting, can be seen as the feminine aspect of Lucifer: the one who brings the liberating and potentially destructive fire of Wisdom. Hecate played a key role as *Propolos*, or "torch bearer," in the Elusianian mysteries — with her priestesses carrying twin torches as they guided the initiate into labyrinthine underground passageways symbolizing the Underworld.[81] She was said to fill the roads with light at night by her fires.[82]

The question of whether the Law hunts down its victims, the animal passion seen in Joseph's exchanges with the women who offer to aid him, the idea of rebirth into the state of mind of childhood, and Leni as the "nurse" of those who are children before the Law — we shall see how all of these themes hark back to the archetype of Artemis-Hecate portrayed in Titorelli's painting. Even more significantly, Artemis is the twin sister of the god Apollo; together they were the patron deities of the Hyperboreans.[83] After Apollo, Dionysus is the other divinity most associated with Artemis. In addition to being the only two divinities of the wilds predominately worshipped by women, Artemis tamed savage lions for Dionysus and fought on his side in the

77 Ibid., 60.

78 Ibid., 56–57.

79 Ibid., 57.

80 Ibid., 52.

81 Ibid., 56.

82 Ibid., 57.

Indian Wars of Dionysus; she also very uncharacteristically bears no ill will towards him when he seduces her nymphs.[84] While Apollo was Artemis' twin brother, Dionysus was her best friend.[85] Artemis was also particularly associated with big cats, such as lions and leopards. She is often flanked by lions, or holding a lion in her left hand and a leopard in her right hand.[86] The lion was a symbol of Apollo and the Leopard a symbolic representation of Dionysus.[87]

In *The Birth of Tragedy*, Friedrich Nietzsche radically reinterprets the pre-Socratic period of Greek culture and its epitomizing tragic art in terms of the dynamic balance of two seemingly opposed states — the *Apollonian* and *Dionysian*.[88] The former can be understood through the analogy of a dream, particularly a lucid dream, in which both the joys and struggles of life are resolved into a simpler and more perfect form and are thus imbued with greater meaning than a reality that is confusing, contradictory and fragmentary. It is a world of vivid yet merely apparent images. The Apollonian is the basis of the principle of individuation — which provides us with the illusion of a boundary of rational and independent self-hood that guards us from the surging flux of chaos which is the true nature of the world and which would otherwise envelope and swallow us. On the other hand, the nature of the Dionysian can be comprehended through the analogy of intoxication. In this state the forms of rationality that sustain the principle of individuation are compromised and revealed as limited, or they collapse altogether. This results at once in a tremendous feeling of horror in the subject, which is swallowed by chaos, and also a tremendous feeling of ecstasy and rapture, which rises up from the most profound depth of humanity. This ecstasy is really the ecstasy of

---

84   Ibid., 108–109.

85   Ibid., 36.

86   Ibid., 79.

87   Ibid.

nature's self-satisfaction in man. In the Dionysian the son of humanity is reunited in communion with Mother Nature — for whom there is great awe and reverence. Not only do the subjective boundaries between people re-dissolve into a primordial unity, but also the boundary between humanity and the earthly element. Human *being* itself becomes a work of art, a rapturous embodiment of Nature's creative force. We will see how one aspect of Joseph K. is Apollonian, while the other is Dionysian. Reflecting the status of Artemis as a mediate figure intimately related to both Apollo and Dionysus, the three women who embody the spirit of the Huntress try to act as mediators between the Apollonian and Dionysian elements in the character of Joseph K.

The ferocity of Artemis is clearly connected with the defense of her maidenhood and that of her nymph attendants and initiates. The myths unambiguously state that she was by far the most beautiful of all the female divinities, prompting many men to be attracted to her and view her as the ultimate trophy to seize and possess.[89] Yet at the same time, it has been suggested by some researchers that sacred prostitution was ongoing at the Ephesus temple and that her status as "maiden" did not mean so much "virgin" as it meant "unmarried" or not in the possession of any man.[90] This would make a great deal of sense if she were originally an Amazon goddess, since the warrior women did have male lovers who were deemed worthy but they fiercely resisted being claimed as a "wife" by any of these men.[91] In his *Blue Octavo Notebooks*, Kafka writes:

> One of the most effective means of seduction that Evil has is the challenge to struggle. It is like the struggle with women, which ends in bed.[92]

---

89 D'Este, *Artemis*, 48, 63, 103.

90 Ibid., 63–64.

91 Lyn Webster Wilde, *On the Trail of the Women Warriors: The Amazons in Myth and History* (New York: St. Martin's Press, 2000), 72.

92 Max Brod ([Ed.),itor] *The Blue Octavo Notebooks by Franz Kafka* (Cambridge:

Woman, or more precisely put, perhaps, marriage, is the representative of life with which you are meant to come to terms.

This world's method of seduction and the token of the guarantee that this world is only a transition are one and the same. Rightly so, for only in this way can this world seduce us, and it is in keeping with the truth. The worst thing, however, is that after the seduction has been successful we forget the guarantee and thus actually the Good has lured us into Evil, the woman's glance into her bed.[93]

The idea that breathes between the lines of all of these notes is that a perpetual seduction that is not killed by the fixity of possession is potentially redemptive. Joseph encounters such a seduction to Life through all of the three women who are associated with the Law: Fraulein Burstner, the Usher's wife, and above all, the "nurse" Leni. It is in Titorelli's studio that Kafka gives us the key to how exactly these *three* women are related to the archetype of the Goddess in the painting. This key is Titorelli's explanation to K., of *the three ways* or *three paths* that one may take in one's "trial" or *process*: "There are three possibilities, that is, definite acquittal, ostensible acquittal, and indefinite postponement. Definite acquittal is, of course, the best, but…I have not met one case of definite acquittal…"[94] Thus the Goddess of Justice, who always secures Victory, and who is also the Goddess of the Hunt, watches over three paths of the Law.

Hecate was a *triple* goddess, she was represented as *three women in one*, and in this way she watched over the *three ways*; one of her epithets is "Goddess of the Three Roads" (*Trioditis*, Latin *Trivia*) or "Goddess of the Crossroads" (*Enodia*).[95] She stood at the crossroads bearing the keys to the mysteries.[96] Hecate was the divinity of triplicity par excellence, the original Trinitarian, being referred to as

---

93 Ibid., 50.

94 Kafka, *The Trial*, 152.

95 D'Este, *Hekate*, 15, 59–60.

Trimorphos — "three formed" or "three bodied."[97] The "crossroads" can be taken to mean the ordeal wherein K. must decide which of the three paths to follow in his case, and in a deeper sense, the spiritual "crossroads" of his life. I suggest that the three bodies of Artemis-Hecate are the three women who are associated with the Law, namely Fraulein Burstner, the Usher's wife, and Leni. Joseph K. is offered the assistance of these women who, while promiscuous like Hecate, are as unbound to any one man as Artemis. His desire to possess them for himself alone (effectively to "marry" them), leads him ever closer to conviction.

3. THE DUALITY OF JOSEPH K.

The "crossed roads" that Hecate watches over can also be taken to mean two paths that are in opposition to one another, and which seem to force one to choose between them, for lack of a *third way*. This third way is the being of the Goddess as a Trinity that overcomes the apparent duality. The ordeal of Joseph K. in *The Trial* hinges on strife between two aspects of his character, his Apollonian conscious mind and the wild, bestial, shadowy aspect of his Dionysian unconscious. An inherent multiplicity of subjectivity precludes the possibility of the moral judgment of Justice in the sense of *Dike* or proper earthly law and order.[98] If there is no singular subject present then a person cannot be held responsible in the name of Justice, nor can he hold others accountable. The following three passages from Kafka's *Blue Octavo Notebooks* are key to understanding the kind of unaccountable "Justice" at work in *The Trial*:

> Through the door on the right one's fellow men push into a room in which a family council is being held, hear the last word uttered by the last speaker, take it up, with it pour out into the world through the door on the left, and shout out their judgment. The judgment of the word is true, the judgment

97 Ibid., 26.

in itself is void. If they had wanted to judge with final truth, they would have had to stay in the room forever, would have become part of the family council and thus, of course, again incapable of judging. Only he who is a party can really judge, but as a party he cannot judge. Hence it follows that there is no possibility of judgment in the world, only a glimmer of it.[99]

In one and the same human being there are cognitions that, however utterly dissimilar they are, yet have one and the same object, so that one can only conclude that there are different subjects in one and the same human being.[100]

Nobody can desire what is ultimately damaging to him. If in individual cases it does appear to be so after all—and perhaps it always does so appear—this is explained by the fact that someone in the person demands something that is, admittedly, of use to someone, but which to a second someone, who is brought in half in order to judge the case, is gravely damaging. If the person had from the very beginning, and not only when it came to judging the case, taken his stand at the side of the second someone, the first someone would have faded out, and with him the desire.[101]

The dual nature of Joseph K. is apparent from the very beginning of the novel. Upon being arrested, K. at first entertains the possibility that the "ridiculous" spectacle of the two warders may be a "rude joke," one that might be brought to an end by his knowing acknowledgment of it as such: "perhaps he had only to laugh knowingly in these men's faces and they would laugh with him."[102] However, almost immediately, he decides to take the matter seriously so as not to "give away any advantage that he might possess" over the warders. The attempt of Joseph K. to possess people, and to seize or maintain "advantage" over them, persistently resurfaces throughout the course of *The Trial*.

It should come as no surprise that Joseph's attempt to possess advantage is inextricably intertwined with his desire to recover and

99 Brod, *Blue Octavo Notebooks*, 25.

100 Ibid., 93.

101 Ibid., 94.

assert a fixed and unitary identity. Straightaway upon deciding that he
will take the warders seriously, K. searches for his "identity papers,"
and on account of his agitation has trouble finding them in his otherwise orderly desk drawer. Kafka seems to be ridiculing the naiveté of
this search for identity when he has K. contemplate offering his "bicycle license" in lieu of his "birth certificate"—as if to suggest that the
two could be interchangeable as evidence (of equal worth) for one's
existence as a unique being. It may also be of some significance that
a bicycle is a means of conveyance built around *two separate* wheels,
which require *perpetual motion* if the whole apparatus is not to crash
to the ground. In other words, we have here a tension between fixity
of identity and a duality ever in motion. (He might actually have done
better to go ahead and hand the warders the bicycle license.) Joseph
presents his identity papers to the warders and, in exchange, he demands that they clearly identify themselves and present their warrant
for his arrest.

At this point Kafka makes a very interesting suggestion, namely,
that the two warders "stand closer" to Joseph K. "than any other
people in the world."[103] Kafka might be hinting, even at this very early
stage of the novel, that the Court officials are manifestations of an unconscious aspect of Joseph K. that is divided against his conscious and
deliberative self. The suggestion is emphasized by the fact that one of
the warders says: "That's so, you can believe that." The significance of
the warder's words is underlined by the fact that he stops himself from
raising his coffee to his lips in order to give K. "a long, apparently significant, yet incomprehensible look." K. finds himself "decoyed into an
exchange of speaking looks with Franz," but then continues to insist
on identification. The warder who exchanges the speaking looks with
K. is named Franz. The combination of the two names would give
"Franz K." or Franz Kafka. Also note that the letter "K" consists of two
strokes branching off from a third. Furthermore, Franz's affirmation

of the other warder's comment must be taken in the context of the nearly relentless deception that we go on to see from the Court officials in the rest of the novel. Franz is saying that this comment, as opposed to all those that are to come, *can indeed* be believed. It is the truth, as opposed to the other lies. That this speaking glance takes place in the context of Joseph's demand for identification, and that it is incomprehensible to K., may suggest a failure of dialogue between the two aspects of his divided "selfhood."

This would explain why proximity to the two warders makes thought impossible. Thought depends on concepts (*Begriff*) of objects generated and applied by a unitary subject, and it is in this sense that we should read Joseph's insistence on grasping (*Greifen*) the situation as a form of possessiveness, though of a more subtle (and deep-rooted) nature than that which is concerned with material possessions: "Any right to dispose of his own things which he might possess he did not prize very highly; far more important to him was the necessity to understand his situation clearly; but with these people beside him he could not even think."[104] The Apollonian aspect of K. so desperately seeks to reestablish order that he welcomes the command that the warders give him when he is called to see the Inspector. Kafka tells us that "The command itself was actually welcome to him."[105] This means that the content of the command is irrelevant to K., it is the hierarchy (*heiros arche*) implicit in the command *as such* that he craves.

Joseph's failure to recognize an aspect of himself in the warders, and his struggle to define his selfhood in opposition to them ("I am so and so...who are you...") and possess an advantage over their Court, intensifies into open and deadly conflict as *The Trial* progresses. This intensification is seen when Joseph K. contemplates severing his connection with the Lawyer and taking action on his own behalf. He decides that in presenting his own plea to the court, he should follow

---

104 Ibid., 4.

the model of the successful business deals that he has closed for the bank, seeing as "This legal action was nothing more than a business deal such as he had often concluded to the advantage of the Bank."[106] In such a case the "right tactics were to avoid letting one's thoughts stray to one's own possible shortcomings, and to cling as firmly as one could to the thought of one's advantage."[107]

After suffering months of the Court's assault on sound reason and common sense, a mere "birth certificate" apparently no longer suffices to ground his sense of identity. Joseph K. contemplates writing his own defense plea, wherein he would "give a short account of his life, and when he came to an event of any importance explain for what reasons he had acted as he did."[108] He himself would draw up the questions for cross-examination, which his lawyer had henceforth failed to do: "To ask questions was surely the main thing. ... [H]e could draw up all the necessary questions himself." K. believes that in answering such questions he could thereby "intimate whether he approved or condemned his way of action in retrospect, and adduce grounds for the condemnation or approval." Such self-examination clearly evokes the old Delphic injunction of the twin brother of Artemis, the god Apollo: "Know Thyself." In his *Blue Octavo Notebooks*, Kafka writes the following commentary on that maxim:

> 'Know Thyself' [*Erkenne dich selbst*] does not mean 'Observe thyself.' 'Observe thyself' is what the Serpent says. It means: 'Make yourself master of your actions.' But you are so already, you are the master of your actions. So that saying means: 'Misjudge yourself! [*Verkenne dich*] Destroy yourself!' which is something evil — and only if one bends down very far indeed does one also hear the good in it, which is: 'In order to make of yourself what you are.'[109]

---

106 Ibid., 127.

107 Ibid.

108 Ibid., 113.

In his quest for a crystalline knowledge of his own character, Joseph K. ultimately realizes that "to meet an unknown accusation, not to mention other possible charges arising out of it, the whole of one's life would have to be recalled to mind, down to the smallest actions and accidents, clearly formulated and examined from every angle."[110] Though he ultimately decides that the completion of such a plea is a "sheer impossibility," K. decides to dismiss his ineffective Lawyer nonetheless. He opts not to announce the dismissal by telephone or letter because "he did not want to lose the advantage" that a personal interview with the Lawyer might possess.[111] Kafka himself unambiguously expresses the impossibility of the descriptive self-knowledge that Joseph K. contemplates, which mistakenly takes the self to be a thing-object that can be circumnavigated. In his *Blue Octavo Notebooks*, we read:

> How pathetically scanty my self-knowledge is compared with, say, my knowledge of my room. (Evening.) Why? There is no such thing as observation of the inner world, as there is of the outer world. At least descriptive psychology is probably, taken as a whole, a form of anthropomorphism, a nibbling at our own limits. The inner world can only be experienced, not described.[112]

4. POSSESSIVENESS AND PROMISCUOUS WOMEN

So we have seen that there is one aspect of Joseph K. that is perpetually seeking advantage and attempting to assert a clear self-identity. The two are of course inseparable; without a clear sense of self, one cannot know what would be to one's advantage. However, from the very beginning of *The Trial*, Kafka also clues us into the fact that this deadly serious desire for order and judgment is not characteristic behavior

---

110 Kafka, *The Trial*, 128.
111 Ibid., 166.

for Joseph K, who "had always been inclined to take things easily, to believe in the worst only when the worst happened, to take no care for the morrow even when the outlook was threatening."[113] We are told that his decision not to interpret his arrest as a joke is motivated by an uncharacteristic learning from past experiences "when against all his friends' advice he had behaved with deliberate recklessness and without the slightest regard for possible consequences, and had had in the end to pay dearly for it."[114] Even once his decidedly serious trial has gotten underway, examples of reckless behavior by Joseph K. are neither few nor far between. What nearly all of them have in common is some ecstatic or even mystical interaction with promiscuous women. That is, K. compromises his "advantage" when he lets himself be seduced by women that he cannot *possess*.

After hearing about how diligently K. undertakes his work at the Bank, Kafka informs us that "once a week K. visited a girl called Elsa, who was on duty all night till early morning as a waitress in a cabaret and during the day received her visitors in bed."[115] We should bear this in mind in evaluating his response to Frau Grubach's complaints that Fraulien Burstner is engaging in apparently promiscuous behavior. According to the landlady, she comes home very late and has been seen in disreputable "outlying" areas of town, "each time with a different gentleman." Joseph K. defends Fraulein Burstner, a stranger with whom he has hardly exchanged a few words, and responds in exasperation to his landlady's intention to restore respectability to her boarding house by saying: "if you want to keep your house respectable you'll have to begin by giving me notice."[116] This reckless admission to being the greatest rogue of the house stands in stark contrast with the landlady's perception of K., and her unflinching trust in him, as the

113 Kafka, *The Trial*, 4.
114 Ibid., 5.
115 Ibid., 17.

most responsible and respectable of her boarders. After this exchange, K. decides to wait for Fraulein Burstner, whom he has just defended before the landlady, ostensibly to inform her of the disarray that the Inspector threw her room into during that day. He muses that after meeting with her, he will still have time to go visit Elsa. Instead, a shocking exchange takes place between K. and Fraulein Burstner. From the outset, Kafka evokes an air of secret liaison between these two strangers. Joseph K. is sitting in his room, with the lights off and his door cracked open, awaiting her (for hours, we later find out). When she enters the dark hallway, he whispers her name and Kafka tells us that "It sounded like a prayer, not a summons."[117] He then replies to her query by uttering "It is I," as if he were her lover and had arrived at a secret prearranged meeting place. This elicits a response of excited recognition from her: "Oh, Herr K!" Joseph K. hardly knows her, but in the course of half an hour in her room, the two become increasingly intimate. K. finds out that she is going to work for a Law Office, and she offers to help him with his case. When she sinks into the sofa in a surrendered position he kisses her brow. Why does K. feel it is appropriate to take such license with a stranger? Perhaps because, after hearing the landlady complain of her apparently disreputable promiscuity, he realizes that Fraulein Burstner is like him. After this first kiss, she feigns to shoo him away, but only because the Captain is next door and may be listening: "[W]hat are you thinking about, he's listening at the door…" This is less of a "no" than it is a "yes, but…here, now?" K. responds to this by telling her that the landlady takes him to be a scion of respectability, especially since she is financially indebted to him, and she will believe him over the sailor. There should be little doubt that what Kafka leaves unsaid is that the two are on the verge of an erotic act of some sort, and "innocent" Joseph K. is consciously advertising that his air of respectability allows him to engage in such misdemeanors without consequence.

Finally, as Joseph K. leaves her room, Kafka presents us with the following scene in the darkness of the hallway between their lodgings:

'Now, please do come! Look' — she pointed to the Captain's door, underneath which showed a strip of light — 'he has turned on his light and is amusing himself at our expense.' 'I'm just coming,' K. said, rushed out, seized her, and kissed her first on the lips, then all over the face, like some thirsty animal lapping greedily at a spring of long-sought fresh water. Finally he kissed her on the neck, right on the throat, and kept his lips there for a long time. A slight noise from the Captain's room made him look up. 'I'm going now,' he said; he wanted to call Fraulein Burstner by her first name, but he did not know what it was. She nodded wearily, resigned her hand for him to kiss, half turning away as if she were unaware of what she did, and went into her room with down-bent head. Shortly afterwards K. was in his bed. He fell asleep almost at once, but before doing so he thought for a little about his behavior, he was pleased with it, yet surprised that he was not still more pleased; he was seriously concerned for Fraulein Burstner because of the Captain.[118]

One might expect Fraulein Burstner to have slapped Joseph K., or perhaps even cried out for help, upon being assaulted in such a manner by a virtual stranger. Yet, she does not do so, and it is far from an assault. Her weary nod and offer of her hand to be kissed evoke the image of secret lovers hesitantly departing before the light of dawn can reveal their liaison. That she acts "as if she were unaware of what she did," means that she is acting out of her subconscious mind, beyond constraints of conceptual judgment. In fact, her profoundly non-judgmental character may have driven Joseph K. to make the move to culminate, in such an insane manner, the intimate exchange that began in her room.

Just as he is about to leave he asks her if she is angry with him (for keeping her up at such a late hour with his reenactment of the Court proceedings in her room), to which she responds: "No, no, I'm never angry with anybody."[119] Such a spiritual liberation from the impulse to erect artificial barriers of judgment and be constrained by them, is perhaps why K. devours her as an animal would "a spring of long-sought fresh water." The reference to an "animal" is to the aspect of Joseph K. that seeks to escape from his own judgmental advantage-seeking mentality—a mentality that animals are incapable of by nature of their inability to engage in conceptual thought. The archetype of Artemis-Hecate, goddess of wild animals and their wilderness, is at work here.

There are verbal suggestions and innuendoes of sexual intercourse in this passage, both in the actual exchange, and in the exhausted satisfaction of Joseph K. as he returns to his room. He intended to visit Elsa, the prostitute, after his meeting with Fraulein Burstner, yet the latter takes Elsa's place and K. goes straight to bed. However, what is significant is that no such intercourse actually takes place. The encounter is one wherein the ever-virgin goddess of the wild retains her virginity, while manifesting her unbridled wildness. The eroticism here is totally unpredictable, unusual, even inhuman. The deepest kiss is on the throat, like that of a vampire imbibing a person's life essence by night. Hecate was a "nightwalker," a maiden who was nonetheless a "lover and companion of the night," who stalked graveyards wandering among corpses like a succubus thirsting for blood, and striking fear into the heart of mortals with her Gorgonic aspect.[120] She is also connected to the vampire folklore of the Middle Ages through her association with the herb wolfsbane.[121] Medea, who would pray to Hecate while she mixed her poisons, was said to be "naked, shrieking, and wild-eyed" when she cut roots for herbal magic.[122]

---

119 Ibid., 29.

120 D'Este, *Hekate*, 64.

121 Ibid., 95.

Only one thing mars Joseph's perfect enjoyment of Fraulein Burstner. He is concerned that the Captain might have heard their exchange and that, believing her to be an "easy" woman, he might take advantage of her. It is not unreasonable to assume that this is in fact what motivates his letters of apology and explanation to Fraulein Burstner, and finally his unannounced entry into her room before the eyes of the Captain. This may be the real reason why she gives him a cold shoulder, and informs K., via her new roommate, that an interview of the kind that he wanted would accomplish nothing. She does not want him to explain away his actions, and she does not want to be controlled by him. Consequently, he forfeits her legal aid. In respect to this potential "legal advisement," we should remember that she has been seen by Frau Grubach in disreputable "outlying" areas of town with different gentlemen. This could be a suggestion by Kafka that the Law Offices that she is going to work for are the very same ones that are to be found in the attics of impoverished outlying suburbs, where K. travels to be prosecuted.

The dialectic between the desire to possess and an attraction to free-spiritedness, reemerges in Joseph's interactions with two even more promiscuous women who have already been initiated into the service of the Law: the Usher's wife and Leni. K. really meets the Usher's wife when he shows up to Court a week from the first interrogation. He recognizes her as the washerwoman in the entryway who, he believes, was "raped" in the courtroom while he was giving his speech. At first, K. is most disturbed that she does not view the act as a grave violation, even though she is married. She replies that she is justified in the eyes of all who know her. She claims that even her husband has been forced to accept the situation, since the young man that she was on the floor with during the end of Joseph's speech was a law student training to become a Judge. She predicts that he will become an official of great power. However, K. starts to be attracted to her when she expresses interest in his desire to reform the court and offers to run away with him. She only asks K. to be patient while she momentarily addresses the student, who has returned and is watching them:

> The woman bent over K. and whispered: 'Don't be angry with me, please don't think badly of me, I must go to him now, and he's a dreadful-looking creature, just see what bandy legs he has. But I'll come back in a minute and then I'll go with you if you'll take me with you, I'll go with you wherever you like, you can do with me what you please, I'll be glad if I can only get out of here for a long time, and I wish it could be forever.' She gave K.'s hand a last caress, jumped up, and ran to the window. Despite himself K.'s hand reached out after hers in the empty air. The woman really attracted him, and after mature reflection he could find no valid reason why he should not yield to that attraction. He dismissed without difficulty the fleeting suspicion that she might be trying to lay a trap for him on the instructions of the Court.[123]

K. does not think of taking the woman away from the student in order to restore her to the Usher. He wants to possess her for himself. She has told him that now, not only the student, but also the Examining Magistrate has taken an interest in her. K. daydreams that "some night the Examining Magistrate...might come to the woman's bed and find it empty...because she had gone off with K...belonged to K. and to K. alone." He does not mind that she commits adultery, so long as it is with him, *and him alone*. He cannot be patient and he begins to storm up and down the room. This elicits the reaction of the student: "If you're so impatient, you can go away..." To which K. responds that it is the student who should go away and leave him and the Usher's wife alone. The exchange ultimately ends with K. attempting to seize the woman's hand and the student in response carrying her off after he says to K. "no, no, you don't get her." K. is angry that she does not protest more violently, but simply shrugs her shoulders. Against her explicit request "Don't be angry with me, please don't think badly of me...I'll come back in a minute..." K. yells at her "as for you, I never want to see you again." He is even more jealous and enraged at being taken in, when he finds out from her husband that she was no victim in the affair, rather "she simply flung herself" at the student. Significantly, the student is not carrying her off for his own pleasure this time, but for that of the Examining Magistrate.

This is Kafka's way of suggesting that because K. could not patiently await her return, and above all, because he wants to *possess* the woman for *himself alone*, he loses the chance to be with her. His interview with her, interrupted by the timed intervention of the student, is indeed a kind of test set for him by the Court. Had he been patient and willing to share the woman, the student would have in all likelihood gone away and allowed the two of them to be together. Yet once K. betrays his jealousy and possessiveness, the Usher's wife does not appear to be carried away against her will. Her shrug of the shoulders does not show much protest in it, and she has a rather bemused expression.

We should note that the man carrying her off is referred to as a "miserable creature," the same words that Leni later uses to describe the tradesman Block. This would suggest that the Usher's wife is not only in a dominant position over her husband, but even over the student who carries her away. She certainly does not want to be "rescued" or "set free," as if she were a helpless dame looking to the arrival of some knight in shining armor. She has metaphorically castrated her seethingly jealous husband, and K. is rendered equally impotent. Even the student carries her off not for himself, but for the Examining Magistrate's pleasure, and by the looks of it, her own delight as well. The emasculation and castration of men is a major theme in the cult of Artemis. Some have interpreted the many pendulous "breasts" of the statue of Artemis from the temple of Ephesus as the testicles of castrated bulls or even of castrated men.[124] In her conflation with the Mother Goddess Cybele or *Rhea*, who was worshipped at Ephesus before her, barefaced male devotees did indeed have themselves castrated in honor of her and as a way to emasculate themselves so as to become fit receptacles of the overpowering force of the divine feminine; they also grew their hair long.[125] This can be traced back to the practices of archaic shamans, who wore women's clothing as part of an effort to attain "female" spiritual abilities.[126]

In the case of Leni we see a more prominent manifestation of the emasculation of men who threaten possession. The first encounter between Joseph K. and Leni mirrors the encounter with Fraulein Burstner in the darkened entryway of the boardinghouse. Leni breaks a plate against the wall so that she can call K. out of the meeting between his Uncle, the Lawyer, and the Chief Clerk of the Court. She is waiting for him in the darkened hallway, takes his hand and shuts the door to the room where the meeting is taking place. Thus this third meeting with the third woman associated with K. takes place in an entryway or doorway, just as the first two. K. encountered Fraulein Burstner in the entryway of the boarding house, and the Usher's wife as the gatekeeper before the doorway to the Courtroom. As *Propylaia*, Hecate was the one before the gate, with statues of her not only at the entrances to cities, temples, and sanctuaries to other deities, but also outside the front door to many homes, in a protective porch-like shrine known as a *hekataion*.[127] The first thing we learn about Leni is that she is the Lawyer's "nurse." At first, K. simply refers to her as "the nurse." Artemis was the "child's nurse" (*Kourotrophos*) and the "nurse of children" (*Paidotrophos*).[128] Hecate was also the nursemaid goddess who presided over childbirth.[129]

At this point the "nurse" should be even more of a stranger to K. than Fraulein Burstner was when the two of them had their bizarrely passionate encounter. Stranger as she might be, there is a similar

125 Ibid., 97–98.
126 Ibid., 98.
127 D'Este, *Hekate*, 21.
128 D'Este, *Artemis*, 66.

whispering in the dark of a secret mutual recognition, as in the case of Fraulein Burstner:

> 'Nothing has happened,' she whispered. 'I simply flung a plate against the wall to bring you out.' K. said in his embarrassment: 'I was thinking of you too.' 'That's all the better,' said the nurse. 'Come this way.'[130]

The "nurse" of the Lawyer guides K. down the dark passageway to the Lawyer's moonlit office. Again, we see Kafka employing the symbolism of Hecate. Her guiding role here calls to mind Hecate as *Propolos*, or "torch bearer," in the Eleusinian mysteries — with her priestesses bearing twin torches as they lead the initiate through labyrinthine underground passageways symbolizing the Underworld.[131] Regarding the office being bathed in moonlight, the hunting bow of Artemis resembles the new moon; she sometimes wore a lunar crescent as her crown (which, put through her hair, made her appear to have horns); and she was referred to as shooting arrows from her "silver bow."[132] In this connection she was identified with the Greek moon goddess Selene from the second 2nd century BC onwards,[133] and the Roman lunar goddess Diana was in turn identified with her. In his second century work *Philopseudes*, Lucian claims that certain witches and sorcerers were able to "draw down the Moon, and show you Hecate herself, as large as life."[134] When "the Moon was brought down," it "went through a variety of transformations."[135] Like Artemis, Hecate was syncretised with the lunar goddess Selene.[136] Hecate could break open the surface

---

130 Kafka, *The Trial*, 106.

131 D'Este, *Hekate*, 56.

132 D'Este, *Artemis*, 97.

133 Ibid., 114.

134 D'Este, *Hekate*, 147.

135 Ibid., 148.

of the Earth, opening passageways to the Underworld — including the Elysian Fields.[137]

The office in which K. and Leni have their first encounter is bathed and illumined by moonlight alone. Here, Leni tells K. that she is annoyed at him for not having come out of the room on his own accord. She tells him that given the way he had been gazing at her since his arrival, she was surprised to have been made to wait so long for him to come and be with her. K. takes this to mean that she is offering herself to him, for sex, and says: "I couldn't simply walk out and leave them without any excuse, and in the second place I'm not in the least a bold young man, but rather shy, to tell the truth, and you too, Leni, really didn't look as if you were to be had for the asking."[138] Leni's response begins to draw another key parallel to the exchange with Fraulein Burstner: "It isn't that," said Leni, laying her arm along the back of the seat and looking at K. "But you didn't like me at first and you probably don't like me even now."[139] At the end of Leni's explanation of the Examining Magistrate's portrait, Kafka adds:

'But I'm a vain person, too, and very much upset that you don't like me in the least.' To this last statement K. replied merely by putting his arm around her and drawing her to him; she leaned her head against his shoulder in silence...seizing the hand with which K. held her [she began] to play with his fingers.[140]

Whether Joseph K. realizes it or not, what Leni is saying, especially in the first comment beginning with "It isn't that..." is that she was not offering her body to him, despite the clear sexual innuendo in her first comments to him in the hallway and as they enter the Lawyer's office. This is not to say that she is denying her body to him (as we will see), but that she is after something more essential, which oddly and in the

137 Ibid., 151.

138 Kafka, *The Trial*, 107.

139 Ibid.

manner of silly children, she calls *liking*. She wants K. to "like" her. He seems to understand this, at least after her second complaint.

The parallel to the non-sexual erotic encounter with Fraulein Burstner culminates after a discussion where Leni asks K. if he would allow her to replace Elsa, the prostitute that is his "sweetheart." Kafka writes:

> 'If that's all the advantage she has over me I shan't give up hope. Has she any physical defect?' 'Any physical defect?' asked K. 'Yes,' said Leni. 'For I have a slight one. Look.' She held up her right hand and stretched out the two middle fingers, between which the connecting web of skin reached almost to the top joint, short as the fingers were. In the darkness K. could not make out at once what she wanted to show him, so she took his hand and made him feel it. 'What a freak of nature!' said K. and he added, when he had examined the whole hand: 'What a pretty little paw!' Leni looked on with a kind of pride while K. in astonishment kept pulling the two fingers apart and then putting them side by side again, until at last he kissed them lightly and let them go. 'Oh!' she cried at once. 'You have kissed me!' She hastily scrambled up until she was kneeling open-mouthed on his knees. K. looked up at her almost dumbfounded; now that she was so close to him she gave out a bitter exciting odor like pepper; she clasped him on the neck, biting into the very hairs of his head. 'You have exchanged her for me,' she cried over and over again. 'Look, you have exchanged her for me after all!' Then her knees slipped, with a faint cry she almost fell on the carpet, K. put his arms around her to hold her up and was pulled down to her. 'You belong to me now,' she said. 'Here's the key of the door, come whenever you like,' were her last words, and as he took his leave a final aimless kiss landed on his shoulder.[141]

The first thing to note about this key passage is that Leni's question whether Elsa has any physical defect does not seem to be motivated by a concern that she might be more "perfect" than Leni. Rather, like some strange little child, Leni seems to be bragging that she has a freakish oddity, and hoping that Elsa does not have anything out of the ordinary to match it. The particular curiosity that it is, and the way that K. opens and closes the webbed middle fingers, clearly presents us with a sexual metaphor for virginal female genitalia. Yet what does Joseph K. do? He seems to play aimlessly with the "two webbed fingers," in the same spirit in which Leni plays with his fingers after he draws her close to him to reassure her that he "likes" her. The liminal web acts as a metaphor for a spiritual *unity in duality*. Finally K. kisses the two webbed fingers "lightly," which is a sign of profound affection rather than lust or passion.

It is in this child-like spirit that one must read Leni's wish for K. to exchange Elsa for her; it is not imbued with the gravity of possessiveness. Rather, its lightheartedness is meant to mock the very idea of possession, as in: "Oh, look! you have so easily exchanged her for me." Her comment "You belong to me now" rings with a similar connotation as it would were it to have been said by a little girl playing at marrying her father. Note how Leni "sits there on [K.'s] knee as if it were the only rightful place for her!"[142] Incidentally, this passage also attests to the fact that Elsa is no mere prostitute to Joseph K. He admits that she is his "sweetheart" and displays a picture of her that he has been keeping in his wallet. Clearly, *at least one aspect of* Joseph K. is the kind of man that can allow himself to love a woman who prostitutes her body to other men.

The language of the animal is also present here, as it is in the encounter with Fraulein Burstner. Upon further examining her hand, K. calls Leni's "freak of nature" a "pretty little paw." Just as with Fraulein Burstner, the climactic erotic act of the scene is of an animal nature, a vampiric kiss on the neck, which this time actually does turn into a bite. Like the encounter with Fraulein Burstner, it involves the same combination of dark animal wildness and preservation of chastity that characterizes the archetype of Artemis. Except that in this case, it is the woman that kisses K. in this manner, rather than the other way around. Whereas at the *conclusion* of his encounter with Fraulein

Burstner K. wants to call her by her first name but realizes that he does not know it, at the very *beginning* of his encounter with Leni she hastily tells him her first name and demands that he call her by it. K. also seems to receive, *unbidden*, from Leni, what he *demands* but is not granted by Fraulein Burstner—the key to the room and free passage therein at any time. Hecate stood at the crossroads bearing the keys to the mysteries.[143] In her temple in Caria, a "procession of the key" (*kleidos agoge*) was held yearly. Hecate was called *Kleidouchos* on account of bearing the keys to Underworld; it is she who led the soul down into *hades* and opened the Elysian Fields to those who were worthy.[144] The Orphic Hymn to Hecate goes so far as to call her "Keyholding Mistress of the whole world."[145] That Leni offers Joseph "the key" is Kafka's way of suggesting that the side of K. that is seduced by these promiscuous women is growing stronger, though perhaps in tandem with the opposing aspect that seeks to possess the advantages of proper order.

When K. emerges from his first encounter with Leni in the Lawyer's office, he is harangued by his Uncle for having gravely compromised the "advantage" that a good rapport with the Lawyer and the Clerk of the Court could have conferred upon him. He asks how K. could have run off with the mistress of a Lawyer whose help he seeks, and how he could have left the Clerk of the Court, who is actually managing his case, when the official was already running late and had so kindly agreed to stay and offer assistance to K. However, what is most interesting of all here is the following. Joseph's uncle is angry at K. for having stayed "away for hours." Just so that we know this is not a mere exaggeration, Kafka repeats it more explicitly: "And you leave me, your uncle, to wait here in the rain *for hours* and worry myself

---

143 D'Este, *Hekate*, 15.

144 Ibid., 20, 151.

sick, just feel, I'm wet through and through!"[146] As described in the prose of the novel, the whole encounter with Leni, from the time K. leaves the room where the old men are discussing his case to the time he leaves her on the floor of the Lawyer's office, cannot have taken more than half an hour at most — from the perspective of K. and Leni. There is a great deal of missing time here. Kafka is telling us that whatever happened between K. and Leni involves an *ex-static* state of being outside of the continuum of ordinary space-time. It seems that K. had begun to lose him*self* in the labyrinth of knowledge to which she had given him the key.

Alas, Joseph's potential relationship with Leni meets the same fate as that with Fraulein Burstner and the Usher's wife — it is murdered by his possessiveness and jealousy. This time the culprit is the tradesman, Block. On his final visit to the Lawyer's home, as Block opens the door "in his shirt sleeves" after a curious delay, K. sees Leni scurrying away and out of sight down the hall. He at once suspects her of being unfaithful and asks Block if he is her lover. He refuses to accept Block's denial, testing him before the Judge's portrait in the Lawyer's office to find out that she has told Block the same thing about it that she has told him. Taking this as a confirmation of intimacy between them, K. asks Block to tell him where Leni is hiding. Finally, when K. encounters Leni in the kitchen, he interrogates her regarding the matter:

'Good evening, Joseph,' she said, glancing over her shoulder. 'Good evening,' said K., waving the tradesman to a chair some distance away, on which the man obediently sat down. Then K. went quite close up behind Leni, leaned over her shoulder, and asked: 'Who's this man?' Leni put her disengaged arm round K., stirring the soup with the other, and pulled him forward. 'He's a miserable creature,' she said, 'a poor tradesman called Block. Just look at him.' ... 'You were in your shift,' said K., turning Leni's head forcibly to the stove. She made no answer. 'Is he your lover?' asked K. She reached for the soup pan, but K. imprisoned both her hands and said: 'Give me an answer!' She said: 'Come into the study and I'll explain everything.' 'No,' said K., 'I want you to tell me here.' She slipped her arm into his and tried to give him a kiss, but K. fended her off, saying: 'I don't want you to kiss me now.' 'Joseph,' said Leni, gazing at him imploringly and yet frankly, 'surely you're not jealous of Herr Block?' Then she turned to the tradesman and said: 'Rudi, come to the rescue, you can see that I'm under suspicion, put that candle down.' One might have thought he had been paying no attention, but he knew at once what she meant. 'I can't think what you have to be jealous about either,' he said, with no great acumen. 'Nor can I, really,' replied K., regarding him with a smile. Leni laughed outright and profited by K.'s momentary distraction to hook herself on to his arm whispering: 'Leave him alone now, you can see the kind of creature he is. I've shown him a little kindness because he's one of the lawyer's best clients, but that was the only reason…But you're certainly going to spend the night with me.'[147]

There are several significant points here. First and foremost, the explanation that Leni ultimately gives K. in the kitchen, in front of Block himself, is most assuredly more superficial and deceptive than the "everything" that she would have sincerely explained to him in the privacy of the study where they had their first mystical encounter. Joseph K. denies himself that explanation because of the same impatience and jealousy that he exhibits in the case of the Usher's wife. Gestures are all important in Kafka's writing, and it is most noteworthy that Joseph K. begins to manhandle Leni in an almost violent manner. This is a stark contrast to the kind of gestures that they usually exchange — Joseph's soft kisses on Leni's hands, Leni's gentle rubbing of Joseph's temples and running her fingers through his hair, and so forth.

It is significant that Leni's first response to Joseph's refusal to accompany her to the study is to convey the import of what she would have told him there by intimately holding his hand and kissing him. It is only when K. also stubbornly refuses this, that she limits herself to saying something that is aimed at divesting K. of his jealousy by enhancing his feeling of superiority over Block. She does not deny that there has been some kind of sexual relationship between her and "the miserable creature," but attributes this solely to his position as a diligent client of the Lawyer, whereas she hints at a personal affection for Joseph. Block himself reinforces this and, for the moment, it seems to work.

However, it is not long before K. finds out that Block sleeps in the house and Leni has given her room to him, permanently. Where does Leni herself sleep? With Block, or in the other bed, with the Lawyer? K. begins to grow disgusted at Leni:

> 'So you sleep in the maid's room?' asked K., turning to the tradesman. 'Leni lets me have it,' said he, 'it's very convenient.' K. gave him a long look; the first impression he had had of the man was perhaps, after all, the right one...Suddenly K. could no longer bear the sight of him. 'Put him to bed,' he cried to Leni, who seemed not to comprehend what he meant. Yet what he wanted was to get away to the lawyer and dismiss from his life not only Huld but Leni and the tradesman too.[148]

When, moments later, he does go in to see the Lawyer, locking the door and barring Leni's way into the room, what he hears from the Lawyer concerning Leni could only reinforce his jealousy and feelings of betrayal:

> 'Has she been pestering you again?' 'Pestering me?' asked K. 'Yes,' said the lawyer, chuckling until stopped by a fit of coughing, after which he began to chuckle once more. 'I suppose you can't have helped noticing that she pesters you?' he asked, patting K's hand, which in his nervous distraction he had put on the bedside table and now hastily withdrew. 'You don't attach much importance to it,' went on the lawyer as K. remained silent. 'So much the better. Or else I might have had to apologize for her. It's a peculiarity of hers, which I have long forgiven her and which I wouldn't mention now had it not been for your locking the door. This peculiarity of hers, well, you're looking so bewildered that I feel I must, this peculiarity of hers consists in her finding nearly all accused men attractive. She makes up to all of them, loves them all, and is evidently also loved in return; she often tells

me about these affairs to amuse me, when I allow her. It doesn't surprise me so much as it seems to surprise you. If you have the right eye for these things, you can see that accused men are often attractive...Of course some are much more attractive than others. But they are all attractive, even that wretched creature Block.'[149]

Shortly after hearing this speech, K. announces his intention to dismiss the Lawyer, and the latter puts on a display involving Block, which is intended to impress upon K. the fact that he is an extraordinarily well-respected client. This horrifying display of sadistic manipulation by the Lawyer, in concert with Leni, and the masochistic submission of Block, actually acts to finalize Joseph's decision to part company with the whole lot of them. Evidently, as K. watches Block turning into a "dog," begging and pleading on his knees, he grasps Leni even more violently than in the kitchen, to which she responds by saying: "You're hurting me. Let go. I want to be with Block."[150] K. probably interprets this as further evidence of her betrayal and intimate feelings for Block. Yet he is wrong to do so, as his own intuition tells him. As he watches Leni mediating the sadomasochistic interaction between the Lawyer and Block, Kafka gives us an important hint:

> Then Leni, displaying the fine lines of her taut figure, bent over close to the old man's face and stroked his long white hair. That finally evoked an answer. 'I hesitate to tell him,' said the lawyer, and one could see him shaking his head, perhaps only the better to enjoy the pressure of Leni's hand. Block listened with downcast eyes, as if he were breaking a law by listening. 'Why do you hesitate?' asked Leni. *K. had the felling that he was listening to a well-rehearsed dialogue which had been often repeated and would be often repeated and only for Block would never lose its novelty.* 'How has he been behaving today?' inquired the lawyer instead of answering. Before providing this information Leni looked down at Block and watched him for a moment as he raised his hands toward her and clasped them appealingly

---

together. At length she nodded gravely, turned to the lawyer, and said: 'He has been quiet and industrious.' ...

So the lawyer's methods, to which K. fortunately had not been long enough exposed, amounted to this: that the client finally forgot the whole world and lived only in hope of toiling along this false path until the end of his case should come in sight. The client ceased to be a client and became the lawyer's dog.[151]

The initial insight that Joseph K. has (*italicized* above) conflicts with his ultimate conclusion. Block has followed a false path that leads him to become the Lawyer's dog. However, K. makes the mistake of forgetting the great difference between himself and Block, especially in Leni's eyes. Leni would never treat K. in the humiliating manner that Block is being treated in this spectacle of psychological torture and subjugation. K. does not listen well when she tells him that Block "is a miserable creature," and that it would be absurd for K. to be jealous of him. She may have performed sexual acts with Block, but they would have been as rehearsed and as professional as K. observes the dialogue in the Lawyer's sadomasochistic drama to be. In the horrifying scene above, Leni is actually in the dominant position. The sick and withering old Lawyer is in bed, Block is cowering on the floor like a miserable creature, while "displaying the fine lines of her taught figure" Leni towers above and "nurses" both of them. The "rehearsed" nature of Leni's relationship with Block, and even with the Lawyer himself, presents a stark contrast to the magical spontaneity of the encounter between her and Joseph K. in the study—an encounter wherein, as we have seen, ordinary space and time were transcended.

Block pursues his case much more aggressively than K. We hear that the Lawyer has given Block certain "scriptures of the Law," and that Block studies these day and night though he can barely understand them.[152] He carries these studies out in Leni's room. Leni is aware of his diligence and cites this "good behavior" in her mock defense of him to the Lawyer. This must be viewed in the context of Leni's advisory comments to K., during their very first encounter in the Lawyer's study. It is not an accident that the transcendence of space-time by Leni and K. on this occasion, takes place during ongoing discussion between the Lawyer and a Court Official, whose aid Joseph's uncle has enlisted. From the moment when the latter meets K. at the Bank, we are told that he favors an overbearingly active approach to Joseph's case. Yet, in her advisement of K., Leni says: "But must you eternally be brooding over your case?" To which K. responds: "In fact I probably brood far too little over it." The rejoinder by Leni is key:

> 'That isn't the mistake you make,' said Leni. 'You're too unyielding, that's what I've heard.' 'Who told you that?' asked K.; he could feel her body against his breast and gazed down at her rich, dark firmly knotted hair. 'I should give away too much if I told you that,' replied Leni. 'Please don't ask me for names, take my warning to heart instead, and don't be so unyielding in future, you can't fight against this Court, you must confess to guilt. Make your confession at the first chance you get. Until you do that, there's no possibility of getting out of their clutches, none at all. Yet even then you won't manage it without help from outside, but you needn't trouble your head about that, I'll see to it myself.' 'You know a great deal about this Court and the intrigues that prevail in it!' said K... Then she clasped both her hands around his neck, leaned back, and looked at him for a long time.[153]

Whereas Leni encourages Block's day and night study of the false scriptures, feeding him a few scraps of food and a few sips of water along the way, she is telling K. to do just the opposite. The truth about her intentionally misleading Block, is probably what she would have revealed to K. if he had agreed to accompany her to the study where she would "explain everything." This would also have given him profound insight regarding his own "case." The clear implication in the passage above, is that despite the ignorance of Joseph's uncle — who cares only for the "good name" of his family, Leni can actually help K. more than the old men discussing his case in the next room. She refuses to tell him who it was that told her that K. needs to be less unyielding because it would reveal too much. This person could not have been the Lawyer, because taking such a view would put him out of business.

Rather, we should read this mysterious comment in light of the fact that Leni is privy to the information that the "High Judge" in the painting on the wall of the study is actually an Examining Magistrate seated on a "kitchen chair, with an old horse-rug doubled under him."[154] We later find out that Titorelli paints all of the court officials' portraits in his own studio, which is appended to their Law offices.[155] This means that Leni knows Titorelli. She has been to his studio, and was probably there even while the Examining Magistrate was having his portrait painted. Kafka's hint here offers a rare glimpse into the workings of the Court behind the scenes, at a level higher than that of the Lawyer or the Chief Clerk of the Court, whom K. impolitely — but *wisely* — abandons in the room down the hall during his first meeting with Leni.

Like the Usher's wife, Leni is one of the promiscuous women of the Law. Perhaps she was once in training, in a manner akin to one of the three adolescent girls that K. encounters when he visits the Painter. Titorelli is "on the friendliest terms" with them, and informs K. that they "belong to the Court too."[156] The Painter tells K. that he painted one of the girls who "belong to the Court" once, but not one of the three he sees on the stairway. Perhaps it is Leni who was painted, on the occasion of her graduation, as part of an earlier *group of three women*. Titorelli also mentions that he brings ladies to his studio to be painted, in addition to the male officials of the Court. Titorelli informs

154 Ibid., 108.
155 Ibid., 156.

K. that he is "in the confidence of the Court" and says that K. is right when he intimates that "such unrecognized posts often carry more influence with them than the official ones."[157] The three women that offer to help K. all hold, or will hold (in the case of Fraulein Burstner), such unofficial positions of higher authority than that of the Laywers, Chief Clerks, or Examining Magistrates. Note how the words of Titorelli's description of the portrait of the vain Judge that he is painting echo Leni's description of the artifice of the portrait in the Lawyer's study as a testimony to the vanity of the Court officials:

> 'Of course,' said K., who had not wished to give any offense by his remark. 'You have painted the figure as it actually stands above the high seat.' 'No,' said the painter, 'I have neither seen the figure nor the high seat, that is all invention, but I am told what to paint and I paint it.' 'How do you mean?' asked K., deliberately pretending that he did not understand. 'It's surely a Judge sitting on his seat of justice?' 'Yes,' said the painter, 'but it is by no means a high Judge and he has never sat on such a seat in his life.' 'And yet he has himself painted in that solemn posture? Why, he sits there as if he were the actual President of the Court.' 'Yes, they're very vain, these gentlemen,' said the painter. 'But their superiors give them permission to get themselves painted like that. Each one of them gets precise instructions how he may have his portrait painted. Only you can't judge the detail of the costume and the seat itself from this picture, unfortunately pastel is really unsuited for this kind of thing.' 'Yes,' said K., 'it's curious that you should have used pastel.' 'My client wished it,' said the painter, 'he intends the picture for a lady.'[158]

Leni also tells K. that the portraits are "all invention" and then proceeds to tell him that she is as "madly vain" as the court officials who are painted in this ridiculously pompous manner. Could it be that the "superiors" of the "vain…gentlemen," who are the ones that determine how each official is to be painted, are actually women? Is one of these women the lady for whom the portrait above is intended? Kafka is

---

157 Ibid., 148.

certainly drawing our attention to some link between the scene where
Leni explains the portrait in the study to K. and the scene of Titorelli
explaining a similar portrait that is being painted for a lady, by a
painter of the Court who occasionally paints women.

It is very interesting that a Court official would give his commissioned formal portrait to a woman. She must be a woman of some
importance. Perhaps the portrait in the Lawyer's study belongs not to
the Lawyer, but to Leni. She claims to know the "dwarf" of a man who
is depicted in it.[159] Perhaps the portrait was the dwarf's gift to her, just
as the portrait in Titorelli's office will be given to another Lady of the
Court. It makes a great deal of sense that such women would invent
the metaphor of the Great Goddess of Witchcraft standing above all of
the seats in which the male Judges sit — as if to mock their judgments
and intimate the hidden dominion of The Craft over their "Court of
Justice." The Judges and all of the male orderlies beneath them may
in fact be servants of the Triune Goddess as embodied by Her High
Priestesses.

On more than one occasion, K. momentarily realizes despite himself that these women who are in some way involved with "the Law"
can help him with his case, especially during his encounter with Leni,
when he thinks to himself:

> I seem to recruit women helpers, he thought almost in surprise; first
> Fraulein Burstner, then the wife of the usher, and now this little nurse
> [Leni] who appears to have some incomprehensible desire for me. 'And if I
> don't make a confession of guilt, then you can't help me?' K. asked experi-
> mentally... 'No,' said Leni, shaking her head slowly, 'then I can't help you.
> But you don't in the least want my help, it doesn't matter to you, you're
> stiff-necked and never will be convinced.' After a while she asked: 'Have
> you got a sweetheart?' 'No,' said K. 'Oh, yes, you have,' she said.[160]

---

159 Ibid., 108.

Leni's claim that K. is "too stiff-necked" to accept her help is immediately followed by her insistence that he must have a sweetheart. The
implication is that the two are related. As we see a few lines down,
what Leni means by "a sweetheart" is someone to whom one is bound,
one with whom one has a possessive relationship that excludes others. Leni takes Joseph's stubbornness and refusal to accept her help, as
evidence that he is possessive. It ultimately turns out that she is right
in this assessment, but for the time being her hope in helping him is
restored by his lightheartedness in respect to exchanging Elsa for her,
and by the intimate manner in which he holds her and cherishes the
oddity of her "pretty paw" (as discussed above). Even when K. himself
realizes that such women have decisive influence over the malleable
male officials who maintain the façade of the Court, he cannot conceive of their help in any other terms than their being employed by
him as his servants: "Women have great influence. If I could move
some women I know to join forces *in working for me*, I couldn't help
winning through. Especially before this Court, which consists almost
entirely of petticoat-hunters. Let the Examining Magistrate see a
woman in the distance and he knocks down his desk and the defen-
dant in his eagerness to get at her."[161]

5. TWO TRINITIES

K. ultimately prefers to forsake the help of the Three Witches of the
Triune Goddess, rather than abandon his aspirations of possessing
them. In his final, brief, conversation with Leni, over the telephone,
she is concerned that he has been called to the Cathedral. As the priest
there later confirms, she suggests that it is an act of the Court and
that they are goading K. on, in other words, that he should not go.
However: "Pity which he had not asked for and did not expect was
more than K. could bear, he said two words of farewell, but even as
he hung up the receiver he murmured half to himself and half to

the faraway girl who could no longer hear him: 'Yes, they're goading me.'"[162] Despite the admission that Leni is right in believing that the Court has called him to the Cathedral, he acts surprised when the "Prison Chaplain" later tells him the same thing.

This attests to the fact that the division between the conscious and unconscious aspects of Joseph K. persists until the very end of his case. Leni offers K. a way to circumvent a Law that cannot be fought against head-on, but only if he confesses to his guilt. It should be clear by now that Joseph K. *is* indeed guilty, at least in as much as he possess two aspects to his character, each with a different ethos. In so far as his calculative, stubborn and possessive conscious self is not reconciled to his unconsciously free-spirited nature, each of these aspects must always view the other as wrong. The guilt of Joseph K. lies in the unacknowledged duality of his persona. An admission of guilt would thus be a means whereby the two conflicting aspects would have to be acknowledged from a third vantage point of observation, one which encompasses the opposition of the conscious and unconscious mind within its horizon. K. is never able to bring these into the spiritual harmony of such a Trinity. Instead, the deadly duality of their opposition draws him towards his execution.

We should not mistake the three men walking to the execution as such a Trinity. The two executioners, whom K. is awaiting with the self-condemnation of a guilty man, are *two men*. Just as the warders who arrest him are *two men*. K. is not the reconciling third term between them, though the speaking looks he exchanges with the warder Franz are a subtle invitation to become that. Rather, the two men taking him off to be executed stand one on each of his two sides, representing the continuing and ever more deadly strife of duality within Joseph K. Instead of each supporting and making the other stronger, as in a genuine Trinity, "the three of them were interlocked in a unity which would have brought all three down together had one of them been knocked over."[163] They form only "a unity such as can hardly be formed except by lifeless matter."[164] *Physis* was a lower aspect of Hecate, the functioning of the material world that theurgists sought to overcome.[165] In this guise as *Physis*, she sent forth deceptive, earthly *daimones* whose task it was to persuade people to be dragged down into the mindset of materialism.[166] The two Visitors who come for K. are men in black, and with great relevance to the Dionysian persona masks of tragic drama at its origins, K. even asks them whether they are (cheap) actors from a theater. Though he takes their response as an unpreparedness to answer questions (as if they are preprogrammed automata), the gestures involved in their reaction to this question suggest something more like a mime performance.[167] Significantly, K. has also dressed himself all in black and is just slipping on a pair of gloves as he waits for the unannounced Visitors. There are always *three* men in black. Even at the outset of *The Trial*, the warders insist on K. donning a *black* coat to appear before the first of the officials he is to encounter.[168] What is it with *black*?

A variety of classical literary and historical sources attest to black stones of volcanic obsidian, with their inhumanly primordial and terrifyingly abstract and reflective aspect, being the earliest idols of the Amazon lunar goddess.[169] Most interestingly, the Ka'aba at Mecca — which was long known by the pagan Arabs as "the Ancient Woman" and which was originally attended by priestesses — is an example of just such a stone.[170] The word *Ka'aba* is descended from *Kybala* or Cybele — the Amazon mother goddess analogized

---

163 Ibid., 224.

164 Ibid.

165 D'Este, *Hecate*, 174.

166 Ibid., 174–175.

167 Kafka, *The Trial*, 224.

168 Ibid., 9.

169 Wilde, *The Amazons in Myth and History*, 100–102.

with Artemis at Ephesus.[171] This may also be the root of the word *Kabbalah* — the black art or Craft. Inside the Islamic enclosure and beneath the shroud that veils it, the actual Black Stone at Mecca bears an engraved symbol of the Moon Goddess' vulva.[172] Classical Anatolia was the center of the Hecate cult, and Byzantine coins symbolized Hecate by means of a crescent and a star. This lunar goddess symbol was later adopted by the invading Ottoman Turks and has ironically come to be emblematic of Islam.[173]

The three men in black on the road to K's execution stand in contrast to the *trinities of women*, such as Fraulein Burstner, the Usher's Wife, and Leni, or the three "prematurely debauched" girls of the Court at Titorelli's studio, who might grow into the roles played by the older Trinity of witches. K. is willing to be led off to the execution site; he even helps the men lead him to the site, which is one both of his and of their choosing. He then lies down voluntarily, waiting to be killed. It is noteworthy that he initially makes the decision not to resist when a lady who appears to be Fraulein Burstner enters the square, which is a crossroads, while he is preparing to resist his two escorts. He leads the two men to follow her for a time so that "he might not forget the lesson she had brought into his mind."[174] K. then elaborates: "I always wanted to snatch at the world with twenty hands, and not for a very laudable motive, either. That was wrong, and am I to show now that not even a year's trial has taught me anything?"[175] He maintains this resolve until the very last moment, when it is too late, and he raises his hands in protest against his decision not to resist. This is Kafka's way of saying that the lack of mastery Joseph K. has over the two conflicting forces in him has allowed them to conspire to execute

171 Ibid., 99.

172 Ibid.

173 D'Este, *Hekate*, 112–113.

174 Kafka, *The Trial*, 225.

him with a dagger — which is one of Hecate's sacred implements.[176] Its being turned twice in his heart, as he stares up at the two "cheek to cheek" faces of the executioners, is a symbol for his having perished of his unacknowledged duality. He is murdered by the light of the Moon, aura of Artemis and Hecate: "The moon shone down on everything with that simplicity and serenity which no other light possess."[177] Kafka repeatedly tells us that the moon shines on K. and his two escorts all along the way, especially as they cross the bridge to the outskirts of town.[178] Hecate was not only the goddess of the crossroads, but also the divinity "of the wayside" and of the gateways at the outskirts that mark a city's limits.[179] This is the domain of stray dogs.

Virtually all of the animals sacrificed in the Classical world at large came from the four species of bovines, goats, sheep, and swine.[180] It is quite striking then, that *dogs* — a household pet and "man's best friend" — were the animals sacrificed to Hecate.[181] Hecate was accompanied by a black dog or "black bitch" and sometimes took the form of one herself.[182] Black dogs were sacrificed to Hecate, especially at the crossroads.[183] Dogs barking or trembling were considered a sign of Hecate's presence.[184] Dogs were her companions, her heralds, and her offerings.[185] This means that like the tradesman Block who became "the Lawyer's dog" (really, Leni's dog), even amidst (literally) mortifying shame Joseph K. also remains a servant of the Goddess — one who

176 D'Este, *Hekate*, 70.

177 Kafka, *The Trial*, 227.

178 Ibid., 226.

179 D'Este, *Hekate*, 21, 29, 60.

180 Ibid., 24.

181 Ibid.

182 Ibid., 74, 91.

183 Ibid., 114, 124, 154.

184 Ibid., 130, 154.

is killed "Like a Dog!"[186] The "shame" is that, unlike the "miserable creature" Block, he could have been more than a servant or sacrificial dog. Joseph K. was offered intimate companionship so long as he did not demand advantage or possession. Though he failed to do so in this life, his final thoughts betray that he has learned his lesson and might do so in the next. The novel's enigmatic concluding line "it was as if the shame of it must outlive him" has to be viewed in the context of Kafka's allusions to reincarnation, not only in *The Trial*, but also his clearer pronouncements on the matter in his *Blue Octavo Notebooks*.

6. THREE PATHS AT THE CROSSROADS

The first time that Kafka hints at the idea of reincarnation in *The Trial* is after the Student has carried the Usher's wife off to the Examining Magistrate. Kafka writes: "how well-off K. was compared with the Magistrate… True, he drew no secondary income from bribes or percolation and could not order his attendant to pick up a woman and carry her to his room. But K. was perfectly willing to renounce these advantages, *at least in this life*."[187] Later on, Kafka makes another reference to the idea in the course of Joseph's contemplation of whether or not to retain his lawyer. He relates to us that in one of the "harangues" which make him doubt the Lawyer's efficiency, the latter had said that "you felt astonished to think that one single ordinary lifetime sufficed to gather all the knowledge needed for a fair degree of success in such a profession."[188] These hints are somewhat elucidated by the following passages from Kafka's *Blue Octavo Notebooks*:

> A man has free will, and this of three kinds: first of all he was free when he wanted this life; now, of course, he cannot go back on it, for he is no longer the person who wanted it then, except perhaps in so far as he carries out what he then wanted, in that he lives. Secondly, he is free in that he can

---

186 Kafka, *The Trial*, 229.

187 Ibid., 60 — emphasis mine.

choose the pace of the road of this life. Thirdly, he is free in that, *as the person who will sometime exist again*, he has the will to make himself go through life under every condition and in this way come to himself, and this, what is more, on a road that, though it is a matter of choice, is still so very labyrinthine that there is no smallest area of this life that it leaves untouched. This is the trichotomy of free will, but since it is simultaneously also a unity, an integer, and fundamentally is so completely integral, it has no room for any will, free or unfree.[189]

Many shades of the departed are occupied solely in licking at the waves of the river of death because it flows from our direction and still has the salty taste of our seas. Then the river rears back in disgust, the current flows the opposite way *and brings the dead drifting back into life*. But they are happy, sing songs of thanksgiving, and stroke the indignant waters. *Beyond a certain point there is no return. This point has to be reached.*[190]

One of the first signs of the beginnings of understanding is the wish to die. This life appears unbearable, another unattainable. One is no longer ashamed of wanting to die; *one asks to be moved from the old cell, which one hates, to a new one, which one will only in time come to hate. In this there is also a residue of belief that during the move the master will chance to come along the corridor, look at the prisoner and say: 'This man is not to be locked up again. He is to come to me.'*[191]

Not only do these passages establish that Kafka believed in reincarnation of some sort, they also gift us a key to understanding the metaphor of the three paths that are offered to K. by the painter Titorelli. The last of the passages cited above, uses the image of "imprisonment," which is preceded by an "arrest," as a metaphor for the embodiment of the soul by the flesh. It suggests that one body is exchanged for another, as one prison cell for another, until finally one may be released once and for all. There is a clear parallel between this and the path of "ostensible acquittal" described by Titorelli. The Painter explains how

189 Brod., *The Blue Octavo Notebooks*, 95.
190 Ibid., 15–16.

a definite acquittal cannot be granted by the Judges of the Court that K. is involved with, and that Titorelli is able to influence. Rather: "that power is reserved for the highest Court of all, which is quite inaccessible to you, to me, and to all of us. What the prospects are up there we do not know and, I may say in passing, do not even want to know."[192] It seems likely that the Judge of this unknowable "highest Court of all" is the same figure as "the master" in the last of the notes cited above, who tells the other Judges that: "This man is not to be locked up again. He is to come to me." Titorelli goes on to explain the difference between this definite acquittal and ostensible acquittal in the following terms:

> [W]hen you are acquitted in this [ostensible] fashion the charge is lifted from your shoulders for the time being, but it continues to hover above you and can, as soon as an order comes from on high, be laid upon you again....In definite acquittal the documents relating to the cases are said to be completely annulled, they simply vanish from sight, not only the charge but also the records of the case and even the acquittal are destroyed, everything is destroyed. That's not the case with ostensible acquittal. The documents remain as they were, except the affidavit is added to them and a record of the acquittal and the grounds for granting it. The whole dossier continues to circulate, as the regular official routine demands, passing on to the higher Courts, being referred to the lower ones again, and thus swinging backwards and forwards with greater or smaller oscillations, longer or shorter delays. These peregrinations are incalculable. A detached observer might sometimes fancy that the whole case had been forgotten, the documents lost, and the acquittal made absolute. No one really acquainted with the Court could think such a thing. No document is ever lost, the Court never forgets anything. One day — quite unexpectedly — some Judge will take up the documents and look at them attentively, recognize that in this case the charge is still valid, and order an immediate arrest. I have been speaking on the assumption that a long time elapses between the ostensible acquittal and the new arrest; that is possible and I have known of such cases, but it is just as possible for the acquitted man to go straight home from the Court and find officers already waiting to arrest him again. Then,

of course, all his freedom is at an end.' 'And the case begins all over again?'
asked K. almost incredulously. 'Certainly,' said the painter.[193]

In light of the passages from the *Blue Octavo Notebooks*, one could
read "ostensible acquittal" as the soul being temporarily released from
the prison of the physical body. It may remain on the ethereal spiritual
plane for a long time before reincarnating, or it may return almost
immediately. In any case, the "documents relating to" one's case,
i.e. the karmic traces of one's actions in life, are not "completely an-
nulled" as they are if one's soul achieves liberation from the transiently
manifest world of multiplicity altogether. We should remember that
definite and ostensible acquittal are two of the *three paths* that Titorelli
proposes, and we have already suggested how these may be the three
roads that are watched over by Hecate, the Triune "Goddess of the
Crossroads."

It is also notable that the metaphor Kafka employs in his *Blue
Octavo Notebooks* is that of being locked up. Again, one of the three
implements held by Hecate is a key. Two others are a rope and a
knife.[194] [195] These originally signified her role as the Goddess of child
labor, where the knife was used to cut the umbilical cord. In the mystery cults, however, her cutting of the "rope" by the "knife" alluded to
the severing of the soul's ties to the physical body. Thus Hecate is the
goddess who presides over the kind of entry and exit of spirits to and
from the physical world that is described in the first quote above from
the *Blue Octavo Notebooks*. Hecate was connected to Orpheus and his
mysteries, and she was central to the Orphic belief in reincarnation.[196]

---

193 Ibid., 159.

194 D'Este, *Hekate*, 157.

195 Unlike other Greek divinities, and very much like Indian ones, she had multiple
arms to hold all of these implements, with her lower arms sometimes being
depicted as serpentine — another, particularly Indian, affinity to *Shakti*.

Many of her devotees were vegetarians on account of the credence they gave to transmigration of the soul.[197]

There is an essential difference between Kafka's notion of reincarnation and that present within (non-tantric) Vedanta or (orthodox schools of) the Buddha Dharma. Kafka believes that one should choose not to avoid subjection to all kinds of experiences, whether nominally "good" or "evil," but experience all of them as fully as possible within one single lifetime. Otherwise, it is implied, one will have to return to the prison cell. We see this idea more clearly expressed in other passages of the *Blue Octavo Notebooks*:

> You can hold yourself back from the sufferings of the world: this is something you are free to do and is in accord with your nature, but perhaps precisely this holding back is the only suffering that you might be able to avoid.[198]

> Your will is free means: it was free when it wanted the desert, it is free since it can choose the path that leads to crossing the desert, it is free since it can choose the pace, but it is also unfree since you must go through the desert, unfree since every path in labyrinthine manner touches every foot of the desert's surface.[199]

> In the struggle between yourself and the world second the world. One must not cheat anyone, not even the world of its victory. There is nothing besides a spiritual world; what we call the world of the senses is the Evil in the spiritual world, and what we call Evil is only the necessity of a moment in our eternal evolution.[200]

> Not shaking off the self, but consuming the self.[201]

---

197 Ibid., 46.
198 Brod, *The Blue Octavo Notebooks*, 97.
199 Ibid., 50.
200 Ibid., 91.

Joseph K. is guilty because there *is* an aspect of him that has preferred to "consume the self" rather than "throw it off" as an ascetic might do. What he does not understand, at least with his conscious mind, and what Leni attempts to convey to him, is that he should not be trying to prove that he is "innocent." The Court and its officials, including the promiscuous women who hold sway over them, are all bathed in sin. Their aim is not to prevent a person from doing "Evil," it is to drive a person to the spiritual depths beyond Good and Evil. In his *Blue Octavo Notebooks*, Kafka has this to say about binary moral oppositions:

> Evil is a radiation of human consciousness in certain transitional positions.[202]
> There can be knowledge of the diabolical, but no belief in it, for more of the diabolical than there is does not exist.[203]
> One cannot pay Evil in installments — and one always keeps on trying to.[204]
> Evil knows of the Good, but Good does not know of Evil.[205]
> Evil is the starry sky of the Good.[206]

The way beyond Good and Evil may be the *third way* proposed by Titorelli, the path of "indefinite postponement." Titorelli proposes this option when it appears to him that "ostensible acquittal" is unappealing to K. He explains that in this procedure, one must maintain occasional contact with the Court, but the interrogations and hearings become a mere formality and may be conducted at one's own leisure, and "the case will never pass beyond its first stages."[207] What could this mean in the context of the transmigration of the soul? One is "arrested," therefore incarnated, but one is indefinitely prevented

---

202 Ibid., 94.

203 Ibid., 96.

204 Ibid., 90.

205 Ibid., 24.

206 Ibid., 29.

from departing from this physical embodiment and being newly reincarnated ("ostensible acquittal"), or alternatively, being permanently liberated from the physical plane and annihilated as an individual ("permanent acquittal"). Metaphorically, there is only one condition of being that would allow for this: indefinitely prolonged *childhood*.

The theme of an artificial eternal childhood surfaces repeatedly throughout *The Trial*. We have already seen how Leni exhibits childish behavior in her encounter with K. in the Lawyer's study. The initial mention of children occurs when K. arrives at the Courthouse for the first time. Children and adolescents are everywhere, and we see the duality of Joseph K. yet again in his split reaction to them:

> On his way up he disturbed many children who were playing on the stairs and looked at him angrily as he strode through their ranks. 'If I ever come here again,' he told himself, 'I must either bring sweets to cajole them with or else a stick to beat them.' Just before he reached the first floor he had actually to wait for a moment until a marble came to rest, *two children with the lined, pinched faces of adult rogues* holding him meanwhile by his trousers; if he had shaken them off he must have hurt them, and he feared their outcries…His real search began on the first floor…almost all the doors stood open, *with children running out and in*…Many of the women were holding babies in one arm and working over the stove with the arm that was left free. Half-grown girls who seemed to be dressed in nothing but an apron kept busily rushing about. In all the rooms the beds were still occupied, sick people were lying in them, or men who had not wakened yet, or others who were resting in their clothes.[208]

Finally, when K. meets the Usher's wife for the first time, Kafka describes her as "a young woman with sparkling black eyes, *who was washing children's clothes in a tub*…"[209] On his second encounter with the Usher's wife, after the Student has carried her up the narrow flight of stairs to the garret of the Examining Magistrate, K. notices that there are indeed law offices upstairs, as indicated by a sign on

---

208 Ibid., 37.

the stairway, *written in children's handwriting*: "K. noticed a small card pinned up… he read in childish, unpracticed handwriting: 'Law Court Offices upstairs.'"[210] The "half-grown girls" are running around half-naked as if they were still little girls who had no shame. Note the juxtaposition of old age and childhood in the description of the playing children's faces. It is not that their faces show the maturity of adulthood, but rather, the aspect of "adult *rogues*." Later on, as he walks up another stairway to Titorelli's studio, located in a similar poor house, Joseph K. is met by three adolescent girls. According to K. "All their faces betrayed the same mixture of childishness and depravity which had prompted this idea of making him run the gauntlet between them."[211] This is the same combination of child-like innocence, and a debauchery that is tempered and transformed by it, which is characteristic of Leni's bizarre behavior. Also, like the elderly children in the Courthouse's stairway, the leader of the band of three adolescent girls has a mark of old age — she is hunchbacked: "The girl who was slightly hunchbacked and seemed scarcely thirteen years old, nudged him with her elbow and peered up at him knowingly. Neither her youth nor her deformity had saved her from being prematurely debauched. She did not even smile, but stared unwinkingly at K. with shrewd, bold eyes."[212] The girl has already learned the soul-piercing stare that Leni gives K. in the study, as she clasps her hands around his head and looks at him "for a long time." Like Leni, the three girls outside Titorelli's studio also "belong to the Court."[213]

The method of "indefinite postponement" seems to render the Court proceedings a farce or joke, as one aspect of Joseph K. is tempted to interpret them from the very outset of his arrest. Indeed, if this postponement is a metaphor for someone indefinitely retaining

---

210 Ibid., 59.

211 Ibid., 142.

212 Ibid.

or *returning to* a state of childhood, despite one's wisdom and one's debauchery, then it calls for the kind of "wise innocence" or grave playfulness that the Lawyer claims is often the only behavior to which the Court officials are responsive:

> But then, suddenly, in the most surprising fashion and without any particular reason, they would be moved to laughter by some small jest which you only dared to make because you felt you had nothing to lose, and then they were your friends again. In fact it was both easy and difficult to handle them, you could hardly lay down any fixed principles for dealing with them. Sometimes you felt astonished to think that one single ordinary lifetime sufficed to gather all the knowledge needed for a fair degree of success in such a profession.[214]

Instead of being perpetually reincarnated, or annihilating themselves together with their guilt in "permanent acquittal," these beings have chosen to live an extraordinary lifetime, where, as old wise men of knowledge, they have become children again. In his *Blue Octavo Notebooks*, Kafka writes: "There is a down-and-outness under true knowledge and a childlike happy arising from it!"[215] This is the same paradox involved in the fact that, like the Goddess Artemis, the three women of the Law remain virgins despite their promiscuity.

It seems that in being offered "indefinite postponement," K. is being given the chance to be reborn into childhood the way that the Court officials have been. The three women, especially Leni, in the guise of Artemis-Hecate, are the midwives of this spiritual rebirth and the nursemaids of the soul reborn into playful innocence, despite the burden of knowledge. K. would then indeed playfully remain engaged with the Court, but in recognition of it as a kind of farce. That K. recognizes this as an option from the very start is Kafka's way of telling us that he *is* at the crossroads of this transformation of consciousness, and that is why he is called before the Law and offered the assistance

---

214 Ibid., 122.

of the Triune Goddess — who is also the nursemaid presiding over childbirth.

So much for "ostensible acquittal" and "indefinite postponement." What of the third path that is watched over by the Triune Goddess of the Crossroads? For an understanding of "definite acquittal" we must look to Kafka's parable "Before the Law." It should not surprise us that K. agrees with the third interpretation of the parable conveyed by the Priest. Not only is it the most detailed and thoroughly argued of the interpretations, it also offers K. what he had been seeking from this prison chaplain. Before the latter descends from his pulpit to speak privately to K. and relate the parable to him, Kafka tells us that

> it was not impossible that K. could obtain decisive and acceptable coun-
> sel from him which might, for instance, point the way, not toward some
> influential manipulation of the case, but toward a circumvention of it, a
> breaking away from it altogether, a mode of living completely outside the
> jurisdiction of the Court.[216]

The third interpretation of the parable elaborates the many reasons why the doorkeeper is himself deceived, and perhaps even inferior to the man from the country. K. is convinced by these reasons and asserts that the doorkeeper should be dismissed from his duty. Whereupon the Priest tells him that, according to certain interpreters, to criticize the doorkeeper, who, deceived as he may be, is nonetheless an em-ployee of the Law "is to doubt the Law itself." Joseph's response to this, and the Priest's rejoinder, is one of the key passages of the novel:

> 'I don't agree with that point of view,' said K., shaking his head, 'for if one
> accepts it, one must accept as true everything the doorkeeper says. But you
> yourself have sufficiently proved how impossible it is to do that.' 'No,' said
> the priest, 'it is not necessary to accept everything as true, one must only
> accept it as necessary.' 'A melancholy conclusion,' said K. 'It turns lying into
> a universal principle.'[217]

---

216 Kafka, *The Trial*, 212.

The last statement by K. is of course intended to be paradoxical. Lying cannot be a universal principle. For lying to be a universal principle, would in fact mean that there are no universal principles at all. There is a link between this passage and the scene of "The Whipper," early in the novel. The injustice of Joseph's willingness to judge others in order to preserve his advantage is forcefully depicted by Kafka in this scene. The men who seem to be perpetually damned to punishment in the lumber room of the Bank, are only there because K. judged them. His horrified regret shows that he was not in command of himself, he did not even know himself, when in the course of the First Interrogation he nonetheless felt confident in judging others. The excessive and interminable nature of the punishment is meant to emphasize the arbitrariness of such deadly judgments that we make of others without even knowing ourselves. The whipping is another sign of Hecate, who carries a whip as one of her trademark sacred implements.[218] The priestesses of Artemis were also armed with flagellating whips.[219] The rites of *Artemis Scythia* involved whipping men until blood flowed freely from their wounds and could be smeared onto her altar.[220] In Sparta, so as to prove themselves courageous enough to be warriors, young men had to endure a ritual known as *diamastigosis,* where they were scourged so severely that they bled onto the altar of *Artemis Orthia.* The priestesses of Artemis would encourage those who administered the initiation not to be lenient to the boys seeking to enter manhood.[221]

Joseph K. defends his criticism of the two warders who wind up being whipped on his account in the following words: "I had no idea of all this, nor did I ever demand that you should be punished, *I was*

---

218 D'Este, *Hekate*, 62, 70, 165.

219 Wilde, *The Amazons in Myth and History*, 92.

220 D'Este, *Artemis*, 56.

only defending a principle."[222] There are numerous passages in Kafka's *Blue Octavo Notebooks* that are relevant to the idea of the relationship between universal principles, truth, and deception:

> Everything is deception...[223] *Can* you know anything other than deception? If ever the deception is annihilated, you must not look in that direction or you will turn into a pillar of salt.[224]

> Truth is indivisible, hence it cannot recognize itself; anyone who wants to recognize it has to be a lie.[225]

> Believing means liberating the indestructible element in oneself, or, more accurately, liberating oneself, or, more accurately, being indestructible, or, more accurately, being.[226]

> The indestructible is one: it is each individual human being and, at the same time, it is common to all, hence the incomparably indivisible union that exists between human beings.[227]

> One can disintegrate the world by means of very strong light. For weak eyes the world becomes solid, for still weaker eyes it seems to develop fists, for eyes weaker still it becomes shamefaced and smashes anyone who dares to gaze upon it.[228]

> Since the Fall we have been essentially equal in our capacity to know Good and Evil; nevertheless it is precisely here we look for our special merits. But only on the far side of this knowledge do the real differences begin. The contrary appearance is caused by the following fact: nobody can be content with knowledge alone, but must strive to act in accordance with it. But he is not endowed with the strength for this, hence he must destroy himself,

---

222 Kafka, *The Trial*, 84.

223 Brod, *The Blue Octavo Notebooks*, 91.

224 Ibid., 97.

225 Ibid., 94.

226 Ibid., 27.

227 Ibid., 93.

even at the risk of in that way not acquiring the necessary strength, but there is nothing else he can do except make this last attempt. (This is also the meaning of the threat of death associated with the ban on eating from the Tree of Knowledge; perhaps this is also the original meaning of natural death.) Now this is an attempt he is afraid to make; he prefers to undo the knowledge of Good and Evil (the term 'the Fall' has its origin in this fear); but what has once happened cannot be undone, it can only be made turbid. It is for this purpose that motivations arise. The whole world is full of them: indeed the whole visible world is perhaps nothing other than a motivation of man's wish to rest for a moment — an attempt to falsify the fact of knowledge, to try to turn the knowledge into the goal.[229]

All individuals, as beings with a unique ego, are a lie in the sense that they have only a relative, dependent, and temporally transient character. They are not unified within themselves, as exemplified by the duality of Joseph K., and they are firmly intertwined with others who appear to be outside them. This sheds light on the innuendo of the mutual recognition of secret lovers, and the intimacy of perfect strangers, that we see between K. and Fraulein Burstner, and K. and Leni. The women, especially Leni, invite K. to recognize the guilt of his imprisonment in the lies of duality, and to win his Trial by becoming One with them. Yet the attainment to Oneness, and the passage beyond illusory knowledge, is tantamount to self-destruction (as the last quote above suggests). It is also "the liberation of the indestructible element in oneself," which is again the same as realization of "the incomparably indivisible union that exists between human beings."

This self-destruction is what the man from the country is threatened with if he disobeys the commands of the doorkeeper and tries to enter into the Law by force. The third interpretation, which K. accepts, is correct to discern that the doorkeeper has no interior knowledge of the Law. If he did, he could not maintain his post. This is because the interior of the Law is the *Truth of the One*, which denies consciousness of multiplicity. The Priest tells Joseph K. that "the scriptures are unalterable,"[230] but this parable, which is "a preface" to the Law, suggests that the interior of the Law destroys all of the principles of the scriptures in which knowledge of the Law is enshrined. We should remember that in observing their strange sense of humor, the Lawyer tells K. that one could not "lay down any fixed principles" in dealing with the Court officials.[231] The Priest is right in reproaching K. for suggesting that the doorkeeper's ignorance should be grounds for his dismissal and the appointment of a wiser man to his post. The doorkeeper can only fulfill his position *because* he is ignorant. Only the self-deluded can preserve the principles of the Law, and only by contrived force. This does not mean that its principles should not be preserved. Should they be abandoned altogether, the world would not exist.

Entry into the interior of the Law is synonymous with the metaphor of "definite acquittal," one of the three ways proposed by Titorelli. It is final liberation from reincarnation in the merely apparent manifest world of ceaseless flux. In connection to Titorelli, it should also be noted that the metaphor of entering unbidden is presented in the spectacle of the three prematurely debauched girls: "As for the girls, he turned them off, he would not admit one of them, eagerly as they implored *and hard as they tried to enter by force if not by permission.* The hunchback alone managed to slip in under his outstretched arm, but he rushed after her, seized her by the skirts, whirled her once round his head, and then set her down before the door among the other girls, who had not dared meanwhile, although he had quitted his post, to cross the threshold. K. did not know what to make of all this, for they seemed to be on the friendliest terms together."[232] This seems to be an intentional foreshadowing of the man from the country debating whether or not to enter the doorway into the Law without permission,

---

230 Kafka, *The Trial*, 217.

231 Ibid., 122.

especially as Titorelli is a man in the confidence of the Court, with a higher unofficial position than many of the Court officials. It has been suggested that the three girls who storm his studio by force, like the three women who offer K. help, are symbolic references to the Goddess Hecate. Titorelli is, of course, the painter of the image of the War Goddess of Justice who is also the Goddess of the Hunt.

The Law maintains the firm ground of "the country," even if those who live there are free from having to deal with the law. The Priest explains that the man from the country was not compelled to remain at the side of the doorway into the Law. He could have gone back into the country and lived his life as he wished. Nevertheless, he lives because there is a Law. The man from country, for whom alone this entryway to the Law has been forged, is a man who is called *before* the Law — as in to the primordial understanding that *precedes* principles of limited relevance. He is called to a wisdom before the scriptures, a wisdom that surpasses the deception of the Law, in a word, to Witchcraft. The parable is clear enough that unlike the doorkeeper, it is his destiny to enter, but he may choose the time of this destiny's fulfillment. If he were to storm through its entrance without permission, the Law would not be destroyed. Rather, he would be ecstatically annihilated by the understanding that the scriptures are a lie and the essence of the Law is the unknowable Oneness of Being.

The same is true of Joseph K. The very first line of *The Trial* is "someone must have been telling lies about Joseph K., for without having done anything wrong he was arrested one fine morning."[233] The passages above suggest that this view, implicitly attributed by Kafka to the perspective of Joseph K., is a naïve presumption. No one has been telling lies about Joseph K., rather the wrong that Joseph K. has done is that he has believed himself to exist at all. Joseph K. *is* a lie, he *exists* a lie. There is some aspect of him that suspects this, and his arrest is not so much a condemnation (of his possessiveness and desire to gain advantage) as it is an invitation into the devastating revelation of the triune goddess that is already seducing him from within. Yet it remains true of Joseph K. that, as Kafka writes in his *Blue Octavo Notebooks*: "His answer to the assertion that he did perhaps *possess*, but that he *was* not, was only trembling and palpitations."[234]

WITTGENSTEIN'S INCOHERENT ETHICS

The most highly reputed philosophers in Western history, from Plato and Aristotle to Locke, Kant, and Hegel, did not confine their work to epistemology or metaphysics. Ever since conservative mobs set fire to the Pythagorean schools and condemned Socrates to death for confronting the likes of Euthyphro and Thrasymachus, the quest to justify some universal standard of ethical conduct has been central to philosophy's defining struggle against religious dogma and the blind rule of force.

While Ludwig Wittgenstein is hailed by some as the preeminent philosopher of the 20th century, or even as the greatest thinker since Immanuel Kant, he never developed a coherent ethics. Perhaps this could be overlooked if Wittgenstein were simply uninterested in ethics, but the fact is that he always believed there to be nothing more important. The theory of meaning in the *Tractatus Logico-Philosophicus*[1] rejects the ethical as nonsensical. Yet the young Wittgenstein attempts,

---

1   Ludwig Wittgenstein, *Tractatus Logico-Philosophicus* (New York: Barnes and

both in that work itself and in his early wartime notebooks,[2] to stow away and protect ethics on a mystically transcendent plane.

In the first section of this paper I argue that this attempt is ineffectual and incoherent from both an ontological and an epistemological perspective. So far as his latter work, as best exemplified by *Philosophical Investigations*[3] and *On Certainty*,[4] Wittgenstein's views on the rational incommensurability of diverse "language games" precludes any understanding of Justice that transcends cultural conditioning or coercion. I hope to make clear why that is so in the second section of this paper. I conclude, in the paper's third section, by considering the late Wittgenstein's often passionate remarks on religion. These remarks accord religious beliefs a unique linguistic, cultural, and psychological status that cannot be accounted for within the framework of the *Investigations* or *On Certainty*. They may have been the attempt of a person with deep moral sentiments to emotionally compensate for, or even to momentarily escape from, the amoral character of his rigorous philosophical work.

1. THE INCOHERENT "ETHICS" OF THE *TRACTATUS*

In his "Letter to Ficker," a potential publisher of the *Tractatus*, the young Wittgenstein claims that the work's main point is ethical, but that it addresses the Ethical by delimiting it from within, which "strictly speaking," is the only way that he believes it could be delimited. The letter reads in part:

> I once wanted to give a few words in the foreword [to the *Tractatus*] which now actually are not in it, which, however, I'll write to you now because

2 Ludwig Wittgenstein, *Notebooks 1914–1916* (Chicago: University of Chicago Press, 1979).

3 Ludwig Wittgenstein, *Philosophical Investigations: The German text, with a revised English translation* (Oxford: Blackwell Publishing, 2001).

they might be a key for you: I wanted to write that my work consists of two parts: of the one which is here, and of everything which I have *not* written. And precisely this second part is the important one. For the Ethical is delimited from within, as it were, by my book; and I'm convinced that, *strictly* speaking, it can ONLY be delimited in this way. In brief, I think: All of that which *many* are *babbling* today, I have defined in my book by remaining silent about it.[5]

However, despite Wittgenstein's claim in this letter, the so-called "ethics" of the *Tractatus* is both ineffectual and incoherent, especially when one traces its origins to remarks within Wittgenstein's wartime *Notebooks of 1914–1916*.

At the core of the ethical problem of the *Tractatus* is its model of an isomorphic, or one-to-one, relationship between linguistic propositions and worldly facts. The correspondence between any statement and the facts that it intends to represent is reducible to one between elementary propositions and states of affairs, and these are in turn respectively reducible to simple names and simple objects. "Meaning" in the sense of "sense" is a function of the way that simple names intend or point to certain simple objects that are elementary constituents of states of affairs. The names out of which all propositions are ultimately constituted function as proxies for objects. We use them in lieu of having to find and point to something every time we want to make reference to it. It is in this sense that a name is supposed to (proximally) *mean* an object. The early Wittgenstein says that "we feel that the world must consist of elements" that are its non-composite "substance," all change being precisely describable in terms of the "configuration" of these "unalterable and subsistent" objects.[6]

The tractarian Wittgenstein rejects any nexus of necessary connections outside of those constitutive of logic. Like Hume, he views the relationship between empirical "causes" and their apparent "effects"

---

5   Brian R. Clack, *An Introduction to Wittgenstein's Philosophy of Religion* (Edinburgh: Edinburgh University Press, 1999), 33.

as a contingent one. "Causation" is no more than a useful concept employed under a given paradigm of representation, not an absolute ontological reality true of the world in itself.[7] This means that there is no logically necessary connection between my willing p and the fact that p actually does come about as an empirical event. According to Wittgenstein, this is true at a level more fundamental than that which differentiates the movements of voluntary and involuntary muscles.[8] My body is a mere phenomenon that cannot be ontologically separated from the rest of the phenomenal world over which I have no control.[9]

If Wittgenstein had not gone on to make any explicit references to ethics, the straightforward ethical implications of such a worldview would clearly be that propositions concerning rape, pillage, and genocide have the same status as those referring to an avalanche. To talk of such "terrible" incidents in ethical terms cannot even be "false," because the statements involved are not reducible to simple names of elementary particulars that stand in precise relations to other such simples in order to constitute a certain state of affairs that either obtains in fact or is found not to be the case, by means of scientifically precise empirical observation. Propositions that cannot be translated into scientific statements of fact do not even refer to *possible* but factually false states of affairs — they are, according to the *Tractatus*, quite literally *sense-less*. In other words, Wittgenstein assumes that no *sensory* experience could serve to verify or falsify them. Such statements violate the isomorphism of language and reality: "the limits of that language (the language which I understand) mean the limits of *my* world."[10]

---

7 Wittgenstein, *Tractatus*, 6.33–6.341, 6.36f., 6.362.

8 Ibid., 5.631.

9 Ibid., 5.641; *Notebooks*, 2.9, 12.10, 4.11.16.

Though it is wholly non-ethical, this position is clearly comprehensible. However, the tractarian Wittgenstein descends into incoherence when he tries to salvage ethics by means of an ill-defined transcendental mysticism concerning the relationship between Will and the World. Wittgenstein acknowledges how profound dissatisfaction with the inhuman doctrine above could motivate a recourse to the mystical: "The urge toward the mystical comes of the non-satisfaction of our wishes by science. We *feel* that even if all *possible* scientific questions are answered our *problem is still not touched at all.*"[11] Although this sounds like a warning against taking recourse to the mystical, if that is what it is Wittgenstein himself apparently fails to heed it.

In the *Tractatus*, from 5.62–5.641, Wittgenstein lays out a doctrine of a metaphysical subject that lies at the "limits of the world." In 6.373 and 6.374, Wittgenstein attributes a "will" to this metaphysical subject, but claims that the facts of the world are independent of this so-called "will." In 6.423 he draws a distinction between two senses of "will," namely, the will as a mere phenomenon, and "the will as the bearer of the ethical." The former would be part of the world of facts, which, according to 6.4 and 6.41, means that it can have no value. However, "the will as the bearer of the ethical" is something of which "we cannot speak" because: "It is clear that ethics cannot be expressed. Ethics are transcendental."[12] Most significantly, Wittgenstein does not take this to mean that the ethical will does not exist: "There is indeed the inexpressible. This *shows* itself; it is the mystical."[13] "Whereof one cannot speak, thereof one must be silent."[14]

Despite this injunction to reverent silence, Wittgenstein does try to use words to gesture towards the significance of the ethical will. Presumably, this is one of the instances of his using propositions that

---

11 Wittgenstein, *Notebooks*, 51; cf. *Tractatus*, 6.52.

12 Wittgenstein, *Tractatus*, 6.421.

13 Ibid., 6.522.

are, strictly speaking, nonsensical, as a ladder that can be cast away once it has been used to see the world rightly.[15] What Wittgenstein abuses his own criteria of proper language use to mumble about the ethical will is that, while it cannot change the facts of the world, the true self circumscribes the world in such a way as to allow one to encompass the amoral facts of the world and assume an *ethical attitude* towards them.[16] This attitude, in turn, somehow *qualitatively* changes one's experience of the world as a whole.[17] What supposedly makes this possible is that, ultimately, the only world is one's own world of experience, which is why Wittgenstein believes that the entire world comes to an end at the death of the true self.[18]

This true "I" is neither the physical body nor the psychological character (the individual ego). It is, rather, a microcosm of some "God" consciousness that can contemplate the world "as a limited whole" from "*outside* of space and time."[19] It seems that to Wittgenstein, this is somehow synonymous with living wholly in and for the present moment, which is a kind of eternal life that relinquishes any regret over the past or hope to change the future.[20] Thus the qualitative change wrought by the ethical will, whereby one's life becomes "happy" rather than "unhappy," occurs on account of aligning one's will with the divine will that the facts of the world be just as they are. This can only be read from in between the lines of the *Tractatus*, but it is repeatedly stated in wartime Notebooks that were obviously the matrix for all of those passages in the *Tractatus* that are cited above:

---

15   Ibid., 6.54.

16   Ibid., 6.422.

17   Ibid., 6.43.

18   Ibid., 6.431–6.4311.

19   Ibid., 6.4312–6.45.

I cannot bend the happenings of the world to my will: I am completely powerless. I can only make myself independent of the world — and so in a certain sense master it — by renouncing any influence on happenings.[21]

The thinking subject is surely mere illusion. But the willing subject exists. If the will did not exist, neither would there be that centre of the world, which we call the I, and which is the bearer of ethics. What is good and evil is essentially the I, not the world. The I, the I is what is deeply mysterious![22]

The will is an attitude of the subject towards the world. The subject is the willing subject.[23]

And in this sense Dostoievsky is right when he says that the man who is happy is fulfilling the purpose of existence. Or again we could say that the man is fulfilling the purpose of existence who no longer needs to have any purpose except to live. That is to say, who is content.[24]

To believe in a God means to understand the question about the meaning of life. To believe in a God means to see that the facts of the world are not the end of the matter. To believe in a God means to see that life has a meaning. The world is *given* me, i.e. my will enters into the world completely from outside as into something that is already there… That is why we have the feeling of being dependent on an alien will. *However this may be*, at any rate we *are* in a certain sense dependent, and what we are dependent on we can call God… In order to live happily I must be in agreement with the world. And that is what 'being happy' *means*. I am then, so to speak in agreement with that alien will on which I appear dependent. That is to say: 'I am doing the will of God.'[25]

In these passages, as in the propositions of the *Tractatus* that emerge from out of them, Wittgenstein claims that the ethical will is that which renounces the thinking subject's illusion of being able to change

---

21   Wittgenstein, *Notebooks*, 11.6.16.

22   Ibid., 5.8.16.

23   Ibid., 4.11.16.

24   Ibid., 6.7.16.

the world according to one's personal wishes. There is a strikingly obvious fallacy here. How can one "renounce" any influence on the happenings of the world if one does not have any influence over those happenings to begin with? The so-called change of "horizon"—that qualitatively transforms the world of the man who does God's will into a "happy" world—cannot be anything that one could possibly bring about by any means. Surely, if the world is at all different, even qualitatively, this affects one's thoughts about one's experience, and these thoughts are themselves facts of the world that are supposedly independent of any personal will.

In the *Tractatus* Wittgenstein clearly states that what cannot be said in logically clear language cannot be *thought* either. However, in the passages above Wittgenstein conveniently claims that the thinking subject is an illusion. But then what is it that re-cognizes that one bears one attitude towards the world, such as renunciation, rather than another attitude, such as striving? What is it (if not some kind of *thought*) that is cognoscente of the qualitative difference of one's experience of the world in the two cases? If we "*are* indeed dependent" on the will of God that wills the facts of the world as if from beyond the world, then we are *always so* dependent. Wittgenstein makes that a conclusion which follows inevitably from his definition of "God" and of the "facts of the world" as two sides of the same coin, as it were. There is nothing "in between" them. Therefore it is not possible for me to change my attitude towards the world, or to resolve to have an ethical will as if I have ever had an unethical one. To the extent that I have a will at all, I will everything that does indeed happen—mine is the solitary "spirit" behind all "material" facts:

> A stone, the body of a beast, the body of a man, my body, all stand on the same level. That is why what happens, whether it comes from a stone or from my body is neither good nor bad. ...

It is true: Man *is* the microcosm: I am my world.[26]

Only remember that the spirit of the snake, of the lion, is *your* spirit. For it is only from yourself that you are acquainted with spirit at all... The same with the elephant, with the fly, with the wasp... Is this the solution of the puzzle why men have always believed that there was *one* spirit common to the whole world? And in that case it would, of course, also be common to lifeless things too. This is the way I have traveled: Idealism singles men out from the world as unique, solipsism singles me alone out, and at last I see that I too belong with the rest of the world, and so on the one side *nothing* is left over, and on the other side, as unique, *the world*. In this way idealism leads to realism if it is strictly thought out. [See TLP 5.64] And in this sense I can also speak of a will that is common to the whole world. But this is in a higher sense *my* will.[27]

Everything from cats torturing mice to Nazis experimenting on starved children, is all my will because I have no conscious self other than a "God" who wills the facts of the world (including my thoughts) just as they stand. I am deluded if I think, wish or appear to will otherwise, but this "delusion" must itself be the will of God. Such is the so-called "ethics" of the tractarian Wittgenstein; it voids any coherent meaning of the word.

2. THE MISSIONARIES AND THE NATIVES

In the preface to *Philosophical Investigations*, Wittgenstein writes that he has been "forced to recognize grave mistakes" in what he wrote in the *Tractatus Logico-Philosophicus*. For the purposes of this paper, the question is whether his running critique of these mistakes is equally destructive of any notion of Justice that would transcend mere cultural conditioning or coercive force. So as to set the stage for answering this question, a brief and general discussion of Wittgenstein's critique of some of the central claims of the *Tractatus* would be in order.

---

26 Wittgenstein, *Tractatus*, 5.63; *Notebooks*, 12.10.16.

According to the *Tractatus*, there is one essential function of language, namely, the description of reality by means of *reference*. As we have seen, this notion that only "stating the facts" of the world is sensibly meaningful has grave implications for ethics. In the *Investigations*, Wittgenstein notes that there are many other functions of language, such as joking, acting, questioning, thanking, swearing, commanding, speculating, evaluating, and storytelling.[28] Language is instrumental.[29] Its words are tools whose meaning is not an object to which they refer, but is rather the manner in which the word is *used*.[30] There is no essence of all language.[31]

To think that words *always* function as the names of things or that they *always* refer to objects (which is in fact only one type of language use) leads to the abstract reification of nouns like "time," "being," "nothing," and "number" as if we could meaningfully inquire into what these "things" are — as if we, as knowing subjects could determine to what objects they actually refer. This causes these unusual "objects" to assume the pretensions of an occult significance. According to Wittgenstein, Philosophy — including his own earlier efforts in the *Tractatus* — consists of over-generalization, over stretching of analogies and the abstraction of words from the context of their normal usage in our ordinary practical lives.[32] We are bewitched by words on account of paying attention only to their surface grammar or apparent place in the structure of a sentence, rather than to their depth grammar or usage in everyday life.[33] Philosophy's "problems" arise only because Philosophy is divorced from the practical tasks of everyday life.[34] These specious perplexities of the annoyingly confused

---

28 Wittgenstein, *Philosophical Investigations*, 23.

29 Ibid., 569.

30 Ibid., 108, 421.

31 Ibid., 16–27, 65, 92, 110.

32 Ibid., 38, 60.

33 Ibid., 664.

pedant are not to be "solved," but rather *dissolved* by remembering the everyday practical employment of language that appears philosophically problematic.[35]

Generality is a matter of degree, and "logical" words are not any more "sublime" or significant than other words.[36] The *Investigations* call the reductionist foundationalism of the *Tractatus* into question. Wittgenstein admits that he was mistaken to believe that there are basic terms from which all others are defined, or that there are any absolutely simple entities of which all others are composed. While it may be said that logic characterizes the basic structure of what is possible within a language (even what it is possible to think), this is a vacuous observation, since there are different ways of stipulating the meaning of terms such as "basic," "structure," and "possible."[37] On this view, what is taken to be "basic" and how one construes a "structure" is never a matter of objective fact, it depends on the aims and motivations of those doing the defining.

All that is universally basic to language, and can never be eliminated, is its *indeterminacy*. Such indeterminacy or vagueness of linguistic terms, and the open texture of language in which they function, does not in practice detract from their utility.[38] The meaning of the same word will differ based on the variety of ways in which it is used.[39] The various ways in which we use words can be thought of on the analogy of *language games*.[40] While the rules of any given language game are arbitrary, these "rules" are what render the game meaningful and they should not be violated so long as one is playing that game and not some other. The practical nature of the rules and the function that they confer on words (and expressions) means that language games

---

35 Ibid., 116.
36 Ibid., 114.
37 Ibid., 89–106.
38 Ibid., 69, 71.
39 Ibid., 43.

should not be judged based upon how successfully they mirror reality. This would be like evaluating soccer on the basis of how successfully it refers to the world. It also does not make sense to judge one game by the standards of another, as if one could sensibly say that poker is inferior to sprinting because it is slower. Each language game has its own aims and standards.[41]

Wittgenstein does, however, observe that there are *family resemblances* between the various applications of certain words. The analogy is to the fact that certain members of a family share their build and gait with others, but not their eye color and facial features, while others share their build and features but not their hair color, and so forth.[42] These irregular overlapping similarities and dissimilarities are also found among games.[43] Soccer and tennis both involve coordinated control of a ball and are similar in this respect, but soccer is also similar to racing because it involves running, and tennis is similar to volleyball in so far as it involves sending a ball *over* a net whereas in soccer one tries to get a ball *into* a net. To the extent that it involves a net at all, however, soccer shares a similarity with tennis and basketball that it does not share with American football (which involves running and controlling a ball, but no net). Games of the aforementioned type are all more similar to each other than they are to board games, and some card games bear a greater resemblance to certain board games than they do to other card games like solitaire (where there are no fellow players or opponents).

By means of this analogy to games and family resemblances, Wittgenstein also critiques the mistaken "ostensive definition" picture of language forwarded in the *Tractatus*.[44] The reader will recall that this notion that words somehow "mirror" objects in the world, so that the

---

41   Ibid., 23.
42   Ibid., 67.
43   Ibid., 66.

former can be distinct enough from the latter in order to *refer* to them, ultimately involved Wittgenstein in a bizarre parallelism between an impersonal immaterial consciousness and an unconscious world of facts. This metaphysical parallelism was shown to be detrimental to the individual's capacity to exercise choice, which capacity must be the basis of any and all coherent notions of ethical responsibility. The heretofore explicated remarks in *Philosophical Investigations* amount to a rejection of this tacit metaphysical dualism of the *Tractatus*.

Now Wittgenstein insists that like all other games, language games only develop their significance within the context of the collective cultural *activities* of a particular society.[45] We are not immaterial minds trapped within physical bodies, waiting only to learn the right words to express our innermost thoughts.[46] We cannot even think, let alone talk to ourselves before we have been taught the *practical* uses of words. For a child to learn language is not at all the same type of phenomenon as for an already linguistically adept British adult to travel in a foreign country and try to learn its language by means of guessing at whether certain words that the non-English speaking locals try to teach him refer to the same object-concepts as certain words in his native language do.[47] It is Wittgenstein's contention that a child first acquires the capacity for any conceptual thought at all only as she is taught language in the context of the shared cultural practices of her society.

The problem, from an ethical perspective, is that while the standards of certain cultures may overlap, people brought up in very different cultures may be unable to find any rationally objective standard of ethical conduct to arbitrate in their relations with one another. Indeed, in *On Certainty* Wittgenstein claims that where there are really two (or more) fundamentally different worldviews there will

---

45 Wittgenstein, *Philosophical Investigations*, 23.

46 Ibid., 32.

be a "combat" that can only end with the destruction of all but one party, or with an irrational persuasion (*Überredung*, literally to "out talk" / "over speak" or verbally dazzle) that converts (*bekehren*, literally "turns") one of the combatants:

> Where two principles really do meet which cannot be reconciled with one another, then each man declares the other a fool and a heretic. I said I would 'combat' the other man, — but wouldn't I give him *reasons?* Certainly; but how far do they go? At the end of reasons comes persuasion. [*Überredung*]. (Think what happens when missionaries convert [*bekehren*] natives.)[48]

Could it be that Wittgenstein's thoroughgoing critique of the inhuman worldview of the *Tractatus* has no greater ethical implication than a return to Thrasymachus's doctrine of "might makes right'? Wittgensteinians who wants to avert this conclusion might claim that it overlooks the fact that Wittgenstein does not see all empirical propositions as holding the same status.[49] "Not all corrections of our views are on the same level."[50] The sense of certain propositions hinges on certain others already being presumed. These "hinge propositions" are more fundamental than others:

> That is to say, the *questions* that we raise and our *doubts* depend on the fact that some propositions are exempt from doubt, are as it were like hinges on which those turn.[51]

Wittgenstein also uses a river's water flow, the sand on its banks and bed, and the more solid bedrock of the river as an analogy for different types of empirical propositions.[52] The analogy is intended to suggest that these different types of empirical propositions admit of

---

48 Wittgenstein, *On Certainty*, 611–12.

49 Ibid., 213, 167, 308, 401.

50 Ibid., 300.

51 Ibid., 341.

significantly different degrees of susceptibility to change over time, even if no sharp distinction can be drawn between them (even if the bedrock can be eroded by the water currents). None of them have the timeless certainty of a priori logical truths. The beliefs according to which we act are not based upon logical tautologies. Rather, our actions are grounded on empirical propositions, some of which are analogous to the river bed and act as tacit background assumptions that lend more derivative propositions the context that allows them to be meaningful — as the hidden river bed shapes the visible flow of the water.[53]

"Earth is older than fifty years" is such a proposition, whereas "Earth is 4.5 (rather than 4.8) billion years old" is not. The latter of these two is always open to reevaluation based on new scientific evidence, while the former is assumed by the very activity of collecting and assessing such evidence. The former is not a logically certain truth, but if it were false it would mean something like our world is a computer simulation that was just started up and all of our "memories" are programmed and so forth, in which case no empirical "evidence" that we amass would tell us anything about what the world (outside the simulation) is *really* like. Our whole "system of evidence" would have to be called into question. That the Earth is older than fifty years is tacitly assumed by the fact that either I am over fifty years old or my parents (or their parents) are. To question such operating assumptions as "Earth is older than fifty years" is to be involved in viciously "going around in a circle."[54]

There is some evidence to suggest that Wittgenstein identified *the* fundamental hinge proposition as the fact of our being *human*, and that this is even more fundamental than "Earth is older than 50 years," the latter deriving its certainty from the fact that a human

---

being has forbearers.[55] There are a handful of passages in *Philosophical Investigations* where Wittgenstein makes reference to a *singular* human "form of life" or "common behavior of mankind" that acts as our most fundamental "system of reference." It does not tell us what human beings *are* contingently at present, but where the limits of possibility lie for any and all *human* thought and action. These limits are defined by phenomenological conditions of existence that are so obvious as to escape notice unless we compare ourselves, collectively, to other *forms of life* — such as various animals or other intelligent beings very different from ourselves. Note these passages in the *Investigations*.[56] In the last of them[57] the reference to "*this* complicated form of life" is clearly indicative of the same thing that Wittgenstein refers to in the first passage[58] as the "*common* behavior of mankind."

While on other occasions he may loosely use "form of life" synonymously with "language game," so that we humans have as many forms of life as language games, it is not these which are the "given" that "has to be accepted." Individual human beings can grow up in more than one culture, or choose to move and live in a different culture than that in which they grew up. Thus when Wittgenstein refers to form*s* of life as that which must be accepted without any further grounds of justification,[59] what he means is that we could not understand a talking lion[60] because lions are "beings different from ourselves."[61] Some intelligent, language-using *feline* species would still remain largely incomprehensible to us, because it is another *form of life*. While we might be able to have limited communication with something like talking lions, since we broadly share with them some

---

55   Ibid., 211, 234.

56   Wittgenstein, *Philosophical Investigation*, 206, 415; xi, 190, 192, 193; II:i, 148.

57   Ibid., II: i, 148.

58   Ibid., 206.

59   Ibid., II: xi, 192.

60   Ibid., xi, 190.

mammalian behavior, Wittgenstein believes that communication with certain intelligent alien life forms would be utterly impossible:

'These men would have nothing human about them.' Why? — We could not possibly make ourselves understood to them. Not even as we can to a dog. We could not find our feet with them.
And yet there surely could be such beings, who in other respects were human.[62]

What Wittgenstein means by "who in other respects were human" is that these beings undertake certain activities that only superficially appear similar to human activities as opposed to those of mere animals who lack intelligent consciousness. Presumably, these activities would include sophisticated purposive manipulation of the natural environment, something like agriculture, city building, and so forth. This causes the interlocutor to refer to them as "men" who nevertheless "have nothing *human* about them."

The key sentence of the passage above is very badly translated as: "We could not find our feet with them." In the original German it reads: "Wir könnten uns nicht in sie finden." This should be literally translated as: "We could not *find ourselves within them.*" Wittgenstein is referring to a phenomenological quality of conscious interiority that contrasts with the outward, merely superficial man-like activities of these intelligent aliens. As noted above, the "soul" does not preexist language games but emerges from out of them, and language games are in turn defined by certain facts of nature. Consequently, "The human body is the best picture of the human soul."[63] Non human beings, such as those from this passage in *Zettel*,[64] have different "souls" than human beings, not on account of their culture but on account of the

---

62 Ludwig Wittgenstein, *Zettel* (Berkeley: University of California Press, 2007), 390.

63 Wittgenstein, *Philosophical Investigations*, II: iv, 152.

different facts of nature that frame their form of life and the language games that they can play within it.

This last point is also the undoing of any attempt to weave an ethics out of the thought of the latter Wittgenstein. Wittgenstein claims that: "What has to be accepted, the given, is — so one could say — *forms of life*."[65] This idea that forms of life are "the given" and must be "accepted" would seem to in itself preclude ethics by denying individual responsibility. While the following passage from *On Certainty* checks this misinterpretation, it only does so in a way that is equally destructive of the idea of Justice:

> 'But is there then no objective truth?' ... 'An empirical proposition can be *tested*' (we say) But how? and through what? What *counts* as its test? — 'But is this an adequate test? And, if so, must it not be recognizable as such in logic?'
> — As if giving grounds did not come to an end sometime. But the end is not an ungrounded presupposition: it is an ungrounded way of acting.[66]

The beliefs according to which we act are not based upon such logical tautologies as A = B, B = C, therefore A = C or 2+2 = 4 = 1+3. None of them have the timeless certainty of a priori logical truths, they can only be affirmed in deed. In other words, by saying that we cannot get outside of the "form" within the context of which we *always already* experience "life," Wittgenstein only means that we cannot do so until and unless we *in fact* cease to be human beings and become some other kind of creatures.

We so-called "human" beings could technologically modify ourselves into becoming life forms as "alien" to what we are now as any beings lurking in the depths of uncharted space. The Wittgensteinian "human form of life" is not, in the end, an inviolable "given" that must be "accepted." It is not a "form" of life in the Aristotelian sense, not an immanent universal that guides the development of specific biological

---

65   Wittgenstein, *Philosophical Investigations*, II: xi, 192.

genera in accordance with some predetermined end. The quote from *Zettel* above certainly makes it clear that Wittgenstein does not view it as a "form" that guides convergent evolution across the cosmos. Man's technological prowess has attained mastery not only over all other life forms on Earth, but now even over his own, which was supposed to have been the most sacredly fixed idea in the Divine Intellect.

Human history thus far does not suggest that our common "humanity" has yet been understood as the basis for a universal ethics of the kind sought by Pythagoras and Socrates at the dawn of Philosophy. Furthermore, it is not as if "Humanity" is something that we must all ultimately realize that we share in common, and that it is only a matter of time before we come to sufficient self-knowledge so as to stop tearing each other to pieces in ever more violent and expansive wars. The twentieth century was the most violent, and the twenty-first has not gotten off to a good start. In the *end*, the ultimate realization of our so-called "humanity" will really be an awakening to the terribly liberating fact that Man alone among the animals is that creature who will be whatever he wills himself to be. We are likely to disagree amongst ourselves about what that is, to disagree more violently than ever because there will be more at stake than in any previous conflict of ideals, and thence could ensue the most total war of all — ending perhaps in an artificial speciation of the human race. This need not happen, but it is possible. Wittgenstein certainly makes no case for it being anything other than a contingency of history whether or not this happens.

The packed earth not only channels the river's water, but may be eroded by it as well. A door cannot be opened or shut without hinges, but swinging a door hard and fast enough could warp or break the hinges. The point of these Wittgensteinian analogies is that the human form of life has thus far provided the context for our cultural development, culminating in advanced technologies such as genetic engineering and artificial intelligence, but our use of these technologies may in turn so drastically change the human form of life that it becomes some other life form altogether. This means that Wittgenstein's notion of a *form of life* is not something that can ground a new Humanist ethics. Patterns of behavior may as a matter of fact overlap significantly enough to allow for mutual cooperation, or they might not — in which case we are left with cunning, coercion or brute force.

What is worse is that Wittgenstein seems never to have been able to reconcile himself to the grave ethical implications of his deconstructive method. There are a number of passages in the notes and transcribed lectures of Wittgenstein's latter period that echo the mystical deference to a "God Almighty" that I have argued, in the first section of this paper, is central to his failure to develop a coherent ethics within the context of the worldview of the *Tractatus*. The tenor of these notes attests to their being at least as important to Wittgenstein as his formal philosophical writings, such as the *Investigations* and *On Certainty*.

3. WITTGENSTEIN'S PERSISTING BELIEF THAT ETHICS REQUIRES THEISTIC FAITH

Wittgenstein's tractarian views on God and the necessarily theistic grounds of ethics were basically unchanged when he returned to Cambridge in 1929. In his "Lecture on Ethics" he discusses his personal experiences of feeling absolutely safe from any possible harm on account of being in the hands of God, as well as his wonder at the existence of the world as if it were God's creation and, finally, of his feeling absolutely guilty in the eyes of God. Even after his return to philosophy in 1929, Wittgenstein seems to believe that ethics treats only of "absolute value," and that otherwise there is no ethics at all.[67] Wittgenstein claims that ethics is supernatural, and that the writing of a book that really treated ethics could not but be a divine miracle.[68] In

67 "Lecture on Ethics" in Anthony Kenny (Editor), *The Wittgenstein Reader* (Oxford: Blackwell Publishing, 1994/2002), 289–290.

a passage from his notebooks of the same period, Wittgenstein writes: "If something is good it is also divine. In a strange way this sums up my ethics. Only the supernatural can express the Supernatural."[69] At the heart of this outlook is a view that human beings cannot better themselves or treat each other justly without some "God" or higher non-human intervention.

Wittgenstein experienced a religious conversion during the First World War, much inspired by Leo Tolstoy's *The Gospel in Brief* (as well as by the mysticism of Dostoevsky, Kierkegaard, and Schopenhauer).[70] He wanted to enter the priesthood after his completion of the *Tractatus*, and settled for the second best of schoolteacher because it afforded him an opportunity to read the Gospels to young children.[71] He was a lifelong reader of the Gospels. Wittgenstein's confession of his sins to others was surely religiously motivated, and his giving away his inherited wealth probably was as well.[72] He referred to himself as "in a sense a Christian" in conversations with his intimate friend Maurice Drury.[73] He viewed belief in a Last Judgment as profoundly valuable if not altogether personally compelling.[74] All of this may have been motivated by the juxtaposition of Wittgenstein's own austere moral sensibility and his view that a merely *human* ethics is impossible.

What is most significant for the purposes of this paper is that Wittgenstein continued to hold this view even after his deconstruction of the *Tractatus*. According to Norman Malcolm, who was an

---

69 Ludwig Wittgenstein, *Culture and Value* (Chicago: University of Chicago Press, 1980), 3.

70 Norman Malcolm, *Wittgenstein: A Religious Point of View* (Ithaca, New York: Cornell University Press, 1994), 21; Clack, *An Introduction to Wittgenstein's Philosophy of Religion*, 31–32.

71 Malcolm, *Wittgenstein: A Religious Point of View*, 9.

72 Ibid.

73 Ibid., 9–11.

acquaintance of Wittgenstein *during his latter years*, Wittgenstein personally expressed to him "a sense of the helplessness of human beings to make themselves better" without some faith in Divine Judgment and Salvation.[75] At least five passages from his later notes on matters of "Culture and Value" attest that Wittgenstein himself was at the very least strongly tempted into embracing such a faith, and into viewing human endeavor as worthless in the absence of it. The first and second are from 1937,[76] the third from 1944/45,[77] the fourth from 1946,[78] and the fifth from a year later in 1947 has Wittgenstein reflecting on the work of a lifetime nearing its end (in 1951).[79]

We can draw several conclusions from these notes taken collectively. While Wittgenstein stresses the importance of changing one's life, he seems to believe that this is as impossible to do in the absence of religious faith in God as it is to forge cold iron.[80] He views his own life's work as having been entirely in vain unless the Divine has somehow ordained or graced it "from above."[81] This is because "wisdom" is merely speculative human intelligence, and as such it is worth nothing.[82] In fact, it is worse than valueless, it is actually a living hell to be damned to the *uncertainty* of human wisdom.[83] Despite the entire thrust of his analysis in *On Certainty* (discussed above), Wittgenstein seems unable to relinquish the desire for the *absolute certainty* that is characteristic of religious faith. This certainty is above and beyond all language games in the sense that, once one arrives at it no change of life circumstances whatsoever should cause one to reevaluate or

---

75   Malcolm, *Wittgenstein: A Religious Point of View*, 9.

76   Wittgenstein, *Culture and Value*, 32–33.

77   Ibid., 46.

78   Ibid., 53.

79   Ibid., 57–58.

80   Ibid., 53.

81   Ibid., 57–58.

82   Ibid., 33.

abandon it.[84] In terms of Wittgenstein's own latter thought, his attraction to the once-and-for-all certitude of faith amounts to "aspect blindness"—a phenomenon that Wittgenstein discusses towards the end of *Philosophical Investigations*.[85] By analogy, it is as if one is only able to see the duck-rabbit as a duck, even once the rabbit aspect has been pointed out as also implicated by the ambiguous lines in the gestalt figure.

In these passages, Wittgenstein claims that in so far as we experience great suffering in life we are each utterly lost, helpless, and condemned to infernal solitude unless there is a Divine Savior and Redeemer.[86] Even when Wittgenstein writes of making a confession of one's failings to other human beings, as he himself felt compelled to do, it is only a means of purging the heart of human vanity and opening it up to the redeeming grace of the Savior. In 1945, only six years before his death, Wittgenstein clearly believed that God alone may judge us or "save us" (from our sins); we should not judge each other or "be furious even at Hitler," because "we are all wicked children."[87]

This view of worldly human life as a kind of imprisonment away from God's grace, as a cage against the walls of which one must beat oneself senseless, is on a continuum with the ascetic mysticism of the *Tractatus*. It should not have survived Wittgenstein's critique of his early philosophy. The fact that it did calls Wittgenstein's latter thought into question, and it precludes the development of something like a starkly Sartrean existentialist ethics on the basis of the *Investigations* or *On Certainty*. As unpleasant as it might be, these religious writings strongly suggest that Wittgenstein was a fundamentally conflicted thinker who never sorted out the first thing about what he really believed. So far as we can tell from all that he left us, he died a splintered man with a makeshift worldview.

---

84 Ibid., 32–33, 53.

85 Wittgenstein, *Philosophical Investigations*, II: xi, 182.

86 Wittgenstein, *Culture and Value*, 33, 46.

BLACK SUNRISE

Sometime during the last days of the Second World War, as allied air power and artillery reduced Berlin to flaming rubble, and then pulverized that rubble, Adolf Hitler stood deep down in his bunker overlooking a pristine architectural model. It was based on Hitler's own designs for a German National Art Museum to be built in his hometown of Linz, Austria. It is well known that Hitler was a failed painter, rejected by the Vienna Academy of the Arts at the age of eighteen. What is less widely known is that he was also an aspiring architect, and in addition to his watercolor painting he would spend hours drafting designs for new public buildings and civic works.[1] Hitler's dream project was an art museum in Linz that was to be the most impressive in all of Germany and even the center of *Kultur* in the world; he himself would design its monumental structure and select its collection. He updated the plans after the annexation of Austria and a visit to the art treasures of Italy in 1938.

As a poverty-stricken young man living at a Vienna hostel, Hitler had spent so much time poring over architectural plans that, when he toured a conquered Paris in the predawn hours of June 23, 1940, the Führer was able to identify obscure modifications in the design of the

---

1   Peter Cohen, *The Architecture of Doom* (New York: First Run Features, 1991).

Paris Opera, such as a small antechamber eliminated during renovations. As the German armies advanced across Europe, Hitler personally drew up the catalogue of thousands of artworks to be purchased or seized for his museum at Linz, including works by Leonardo da Vinci, Rembrandt, Jacob Jordaens, Vermeer, and Rubens. At the same time he organized exhibitions of "degenerate" art across Germany, to put artists on notice that works of this kind would no longer be tolerated. Sculptors such as Arno Breker and Josef Thorak were seen as something more than "mere artists," they were to convey the image of a new type of man whose creation was the goal of Nazism. Hitler had even chosen to cap his inaugural speech as Chancellor with this reflection on the recent German acquisition of the classical sculpture of the *Discus Thrower*:

> Let us perceive how splendid man's beauty once was, and how we may speak of 'progress' when we have not only achieved such success, but even surpassed it. May we find here a measure of the tasks which confront us in our time. May we strive as one for beauty and elevation, so that our race and our art withstand the judgment of millennia.

Indeed, his artistic vision was on a millennial scale. Hitler saw architect Albert Speer as something of a soul mate, confiding to Speer that he took vicarious pleasure in Speer's work since he had always wanted to be an architect. Speer's first task was building a new Reich's Chancellery, based on Hitler's own designs, to be followed by monumental projects in forty cities. Together with Speer, and in accordance with his millennial vision, Hitler adopted something known as the "ruins principle" to govern these titanic building projects. Specific construction methods and design principles would be employed in order to cause the buildings to collapse into picturesque and awe-inspiring ruins like those of Greece and Rome. It is noteworthy, that when the Germans invaded Greece, Hitler gave express orders forbidding the bombing of Athens and demanding that his soldiers sustain any losses necessary to take the Greek capital without damage to classical ruins and cultural treasures. The most dramatic implementation of the ruins principle was at the Nurnberg Rally Grounds and Zeppelin field, where 16.5 square kilometers were covered with travertine and granite. The arena could hold millions of people and its centerpiece was a 360-meter long tribune based on the *Altar at Pergamon*. Already in 1930, three years before becoming Chancellor and at a time when his political career was far from certain, Hitler envisioned Nurnberg as hallowed ground: "If here, in the distant future, archeologists should delve the Earth and strike granite beneath, let them stand bareheaded before the glorious revelation of an idea that shook the world."

From the very evening that he took power in 1933 until the war broke out in 1939, Hitler devoted the largest single block of his time to working with Speer on architectural designs for monumental building projects in the new Reich. On June 14, 1938 he announced that Berlin was to be reconstructed into a new city, *Welthauptstadt Germania* — a "World Capital" which would eclipse Paris, whose beauty Hitler so admired, and which would be comparable only to Ancient Egypt, Babylon, or Rome at its zenith. It was to feature a triumphal arch twice the scale of the one in Paris, and a domed Great Hall at the terminus of its central avenue that would be the largest assembly hall in the world, some seventeen times as big as St. Peter's basilica in Rome, with seats for 180,000 people. There would be an opening in the dome for heaven's light to shine down on the party faithful.

Speer's model of *Germania* was based largely on sketches that Hitler himself had made as early as 1925, when the Weimer government saw him only as a fringe domestic terrorist. Although they publicly announced the general plans for *Germania*, Hitler and Speer kept most of the details secret. This is because anyone with access to them would have quickly realized that the plans called for a large-scale destruction of the extant city of Berlin that was not the type of destruction one would assign to a demolition crew. Its prerequisite was devastation of a kind wrought only by aerial bombardment.

In his youth, Hitler would go with Auguste Kubicek to see Wagner's Operas. Too poor to afford seat tickets, they would stand through the entire performance. His personal favorite was a lesser-known opera called *Rienzi: Der Letzte der Tribunen*, which Wagner had based on a novel by Lord Bulwer-Lytton, the author also of *Vril: The Coming Race*. It is about a medieval Italian populist who aimed to reestablish the Roman Republic of antiquity. While the people at first support Rienzi in a struggle against the nobility, eventually he is betrayed both by them and the Church, and he takes a last stand in battle with his most faithful followers, as his capital crashes and burns around him. In his memoirs, Kubicek relates that Hitler was overwhelmed by *Rienzi* and would speak of executing similar operas that would eclipse even those of Wagner. The two friends began to write an opera together. Later, as he rose to power, Hitler befriended Wagner's son's wife Winifred. Whenever he would watch *Gotterdammerung* together with her, during the fiery collapse that is the drama's final scene he would reach for her hand in the darkness of their theater box and kiss it with devotion.

Hitler and Speer were not the only "failed" artists in the Nazi regime. The single most apt characterization of the leadership of the Third Reich is that it consisted of men who had been aspiring artists of one kind or another. Joseph Goebbels, the Reich's Minister of Propaganda, who briefly succeeded Hitler as Chancellor, had written a novel as well as some plays, and he occasionally composed poetry. Goebbels held a doctorate in romantic drama from Heidelberg University. Alfred Rosenberg, the party ideologist, was a painter who also entertained literary ambitions. Baldur von Schirach, the leader of the Hitler Youth, was one of the Reich's foremost poets. In 1933, Von Schirach penned this verse based on Hitler's own words, which are obviously inspired by the tragic plot of *Rienzi*: "I will be true, though all have forsaken me, I'll bear my banner ever to defeat. Upon my tongue a madman's words awaken, yet if I fall this banner will be taken, to be in death my glorious winding sheet." Hitler saw his youthful experience of Wagner's *Rienzi* as "that hour it all began."

There is nothing more powerful than Art. This is the insight that all of these morbidly fascinating vignettes have been driving at. What it means to say that there is nothing more powerful is that the aesthetic experience, both of the genius and of others captivated by her, is irreducible. Past a certain point, it resists rational analysis because it is, quite literally, incomprehensible. Art is about forging an intimate, partly unconscious, relationship with that abyssal dimension of existence which encompasses all and which cannot be encompassed by any machination. The Abyssal encountered by the artistic genius can, however, become the wellspring of an extraordinary power that, depending upon how its generative or destructive force is channeled, ultimately proves decisive for the rise and fall of civilizations. Political organization and technoscientific development are subordinate expressions of aesthetic activity in the highest sense. The power of Art remains determinative of their destiny, occulted in a dimension beyond their control.

I.

If the advent of Modernity involves an alteration of temporality, a profound change in our experience of time brought about by technological mediation, then it really came into its own during the French Revolution. The attempt of the French revolutionaries to completely uproot traditional modes of life and to rebuild the world on an entirely rational — i.e. non-historical — ground is epitomized by their replacement of the Christian calendar with a new calendar where the revolution was zero hour. They were attempting to restart time, a notion implicit in the German word for the Modern age: *Neuzeit* or "New Time." This is what horrified conservative thinkers such as Edmund Burke and provoked such a vitriolic response from them.[2] By contrast, Modern*ism* emerges with the increasingly apparent failure

---

2   Roger Griffin, *Modernism and Fascism: The Sense of a Beginning under*

of this project. Once large numbers of ordinary people began to experience time not as "ever new" but as a continual decline or decay from a projected utopia—from a tomorrow that seemed ever more distant rather than ever more imminent—various movements against this decadence began among the intellectual and artistic vanguard of modern societies.[3]

This response to the crisis of the modern world began among intellectuals and artists prior to 1914 but was not widely received by society at large until after the catastrophes of the First World War and the Flu Pandemic.[4] During the First World War many young men and women began to believe that the destruction around them was a purgation and that they were about to witness the dawning of a new postmodern age.[5] The devastation wrought by the war, including the attendant overthrow of three absolutist regimes and a powerful monarchy, as well as a worldwide influenza pandemic that claimed the lives of 100 million people, had opened up an ontological void that needed to be filled.[6] This is the mood that allowed Oswald Spengler's *The Decline of the West*, a two-volume scholastic work, to become an international bestseller.[7]

It is also, ultimately, what fueled the rise of Adolf Hitler. In *Mein Kampf*, Hitler reflects that, "Vienna was and remained for me the hardest, though most thorough school of my life."[8] It was there that he suffered four years of extreme material hardship, as reflected by the chapter in *Mein Kampf* entitled "Years of Study and Suffering in Vienna," where he writes "[I]n this period there took shape within me a world picture and a philosophy (*Weltanshauung*) which became

3   Ibid., 52–53.
4   Ibid., 117.
5   Ibid., 155.
6   Ibid., 162.
7   Ibid., 163.

the granite foundation of all my acts."[9] Turn-of-the-century Vienna was the scene of radical experimentation in every cultural sphere. It was home to Arnold Schoenberg, Otto Wagner, Adolf Loos, Josef Hoffmann, Karl Kraus, Arthur Schnitzler, Robert Musil, Gustav Klimt, Egon Schiele, Oskar Kokoschka, Otto Weininger, Sigmund Freud, and Ludwig Wittgenstein.[10]

Under conditions of extreme stress, such as subjection to economic collapse, natural catastrophes, plagues, foreign occupation, displacement, and so forth, a fringe subculture can become the basis for a revolutionary reorganization of the broader society that had marginalized it.[11] Indispensable to such a development is a charismatic leader, who is initially viewed as a madman by the broader society, and who is at once a visionary artist, a prophet, and a teacher.[12] Above all, the synthetic vision that such a person has for transforming the world — which defies all disciplinary boundaries — will seem not only utopian but also megalomaniacal to the dispassionate academic; he will always appear to believe that the world depends on him or rests on his shoulders.[13] Yet this leader will know what Guillaume Apollinaire wrote in his eulogy of Pablo Picasso:

> Without poets, without artists, men would soon weary of nature's monotony. The sublime idea men have of the universe would collapse with dizzying speed. The order which we find in nature, and which is only an effect of art, would at once vanish. Everything would break up in chaos. There would be no seasons, no civilization, no thought, no humanity; even life would give way, and the impotent void would reign everywhere.

The countermovement to Modernity arose in those metropolitan areas most deeply affected by modernization and by the disillusionment

---

9   Ibid., 282.

10 Ibid., 280.

11 Ibid., 104–105.

12 Ibid., 113–114.

with its promised utopia: Berlin, Vienna, Paris, Prague, and New York.[14] By 1940, the Third Reich encompassed the first four of these five ultra-modernist cities. What was common to the various avant-garde social movements of the time was the search for some ideological basis for the *progress* of Western civilization other than the ahistorical Enlightenment rationalism of the French Revolution.[15] Moreover, this reorientation of Modernity would aim, by one means or another, to remedy the subject's relationship to the maelstrom of technological transformation so that this force would be affirmatively appropriated rather than experienced as a source of alienation.[16] Finally, this would be accomplished not simply by breaking with the past, as the French Revolutionaries had sought to do, but by manufacturing mythic "historical" traditions on the basis of which alternative futures could be projected.[17] In a word, these visionaries were part of what I would call an *Archeovanguard*. Their vanguard futurism was rooted in an archaic, primordial past.

The SS was obsessed with Atlantis, believing it to be the primordial Aryan homeland. In fact, the Nazi Party was only a political action front established by an esoteric group known as the "Atlantis Society." In 1917 in Munich, Baron Rudolf von Sebottendorf founded the *Thule Gesellschaft*. Sebottendorf was an esotericist whose specialty was the Persian Sufi tradition. He was also a student of the runic expert Guido von List, who was in turn influenced by the theosophist Lanz von Liebenfels. List and Liebenfels appropriated certain theosophical ideas of Helena Blavatsky and Rudolf Steiner in order to forge their doctrine of "Ariosophy" or Aryanism.

This was a *biopolitical* movement in the deepest sense; its intention was to replace both the traditional dogmas of revealed religion and

14   Ibid., 68.
15   Ibid., 52.
16   Ibid., 56.

the outdated rationalistic "Enlightenment" concepts of liberal individualism with a new politics grounded on a vitalistic cultivation of the "life force" of evolution. This Force was conceived along the lines of the psychical reinterpretation of Darwinian evolution that had been forwarded by theosophists such as Blavatsky and Steiner with their "root races" and so forth.[18] The reconnecting-forwards characteristic of this movement is an overcoming of decay through a re-rooting in the merciless evolutionary force of *life* as they conceived of it.[19] This vitalism was both futuristic in its techno-scientism, as exemplified by Eugenics, and also primordially pagan in its opposition to the "degenerate" ethos of Judeo-Christianity.[20] It was, in a word, Neo-Pagan. It concentrated and crystallized the eclectic New Age movement that was thriving in 1920s Weimer Germany as an antidote to the spiritual bankruptcy of materialism and rationalism.[21] Just as in post 1968 America, this movement drew together Western esotericism, Eastern yoga, and alternative medicine.[22]

The members of the *Thule Gesellschaft* believed that Atlantis — or "Thule" in the Germanic myths — was the lost homeland of the Nordic-Atlantean master race, which had descended from the Heavens and, during the course of Atlantean civilization, had gradually lost its supernatural powers on account of interbreeding with Earth's native hominid population who had only recently evolved from apes.[23] Initially a society for wealthy aristocrats with an interest in the occult, its largely secret membership included some of the foremost Germanic scientists of the day, such as Ernst Haeckel.[24] They routinely met in luxurious rooms at the Four Seasons Hotel in Munich. In 1919

---

18 Ibid., 317.

19 Ibid., 318.

20 Ibid., 332.

21 Ibid., 258.

22 Ibid.

23 Ibid., 138, 187, 197.

the group sought to compete with the increasing political influence of socialist and communist organizations by establishing its own workers branch—the *Deutsche Arbeiterpartei* (DAP).[25] This public political action front, which met at beer taverns rather than at the posh Hotel, later changed its name to the *Nationalsozialistische Deutsche Arbeiterpartei* (NSDAP), "the National Socialist German Workers Party" or *Nazi* Party for short.[26] Hitler, who was then a corporal in the German army, was sent to spy on this workers party on the suspicion that it might be a socialist organization.[27] He quickly saw through its socialistic veneer to its martial and aristocratic occult underpinnings and joined the group himself, rising to be its charismatic leader.

Although Hitler was still poor and hungry, a shabby embarrassment in the milieu of high society, one of the most prominent of the Thule occultists, the German poet Dietrich Eckart, saw a spark of genius in him. He took Hitler under his wing and introduced him to the elite of Munich society, connecting him to the movers and shakers of finance and industry in Bavaria and helping him to secure foreign backing from European and American industrialists, such as Henry Ford.[28] On his deathbed, after Hitler's failed Beer Hall Putsch of November 8–9, 1923 (which led to the arrest and imprisonment during which *Mein Kampf* would be written), Dietrich Eckart said: "Hitler will dance, but it is I who play the tune... Do not mourn for me, for I will have influenced history more than any other German."[29] Eckart was steeped in the Aryan philosophical traditions of India, and he tutored Hitler for long hours at his occult library.[30]

---

25   Peter Levenda, *Unholy Alliance: A History of Nazi Involvement with the Occult* (New York: Continuum, 2002), 13–107.

26   Griffin, *Modernism and Fascism*, 138–139.

27   Levenda, *Unholy Alliance*, 76–77.

28   Ibid., 94.

29   Ibid., 92, 78.

Yet Eckart and others at the Thule Society can only be seen to have fostered Hitler's longstanding interest in the occult. Around 1911 (at the age of 22), when he was still living at the poor house in Munich, Hitler befriended Josef Greiner, an unemployed lamplighter and fellow border. Greiner recalls having often spent hours discussing occult subjects with Hitler. He recounts Hitler's fascination with Yoga and the attainment of *siddhis* or magical powers by its practitioners, as well as the search for Shambhala in the Himalayas.[31] The young Hitler voraciously read an occult magazine called *Ostara*, and even paid an unannounced visit to the editor's offices where he encountered the magazine's founder, Jörg Lanz von Liebenfels—a follower of Guido von List, whose esoteric writings had been the main inspiration for the Atlantis Society. Liebenfels remembers Hitler looking distraught and pitifully impoverished. He gave the Führer-to-be free copies of *Ostara* and bus fare to get back home.[32]

Hitler's involvement with the occult persisted throughout his political career. In the trenches of World War I, he wrote poetry laced with runes, magic spells, and formulas.[33] When Hitler's political career was on the brink of collapse in 1932, and he was suicidal, he turned to Erik Jan Hanussen, a famous astrologer and master of several occult disciplines who, in addition to providing him with astrological advice, taught Hitler nearly all of what would become his characteristic gestural and body language for speaking to mass audiences.[34] Hanussen was a master hypnotist. At orgies that SA leader Count Wolf Heinrich hosted on his estate, Hanussen would entrance attractive young ladies in attendance to the point where they would be brought to orgasm against their will and without any physical stimulation.[35]

---

31 Ibid., 88–89.

32 Ibid., 87.

33 Ibid., 89.

34 Ibid., 102–103.

That Hitler was a vegetarian who did not smoke or drink was probably connected to the practice of Yoga. His close personal friends during his years as Chancellor contend that he was a psychic medium who would enter into hypnotic trances and at times appear to be possessed.[36] All of them attested to his hypnotic power over others in his immediate vicinity. Hitler's charisma cannot be dismissed as the effect of manipulative brainwashing; it is the totality of his faith that radiated from out of him like a magnetic field.[37] He was a shaman — a term derived from the Tungus noun *saman* meaning "one who is excited, moved or raised" and who "knows in an ecstatic manner."[38] As Roger Griffin explains in *Modernism and Fascism*, in traditional cultures such an "inspired figure is always one who stands apart, completely focused on his inner vision. This sets him on a level above ordinary humanity. He is seen to be in the liminoid state, halfway between Heaven and Earth. It means that he speaks with the conviction of higher authority, which puts his followers in awe of him."[39] Hitler's shamanic drumbeat put Germany into a collective trance that could never have been achieved through shrewd propaganda alone.[40] His listeners felt personally addressed by him and could sense his conviction that he was tasked with a mission that transcended the political.[41]

Although he almost never finished his speeches early, Hitler survived a bombing attempt by Georg Elser on November 8, 1939 when — acting on intuition — he cut his speech at a beer cellar short by a few minutes and walked off just before the explosion of a bomb planted in a pillar right beside where he was speaking.[42] This attack was predicted by the Swiss astrologer Karl Ernst Krafft, but Krafft's

---

36 Ibid., 82.
37 Griffin, *Modernism and Fascism*, 273.
38 Ibid., 274.
39 Ibid.
40 Ibid., 278.
41 Ibid., 283.

warning had gotten lost in the Reich's bureaucracy.[43] Krafft, who made the mistake of drawing the Nazis' attention to his accurate prediction after the fact, was rounded up and met his demise in transit between two concentration camps in January of 1945.[44] Hanussen, who knew too much about how Hitler had acquired his art, also ended his days in a concentration camp.

Hitler's library at his "Eagle's Nest" mountain retreat *Berchtesgaden*, which he had remodeled from an alpine lodge into a chateau as an architectural pet project, was found to contain many volumes on occultism.[45] In one of these books, entitled *Magic: History, Theory, and Practice*, the Führer had emphatically marked the margin beside the line: "He who does not carry demonic seeds within him will never give birth to a new world."[46] We are reminded of Kandinsky's *Concerning the Spiritual in Art*, when Hitler remarks that art is the source of "the eternal, magic strength... to master confusion and restore a new order out of chaos."[47] In a speech he gave at the ceremonial opening of the House of German Art, Hitler explicitly linked the New Age movement with the aestheticism of the Nazi regime: "The new age of today is at work on a new human type."[48] It is through this occult understanding of the power of art or craft that we should interpret another of the Führer's tremendous statements: "Anyone who interprets National Socialism merely as a political movement knows almost nothing about it. It is more than religion; it is the determination to create a new man."[49]

Hitler believed that the base matter of mundane reality could be melted down and willfully forged into a work of art based on a total

---

43 Ibid., 236–237.

44 Ibid., 239.

45 Levenda, *Unholy Alliance*, 80.

46 Griffin, *Modernism and Fascism*, 261.

47 Ibid., 289.

48 Ibid., 308.

Weltanshauung.[50] The Nazi Revolution was not just political — it was anthropological in its aim of using, not only state power, but *Technik* (Technology or Craft) to reshape minds, bodies, and machines into a *Gesamtkunstwerk* (Total Work of Art).[51] The term is often taken to be a Wagnerian one. The operas of Richard Wagner epitomize that brand of modernism that the Nazis forwarded with its mythic reimagining of the past as a basis for a projection of the future. Even when recanting his youthful praise of Wagner as the rebirth of Dionysian art that allows for the "spirit's return to itself through the purifying power of myth," in *The Case of Wagner*, Friedrich Nietzsche writes: "Wagner sums up modernity. There is no way out, one must first become a Wagnerian."[52] What is so quintessentially modernist about Wagner is his aspiration to synthesize all of the arts into a single Master Craft that expresses the mythic world-view of his society in a more total and all-encompassing way than had ever been possible in pre-modern times.[53]

As in the case of his artistic aspirations, Hitler was not alone in his occultism. Numerous members of Hitler's inner circle were avid practitioners of the black arts, most notably: Heinrich Himmler, Rudolf Hess, Alfred Rosenberg, and Wilhelm Gutberlet.[54] Among these, Heinrich Himmler's esotericism far surpassed even that of Hitler. Himmler was the head of the SS — the most feared institution in Nazi Germany. Even the *Geheime Staatspolizei* or Gestapo came under the jurisdiction of the SS.[55] Together with Hermann Wirth and Walther Darré, Himmler founded the *SS Ahnenerbe*, whose full name in German translates as "Research Society for the Primordial History

---

50 Ibid., 289.

51 Ibid., 308–309.

52 Ibid., 298.

53 Ibid., 299.

54 Levenda, *Unholy Alliance*, 107.

of the Spirit."[56] The organization's two-fold purpose was 1) to launch archeological and ethnographic expeditions in search of the Atlantean origin and worldwide influence of the Aryan race; 2) scientific research into the paranormal with a view to weaponization of psychic abilities. The SS was the most elite military-industrial institution in Nazi Germany, and the Ahnenerbe was its highest-level think tank. Many of the German intellectuals who belonged to the Ahnenerbe were inspired by the adventure writings of the famous Swedish explorer, Sven Hedin.[57] Hedin maintained continuous contact with his friends in the Ahnenerbe, even though by 1942 it had begun scientific experiments at the camps on account of which its director, Wolfram Sievers, received the death penalty at Nuremberg.[58] As late as July 27, 1942, Hedin was maintaining a correspondence with Schäfer where he forwards greetings from his sister to Schäfer's wife, as well as to Dr. Wüst, and signs "Your faithful and sincerely devoted…"[59]

Dr. Ernst Schäfer of the Ahnenerbe led the SS-Tibet Expedition, which was extensively chronicled in German newspapers.[60] The Ahnenerbe is the actual Nazi group of world-traveling adventurers seeking occult power that was fictionalized in Steven Spielberg's *Indiana Jones* films. These SS officers visited the Dalai Lama in the Tibetan capital of Lhasa as well as the Panchen Lama in Tibet's second largest city of Shigatse. They made pilgrimage to prominent monasteries and they used nine animal loads to bring back a complete 108-volume edition of the *Kangschur*, the sacred scriptures of Tibetan Buddhism.[61] The whereabouts of this particular Nazi acquisition after the conclusion of the Second World War remains unknown.[62] One

---

56   Griffin, *Modernism and Fascism*, 256.

57   Levenda, *Unholy Alliance*, 173, 199.

58   Ibid., 174.

59   Ibid., 192.

60   Ibid.

61   Ibid., 195.

very practical strategic aim of the Tibet Expedition was to organize a joint Tibetan-North Indian strike force tasked with expelling the British from India.[63] Geophysical and earth-magnetic research was also conducted at the behest of Heinrich Himmler himself.[64] Although he realized that many Germans were devout Christians and that he would have to play politics with the Church for the time being, the ultimate dream of the head of the SS, the second most powerful man in the Reich after Hitler, was to replace Judeo-Christianity with a New Age revival of the Aryan Ur-religion of India, Iran, and Europe.[65] Members of the SS were pressed to formally renounce Christianity and a whole set of alternative holidays and ceremonies were devised for them to replace Christian ones.[66] Even the word "Christmas" was prohibited on SS documents after 1939, which made reference to the Solstice instead.[67] Himmler's dealings with the Vatican were as cynical as his dealings with the capitalists were pragmatic.[68] The National Socialists were in principle against capitalism on account of its materialism, which they associated with the Judaism of its foremost financiers, and they only placated capitalistic industrialists as a means to seize power.[69] They opposed Communism, in part, because it retained the materialist delusion at the core of capitalism. Himmler spoke often of India and Indian philosophy.[70] Thus it is perhaps unsurprising that the Humanities chairman at the Ahnenerbe was one Walther Wüst, an expert on Sanskrit — the closest language to the Aryan root tongue. He was also acting president

---

63 Ibid., 192–193.

64 Ibid., 195.

65 Ibid., 215.

66 Ibid., 176–177.

67 Ibid.

68 Ibid., 215.

69 Ibid., 206.

of the *Deutsche Akademie* and Rector of the University of Munich.[71] Since the Ahnenerbe was officially part of the SS, Wüst held the rank of *Oberführer* or Brigadier.[72]

A book that Wüst co-authored with R. Schrötter, and which bore a foreword written by Heinrich Himmler himself, gives us some insight into what the Ahnenerbe considered the canon of Aryan civilization. Published in Berlin in 1938, *Death and Immortality in the Indo-Germanic Thinker's Worldview* treats these Indian, Greek, Italian, German, and Persian thinkers as Aryan forefathers whose knowledge ought to be preserved: the nameless authors of the Eddas and of the Vedas, the Upanishads, and the Bhagavad-Gita, Homer, Socrates, Plato, Cicero, Seneca, Marcus Aurelius, Empedocles, Meister Eckhardt, Jacob Böhme, Angelus Silesius, Giordano Bruno, Omar Khayyam, and Rumi.[73] The Judeo-Christian Bible is conspicuously absent. Himmler identified with the medieval witches who were burned at the stake by the Holy Inquisition of the Church for upholding their pagan practices.[74] He had researched the witchcraft trials to the point that he considered himself an expert on the subject and this, among other things, had led him to view Catholicism as "monstrous."[75] He held the same view of Calvinism.[76] At the root of the persecution of witches was, of course, not any teaching of Christ but the Old Testament Jewish injunction that "You shall not tolerate a sorceress." (Exodus 22:17)

Himmler was also very interested in the Grail legend and tasked certain members of the Ahnenerbe to discover its true meaning. The Grail was originally a pagan symbol that was adopted by Christianity,

---

71   Ibid., 174.

72   Ibid., 175.

73   Ibid., 181.

74   Ibid., 180.

75   Ibid., 206.

like so much of the rest of its symbolism.[77] Wolfram von Eschenbach's *Parzival* and Richard Wagner's adaptation of it inspired Otto Rahn's researches, which came to the attention of Himmler who offered the impoverished young scholar a commission with the SS to continue the studies that had led to *Crusade Against the Grail*.[78] A number of elements of Rahn's Cathar reading of the Grail legend appealed to the Nazis. According to Rahn, the Grail was in the possession of the Cathars of Montségur, whose eradication was *the* principal motivation for the Catholic Church's establishment of the Holy Inquisition.[79]

First of all, *Cathar* is a word of Greek origin, meaning "pure." The Cathars were Gnostic Dualists, probably of Persian Manichean origin, who thought that the material world had to be transcended altogether and that Jesus was not a corporeal being, but an emissary of the Light, who had come to teach the elect how to purify themselves and attain his state of being. He most certainly was not a Jew, since the God of the Jews is the demiurge who created the material world in order, together with his Archons, to blind and imprison the souls of the elect.[80] For example the Cathar saint, Esclarmonde, whom Rahn takes to have been "one of the noblest women of the Middle Ages" believed that Jehovah was actually Satan himself.[81] Moreover, the Cathars were the perfect underdogs or martyrs. They fought against the Judeo-Christian perversion of Christ's true teaching knowing that it was a futile battle, at least *in this world*, one that could only end in martyrdom.[82] Ritual suicide was prominent among them as a more noble death than falling into the impure hands of the enemy, and it is

---

77   Ibid., 223.

78   Ibid., 209, 211, 219.

79   Ibid., 208.

80   Ibid., 204–205.

81   Ibid., 218.

interesting to note just how many Thulists and Nazi leaders also committed suicide.[83]

According to Rahn, the Cathars were Luciferians.[84] He argued that certain Cathars escaped the destruction of Montségur with the Grail — which came into the hands of the Templars, who then used it to finance and build so many of the great cathedrals of Europe in only a hundred years (1170–1270 AD).[85] This Templar tradition was bolstered by Fulcanelli in his 1925 *Le Mystère des Cathédrales*.[86] Before founding the *Thule Gesellschaft*, Baron Sebottendorf was a member of a *Germanenorden* occult lodge that claimed to be an underground survival or revival of the Knights Templar.

In his second book, *Lucifer's Court*, which was commissioned by Himmler's Ahnenerbe, Rahn also furthers the Nazi belief in the special significance of Latin America to the Aryan race. He recounts the Mexican legend of how Montezuma mistook Cortez and his conquistadors for the "White God" who had promised to return some day with his entourage of refugees from Tullan — the homeland of the White Gods that had been subsumed by ice, i.e. Thule or Atlantis.[87] The "feathered serpent," or dragon, was the symbol of these gods. This is also an ancient Germanic symbol; it appeared, for example, on the flag of the Saxons (in gold on a blue field) at the battle of Hastings.[88] Incidentally, Himmler believed that he was the reincarnation of the Saxon king, Heinrich the Fowler. The Serpent, which is one of the Judeo-Christian representations of the devil, is a sacred symbol of the Aryans.[89] According to Rahn, these gods had also gone to the Andes Mountains in South America, because they

---

83 Ibid., 207.

84 Ibid., 213.

85 Ibid., 208.

86 Ibid.

87 Ibid., 183, 197.

88 Ibid., 179.

stood above the floodwaters unleashed by the great cataclysm that had rendered their homeland uninhabitable.[90] Rahn heaps scorn on Cortez and his gang as emissaries of the Church, rather than of the Light-Bringer, Lucifer, whose return the Aztecs had been expecting.[91] Rahn also discovered other traces of the way of the stars and doctrine of the Light, for example among the Celts and the Persian mystics, and took these to be signs of a suppressed Aryan tradition of reverence for Lucifer, the Light-Bearer.[92] Rahn concluded that the God of love, i.e. Venus/Mehr, and the Light-Bearer Apollo/Mithras, were the same figure as Lucifer — who is the accursed "Apollyon" that appears in the *Apocalypse* of John as the Anti-Christ ruling the world in the end times.[93]

As late as January 1938, Rahn gave a lecture based on *Lucifer's Court* at the Dietrich Eckart House in Dortmund, Westphalia, which a local newspaper summarized in the following terms: "The Albigensians were exterminated. 205 leading followers of Lucifer were burnt on a huge pyre by the Dominicans in the South of France after a large-scale priestly Crusade in the name of Christian clemency. With fire and sword, the Lucifer doctrine of the Light-Bearer was persecuted along with its followers."[94]

The Ahnenerbe's most significant work was not, however, in the realm of research into the esoteric literature and history of Aryan survivors from Atlantis, but in the practical development and use of paranormal abilities — especially with a view to military application. Here are just a few examples. The most secretive group within the Third Reich was that of twelve SS Gruppenführers selected by Himmler to sit at the Round Table in Wewelsburg Castle.[95] During the course of

---

90   Ibid., 183, 197.

91   Ibid., 182–183.

92   Ibid., 209, 217.

93   Ibid., 217.

94   Ibid., 220.

an investigation of a German Army General, the Foreign Intelligence
Chief Walter Schellenberg accidentally observed Himmler and the
others at the round table sitting silently and in deep concentration.
Apparently, Himmler had ordered them to exert their psychic influence on the General, who was being interrogated in a nearby room, so
as to encourage him to tell the truth.[96]

The successful allied invasion of Italy had led to the ouster of
Mussolini by his own Fascist grand council. He was subsequently
arrested and was being held at an undisclosed location. Himmler
sequestered practitioners of the "occult sciences" in a Wannsee country house, stocked with the best food, wine, cigars, and so forth, and
tasked them to find Mussolini.[97] This they did with pinpoint accuracy,
despite the fact that Mussolini — who was being held on the island
of Ponza — had no apparent contact with the outside world and all
conventional intelligence methods at the disposal of the Reich had
come up empty.[98] It appears that the two participants with paranormal
abilities who contributed most to finding Il Duce were a Dr. Wilhelm
Gutberlet, a "Master of the Sidereal Pendulum" and a confidant of
Adolf Hitler, and the astrologer Wilhelm Wulff.[99] On the basis of their
information, Austrian-born Luftwaffe officer Otto Skorzeny led a
team of Special Forces glider commandos to swoop down onto the
roof of the building where Mussolini was being held and successfully
extract him.[100]

In the days before AWACS and satellites, it was very difficult for
naval forces to accurately locate enemy warships. Himmler and his
associates created a special department of the German Navy responsible for using every manner of paranormal research to track allied

96   Ibid., 176.

97   Ibid., 227.

98   Ibid., 228.

99   Ibid., 229, 106.

convoys.[101] The man in charge of this top-secret department, which was given the inscrutably vague name of "Naval Research Institute," was Captain Hans A. Roeder, and under his command psychics and astrologers worked together effectively with ballistics experts and astronomers to launch devastating U-boat attacks on otherwise undetectable British vessels.[102] The project was launched after a test wherein the prospective paranormal adepts were shown photographs of the two most vital German naval assets, whose locations were the most highly classified: the *Bismarck* and the *Prinz Eugen*. The British Admiralty was obsessed with destroying these ships, but could not find them. The team of occult practitioners did do so from a room in a Berlin office building equipped with little more than their minds, and they did it with such an exactitude that even the staunchest skeptics in German Naval Intelligence had to consent to opening a department devoted to developing paranormal capabilities — if only so as not to fall behind any potential Allied efforts to discover the coordinates of German ships by such unorthodox means.[103]

In 1938, Karl Wiligut delivered a report on a lecture that Baron Evola had presented before SS circles to Heinrich Himmler. Signed K. Weisthor, the report was entitled "The Restoration of the West on the Basis of the Original Aryan Spirit." Wiligut or Weisthor was also known as "Himmler's Rasputin." Officially, he was head of the Department for Pre- and Early History and a member of the Central Bureau for SS Race and Settlement. He was Himmler's foremost advisor on esoteric matters, such as the redevelopment of Wewelsburg Castle into the ritual headquarters of the SS. A German translation of Julius Evola's *Revolt Against the Modern World* had been published in 1935. Wiligut's report to Himmler basically endorses Evola's view that ethical degeneracy as exemplified by evils such as materialism,

---

101 Ibid., 229–230.

102 Ibid., 230.

relativism, and egalitarianism signaled the West's decline into the Dark Age or *Kali Yuga*.

This crisis was also a moment of opportunity. It could be followed by the dawn of a new Golden Age of Purity or *Krita Yuga*, but only provided that the leaders of Fascism and Nazism recognized the fundamentally metaphysical dimension of their revolutionary struggle. The socio-political activity of the movement, namely its "Aryan Imperial Idea," was only an exoteric manifestation of a spiritual struggle to dominate matter on the part of "the bearers of the Aryan heritage" with their cyclically eternal "Solar conception."[104] It is Evola who submitted his "doctrine of race" to Mussolini and played the key role in rendering Italian Fascism racist, albeit in a spiritual sense.[105] The cosmic vision of history as a perennial alteration between *Untergang* and *Wiedergeburt* that we see in Evola was central to Hitler's worldview.[106] So was the idea of the Aryan origin of heavenly knowledge, which was defused around the world by colonizers from Atlantis. Witness this passage from *Mein Kampf*:

> All the human culture, all the results of art, science, and technology that we see before us today, are almost exclusively the creative product of the 'Aryan.' … He is the Prometheus of mankind from whose bright forehead the divine spark of genius has sprung at all times, forever kindling anew that fire of knowledge which illumined the night of silent mysteries and thus caused man to climb the path to mystery over the other beings of this earth.[107]

Evola was a painter and the foremost practitioner and expositor of Dadaism in Italian Futurist circles between 1920 and 1923.[108] In his autobiography, *The Path of Cinnabar*, whose title references the practice

---

104 Griffin, *Modernism and Fascism*, 15–16.

105 Ibid., 336.

106 Ibid., 282.

107 Ibid., 316.

of Alchemy, Evola explains that it was the purgative destructive force of Dada that attracted him: "Dadaism did not just want to be a new trend in avant-garde art. Rather, it asserted a general vision of life in which the impulse towards an absolute emancipation, which threw into disarray all logical, ethical, and aesthetic categories manifested itself in paradoxical and disconcerting ways."[109] In other words, Dada was for Evola a form of *active* nihilism (in Nietzschean terms) or "deconstruction" (*Abbau*, in Heideggerian terms) that served to clear the canvas for creating a new world beyond the filthy ruins of modernity. As Nietzsche put it in *Thus Spoke Zarathustra*: "And whoever must be a creator of values in good and evil: verily, he must first be an annihilator and shatter values."[110] Moreover, although Evola dubbed his vision of a postmodern world "Traditional" it was in fact an extremely eclectic and innovative synergy of nearly every form of esoteric spirituality in the world. It was, however, a syncretism that passed through the crucible of visionary gnosis in such a way that what was forged could not be picked apart in the manner of a merely scholastic work indefinitely open to dilution through relativistic critique and qualification. Evola's understanding of knowledge *as vision* is key to understanding the connection between his Dadaist venture and his pro-Nazi ultra-Fascism.[111]

Fascism characteristically blends "the technocratic with the mythic, the ultramodern with the primordial."[112] The primordial past that the Nazis were reaching back towards was a mythic projection of a different order than that of Fascist Italy, which did bear a quasi-historical relationship to Ancient Rome. The Nazis invented or discovered their primordial Aryan past, as Promethean world-colonizers from Atlantis, on the basis of a radically futural projection

---

109 Ibid., 40.

110 Ibid., 43.

111 Ibid., 41.

of revolutionary social transformation.[113] Although National Socialism was, by definition, "nationalist" it was not so in an insular sense. The leading Nazis certainly saw their ultimate mission as the salvation of Western civilization at large from the degenerative effects of the twin evils of liberal capitalism and communist materialism. Yet their vision of social transformation was so radical and drew on so many "Eastern ideas" — albeit ones with origins in Aryan India — that the civilization they were seeking could really be called *post-Western*.[114] The future world that they wished to bring about was substantively different both from the present and from any conventionally acknowledged past epoch.[115]

In his essay "Total Mobilization" (1930) and his book *Der Arbeiter* (1932), Ernst Jünger futuristically predicts the coming of *Homo technologicus* — "The Worker" that has evolved into a new, post-human *type*. After having served on the Western Front continuously from December 1914 until he was seriously wounded and hospitalized in August of 1918, Jünger wrote that since the armistice "a new constellation" had appeared over the horizon "betokening a turning point in world history, just as it once did for the kings of the East… From this point on the surrounding stars are engulfed in a fiery blaze, idols shatter into shards of clay, and everything that has taken shape hitherto is melted down in a thousand furnaces to be cast into new values." Jünger believed that "those still capable of a solution" would, in a "prosecution of the war by other means," alchemically transform Man and his world in the forge of Vulcan and bring forth a New Culture, a New Man, a New World Order. Through technological mastery of his terrestrial home, *Homo faber* (the Worker who is a fusion of technocrat and solider) would become *Homo transcendens* — a new type of

---

113 Ibid., 257.
114 Ibid., 267.

being. This is a Promethean vision of perfecting or transmuting matter in such a way as Man is also thereby perfected.

The same thing that drew Ernst Jünger and other militaristic modernist artists to National Socialism is what appealed, on a more unconscious level, to many other academics working in the natural and applied sciences: not a romantic rejection of the technological development that had uprooted traditional society, but a vitalistic and onto-theological understanding of apparently dehumanizing Technology as a fateful expression of a uniquely perilous and promising human existence. They felt that applying their positivistic techno-scientific knowledge could be integral to the project of forging a new world civilization, rather than becoming a force that is merely corrosive to old forms of life. These were people who understood that the destructive force of technological instrumentalization was such that nostalgia for undermined traditional communities had become futile, and so instead they longed for the revolutionary advent of a new *Volksgemeinschaft* of the future.

Julius Evola concurred with Ernst Jünger's metaphysical interpretation of the essence of Technology. In *The Path of Cinnabar*, Evola offers this affirmative explication of the positively destructive force of technology as it had been "revealed" to Jünger and other German visionaries amidst the mechanized slaughter of the First World War:

> Technology in its elemental aspect operated like a non-human force awakened and set in motion by Man. He must face up to this force, become the instrument of the machine, and yet at the same time master it, not just physically, but spiritually. This is only possible if human beings make themselves capable of a new form of existence, forging themselves into a new type of human being, who, precisely in the midst of situations which are lethal to anyone else, is able to derive from them an absolute sense of being alive. To this end it is, however, necessary to transcend entirely the way of being, the ideals, the values, and, the whole world view cultivated by the bourgeoisie.

The destruction of traditional values and the rise of the bourgeoisie, which began with the birth of Cartesian subjectivity and culminated in the French Revolution, did not lead to a rational "Enlightenment" as it was supposed that it would. The Enlightenment thinkers, especially the most radically atheistic ones who prepared the way for the revolutionary Cult of Reason, were deluded in thinking that after dynamiting the edifices of centuries of tradition they would reach a solid bedrock of rationality — the Laws of Nature, Human Nature, and so forth — on which to build a new order. Once this foundation was, at least subconsciously, discovered to be lacking, the anti-traditional character of the Modern embrace of technical innovation became expressive of a merely passive nihilism.

In response to this, modern*ist* progenitors of postmodernity such as Friedrich Nietzsche called for an *active nihilism* of creative destruction. This meant the affirmative embrace of the destruction of traditional values or at least an active encouragement of the disintegration of the decayed sacred canopy that they had held together to shield human life from the terrifying boundlessness of a "Cosmos" that may truly be a Chaos. However, this affirmation would now be coupled with a sober realization of the groundlessness of our existence and yet, in the face of the ineradicable human need for meaning, it would also rise to the demand to *create* new values and to write a new mythic history on the basis of which one could build a new world *as one creates a work of art.*[116]

II.

That a group of aspiring artists and esoteric occultists would seize power in some fourth world wasteland would not be so incredible. The Third Reich was, however, no cult contrived in the midst of a jungle or on some desert island. In the early 20th century, Germany was the most scientifically advanced country on the face of the Earth.

The *Technische Hochschulen* and Kaiser Wilhelm Institutes were widely regarded as the best scientific research centers in the world. The submarine or *U-boat*, which spectacularly sunk the *Lusitania*, was the first wonder weapon to be yielded by this superior technical establishment. The original Volkswagen, a car designed to turn the motorway into a mass transit system, was so sleekly crafted that it has since been celebrated as a paragon of modernism.[117] Nazi "macro-planning" for modernization of the Reich was decades ahead of its time with its projected infrastructure to accommodate nine million private cars while routing motorways in a nature-sensitive way and providing for pedestrian zones and cycle-lanes within vast "cities of the future."[118] Socialistic aspects of German National Socialism included dramatically improved sports and public recreation facilities, subsidized holidays, and "hygienic" factory conditions and housing estates.[119]

In 1936 Hitler broadcast the Berlin Olympics to televisions set up in public places. This was the first wireless transmission of moving images in recorded history. By 1939, at a cost of 650 Marks the Fernseh-Volksempfänger became the first television set available for private use. It made its entrance at the 16th Great German Wireless Exhibition, where only two years later — in 1941! — color TV transmission was demonstrated.[120] By 1939, German rocket technology was a full generation ahead of similar developments anywhere else. The Horton Brothers Flying Wing incorporated most of the essential design principles of the Northrop B-2 Stealth Bomber, some thirty years before its time. Nearly all of the leading quantum physicists of the early twentieth century were of German extraction: Max Planck, Max Born, Werner Heisenberg, and Erwin Schrödinger.

---

117 Ibid., 337.

118 Ibid., 328, 337.

119 Ibid., 331.

Computer technology in Nazi Germany was far in advance of
that of any other industrial nation. Alan Turing's breakthroughs in
the field, which culminated in his seminal 1950 paper on "Computing
Machinery and Intelligence," were largely driven by his services in the
effort to break the code of the Enigma Machine used by the Germans
for encrypted communications during the war.[121] In 1945 advancing
allied forces discovered, in a hidden cellar in a small Bavarian village,
the fourth prototype of the first fully operational modern program-
controlled electronic computer manufactured in 1941 by Konrad
Zuse.[122] The particular model discovered by the Allies had been fund-
ed by the Third Reich's military-industrial Aerodynamic Institute for
stress-testing vibrating airframes, such as those of the aforementioned
exotic aircraft being developed by the *Luftwaffe*.[123]

What had initially driven German scientists to lead in the development of electronic computers, as opposed to glorified mechanical
calculators, was the need to draw the solution curve for problems
of quantum physics — another cutting-edge scientific field where, as
noted above, almost all of the leading contributors were German.[124]
In the same year, nearly a decade before Turing's paper, the May 18,
1941 issue of *Koralle* — a magazine for "Knowledge, Entertainment,
and *Lebensfreude*" that was something like *Wired* for Aryan house-
holds — ran a lead article on Artificial Intelligence under a headline
asking "Can Machines Think?"[125] The darkest side of computer
technology development in the Reich was punch card sorting equipment custom designed by Dehomag, the German subsidiary of IBM,
on commission for the SS. Billions of specially printed punch cards
were used to keep track of the millions of prisoners and slave laborers

---

121 Ibid., 310–311.

122 Ibid., 311.

123 Ibid., 312.

124 Ibid., 311.

of the Reich.[126] All of the sophisticated equipment developed for this purpose was subsequently moved to IBM New York, which had consistently made millions of Reichsmarks on its subsidiary's work for the SS.

In the late 19th century Nikola Tesla laid the groundwork for wireless or remote radio control of mechanical devices, including a remote-controlled motorboat armed with torpedoes that he unsuccessfully tried to sell to the US military.[127] Instead, it would be the Germans who, two decades later, in 1916 first deployed Tesla's technology in unmanned systems in order to compensate for their being outnumbered by their enemies.[128] The Germans also led the use of robotics for warfare during the Second World War when their Goliath robot of 1940 became the first battlefield-deployed device capable of taking out enemy tanks and bunkers with the 132 pounds of explosives carried by each unit. The Germans fielded 8,000 of these on the Eastern Front where their troops were outnumbered 3-to-1 on the way to Moscow.[129]

The Goliath is remarkably close in design to the Foster-Miller Corporation's Talon robot, despite preceding it by six decades. Remember that the Germans deployed the world's first cruise missiles (V-1), ballistic missiles (V-2), and jet fighters (Me-262).[130] Then it should not come as a huge surprise that the very first remotely piloted drones, the FX-1400 also known as "the Fritz," was a German-designed 2,300 pound bomb driven by a rocket motor, propelled by four small wings, and fitted with tail controls.[131] The device, which was radio controlled by a remotely located operator using a joystick,

126 Ibid., 312.

127 P.W. Singer, *Wired for War: The Robotics Revolution and Conflict in the 21ˢᵗ Century* (New York: Penguin Books, 2010), 46.

128 Ibid., 47.

129 Ibid., 47.

130 Ibid., 48.

was released from out of a plane flying at a high enough altitude, at a sufficient distance from the target, and at an angle that deceptively convinced the enemy that it was not a bomber coming in for a strike.[132] The first drone strike using the Fritz system was on the Italian battle-ship *Roma* that tried to defect to Allied forces in 1943.

Germany was also on the cutting edge in the fields of Psychiatry and Medicine. The world's most prestigious research center for the mind sciences was the Kaiser Wilhelm Institute of Psychiatry in Munich. The medical establishment of Nazi Germany was home to the highest-quality epidemiological research in the war on cancer. The Nazis waged an aggressive anti-smoking public-information campaign in an effort to decrease incidents of lung cancer.[133] They were at least two or three decades ahead of the rest of the Western world in this respect. It is a little-known fact that the Nazis were quite interested in holistic herbalist and homeopathic alternatives to reductionist modern medical practices.[134] Himmler was receiving reports from a certain army captain, Emmerich von Moers, who had been sent to live with various tribes in the Amazon basin so as to learn what rainforest plants could be used as cures for malaria, syphilis, and serious skin conditions, as well as in the creation of aphrodisiacs and natural sweeteners. Himmler declared that organizing an SS expedi-tion to Amazonia in order to conduct extensive field research and bring back resources for pharmacological development ought to be "one of the first tasks to be undertaken in peace time."[135] This was justi-fied on account of the supposedly "enormous" economic advantage that would accrue to Germany for making scientific breakthroughs in pharmacology.[136]

---

132 Ibid., 48.

133 Griffin, *Modernism and Fascism*, 267, 337.

134 Ibid., 258–259.

135 Ibid., 259, 337.

So, Eugenics is not the only biomedical field in which Nazi Germany took the lead, although that is also worth mentioning—since, at the time, Eugenics was widely regarded across the Western world as a progressive techno-scientific project. What was different about Nazi Eugenics was that the structure of the regime allowed for the same ideas that predominated among the Western political elite in general at the time to be much more ruthlessly and efficiently implemented in Germany than in liberal democracies.[137] With programs such as *Lebensborn* the Nazis could accomplish what Winston Churchill could not when, in his term as British Home Secretary, he introduced a Eugenics bill into Parliament that included enforced sterilization. The concerns that led him to do so are summarized in this passage of a memorandum that Churchill had written to Prime Minister Henry Asquith:

> The unnatural and increasingly rapid growth of the feeble-minded and insane classes, coupled as it is with a steady restriction among all the thrifty, energetic and superior stocks, constitutes a national and race danger which it is impossible to exaggerate. … I feel that the source from which the stream of madness is fed should be cut off and sealed up before another year has passed.[138]

That within less than a decade the National Socialists were able to transform an economically bankrupt, socially humiliated, and politically dysfunctional Germany into the world's leading techno-scientific and industrial power is a testimony to their futuristic ethos.[139] Conservative luddites would never be capable of such an accomplishment. One should not make the mistake of thinking that the military defeat of Nazi Germany is any indication of American military-industrial superiority. The Nazis were defeated only by the United States *and the Soviet Union together.* Stalin's totalitarian state sacrificed *thirty*

---

137 Ibid., 330.
138 Ibid., 329.

million Russian lives to resist and finally overcome the Germans on
the Eastern Front. Had we in the United States shared a border with
the rapidly expanding Reich, as Russia did, the war might have ended
very badly for us. From the audacious launch of Operation Barbarossa
in 1941 through to the Battle of Berlin in 1945, Nazi Germany *simultaneously* fought against *both* of the two "superpowers" that divided the
Earth between themselves in the second half of the 20th century.

Furthermore, the rise of the United States to a position of techno-
scientific global dominance from 1945 and onwards is largely a function of the willingness of the American Intelligence establishment to
seek out and recruit the brightest Nazi German "war criminals" in
violation of both domestic US law and the Allied Potsdam and Yalta
agreements with the Soviet Union.[140] Those who were tried and punished for war crimes at Nuremberg were not the worst Nazis — they
were simply the most dispensable. Beginning in May of 1945, the Joint
Intelligence Objectives Agency under the auspices of the Office of
Strategic Services (the precursor of the CIA) began recruiting Nazi
rocket scientists, engineers, psychiatrists and doctors to continue
their research in the United States. With their corporatist background,
these scientists and technicians were far more amenable to striking a
deal with American capitalists than they were with Soviet communists
who also had a more profound hatred of Germans for having invaded
their homeland and spilled so much Russian blood.

The project was codenamed "Operation Paperclip" in a reference
to the paperclips used by American intelligence to attach almost
wholly fabricated employment records and false political biographies
to the dossiers of the imported Nazi German scientists, so that they
would be granted security clearances to work at sensitive military-
industrial installations in the United States.[141] The most famous of

140 Linda Hunt, *Secret Agenda: The United States Government, Nazi Scientists, and
    Project Paperclip, 1945–1990* (St Martin's Press, 1991).

141 Annie Jacobson, *Operation Paperclip: The Secret Intelligence Program That*

these imported Nazi scientists is, of course, Werner von Braun — the founder of NASA, who was responsible for beating the Soviets in the space race by landing American astronauts on the Moon. Von Braun was an SS Major and the majority of his Apollo program scientific team consisted of card-carrying members of the Nazi party who were exempted from prosecution. The glory of Apollo was an afterglow of the Faustian project of National Socialist Germany.

The German scientists recruited into anti-Soviet American military research and development via "Operation Paperclip," organized by Dulles' nascent half-Nazi CIA, were far from loyal to the United States. The rocket scientists continuing their work on V-2 rockets in New Mexico would routinely sabotage tests, even deliberately misdirecting these ballistic missiles — on one occasion to a populated area in Mexico.[142] They received money and coded messages from unknown foreign sources at illegal mail drops in Texas.[143] Sometimes they would even cross the border into northern Mexico to directly communicate with their counterparts who were spread throughout Latin America, especially Argentina and Chile.[144]

These men, who would go on to leadership positions within NASA and direct the Apollo Program, included SS Major Wernher von Braun, who had been using slave labor to construct V-2 rockets at Peenemünde, Arthur Rudolph, who had been designing an ICBM for the Reich and went on to direct the Saturn V rocket project, and last but certainly not least, a certain Kurt Debus who did even more sensitive work for the SS (which we will come to shortly) before becoming the first director of NASA's Kennedy Space Center.[145] How long these men remained hardcore Nazis is attested by the fact that they would set key NASA missions for dates commemorating events that were

---

142 Joseph P. Farrell, *Roswell and the Reich: The Nazi Connection* (Kempton, IL: Adventures Unlimited Press, 2010), 353.

143 Ibid., 355.

144 Ibid., 354.

particularly meaningful to the Reich. For example, two of the Apollo missions landed on the Moon on April 20th, Adolf Hitler's birthday. The first was the unmanned Surveyor 3, on April 20, 1967, and the second was Apollo 16, which was even delayed for a number of hours by ground control, purportedly for troubleshooting, until the problem somehow cleared itself up just after midnight on April 20, 1972.[146]

But why would the Americans allow such a deep penetration of their intelligence-military-industrial complex by enemy agents? Because they had no choice. The United States did not win the war. In fact, the war is not over. While the Reich's elite lost the battle, they did so in a way that has positioned them to win the war with overwhelming force. To understand how this is the case, we have to familiarize ourselves with a German idea known as *Weltanschauungskrieg*. Although poorly translated by American military officers as "psychological warfare" (and later, psychological operations or PsyOps), the German term actually means something quite different: worldview warfare.

Since "Reality" is not directly ascertainable and is reconstructed by the synthesis of perceptual patterns in our minds, the construction of a simulacrum or virtual "reality" essentially concerns the manipulation of this information processing.[147] Orson Welles' 1938 radio adaptation of H.G. Wells' *War of the Worlds* was an early mass experience of the barrier between reality and virtual reality dissolving.[148] Although, unlike today, control over radio broadcasting rested in the hands of only a few supposedly responsible and rational actors, like CBS, millions of people who turned on the program at some point after the explanatory introduction became hysterical over an event that turned out to be fictional. The highways were jam-packed with people fleeing in

146 Richard C. Hoagland and Mike Bara, *Dark Mission: The Secret History of NASA* (Port Townsend, WA: Feral House, 2009), 322–323.

147 Jim Blascovich and J. Bailenson, *Infinite Reality: The Hidden Blueprint of our Virtual Lives* (New York: William Morrow, 2011), 14.

their cars. Some aimed their shotguns at water towers that resembled the radio program's description of the alien invaders' tripod-shaped crafts. Others wrapped their heads in towels as a safeguard against mind control. Even scientists rushed to the scene in New Jersey, to examine the environs of the alleged first contact.[149]

The limits of human perception are central to the question of the line between reality and virtual reality. An experiment carried out by Dan Simons at the University of Illinois demonstrated that nearly half of people who watched videos of team members passing a basketball back and forth to each other, and who were asked to count the number of passes, missed a person in a gorilla suit walking right into the middle of the players, stopping, beating his chest for around seven seconds, and then walking off the scene.[150] Researchers refer to this phenomenon as "inattentional blindness" or not seeing things that are there. This manipulation of reality features prominently in the sleight-of-hand tricks practiced by stage magicians.[151] But in the case of the gorilla suit, I suspect that something else is at work as well. The gorilla-suited man can "disappear" because in that particular context he is absurd. People *do not want* to see him. Something that badly violates our perceptual expectations and is too demanding on our interpretive matrix is simply filtered out by many, if not most people. SS experts in worldview warfare would have understood this well. Absurdity of the kind that has been characteristic of close encounters for decades could act as a kind of stealth cloaking device, bypassing the scientific establishment of the target society, who will dismiss such high strangeness. This grants direct operational access to elements of society that have been rendered all the more vulnerable and isolated on account of the dismissal and disbelief of authorities.

149 Ibid., 6.

150 Ibid., 12.

What am I driving at? The fact that flying saucers were invented
in Nazi Germany. They were a response to a very concrete problem
tackled by world-famous German engineering. In aeronautical engineering there is something known as the "boundary layer," a thin layer
of air that clings to an airframe, causes turbulence, and results in a
drag on the aircraft that limits its speed and maneuverability. Initially,
German engineers working on contract for the *Luftwaffe* approached
this problem by cutting slots into experimental aircraft and installing auxiliary engines that would suck in the boundary layer through
these slots. However, this proved unworkable on an airframe that has
wings sticking out of it or other protuberances.[152] At the same time,
the Horton Brothers were experimenting with more aerodynamic
designs such as their Ho-229 flying wing (which was retrieved by the
Americans in 1945, and eventually became the basis for the B-2 stealth
bomber). It was found that these designs, which eliminate protuberances and lower the aspect ratio of the aircraft, also dramatically reduce the boundary layer and help to minimize drag.

Consequently, around 1941 a design team initially based at
Peenemünde realized that if the Horton aerodynamics were pushed
even further from a conventional airframe beyond a flying wing and
to the point of a circular wing or disc shaped airframe, it would also be
easier to suction what little was left of the boundary layer.[153] A ramjet
engine could be installed inside the saucer in such a way that it rotates
around the central cabin and suctions the boundary layer through
slots built into the periphery of the saucer.[154] This would mean an aircraft with *no* drag, *no* turbulence, and thus fantastic maneuverability.
The exhaust thrust would be vectored so that the craft could hover
(something airplanes cannot do) and execute an essentially vertical
takeoff and landing from almost any type of terrain, which would

---

152   Jospeh P. Farrell, *Roswell and the Reich*, 472.

153   Ibid., 489, 493–494.

become increasingly useful as German airfield runways came under heavy allied bombardment.[155] The German engineers involved with this project included Viktor Schauberger, Walter and Reimar Horten, Heinrich Fleissner, George Klein, Richard Miethe, Rudolf Schriever and Klaus Habermohl; the Italian Giueseppe Belluzzo was also involved as a liaison to Mussolini's regime.

But these jet aircraft, although brilliantly unconventional in design, did not become potentially time-warping anti-gravity devices until they were appropriated by, and fused with, another even more highly classified wartime German research project. In 1944, an SS think tank under the command of Dr. Hans Kammler seized control of the *Luftwaffe* saucer project at Peenemünde and relocated it to a Top Secret facility at the Skoda Works industrial site located at Pilsen in Nazi occupied Czechoslovakia.[156] Among the team of engineers, Viktor Schauberger was very resistant to work under SS conditions and despite being threatened with his life, demanded that the slave labor force of technicians from the nearby Mauthausen concentration camp that was being employed at the facility be removed from the camp and properly treated like civilians.[157] It is here on the western outskirts of Prague, where the project's administrators were based, that on the 14th of February in 1945, the first jet-powered flying saucer was successfully test flown at a speed of around 1,250 miles per hour and at a maximum altitude of 40,000 feet.[158]

What is more important is that Obergruppenführer Kammler aimed to synthesize the saucer airframe with an incomparably more advanced power plant and propulsion device that was under development by his research group, the *Kammlerstab*. This device was known as *Die Glocke* or "the Bell," and the codename of the program to

---

155 Ibid., 366, 401, 489.

156 Joseph P. Farrell, *Roswell and the Reich*, 493.

157 Joseph P. Farrell, *Reich of the Black Sun: Nazi Secret Weapons and the Cold War Allied Legend* (Kempton, IL: Adventures Unlimited Press, 2004), 209.

develop it was *Projekt Chronos* — referring of course to Father Time, the progenitor of the Greek race of Titans such as Prometheus and Atlas, whose name is the root of our words "chronology" and "chronometer." The Romans referred to him as Saturn. This project had the highest level of classification in all of wartime Nazi Germany, a classification that was in fact unique to the Bell. Of all of the *Wunderwaffe* or "wonder weapons" being designed at the time, this is the one that was designated *Kriegsentscheidend* or "decisive for the war."[159]

The Bell was a bell-shaped ceramic container about twelve feet high and nine feet wide.[160] It housed two counter-rotating cylindrical metal drums coated with pure mercury and centered on a hollow hard metal axis that acted as a receptacle for a radioactive compound of an isotope of mercury mixed with thorium and beryllium that was violet-gold in color and had a jelly-like consistency at room temperature.[161] One cylinder was set inside the other and they were sent spinning in opposite directions at a tremendous speed by continuous AC power while the device was periodically pulsed with high voltage DC.[162] This DC pulsing produced a beehive-like buzzing sound that got the Bell nicknamed "the Hive."[163]

Initial testing of this device resulted in the death of five out of the seven scientists on the original research team, which consequently had to be disbanded and replaced with a second team.[164] The Bell totally broke down the cellular structure of their bodies. Why it did so can be surmised from the effect that it had on other organic materials, such as plants that were deliberately placed in its environs during the

---

159 Joseph P. Farrell, *Reich of the Black Sun*, 178.

160 Nick Cook, *The Hunt for Zero Point* (London: Random House, 2001), 191–192.

161 Igor Witkowski, *The Truth About the Wunderwaffe* (Farnborough, England: European History Press, 2003), 232–233.

162 Joseph P. Farrell, *The SS Brotherhood of the Bell* (Kempton, IL: Adventures Unlimited Press, 2006), 253.

163 Ibid., 252.

tests. These first turned grey, as if the chlorophyll in them had totally decayed, and then they would go on living for about a week, at which point the plants would decompose into a grey goo within eight to fourteen hours without any of the characteristics of normal decomposition, such as the smell of rot.[165] Mosses, ferns, fungi, molds, animal tissues, egg white, blood, meat, and milk, as well as a wide variety of insects, snails, lizards, frogs, mice, and rats, that were subjected to the Hive also demonstrated signs of enduring some distortion in the flow of time.[166] Before dying the members of the first team suffered severe disorientation, including their sense of the passage of time, memory problems, sleep problems, loss of balance, muscle spasms, and a permanent metallic taste in their mouths.[167] Developing methods to minimize these effects became a priority, and they eventually succeeded in doing so.[168]

Meanwhile, the effects led to a safety protocol that included the following precautions.[169] Experiments were conducted in an underground chamber, which featured a pool. This chamber was lined with ceramic bricks and rubber matts that served to insulate it. The Bell was run for only a few minutes at a time. The rubber matts were removed after each test, and then the ceramic bricks were washed down with brine by concentration camp inmates (who probably had to be regularly replaced). On account of the fact that they could not be electrically grounded while the Bell was in operation, the Project Chronos technicians had to be in rubber suits even at a distance from the device. Their eyes needed to be protected by red visors, and in this regard it is noteworthy that the Bell radiated a blue light while it was operational. This was witnessed by inmates of the nearby Mauthausen

---

165 Ibid., 178–179.

166 Nick Cook, *The Hunt for Zero Point*, 192.

167 Ibid., 193.

168 Joseph P. Farrell, *The SS Brotherhood of the Bell*, 178.

camp, who could see a bluish-glowing barrel levitating above the tree line at night.[170] In fact, a massive circular test rig or "henge" with giant hooks in its concrete pylons had to be constructed around the underground chamber, in order to chain the Bell so that its ascent and descent could be more tightly controlled.[171] So in addition to distorting the time frame of biological processes, the Bell was also an anti-gravity device.

More precisely, what it did was establish a local gravitational field. This does not appear to have been the intention of the *Kammlerstab*. Instead, the field propulsion potential of the Bell seems to have been a fortuitous fringe benefit of what they were really after: an exotic power plant based on tapping what is now widely referred to as the Zero Point Energy (ZPE) field. In the Physics that became conventional after the apparent defeat of the Reich, the existence of a hidden background energy in the universe is accepted. However, this Zero Point Energy is conceived of as fluctuations taking place in a quantum vacuum. Hendrik Casimir famously proposed searching for it by placing aluminum plates so close together that the gap between them was less than the wavelengths of the hypothesized quantum fluctuations and observing how, at that point, separated by less than one micron, the plates snap together.[172] Although this was finally achieved in 1997, there is a more coherent way to conceptualize what the Casimir Effect is actually demonstrating, to the extent that it is any evidence for "Zero Point Energy."

It must be recalled that quantum mechanics was invented by Germans and that, in the open source literature, there is still no solution to certain contradictions between it and the relativistic model of space-time famously developed by Albert Einstein. The Reich, which it bears repeating was the most scientifically and technologically

---

170 Igor Witkowski, *The Truth About the Wunderwaffe*, 263.

171 Joseph P. Farrell, *The SS Brotherhood of the Bell*, 165.

advanced regime on the planet in its time, considered Einsteinian physics to be a reductively and crassly materialistic "Jewish physics." Consequently, advanced research programs such as this one under the auspices of the SS embraced and attempted to further develop a physical model that preceded and rivaled that of Einstein, one which they believed could offer a different interpretation of quantum physical processes while also accounting for the empirical data set marshaled by Einstein in defense of relativity theory, such as the Doppler Red Shift.[173] The key German physicists involved in the development of the paradigm on the basis of which the Bell was engineered were Nobel laureate Walther Gerlach, his student O.C. Hilgenberg, and Carl Friedrich Kraft, who in the 1940s condensed Hilgenberg's many highly technical papers into a systematic presentation in his book *Ether and Matter*.[174]

According to these physicists the failure of the Michelson-Morley experiment to detect the aether wind was not, as Einstein maintained, a disconfirmation of the existence of an aether as such — it only disconfirmed a static aether.[175] The aether is, however, not a static plenum or background to independently existent subatomic particles. Rather, a proper conception of the aether is one wherein what appear to us to be subatomic particles are vorticular structures in a dynamic energetic medium.[176] Such thinking about fundamental Physics is non-linear and purely topological; time is not conceived of as a fourth dimension that plots the linear efficient-causal interactions between discrete entities in three-dimensional space, unless one wants to posit a fifth dimensional aether whose relation to discrete time-frames is quasi-spatial.[177]

---

173 Joseph P. Farrell, *The SS Brotherhood of the Bell*, 202, 259.

174 Ibid., 258, 305.

175 Ibid., 259.

176 Ibid., 260.

This is a Heraclitean view of the cosmos, one wherein there is perpetual flux. The way in which we are required to turn our view of the cosmos inside out so as to see how what appear to be material structures in the void of space are actually complex vortices in a plenum, also calls to mind the Buddhist metaphysics of *Shunyata* or the void that is a plenum and in light of which nothing has any inherent essence or ultimately independent existence. Nature is not constituted of discrete building blocks. Things take shape as vortices in the void and eventually dissolve into this ocean of invisible energy. Tapping that unbounded ocean as a power source for human endeavor, on the basis of this very Aryan Physics, was the ultimate aim of the Bell technology.

Based on Kraft's groundbreaking research, Hilgenberg went so far as to develop a version of the periodic table of elements that modeled each and every element as a compound structure of vortices; he even speculatively, but accurately, included aetheric models of super-heavy elements that had not yet been discovered.[178] But the ultimate aim of this work was practical, not theoretical. As opposed to Einstein's physics, this dynamic aetheric physics allowed for the local engineering of the curvature of space-time without the need of a large object. One does not need a black hole to warp space-time, one can engineer a supermassive black sun on a small scale through stressing the vorticular structure of certain elements to such a degree that the fabric of space-time is sheared.[179]

Since both the structure and the mass of what we take to be a "particle" are determined by vorticular motion, the violent compression of vortices in an appropriate plasma through the application of electro-magnetically charged counter-rotational stress can result in an implosion that opens a super-massive mega-vortex or singularity. In accordance with what is commonly referred to as "wave-particle

---

178 Joseph P. Farrell, *The SS Brotherhood of the Bell*, 263–265.

duality," this forced compression of vortices in the plasmatic medium, like any particular vorticular structure taken to be a "particle," will also have a standing wave scalar signature.[180] It is probably such scalar waves that destroyed the cells of the Bell scientists on a molecular level.

At any rate, put in layman's terms, the implications of this are that the Bell was not only an experimental Zero Point Energy power plant that turned out to have field propulsion potential, by generating a local gravity field (i.e. "anti-gravity"), but it could also be adapted into the most destructive weapon imaginable. This makes perfect sense when you think about it, which is something that advocates of "free energy" to end war and save the world apparently have not done. Every form of explosive weaponry thus far has been developed on the basis of a physical and chemical technology that is dual-use. Gunpowder can be used for fireworks or for firearms. Nuclear fission can be controlled for power generation, but it can also be adapted into an atomic bomb. It follows that any source of energy that is potentially unlimited, could be converted into a weapon whose destructive force is potentially unlimited.

Hal Puthoff, a physicist who did decades of classified research for Naval Intelligence and the National Security Agency, and who worked on contract for the CIA at the Stanford Research Institute, now researches Zero Point Energy at his Institute of Advanced Studies in Austin, Texas. Puthoff maintains that ZPE devices could eventually be miniaturized for use in a wide variety of vehicles, or even for installation in anyone's back yard. However, if such a ZPE system were to be weaponized there would be "enough energy in the volume of your coffee-cup to evaporate all the world's oceans many times over."[181] Compare this to the ratio between mass and explosive force that we are dealing with in the case of the uranium or plutonium core of a

---

180 Ibid., 269-270.

nuclear bomb. Intercepted wartime Japanese communiqués with their Axis partner, reveal that German researchers were working on a project that produced matter with a density comparable to that found inside certain types of stars.[182] When poor Victor Schauberger — who if you recall had already been forced by Kammler to work for the SS — was held under duress by American military-industrialists in the 1950s, it occurred to him that perhaps he ought to resist passing on certain information because the work he had done for Kammler in 1944–45 could be used to produce an "implosion" bomb many orders of magnitude more destructive than the most powerful hydrogen bomb.[183]

III.

The problem with accepting that the Germans had, in principle, developed such a weapon is that according to the official Allied narrative of the war's end, Germany had failed to even develop a nuclear weapon comparable to those dropped on Japan. This could not be further from the truth. In fact, the highly-enriched uranium for the bomb dropped on Hiroshima was transferred from Germany to the United States, via a planned U-Boat surrender, under a deal brokered by Hans Kammler and his associates.[184] It is the United States that lagged behind Germany in the race for nuclear weapons — far behind. The Reich carried out several successful tests of nuclear weapons late in the war, months before the American test at Trinity.[185] The most significant of these is the nuclear test carried out on March 4, 1945, at the troop parade ground near the village of Ohrdruf.[186] This is because

---

182 Joseph P. Farrell, *The SS Brotherhood of the Bell*, 294–295.

183 Nick Cook, *The Hunt for Zero Point*, 250–251; Joseph P. Farrell, *Reich of the Black Sun*, 207, 219.

184 Joseph P. Farrell, *Reich of the Black Sun*, 60–65.

185 Ibid., 66–80.

the bomb tested there was only 100 grams in mass and yet produced blast damage, including to concentration camp victims, extending out to a radius of 1.2 kilometers. According to the atomic physics of the Hiroshima era, referred to as the era of "first generation" nuclear weapons, one needed a minimum of 50 *kilo*grams of enriched uranium to serve as an effective critical mass.

The second-generation nuclear weapon of the 1960s and 70s, namely the hydrogen bomb, accomplishes a fusion reaction using a fission reaction as a trigger. It was only with the advent of "third generation nuclear weapons," supposedly in the 1980s, that the USA and USSR discovered it is possible to engineer a pure fusion device using what is known as a "ballotechnic" explosive compound, such as a certain isotope of mercury that can boost a conventional explosive to the extent that it is capable of compressing heavy hydrogen into a fusion reaction.[187] Red Mercury can double the yield of a hydrogen bomb while reducing its weight by a hundredfold. Unless it is deliberately salted, the weapon is also much cleaner in terms of radioactive fallout (the fallout caused by hydrogen bombs is on account of the built-in atomic bombs that they use as a trigger). The Reich probably developed the ballotechnic mercury isotope used as a trigger in this weapon as a derivative of the work being done on the Bell by the *Kammlerstab*, which as we have seen yielded its own doomsday weapon by comparison to which atom bombs would be relatively uninteresting to the SS. So far from the popular view that a rejection of "Jewish Physics" shows the dangers of ideological science, because it put Nazi Germany at a disadvantage, pursuing research and development based on an alternative physical model actually allowed the SS to hold the Allied powers hostage in 1945.

I say the SS, and not Germany, because unlike the various branches of the German armed forces (Army, Navy, Air Force, etc.), no representative of the SS or even of the Nazi Party ever signed the

instruments of surrender; these very carefully drafted legal documents make no reference to any *Schutzstaffel* surrender to the Allies.[188]
In fact, whereas the Victory Japan instruments clearly indicate the
surrender of the Imperial government of Japan, the texts of the two
German instruments of surrender, the one to the Soviet Union signed
on May 7, 1945, and the one to the French and Americans a day later,
do not even make any reference to the Reich's government. This is terribly significant because the Reich's government still existed, albeit in
the deterritorialized sense relevant to a government of pirates on the
high seas.

While it is widely believed that Joseph Goebbels very briefly succeeded Hitler as the leader of Nazi Germany, the fact is that Adolf
Hitler's last orders as Führer included the reinstatement of the Weimer
office of Reich's President as head of state — superseding the authority of the Reich's Chancellor, which had been conferred to Goebbels.
Who did Hitler appoint as his successor, namely as the President of
the Reich? Grand Admiral Karl Dönitz of the Navy. Dönitz was the
Reich's President for one week before he himself initiated the surrender of the German national armed forces — a "surrender" in which his
government never actually surrenders and no mention is made of the
tens of military divisions of the SS.[189]

We must set this in the context of a *Kriegsmarine* project to
construct a submarine base in New Swabia (*Neuschwabenland*), the
colonial territory that Germany had claimed in Antarctica in 1938. Of
this base Admiral Dönitz said in 1943: "the German submarine fleet
is proud of having built for the Führer, in another part of the world,
a Shangri-La on land, an impregnable fortress." Dönitz later added
some even more revealing details when he described "an invulnerable
fortress, a paradise-like oasis in the middle of eternal ice."[190] So the

188 Joseph P. Farrell, *The Nazi International* (Kempton, IL: Adventures Unlimited
      Press, 2008), 6–12.

189 Joseph P. Farrell, *Reich of the Black Sun*, 238.

place is a *naval* base, an oasis *on land*, and is impregnable at least in part because it is in the middle of ice that never melts. The reference to land rules out the North Pole, and leaves us with the southern polar region. A huge rift valley runs through Antarctica, a valley that is full of geothermal activity and consequently features cavities in the ice cap where there are warm water ponds each colored by a different type of algae.[191] In the summer of 1945 numerous German U-Boats were intercepted near Patagonia, the region of Argentina just across from the part of Antarctica that was declared a colonial territory of the Reich in 1938 (well before the UN Antarctic Treaty of 1959 prohibited claims of national sovereignty over territories in Antarctica).[192]

In 1946 US Navy Admiral Richard E. Byrd led a catastrophically failed military mission to Antarctica, specifically to that part of the frozen continent claimed by the Reich as New Swabia.[193] It was disguised as a mapping expedition, but the assets devoted to "Operation Highjump" reveal its true nature. The outfit consisted of the *Philippines Sea* aircraft carrier escort, the *Pine Island* and *Curritich* seaplane carriers, the *Brownsen* and *Henderson* destroyers, the *Yankee* and *Merrick* escort ships, the *Canister* and *Capacan* fuel carriers, and the *Sennet* submarine. They were provisioned for what was supposed to be an eight-month long mission, but after massive damage to the ships and aircraft, as well as casualties, Admiral Byrd wound up ordering a retreat after only two months. Upon return to Washington, D.C. both his personal and operational logs were classified and remain so to this day. The reason for this classification can be clearly deduced from a statement that he gave to the Chilean press on the way back home, before he was debriefed and gag ordered. In the March 5, 1947 edition of the Santiago-based Chilean paper *El Mercurio*, journalist Lee van Atta, wrote:

---

191 Ibid., 511.
192 Ibid., 242.

Byrd announced to me today that it is necessary for the United States to put into effect defensive measures against enemy airmen which come from the polar regions. The Admiral further explained that he did not have the intention to scare anyone but the bitter reality is that in case of a new war the United States would be in a position to be attacked by flyers which could fly with fantastic speed from one pole to the other.[194]

So, whatever happened to that fantastic German field propulsion technology, the Bell, and the saucer shaped airframes that it was being integrated into by the *Kammlerstab* near Prague in 1945? After faking his death (of which three conflicting accounts exist), Obergruppenführer Hans Kammler organized the evacuation of all high-level scientific personnel, the execution of the rank and file project members, and aerial transport of the Bell itself to Argentina via a Junkers 390 heavy transport plane.[195] This was facilitated by a "Special Evacuation Command" under the direction of another prominent official who faked his death, Martin Bormann, the head of the Reich's Chancellery and Adolf Hitler's private secretary.[196]

At the very end of the war, the Reich's leadership asked their unofficial ally, the quasi-fascist Argentina of Juan Peron, to declare war on Germany so that, as a member of the Allied Powers, Argentina would have the right to fly aircraft to and from German-occupied territory.[197] Bormann was a mastermind of financial manipulation connected to magnates of industry, especially at I.G. Farben.[198] Partly with the use of unmarked or black ops submarines handed over to him by Admiral Dönitz, he smuggled $800 million (at 1945 value) and 95 tons of gold to Peron's Argentina via Franco's Spain.[199] Bormann has been described

---

194 Ibid., 247–248.

195 Joseph P. Farrell, *The SS Brotherhood of the Bell*, 39, 167–170.

196 Nick Cook, *The Hunt for Zero Point*, 198–199.

197 Joseph P. Farrell, *The Nazi International*, 172.

198 Ibid., 69.

as something akin to a Nazi John D. Rockefeller or J.P. Morgan.[200] Interestingly, Bormann's signature appears on a J.P. Morgan Chase Manhattan bank check drawn up *in his own name* in Argentina as late as 1967.[201] That check cleared through the local Deutsche Bank in Buenos Aires. This lack of any attempt to remain anonymous bespeaks tremendous confidence, at least by that point — some two decades after he orchestrated the evacuation of the Bell and other assets between 1945 and 1947. The Rockefeller banking elite had backed the rise of the Nazi Party in Germany, and Bormann's post-1945 plan included reconnecting with sympathetic elements within the Anglo-American banking and corporate elite that had been cut off from their German contacts after the American declaration of war in 1941.[202] It is more than a coincidence that the Chase Bank logo remains, to this day, a swastika.

High finance was not the only target for infiltration within the United States. Perhaps even more significantly, both the vast and deep state intelligence apparatus set up by the National Security Act of 1947 and the military-industrial complex were — from their inception — so deeply penetrated by unprosecuted (and unreconstructed) elites of the Reich that the latter could even be said to have co-constituted these structures. This is the true and hidden context for Former Supreme Allied Commander Europe, President Dwight Eisenhower's famous farewell speech warning the American people about an occulted state within the state ostensibly tasked with National Security but actually posing a mortal danger to the United States.

In the late 1930s Allen Dulles was a lawyer for, and board member of, a German-Anglo-American corporate consortium called Schröder, Rockefeller, and Company, that *Time* magazine described as "the

---

200 Ibid., 81.

201 Ibid., 304.

202 Joseph P. Farrell, *Saucers, Swastikas, and Psyops* (Kempton, IL: Adventures

economic booster of the Rome-Berlin Axis."[203] Avery Rockefeller in New York, nephew of Chase Bank's John D. Rockefeller, owned 42% and the Europe-based Fascists owned 47%. Dulles would of course go on to serve the OSS, America's wartime intelligence agency, which he transformed into the Central Intelligence Agency under authorization granted by the National Security Act of 1947. What few people know is that what essentially transformed the OSS into the CIA was Dulles' assimilation and incorporation of the *Fremde Heere Ost* or Foreign Armies East, which was under the command of General Reinhard Gehlen and was consequently also known as the *Gehlenorg*.[204] This was the rabidly anti-Russian Nazi German espionage network in increasingly Soviet-occupied Eastern Europe, which consisted of Czechs, Lithuanians, Estonians, Belarusians, and Ukrainians.

A deal brokered with General Gehlen in 1945, by then OSS Zurich station chief Allen Dulles, allowed these extraterritorial German assets to continue operating in a fashion that assisted the Americans in a common cause against Russian Communism but that did not require these assets to work "for" or "under" the Americans; in fact, the agreement explicitly stated that "should the organization at any time find itself in a position where the American and German interests diverged, it was accepted that the organization would consider the interests of Germany first."[205] What "Germany" are we even talking about at this juncture, amidst the smoldering rubble of 1945? An extraterritorial "Germany" in Fascist Spain and Argentina, in Antarctica, and even deep within the American military-industrial complex.

IV.

Sometime in 1944 SS Colonel Otto Skorzeny, who was the ace commando in charge of all false-flag and Black Ops in the Reich, was

---

203 Ibid., 159.

204 Joseph P. Farrell, *Roswell and the Reich*, 346–347.

shown the Bell and associated Saucer aircraft. According to testimony obtained through the American interrogation of his commandos, at this point Skorzeny lost interest in his mission of carrying out acts of sabotage behind enemy lines in Europe. Instead, after having seen "the wonder weapon" he became maniacally "possessed" by the idea of using it in a *Sonderkampf* or special operation behind enemy lines *in America* that was sure to win the war, the real war — of worldview.[206] *Weltanschauungskrieg* does not mean a conflict between different subjective views or ideologies contending over control of an objectively existent world, including not just Nature but also a fixed human nature. Rather, it is a concept based on the insight of Heraclitus into strife as integral to the creative process of the Cosmos and the related perspectival thought of Nietzsche. *Weltanschauungskrieg* determines the way that the world reveals itself out of a predominating occultation. The strife of conflicting vital perspectives or existential standpoints does not solely concern political constitutions in the derivative legal sense but the very constitution of the world of a folk.

One of the operative principles of this war of the worlds over Earth, is to capture or captivate the enemy on an existential level by inculcating fear without a definite object and attendant hopelessness in the target population while at the same time offering a salvific sense of direction and promise of security to people whose trust in established authority has been shattered.[207] The aim is to create a matrix of perception and interpretation that only leaves certain lines of thought and avenues of action open to the target population, not by hiding others but by making them disappear.[208] A key means to accomplish that is the use of false alternatives or the deliberate polarization of the target's decision-making process in such a way that two alternative ideologies or interpretive paradigms, which are both false constructs,

206 Joseph P. Farrell, *Saucers, Swastikas, and Psyops*, 94–95.
207 Ibid., 95–96.

are designed to dialectically drive the enemy towards a third position that remains occulted.[209]

Ultimately, anyone who cannot think outside of binaries such as "good and evil" can be manipulated by the use of such a methodology to lure them into a simulacrum, a false world that has been crafted to encompass their existential horizon like a total work of art. Throughout the course of history, the lore of any folk has served as the fundamental architectonic for both their mundane crafts and monumental constructions. *Weltanschauungskrieg* had taken place only on an unconscious level, as strife between divergent cultures or what Samuel Huntington calls the clash of civilizations. What was different about the idea that possessed Skorzeny was the deliberate use of folklore or the engineering of mythology for the purpose of bringing forth a new world order.

What is most interesting about this diabolical stroke of genius is that it presupposes the ability, not to stand outside of any and all worldviews, which is not possible, but to be able to assume a variety of different existential standpoints or vital perspectives to the end of not being captivated by any one of them, including that of one's "own culture." Nietzsche understood this well and identified it as one of the characteristics of the Superman.[210] It also lies at the core of Heidegger's conception of *Abbau* or "deconstruction," which is very Nietzschean. This term, which has become synonymous with the passive nihilism of postmodern "thought" originally had a much more active and archeo-futuristically postmodern meaning.

If we were to want to retain the designation "postmodern" we would have to conclude that Nazi Germany was the first attempt at a postmodern political system. From the viewpoint of its own leaders, however, it was the culmination of the "modern" in the German sense of *Der Neuzeit* or "the New Age." From this standpoint, Neo-Cartesian

---

209 Ibid., 99–100.

210 Friedrich Nietzsche, *The Will to Power* (New York: Random House, 1968),

Rationalism and Materialism were an incomplete or imbalanced reaction against the medieval Judeo-Christian Scholasticism that began to be overcome in the Renaissance. Even more than Mussolini, with his vision of a Second Italian Renaissance, the Nazis forwarded the occult current of the Renaissance epitomized by Giordano Bruno in their vision of a new post-Judeo-Christian age. What made this age "new" is that it would reconnect with the primordial Aryan wellspring of Western civilization after having withstood its uniquely destined encounter with the destructive and yet essentially revealing force of technological instrumentality. This fiery alchemical force is, after all, a product of the Promethean genius of Aryan Man.

It is as a deconstructive thinker in the vanguard of postmodernity that, in one of his arcane lectures on logic and the essence of language, Heidegger explains that World War I was not "the true world war" if one takes it to have ended in 1918.[211] Likewise the true World War did not end in 1945. The only real world war is the war of the worlds over the Earth, the *Weltanschauungskrieg*, and unlike Nietzsche who could only prophesy it, Heidegger knew that although this war had begun in his time, he would not live to see the end of it. This is that war of which Nietzsche wrote in *Ecce Homo*:

> I know my fate. One day my name will be associated with the memory of something tremendous — a crisis without equal on earth, the most profound collision of conscience, a decision that was conjured up *against* everything that had been believed, demanded, hallowed so far. I am no man, I am dynamite. ...

> The concept of politics will have merged entirely with a war of spirits; all power structures of the old society will have been exploded — all of them are based on lies: there will be wars the like of which have never yet been

---

211 Martin Heidegger, *Logic as the Question Concerning the Essence of Language*

seen on earth. It is only beginning with me that the earth knows *grand politics.*[212]

Dynamite, indeed. War of spirits, indeed.

What Nietzsche, qua apocalyptic prophet, is seeing through a glass darkly here and what was adopted as a plan of action by Skorzeny and his comrades is something that I would conceptualize as *Abbauende Aufbruch ins Weltanschauungskrieg.* Heidegger was right that some things can only be thought in German. *Abbau* is the term "deconstruction" from Heidegger's thought, so that *Abbauende* literally means "un-building" or dismantling. But through its connection with the "destruction of the history of ontology" that was the projected aim of *Being and Time,* and in light of the socio-politically dangerous implications of such dynamiting of the paradigmatic principles of a world-epoch, I suggest rendering *Abbauende* as "destructive," which carries within it the sense of de-structuring. The idea of *Aufbruch* has a rich philosophical and literary history in modernist German thought. It is alternatively translated as "breakup" in the sense of a breaking-with or divorce, or "breakthrough" in the sense of a revolutionary discovery rather than an incremental increase in knowledge, and finally, as "breakaway" in the sense that such discoveries can represent a rupture wherein something or someone heads out of bounds in a different direction. In other words, a "breakout" or "departure."

Thus my concept for what Skorzeny, Kammler, Gehlen, Bormann and company did in deed, even if it remained imprecisely conceptualized, could be loosely translated as "destructive departure in world-view warfare." Although, based on the alternative meaning of the terms, it is also possible to translate it as "deconstructive breakthrough in psychological warfare" or "dismantling breakaway in the worldwide ideological war." This is the worldwide constitutive or emergent state of a breakaway civilization. It is based both on a breakthrough in the

212 Friedrich Nietzsche, *Ecce Homo* in *Basic Writings of Nietzsche* (New York: The

positive sense and on a negative breaking-down and a breaking away. This allows those who have broken through to come back and conquer what they have broken-down in a way that is *Kriegsentscheidend* for the *Weltanschauungskrieg*. Recall that this term, *Kriegsentscheidend* or "war-decisive," was a classification at the highest level above Top Secret uniquely given to Project Chronos.

Otto Skorzeny initiated his special operation against the United States from Spain. By design, the alien contact mythos has been so built up over the past seventy years that hardly anyone remembers that when flying saucers first invaded the skies over the United States in 1947, it was being speculated that they were of German construction and being launched from Fascist Spain. Moreover, consider the fact that President Truman's policy regarding the flying saucers would have been colossally stupid if the US intelligence actually believed them to be alien spacecraft. According to Air Force information officer, Lt. Colonel Moncel Monts, as reported by news wire services at the time, the Truman administration policy was that: "The jet pilots are, and have been under orders to investigate unidentified objects and *to shoot them down if they can't talk them down*."[213] Rather than assuming that Truman was willing to risk an interplanetary war with a superior race of extraterrestrials, it makes much more sense to recognize that at the highest levels it was believed that these UFOs represented terrestrial enemy aircraft.

Two classified memoranda speculate on German technology as the matrix for UFOs. The first is a September 23, 1947 letter of General Nathan Twining to Brigadier General George F. Schulgen, widely known as the *Twining-Schulgen Memorandum*.[214] The second is an October 28, 1947 intelligence collection memorandum prepared by General Schulgen in response to General Twining's analysis,

---

213 Joseph P. Farrell, *Roswell and the Reich*, 368–369.

recommendations, and request for further study.[215] It should be noted that, with great relevance to the issue of concern here, a faked version of the second of these documents was widely circulated within the Ufology research community. This forgery both interpolated lines not in the original and censored text from the original in order to make it appear as if Schulgen and the USAF were considering an extraterrestrial or "interplanetary" origin of flying saucers.[216]

In fact, both memoranda clearly indicate German aeronautical engineering and propulsion research and development as the most likely source for the UFOs, with specific concern about the post-war whereabouts of the Horten Brothers. While Twining's summary of the USAF technical analysis of the craft certainly involved futuristic concepts in the context of 1945 technology, all of them are still within the theoretical scope of terrestrial engineering. Although Schulgen speculates that Russia may be the geographical point of origin for this presumably captured German technology, this seems to be only because the other possibility is even more terrifying — namely the postwar survival of an independent, extraterritorial Reich of some sort.[217] Still, if one reads between the lines, Schulgen remains open to this possibility since he is especially concerned with determining, based on the aircraft's landing gear, what kind of terrain they might be taking off from.[218]

The headline of the *Denver Post* for November 9, 1947 reads "Spies Bid for Franco's Weapons: Agents Ascribe 'Flying Saucer' to New Rocket."[219] The article explains that "German scientists working under the personal sponsorship of Generalissimo Francisco Franco have developed" saucer-shaped "rockets" that are "responsible for the flying

---

215 Ibid., 375–387.

216 Ibid., 388–389.

217 Ibid., 409.

218 Ibid., 403.

saucers seen over the North American continent last summer and for at least one and perhaps two hitherto unexplained accidents to transport aircraft." Journalist Lionel Shapiro, writing from Geneva, goes on to reveal that according to his sources these "weapons" were first flown in the presence of Franco on the south coast of Spain, just east of Gibraltar, early in the summer of 1947. Note the date. The saucer-shaped "rockets were directed over North America…"[220]

July 8, 1947. Roswell, New Mexico — home to the 509th Bombardment Group, at that time, before the Russian acquisition of an atomic bomb, the only bomber wing in the world known to possess nuclear weapons. Roswell Army Air Field was the point of origin for the airstrikes on Hiroshima and Nagasaki. In other words, we are dealing with the most classified military installation in the entire United States. In the vicinity of this installation, during what Roswell residents remember as a terribly stormy night, a disc-shaped aircraft crashes onto a ranch. In the morning, the debris is witnessed by the rancher, Mac Brazel, and his son, as well as a few other startled civilians. Then the military swoops in and sweeps up the evidence.

An initial USAF authorized press release by Major Jesse Marcel admits the capture of a flying saucer, but then the official story changes — over and over again. At this point, the United States government has offered three contradictory accounts of what crashed on the Brazel ranch that night. Something is certainly being covered up, but not debris from an extraterrestrial craft or alien corpses. Something far more terrifying from the standpoint of the United States government, and worthy of above Top Secret classification all the way down to our own time. Something that catalyzed a fundamental transformation of the American power structure with the National Security Act of 1947. What crashed was one of those flying saucers launched from Spain that summer, one with the special mission of radicalizing worldview warfare.

The debris recovered at Roswell was not alien enough to be extraterrestrial, but it was exotic enough to fit within the context of the most cutting-edge German research and development. There is a 1940s German technological context for at least seven different types of material recovered at Roswell, and mistakenly or misleadingly identified as "alien" by the Pentagon's Foreign Technology division head, Colonel Philip J. Corso.

So-called "memory metal" which restores its original shape after being bent or folded is a nickel and titanium chemical compound whose properties were discovered as early as 1932 in Sweden; it became a part of the Reich in the early 1940s.[221] This technology was not re-developed within the Allied world until 1962. The super-strong metal that could not be dented with a sledgehammer could have been a cold-formed and heat-treated stainless steel like alloy of iron, nickel, chromium, manganese and carbon that was developed in Bavaria in 1935–36.[222] German metallurgists had also developed other methods of bonding nitrogen to the surface of steel and aluminum in order to harden them so much that the weight of an aircraft could be cut in half without compromising its durability.[223] Such hardening would be necessary if one were going to perforate the metal of the airframe in order to minimize drag, an improvement on the suction methodology described above in the context of early saucer airframe research. Apparently, metal that you can blow air through was found in the Roswell wreckage. This porous metal, permeated by microscopic holes, was referred to as *Luftschwamm* or "aerosponge."[224]

Besides these exotic but solidly German metals, the Roswell wreckage included fiber optics, Kevlar, night vision, lasers, miniaturized transistors and integrated circuits. For 1947 America these were

221 Joseph P. Farrell, *Roswell and the Reich*, 458.

222 Ibid., 466–467.

223 Ibid., 469–471.

materials from science fiction. In early 1940s German military R&D programs they were technological fact. The basic concept for fiber optics dates back to the late 19ᵗʰ century, when it was conceived of by the inventor of the telephone, Alexander Graham Bell, who saw it as the more important of his inventions and referred to it as the "photophone." Among the German military technology papers seized by the allies in 1945 are casual references to an apparently existing but unexplained technology called "optical telephony."[225] The synthetic fabric now known as Kevlar was being tested at I.G. Farben, and both Panther tanks and German naval vessels employed "night vision" infrared sight equipment.[226] In Germany, where quantum physics was developed, classified research was already being done on lasers in the 1930s, three decades before their public invention in 1960, specifically with a view to substituting centrifuge enrichment (which requires large-scale facilities) with much more efficient and potentially clandestine laser isotope enrichment of uranium.[227] The prerequisites for integrated circuits also existed insofar as circa 1941, Germans already had semi-conductor chips and the firm Telefunken was manufacturing a klystron tube that was one-tenth the size of the ones produced in Britain and the United States, years later, at the war's end (probably via an attempt at reverse engineering).[228]

As for the allegedly recovered bodies, there is also an all-too-terrestrial explanation for the physiological descriptions of them: Fascist human experimentation, both in Germany and Japan. The alleged witness accounts of the bodies are consistent with the physiological manifestations of Progeria Syndrome: enlarged heads, baldness, protruding eyes, a beaklike nose, elongated arms, the wrong number of digits on their hands, and a short stature that reflects the late

225 Ibid., 478–479.
226 Ibid., 479–480.
227 Ibid., 483–484.

childhood maximal life expectancy of Progeria victims.[229] Some of the witnesses also described the facial features of the corpses as "oriental," which is interesting in light of the fact that Japan has one of the highest incidences of a rare form of Progeria that effects adults. These poor people were experimented on by the infamous Japanese Unit 731 as part of its biological weapons research and development program.[230] In 1945 there was an intensification of the already extensive exchange of both intelligence and material between Germany and its Axis-ally of Imperial Japan.[231] It should also be recalled that Dr. Joseph Mengele, the infamous director of human experimentation at Auschwitz, was among those Reichs officials who was able to successfully evade Allied prosecution and relocate to South America.

Although it is possible that the flying saucer that crashed at Roswell was on a surveillance mission, offering intelligence regarding the most classified USAF base, I think that is doubtful — especially if the deformed bodies were indeed part of the wreckage. What is more likely, and consistent with Skorzeny's vision for the ultimate black-flag special operation for waging worldview warfare within American territory, is that the craft was deliberately crashed in order to provoke fear, panic, and wonder. The initial press release was probably quite deliberate in suggesting that an alien craft had been captured, so that once this was "covered up" by the weather balloon story, and this story was in turn called into question by the even later Project Mogul explanation, a significant segment of the public would assume that something extraterrestrial was being concealed.

Suggesting that what came down in Roswell could have been a scout for an impending alien invasion was better than admitting the truth, namely that the United States had not really won the war and that there was a Fourth Reich somewhere with vastly superior science

---

229 Ibid., 445.

230 Ibid., 440, 445.

and technology. This is exactly the thought process that Skorzeny and his comrades would be counting on. Only those at the very highest level would know the truth, but beneath them a vast military-intelligence apparatus would be implicated in the "cover-up" of what even they had been led to believe was an extraterrestrial threat. This would catalyze the creation of a gigantic machinery of undemocratic National Security institutions, a military-industrial complex with no real oversight that — in light of Operation Paperclip and the CIA's absorption of the *Gehlenorg* — would actually allow for a Nazi take-over of this only nominally "American" deep state from its deepest level. This is the true nature of the connection between UFOs and the National Security State. The plot was meant to buy time for the development of a Fascist breakaway civilization, for a destructive departure in worldview warfare made possible by Project Chronos.

V.

Although the Roswell incident has been a lightning rod of controversy even within the UFO research community, it features in one of the most rigorous and reputable scientific studies of the phenomenon. After nearly twenty years of official study of UFO cases by the government of France, in 1996 officials within the high-level French think tank IHDEN or "Institute of Advanced Studies for National Defense" decided to found a "Committee for in-depth studies," abbreviated COMETA, in order to come to some conclusion on the matter especially with a view to strategic implications.[232] Comparable to the RAND Corporation in the United States, IHDEN consists of officers and officials who have held the most sensitive command posts and corporate positions in the armed forces and aerospace industry of France.

232 Leslie Kean, *UFOs: Generals, Pilots, and Government Officials Go On the Record*

COMETA at IHDEN completed its report in 1999 and entitled it *Les OVNI Et La Défense: À quoi doit-on se préparer?* (UFOs and Defense: For What Must We Prepare?). COMETA's elite twelve-member committee was chaired by Major General Denis Letty, a renowned former fighter pilot who headed the southeast zone of French Air Defense as well as the French military mission for the Allied Air Forces of Central Europe.[233] The study begins with a preface by General Bernard Norlain, the former director of *L'Institut des hautes etudes de défense nationale* — a most prestigious military academy that is France's equivalent of West Point or Annapolis. The report's preamble is written by none other than André Lebeau, former President of CNES — *Centre National D'études Spatiales*, the French NASA. In his conclusion to the COMETA Report, General Norlain mentions the Roswell incident and claims that the United States government has attempted to carry out foreign-technology reverse-engineering projects on the basis of recovered materials.[234] He seems somewhat miffed that the Americans have not shared whatever they have learned with their French allies, although he understands the need to maintain public denial because of what he takes to be the potential for mass panic attendant to the disclosure of alien contact.

In fact, Chapter 13 of *UFOs and Defense*, entitled "Implications politiques et religieuses," features several subsections evaluating the social and political impact of the UFO phenomenon on "pre-industrial civilizations of Earth," where the suggestion is made that what have long been taken to be "religious manifestations" of past times may have been UFO-contact related events. COMETA expresses grave concerns about the social impact of such an immanent scientific discovery, considering the real possibility that events constitutive of revealed religions were in fact interventions by some "alien" intelligence with, at best, dubious intentions among the various UFO-related

233 Kean, *UFOs*, 122.

234 COMETA, *Les OVNI et La Défense: A quoi doit-on se preparer?* (France:

defense considerations for which it advises the French government to prepare.[235] The COMETA Report suggests a possible alien influence on "pre-industrial civilizations" of Earth, but just how far back in time might this influence extend? Could it account for traces of a lost civilization with otherwise inexplicably advanced technology?

In his writings on Atlantis, the British existentialist and occult philosopher Colin Wilson makes much of the *Book of Enoch* and its connection to the passages in Genesis on fallen angels spawning giants with their lovers among earthborn women.[236] As Wilson notes, the Hebrew word *elohim* is the plural of *el* and its translation as "God" in the Old Testament is terribly misleading. It means "the gods," so that "the gods made man in *their* image," "the gods planted a garden in Eden," and Enoch "walked with the gods." The word *elohim* is derived from *ellu*, which means "the shining." So the gods of the Old Testament are literally "The Shining Ones."[237] Jehovah is the chief of the Shining gods, and the "Watchers" of Genesis 6 and *The Book of Enoch* are rebel gods — the "fallen angels" of Christianity and Islam — who descended to Earth at Mount Hermon to sire a titanic race of hybrids and establish a worldwide civilization, the "Atlantis" of Plato, where heavenly knowledge is put to the profane use of improving the lot of humans so that they can stop being lorded over by the tyrannical Jehovah and his cronies.

Wilson points out that Mount Hermon, from which the rebel Watchers set out on their civilizing mission, is in Lebanon where the nearby Bequa'a Valley features Earth's most enigmatic monumental site: the so-called "Temple of Jupiter" at Baalbek.[238] Here the Romans found an incredibly solid platform of unknown antiquity and origin, and chose to build the grandest temple in the entire empire atop this

---

235 COMETA, *Les OVNI et La Défense*, 149–163

236 Colin Wilson and Rand Flem-Ath, *The Atlantis Blueprint* (New York: Random House, 2002), 189–190.

237 Ibid., 196–197.

unshakeable foundation. As it turns out, an earthquake in modern times left the Roman temple in ruins but the megalithic foundation remained unscathed. We know that the Romans did not build the foundation courses at Baalbek because they mention nothing whatsoever about them and any Caesar who had been capable of the task would not have neglected to glorify himself on that account, given that moving Egyptian obelisks weighing a small fraction of what the Baalbek stones do, were meticulously recorded as great accomplishments.

The foundation courses at Baalbek consist of a platform of six stones thirty feet long, fourteen feet high and ten feet deep, each weighing 450 tons, surmounted by three larger stones known as "Trilithons" — each of which is a staggering 1,000 tons. Engineers using modern cranes have great difficulty moving even the 200-ton blocks employed at Giza in Egypt, whereas by placing the heavier 1,000 ton stones on top of the "smaller" 450 ton ones, it is as if the unknown builders at Baalbek were making a point of how easily they could accomplish their task and insisting that practicality was of no concern to them. These stones are cut and fit together with such precision that a razor blade cannot be slipped between their joints. The quarry from which they were cut is at a considerable distance; it has been clearly identified, since one of the largest stones was left in the ground there — perhaps deliberately. According to the pre-Islamic folklore of the natives of the Bequa'a Valley, the citadel dates from before the great flood and, afterwards, a race of giants restored it.

Baalbek is not the only mysterious archeological site that Wilson suggests is a trace of the transatlantic antediluvian civilization that Plato called "Atlantis." On a vast plain in the Andes Mountains of present day Bolivia lies what may be the oldest city in the Americas.[239] Archeological excavations at Tiahuanaco (sometimes also spelled Tiwanaku) reveal that it was once a port on the nearby lake Titicaca; it seems to have been built when the sea level was two and a half miles

higher than it is today. Metal I-shaped clamps were used to fasten the
blocks in the city's structures together and microscopic examinations
have revealed that the metal was poured into the joints in a liquefied
form, which means that the builders would have needed something
like a portable forge.

Tiahuanaco features an expansive step pyramid, known as the
Akapana, whose facing stones have lamentably been stripped over
time for building material. Despite its vandalized state, excavations
have discovered that its seven terraces were built in something like
a modernist style and featured an intricate system of waterworks
that channeled rain between a pool in the central court on the roof,
through a drainage system that ran around and down the sides of
the various terraces and into a moat surrounding the pyramid. The
heart of Tiahuanaco is the Kalasasaya, an austere rectangular open-air
temple with megalithic walls of 100-ton stones perfectly cut and, as at
Baalbek, so tightly fitted together without mortar that a razor blade
cannot be slipped between their joints.

Wilson recounts how Professor Arthur Posnansky spent the better
part of his life studying these ruins before publishing his findings in
an encyclopedic multi-volume work entitled, *Tiahuanacu: The Cradle
of American Man* (1915). It has been recognized that, like many ancient temples elsewhere, the Kalasasaya is an astronomical observa-
tory. Measurements of the sunrise and sunset from markers inside the
Kalasasaya are as persistently precise as the stonework of its builders.
Two observation points in the enclosure mark the summer and winter
solstices. Posnansky noted that these measurements were uncharacteristically off the mark. Due to a slight rolling motion of the earth
over very long periods of time (the obliquity of the ecliptic), the two
tropics are slightly further from the equator than they once were.

If one takes this into account, the builders at Tiahuanaco could
have marked the solstices accurately at the precisely constructed
Kalasasaya, but long before the date that conventional archeologists
assign to the structure. Posnansky put this date at 15,000 BC. More

recently another archeologist, Professor Neil Steede, replicated Posnansky's methodology with more refined contemporary instruments and corrected that to 12,000 years ago — roughly the date that Plato gives us for the zenith and catastrophic collapse of Atlantis. When Dr. Oswaldo Rivera, the Director of the Bolivian National Institute of Archeology, was initially presented with these refinements of Posnansky's analysis he was skeptical, but after taking his own meticulous measurements, he came to agree with the assessment that the megalithic city was built long before the rise of the known native historical culture that revitalized the site nearly ten thousand years later. The Aymara Indians, who live in the environs of Tiahuanaco and around Lake Titicaca, have a language that is so logical that, when translated into algebraic shorthand, it is the perfect bridge for computers to translate from one language into another.[240] The Bolivian mathematician Rojas de Guzman believes that it was artificially constructed; the Aymara Indians claim that it came from the gods.

The later Mesoamerican culture in Bolivia and Peru as well as that of the Mayans in Mexico and the Aztecs after them, all share the unambiguous tradition that tall white gods coming from across the ocean brought the arts of civilization to the highlands of what is now Latin America after their own island homeland was destroyed by a cataclysmic upheaval and a great flood that washed over the Earth. The bearded leader of these sagacious gods, symbolized by the feathered serpent or dragon, is variously called Quetzalcoatl, Kukulkan, Viracocha, and Votan (Wotan?).[241] This civilizer and his cohorts were eventually confronted and defeated by Tezcatilpoca, the "Lord of the Smoking Mirror" by means of which distant places could be seen.

With his smoke and mirrors, Tezcatilpoca instituted the practice of human sacrifice in Mesoamerica. Instead of violently resisting him, Quetzalcoatl and his fellow gods fled in boats without paddles but

---

240 Ibid., 53.

promised to return someday. It was because the arrival of the bearded European Cortez and his plunderers was mistaken for the return of these white civilizer gods that the Mesoamericans were so easily overcome by the conquistadors. Ironically, the Catholic friars who came with the conquistadors identified Quetzalcoatl — the Feathered Serpent who was also symbolized by the Morning Star (Venus or Lucifer) — with Satan or the Dragon of the Apocalypse and on this account, above all others, they rounded up and burned the Mayan scriptures. If they had been a little keener they might also have recognized in Tezcatilpoca the blood-lusting egotistical maniac of their own Bible, the Lord of Abraham and Moses.

As Wilson observes, there is something disturbingly bizarre about the alleged civilizational accomplishments of the Mesoamericans. The "Mayan" solar calendar is more precise than any other pre-modern measure of time; their year was 365.242 days long, only 0.0002 seconds shorter than our modern measurement of 365.2422, which was calculated with a cesium clock.[242] They also had several other calendars: one that calculated according to Venus cycles, another according to Jupiter–Saturn cycles, as well as a Long Count calendar. This by now infamous Long Count calendar that measures world ages, has units of 20 days, its "weeks" consist of 360 days or 18 units, called a *tun*, a *katun* consists of 20 *tuns*, and 20 *katuns* is a *baktun* or 144,000 days, with 13 *baktuns* amounting to a Great Year after which the cycle begins again.

Why did the Mayans need calendars that were so accurate and that calculated such cosmic spans of time? Were the Maya faithful preservers of fragmentary knowledge that they inherited but did not truly understand? Did a culture that put wheels on children's toys but failed to grasp what they would accomplish on cars or chariots really build that vast network of roads that crisscrosses Mesoamerica, or were they built by the same people who set down vast straight lines in the plains of Nazca that can only be seen from the air?

While these potential traces of Atlantis in the Americas are intriguing, Plato tells us that the legend came to him by way of Solon who received it from the priests of ancient Egypt — where the best memory of the Atlantean age had been preserved. Indeed, the Edfu building texts recount the tale of the Seven Sages who brought civilization to Egypt after a worldwide deluge.[243] These *shemasu hor* — Followers of Horus, or more literally "trackers of the Sun" — are described in strikingly similar terms as the civilizer gods of the Americas: tall, statuesque, fair-skinned people, whose men could grow flowing beards, and who wore robes that were emblazoned with feathered or winged serpents. As in Mesoamerica, the winged serpent became *the* ubiquitous sacred symbol of ancient Egypt. Here it took the form of two serpents framing each side of a winged solar disk — the symbol of the secret society of the *shemasu hor*, the initiatory kingmakers and power behind the throne of the Pharaohs, who had it engraved over nearly every doorway in temples and palaces. But what is this reference to a "tracking of the Sun"?

The Belgian engineer Robert Bauval noticed that there is something odd about the three pyramids at Giza. A straight line can be drawn through the corners of the first two large pyramids, but the third much smaller pyramid is not anywhere near aligned with them. Menkaura was no less important a Pharaoh than Cheops and Chefren, so what accounts for this geometry? It occurred to Bauval that the three pyramids of Giza look just like the three stars of Orion's belt, where the third is offset from the alignment of the first two and is less bright than they are. Furthermore, these three stars are in the same basic orientation to the Milky Way as the three pyramids on the ground at Giza are to the Nile River. Bauval was familiar with the fact that the Egyptians associated Osiris with Orion and thought of Egypt as an earthly mirror of the heavens. Yet, if so much trouble was taken to mirror Orion and the Milky Way on the Giza plateau, the builders ought to have come very close to a perfect reflection. This was not the case, but Bauval recalled that on account of a slight wobble of the Earth's axis there is, over the course of 25,920 years, a "precession of the equinoxes."[244]

The signs of the Zodiac turn backwards so that the Sun rises into a different one on the Spring Equinox every 2,160 years. A "zodiacal age" is marked by which constellation the Sun rises into around March 21. From the standpoint of the average lifespan of a civilization, let alone that of an individual human being, this change in the stars is nearly imperceptible. The position of the three stars of Orion's belt with respect to the Milky Way in the heavens is mirrored exactly by the three pyramids of Giza with respect to the Nile River on the Earth at about 10,500 BC.[245]

The Egyptians refer to this period as *zep tepi* or the "first time," when the builder gods founded their civilization. Not only is this the same epoch as Plato's destruction of Atlantis and the new date proposed for the earliest strata at Tiahuanaco, it is also the astrological age of Leo, which ties in the other great monument on the Giza plateau: the Sphinx. With the possible exception of the foundation courses of the Pyramid of Cheops, whose massive megalithic stones are reminiscent of those at Baalbek, the pyramid complex at Giza seems to have been built around 2,500 BC. If it was planned eight thousand years earlier, or at least commemorates that time precisely, who in Egypt was following the movements of the Sun through the astrological ages for so long?

Wilson explains how R.A. Schwaller de Lubicz undertook a detailed study of esoterically encoded Egyptian symbolism that sheds light on how the Egyptian elite of initiates managed to maintain a

244 Ibid., 51, 166.

basically stable high civilization for three thousand years (six times longer than the classical Greeks, four times longer than the Romans, and some ten times the length of modern European civilization to date).[246] Schwaller noted that the Great Sphinx at Giza appeared to be badly eroded *by water* as well as by wind. Thus, he hypothesized that the ancient Egyptians' account of their own prehistory might be more than mythology. Manetho and other Egyptian chroniclers before him had claimed that their civilization was a *legacy* handed down by a Pre-Pharaohonic culture established by the gods after the devastation at the end of the last world age.[247] A single unbroken lineage traced back to these times through the *shemasu hor*, the Followers of the Sun.

Boston University geologist Robert Schoch began to study the water erosion on the Sphinx in the 1990s. He concluded that it was indeed a pattern of erosion quite separate from that produced by wind, and that it was due not to flooding but to sustaining centuries of torrential rainfall. Based on the history of climate conditions in Egypt, where there had not been regular heavy rainfall for many centuries before the known Egyptian civilization, Schoch was ultimately able to convince geologists to re-date the Sphinx to a period *at least* several thousand years prior to the recognized "rise" of ancient Egyptian civilization.[248] Its head, which is dramatically out of proportion with its body and may originally have been a lion's head, that of Leo, could have been re-carved during dynastic times — perhaps because the original was so water eroded by then that its facial features could not be made out. The megalithic Sphinx and Valley temples were built with the same rock hollowed out of the Sphinx trench while that statue

---

246 R.A. Schwaller de Lubicz, *Symbol and the Symbolic: Ancient Egypt, Science, and the Evolution of Consciousness* (Vermont: Inner Traditions, 1978).

247 Gerald P. Verbrugghe and John M. Wickersham, *Berossos and Manetho, Introduced and Translated: Native Traditions in Ancient Mesopotamia and Egypt* (Ann Arbor: University of Michigan Press, 2000).

248 Robert M. Schoch, *Voices of the Rocks: A Scientist Looks at Catastrophes and*

was being carved, and so they are of the same earlier date although the engineering skill involved in them surpasses most anything known to be Egyptian.

The Osireion at Abydos, which is in the same austere style as the Sphinx and Valley temples, is buried under 8,000 years of sedimentation — in other words, that could be the last time it stood above ground. The proposal of establishment Egyptologists that it may have been built underground boggles the mind even further given that the unmarked precision-cut megaliths there are the largest in all of Egypt. The Egyptians believed that this structure was the dwelling place of Osiris, who was represented by the constellation of Orion.

The folklore of Atlantis has it that before the destruction of their civilization, its mariners had colonized the world and that after the cataclysm they took refuge in some of these colonies. If Baalbek, Tiahuanaco, and Giza were among the colonies of Atlantis, where are the remains of Atlantis itself? A plethora of attempts made to geographically locate the homeland of Plato's advanced antediluvian maritime empire, beginning with that of the US Senator Ignatius Donnelly, have all been sunk by this question. Certainly, there are no such remains in the Atlantic — at least not on a continental scale (although recent ocean floor mapping suggests that there might have been another colony somewhere around Cuba, one swallowed by sea level rise). Establishment archeologists have taken this to mean that if Plato's "Atlantis" refers to any historical civilization at all, it is nothing but a vague and embellished recollection of the island culture of Minoan Crete — the cradle of Greek civilization.[249] The palace of Knossos with its labyrinth is supposed to have been that of the ringed city of Atlantis, and the volcanic eruption of Thera on nearby Santorini has been taken for the cause of the earthquake and tsunami that Plato describes.

However, as Colin Wilson recognizes, Plato's account clearly refers to an island *outside* of the "pillars of Hercules" or Straits of Gibraltar and *not inside the Mediterranean*. Subsequent interpreters have assumed that he meant that Atlantis was in what we have come to know as the Atlantic Ocean, between Europe and the Americas. But Plato himself is clear in telling us that "the Ocean" was named after Atlantis and not the other way around. Moreover, he uses the enigmatic phrase "*the* true Ocean" when he describes the location of Atlantis at the center of it, and then he adds that "the whole opposite continent" could be reached across this Ocean on the other side of Atlantis. Finally, he explicitly states that this so-called "island" is actually an immense landmass with its own impressive mountain chains, rivers, lakes, and so forth. There is only one "true Ocean" recognized by oceanographers today — the place on earth where the three major "oceans" converge into a single Ocean that surrounds an island that is indeed the size of a continent: Antarctica.

While this continent is just the right size, and in just the right place, to be Plato's Atlantis, it is now buried under an ice cap that is in some places two miles thick. The conventional geological view is that Antarctica has been within the southern polar region for millions of years. That view has been challenged by the Earth crustal displacement theory of Professor Charles Hapgood, which was endorsed by Albert Einstein.[250] Hapgood was a Harvard graduate in the Philosophy of Science and later went on to teach anthropology at Springfield College in Massachusetts. Hapgood became aware of very old maps that accurately depicted the sub-glacial topography of Antarctica, a continent that was not even supposed to have been "discovered" until the 19th century and was not accurately mapped, under the ice cap, until the middle of the 20th century.

There are some very basic features of Antarctica that one cannot know unless one has mapped its contours beneath the ice, for example, some of its mountain ranges are entirely buried by the ice, it actually consists of two distinct but closely joined landmasses, with one considerably larger than the other, and the so-called Palmer Peninsula stretching towards Patagonia in Argentina is really only an island. The Ottoman Piri Reis map of 1513 and the 1531 Renaissance European map of Oronteus Finnaeus depict these distinct sub-glacial topographical features. These maps, which are thought to have been copied from older ones in the Library of Alexandria, also feature accurate longitudinal measurements despite the fact that longitude was not properly grasped until the 18th century. What primeval mariners already understood it?

After finding a number of other anomalous maps in the US Library of Congress and elsewhere that depicted different parts of the Earth as they were long ago, Hapgood came up with a theory. There are mammoths in Siberia who were frozen so rapidly that they have undigested food in their stomachs, and this food is suggestive of a much warmer climate than obtains there today. What if the earth's crust occasionally slips over its mantle, and does so quite precipitously, so that Antarctica was pulled into the southern polar region from a relatively more temperate latitude just as Siberia was pushed upwards towards the north pole?

Hapgood entered into a lively correspondence with Einstein over this theory, which involved complex calculations of how much ice accumulating during ice ages would be sufficient to periodically make the Earth top heavy, so that the crust would slip. Einstein eventually wrote an introduction to Hapgood's book, *Earth's Shifting Crust*. In this book and its sequel, *The Path of the Pole*, Hapgood hypothesized that the North Pole used to be in Hudson Bay and a large part of Antarctica was free of ice as early as 12,000 years ago. This area, on Antarctica's Atlantic coast, which would then have had the climate of Argentina, is the region that was dubbed Neu Schwabenland (New Swabia) by the aforementioned 1938 German expedition led by Rudolf

Hess and Herman Goering. The *Luftwaffe* claimed it by raining sharp stakes bearing Swastika banners down onto the icy mountainsides.[251]

Hapgood's shift of the pole theory explains, among other things, the fact that the ice sheet in Antarctica is thicker in some areas towards the outer perimeter opposite New Swabia than it is in those areas now most centered on the South Pole. Snow has had less time to glaciate in these areas, whereas the other parts of Antarctica that are now further from the pole were already inside the polar region before the crustal displacement. Of course, with respect to "North" and "South" it should be noted that these are ultimately determined in relation to the magnetic poles, which undergo an inversion at intervals of several hundred thousand years. At the beginning of the anthropological record of Man, Antarctica was a *northern* polar continent. A Nordic polar continent veiled by ice is at the core of the classical myth of Hyperborea — which German esotericists understood to be one and the same as the lost world of Thule.[252]

Hapgood wrote some very significant letters to a young correspondent named Rand Flem-Ath at the end of his life in 1982, letters pointing beyond the thesis of his 1966 book *Maps of the Ancient Sea Kings*, towards the conclusion that Antarctica was Atlantis and that a whole cycle of civilization had been lost with it. Hapgood's theory calls for a very rapid displacement, which would have produced just the kind of massive earthquake and tsunami that Plato describes as the cause of the destruction of Atlantis (and of culture, worldwide). It also would have had another terrifying effect that *is* recorded in the myths of ancient and aboriginal peoples the world over: the sky would have fallen. Wherever it was nighttime, people would have seen the stars, the supreme symbol of the constancy of cosmic order, suddenly come loose and fall through the void.

---

251 Joseph P. Farrell, *Reich of the Black Sun*, 249.

252 Joscelyn Godwin, *Arktos: The Polar Myth in Science, Symbolism, and Nazi*

PRISONERS OF PROPERTY
AND PROPRIETY

In the *Communist Manifesto*, Karl Marx writes that "self-conscious self-determination is the meaning of human freedom," and in the *Manuscripts of 1844* he defines equality as "Ich-Ich" (I-I) or "universal self-consciousness," in other words the collective self-consciousness of the community.[1] Which community? Humanity as such. Marx's conception of freedom arises from a consideration of man's "life-activity." An animal cannot reflect on its activities, which are a means of sustenance that directly *determine* its life. But human freedom consists in the fact that man's consciousness allows him to choose and direct his life-activity reflectively.[2] Marx's conception of equality is based on an understanding of this life-activity as a social product. Even a person's language, and thus also his thought, is a collective product of the community. In his natural state man is not only a social being, but in a deeper sense a person *is* a refraction of the totality of the community's collective Mind or "universal self-consciousness."[3]

---

1   Karl Marx, *The Economic and Philosophic Manuscripts of 1844 and the Communist Manifesto* (New York: Prometheus Books, 1988), 99.

2   Ibid., 76.

What this means is that the tired old arguments about the Marxist denial of the right to private property are totally uprooted from the metaphysical and psychological dimensions of Marx's deepest insights. Few Marxists have appreciated the extent to which Marx's argument that private property is a snare holding one back from an actualization of one's full human potential is also an argument about the very structure of thought. What needs to be overcome is not a property-holding economic and political system. Any attempt to do that is hopeless without a deconstruction of the ego that one takes to be one's *proper* self, reinforced as it is by certain norms of propriety in one or another society. The fully self-conscious and universal human community can only come about by orchestrating an escape from this prison of property and propriety, the prison of what is taken to be proper to oneself as opposed to other individuals and societies.

One of the very few people who has understood this is the physicist David Bohm, whose Marxist political orientation became grounds for his exile from the United States after a federal investigation in 1949. In his late work *On Dialogue*, Bohm develops a method for freeing ourselves from mechanisms of thought that imprison us within a petty ego structured by unexamined beliefs and prejudices. Taken together with the work of the sociologist Erving Goffman on how selfhood is constituted in everyday life, Bohm's dialectical process for attaining self-consciousness promises the kind of radical transformation of the human condition presupposed by Marx's critique of property. It also requires abandoning conventional notions of propriety, for example, monogamy.

It should not come as a surprise that it is a scientist, namely Bohm, who draws out this dimension of Marx. As we shall see, the kind of "objectivity" aimed at by Science as a human enterprise is itself a reflection of universal human self-consciousness and self-determination. For scientific exploration to come into its own and embrace its Promethean promise of liberating Man from every false limitation, a revolt against oppressive ideologies — including and especially religious ones — is indispensable. Science will always be an abortion and miscarriage of what Prometheus intended it to be when he gifted us with *techne*, so long as Olympus keeps us alienated from ourselves through the worship of false gods that take us to be their property. The communist revolution is, as Jacques Derrida recognizes, a revolution that is radically *spectral*.

The possibility of "private property" — i.e. of some-"thing" from nature becoming *mine* to the exclusion of others when I put my labor into it — rests on the assumption that man is separate from and stands against nature. John Locke claimed that the earth is given *to* man, as something separate from him and for his *use* — whereas for Marx nature and man are inseparable. Nature is man's "inorganic body" and so man always *has* nature.[4] Through his sensuous experience (hearing, seeing, smelling, feeling, thinking, being aware, wanting, loving) he always already appropriates nature as his, because in fact his senses manifest the world of nature as a projection of human consciousness.[5] Moreover, man does not have nature as an "individual" but as the collective consciousness of his society or community.

Thus the separation from nature (which is assumed in Locke and European Enlightenment thought in general) is not the inherent state of affairs but consists of an "estrangement" in which man objectifies the entities of the natural world as mere "things" and thereby alienates himself from them. Man is estranged from the exterior manifestation of his own consciousness, which is to say he loses self-consciousness. He forgets that nature is always already given to him and tries to *take* it. In alienating himself from nature he simultaneously alienates himself from others and objectifies himself as "the individual" — in whose eyes the sensuous richness of reality has been reduced to a matrix of

---

4   Ibid., 75.

functional "things" for *use* in the projects of a life-activity which has also been objectified into being merely mechanical.[6]

Only on the basis of this estrangement from nature and others is an appropriation of nature as "private property" to the exclusion of others *even possible*. Such an appropriation is an attempt to bridge a chasm which man himself has created by forgetting his own nature *as Nature*. The more man tries to appropriate the more the chasm of estrangement widens. Thus for Marx the real meaning of private property is as the concrete expression of an estrangement of self-consciousness which more abstractly and broadly includes God and religion as forms of man's alienation from his nature.[7]

In his book *Specters of Marx*, Jacques Derrida rightly recognizes that "Religion... was never [just] one ideology among others for Marx."[8] The most subversive and promising dimension of *Capital* is that therein Marx advances a mode of thinking that, although he takes it to be "scientific," lies beyond scientific "objectivity" by designating Science as that which entails its own radical transformation or mutation — not a scientific "objectivity" whose *end* is *a* revolution, but a Science whose self-reflexive and transformative *process* is *revolutionary*.[9] There has never yet been Science, but only sciences whose "scientificity" has remained dependent on ideologies that they are powerless to reductively exorcise. Even human sciences have not remedied this as a rejoinder to the natural sciences, as if nature and human experience could be separated.[10]

The messianic eschatology of religion cannot simply be classified among other elements of ideology or theology subject to the Marxist critique, or for that matter to postmodern deconstruction,

---

6   Ibid., 75; 77.

7   Ibid., 79.

8   Jacques Derrida, *Specters of Marx* (New York: Routledge, 1994), 131.

9   Ibid., 41.

because Marxist science necessarily carries within itself this messianic eschatology in its formal structure and in such a way that precedes and exceeds the content of the extant religions in its redemptive promise.[11] In a dangerously naïve manner, Derrida plays with the idea that "Abrahamic messianism" was "but an exemplary prefiguration" or "pre-name [*prénom*] given against the background of the possibility" of the messianic that he is evoking as the spectral force of Marxism beyond its ideology.[12] He sees in the desert mindset of "the religions of the Book" a herald of the "open, waiting... a waiting without horizon of expectation" for an undefined messianic salvation.[13]

However, a good case can be made that although Derrida is right to recognize the religious dimension of Marx's scientific thinking, he could not be more mistaken about the identity of Marx's spectral savior and the relationship of this "Messianism" to the essential thrust of the Abrahamic tradition of revelation. Marx *did* have a god, one with a very definite mythic heritage, but from the Abrahamic perspective this god is *the devil* — the Rebel of the International's fiery banner and emblematic star. The sickle moon and the hammer are both symbols of Prometheus in Greek mythology.

In *Prometheus Bound: The Mythic Structure of Karl Marx's Scientific Thinking*, Leonard P. Wessell argues that while some have recognized a religious dimension to Marx's thought and to Marxism in general, even they have been mistaken to think that Marx is mythic and poetic *despite* his "pretensions" to founding a science, in fact to effecting the unification of the sciences in the historically self-conscious and self-correcting Science that Hegel sought. Wessell thinks that it is precisely Marx's scientific thinking that is religious.[14] Moreover, he advances this argument while affirming the scientific status of Marx's thought.

---

11   Ibid., 74.

12   Ibid., 210.

13   Ibid., 211.

14   Leonard P. Wessell, *Prometheus Bound: The Mythic Structure of Karl Marx's*

Of course, many of Marx's theories may have been invalidated, but so have most of the theories ever advanced by practitioners of any acknowledged science.

The basic structure of Marx's thought is not only scientific but is exemplary for Science as opposed to fragmentary sciences that come up against each other's boundaries and the boundaries of non-scientific domains, such as the religious. Scientific thinking takes empirical events and evaluates them against objectivity constants that determine how they are to be ordered in a world model of unlimited scope. How the objectivity constants are constructed will yield different interpretations of the empirical manifold as it is immediately encountered. What is exceptional about Marx's scientific thinking is that "A *mythos* grounds the world hypothesis from which the categorical structure, the most general objectivity constants are derived..."[15] Not only is it the case that "Marx's scientific *logos* is grounded in a religious *mythos*," but the particular mythos that grounds it is determinative of science in general — and has always been so, even if only unconsciously. This is the mythos of Prometheus.

Wessell's study of Marx as a thinker of the Promethean spirit of Science argues that "Marx's thought is dominated by a Prometheanism. Marx believed in the unlimited powers of man for self-emancipation. Prometheus, the fire bringer, is a symbol for such self-divinization."[16] In fact, this is not going far enough: "Prometheus is more than a mythopoetic symbol in Marx's thinking. Prometheus bound, suffering, striving for redemption, indeed, rebelling furnishes the root metaphor used to generate the categorical self-system Marx used in his scientific thinking, including *Capital*."[17] It is not Marx's socioeconomic thought that inclined him to adopt Prometheus as a symbol or rhetorical device, after the fact, but rather a study of the

---

15   Ibid.

16   Ibid., 62.

thinker's youth and, especially, his early poetic writings, reveals that "Marx had to and did discover that the socioeconomic realm is the subject of a redemptive process because his mythico-ontological root metaphor of Prometheus bound so inclined him."[18] Already in his doctoral dissertation of 1840, Marx had quoted the *Prometheus Bound* of Aeschylus in this striking passage:

> Philosophy, as long as a drop of blood shall pulse in its world-subduing and absolutely free heart, will never grow tired of answering its adversaries with the... confession of Prometheus: 'In simple words, I hate the pack of gods,' [which] is its own confession, its own aphorism against all heavenly and earthly gods who do not acknowledge human self-consciousness as the highest divinity. It will have none other beside... Prometheus is the most eminent saint and martyr in the philosophical calendar.[19]

Marx saw Prometheus as the primordial philosopher or as the god who instilled the impetus to philosophizing in those that he made in his own image.[20] The young Marx's poems to his lover Jenny are filled with the Promethean spirit that inspired his own philosophical enterprise.[21] The titanic sense of Justice that breathes through these fiery verses of Marx is the spectral promise of Marx's thought that Derrida seeks, which exceeds the materialist ontology and the failed party ideologies of Marxism in the Soviet Union and elsewhere.

Derrida notes that according to the *Manifesto* of 1844, the "universal Communist Party, the Communist International will be... the final incarnation, the real presence of the specter, thus the end of the spectral."[22] The ontological commitment to substance as contrasted with the insubstantial or unreal is a betrayal of the permanence of

---

18   Ibid.

19   Ibid., 65, 106.

20   Ibid., 104–143.

21   Ibid., 117–122.

"permanent revolution," whose endurance is of a spectral nature.[23] Derrida is seeking a retrieval of the spectral revolutionary force of Marxism beyond the ontology of "dialectical materialism."[24] With reference to Blanchot and the manner of temporality that pervaded the May of 1968 uprising in France, Derrida remarks on the *immanence* of permanent revolution, which is not some determinate final goal but which opens up Time in such a way that one is addressed by an ever-present demand.[25]

This permanent revolution must proceed from out of a radical reorientation of our thought processes to the end of attaining the kind of "open mindedness" that Derrida means to evoke with his suggestion that even our experience of time ought to be revolutionized. David Bohm has developed a dialectical method for bringing this about within small communities. Time is for us, after all, a function of the interplay between memory and representational thought. We are prisoners of past thoughts and patterns of behavior that were never authentically ours to begin with.

David Bohm argues that though human consciousness/cognition is uniform from person to person, human beings also have *thought* (which is responsible for their *social* being). Consciousness/cognition is simply the direct *presentation* of what is before one's senses to the brain. Bohm explains that *thought* however, is a "system" of "symbolic representation." That is, when one sees an object (or a situation composed of various objects) it is presented to the brain, but it is also *recorded* there in memory. Thought then *re-presents* former recorded presentations, in order to determine how a current situation itself will be recorded for future *re-presentation*. The point is that the presentation fuses with the representation. One channel is coming from the senses, the other from memory, and the two mix in experience.

---

23   Ibid., 39.
24   Ibid., 110.

Ultimately, new representations are being created by the criteria of aggregates of old representations, which Bohm calls "assumptions."

Bohm's central point is that we are not aware that *thought* functions in this way, we lack "proprioception (self-awareness) of thought." "Proprioception" is a word that usually refers to the mostly unconscious perception of spatial movement and orientation from within the body itself, whether through the nervous system or canals in the inner ear. By adopting and adapting this term to the context of thought processes Bohm is implying that it is possible for a deeper awareness to become conscious of the typically mechanical function of mental representation as mediated by memory. Bohm suggests that thought functions mechanically on its own, whenever there is an "object" present before the "subject" of a consciousness with a brain capable of memory (and language). Thus it is arbitrary in creating representations, which results in many of them being contradictory (in conflict with each other). We believe that we are obviously looking at what actually *is*, and that we are then free to think about how we respond to it. However, Bohm argues that the content of thought (the representational *assumptions*) constantly effect the thought process—again, unconsciously. This means that when we believe that "we" are thinking-about something our assumptions are actually thinking for us.

This has major implications for the nature of the "Individual Will" of the *ego,* and deconstructs it in such a way that it is opened to a Hegelian unity with communal will. If Thought functions as Bohm claims that it does, then all of the objects that we identify with ourselves, and in turn, which identify us, are illusory and often contradictory. Our wife is not ours, we have been tricked by thought into thinking she is. All of our possessions are not ours either. But most fundamentally our opinions are not our own, for as Bohm suggests, they are nothing but assumptions that have been randomly and reflexively created by thought through a series of (subject-object) interactions. In other words, when consciousness or cognition exists

without thought (as it does in other animals), then there is a fundamental universal self among all that are biologically similar, but when
thought intervenes it creates another constructed self, the "ego." This
ego-identity varies from individual to individual (in fact it creates the
"individual') within a species with thought, because representations
are mechanical and arbitrary and will differ if different entities are
subject to different placements, situations and interactions.

The problem of the psychological "ego" or private self can be seen
as follows. Thought as a system of symbolic representation is arbitrary
in how it represents the world. However, in that it is also tautological
it has to reconcile these representations and guide future representations by their self-asserted criteria. Thus the division between "private"
and "public" and the solipsistic distinction between "self" and "other"
develop so that certain representations or assumptions of Thought can
disappear into a "back" region and be hidden from others, while up
"front" one gives a presentation based on assumptions that contradict
those now hidden in the back. With different people, different aspects
of thought are concealed and others presented. Furthermore, when
one is "with-oneself," the same process of private and public conceal-
ment takes place in a more complex and internalized way in that one
is usually tacitly and subtly relating to oneself in terms of others — or
what George Herbert Mead calls the "generalized Other" of society
(or what Martin Heidegger conceptualizes as the "They" or *Das Man*).
In other words, the coherence of "the self" as circumscribed by the
system of Thought, depends on suppressing the incoherence of that
system through giving conflicting assumptions their own time "on
stage" or in the spotlight, and forcibly concealing others.

Thus in *The Presentation of Self in Everyday Life*, Erving Goffman
suggests that when we enter the presence of others we "define the
situation" in such a way as to indicate how we want to be considered.
We define the situation differently depending on who we are with
and where. Each person makes this definition and by being in tune
with and accepting each other's definitions a given social situation is

created. A performance is divided into what Goffman calls "front" and "back" regions. The "front" is the part of oneself which one presents to certain people and the "back" is what one hides or does not allow them to see. What is in the "front" and what is in the "back" will depend on who our "audience" is. Goffman writes that when engaged in performance (or interaction), for the sake of propriety "each participant is expected to suppress his immediate heartfelt feelings, conveying a view of the situation which he feels the others will be able to find at least temporarily acceptable...each participant concealing his own wants..."[26] This implies that the "back" region, from which the performance of the "front" region is controlled, is home to one's true Self. It is the inner realm which contains what one really feels and "wants" and thus reflects who one really *is*.

Our performance even continues to some degree when we are on our own, because we are thinking about ourselves in terms of something in respect to which we would need to express certain aspects of ourselves and suppress others. Thus we come to identify ourselves with a set of assumptions set within a complex of various degrees of private and public presentation. We see any threat to these assumptions as a threat to ourselves, and so the most profound fear becomes a tenacious guardian of the "ego."

Goffman argues that there are expressions that we "give" purposely as part of the performance, and also expressions that we inadvertently "give off" — those that escape our attempt to prevent what is in "back" from being seen "in front": "The expressiveness of the individual (and therefore his capacity to give impressions) appears to involve two radically different kinds of sign activity: the expression that he gives, and the expression that he gives off." He goes on to further emphasize this distinction when he explains how because the audience's keen perception often outsteps our measures to hide the "back" region, we engage in further steps to prevent its exposure. So a cat and mouse

---

26 Erving Goffman, *The Presentation of Self in Everyday Life* (New York:

cycle develops between the keenness of the audience and the tact of the performer, in which greater measures are employed by each to maintain propriety. Goffman believes that all of our social structures are circularly recreated and maintained by our everyday small-scale interactions with one another in this manner of performance.[27]

In his work *On Dialogue,* David Bohm acknowledges that *thought* currently lacks *proprioception* or the self-awareness to realize that it is perpetually casting a false divide between private and public realms, but for him this is not inherently so. He argues that *thought* does innately have the potential for self-awareness.[28] For Bohm "external forces" such as the expectations of conduct that reinforce the social structure, are only "external" in that they come from many other *individuals* and blindly act together on oneself. Since the representational mechanism of Thought is collective, he argues that the response must also be collective. Thus, Bohm argues that "proprioception of thought" can arise in what he calls a true "dialogue" between people. In his vision of "dialogue" Bohm hopes to bring about a social self-consciousness by exposing Hegel's dialectical process, in its psychological aspect, to those who are undergoing it, and thereby accelerate its dynamic of eroding the illusory individual will, by exposing and negating its contradictions, in favor of the realization of collective unity.

A sufficient number of participants so as to reflect a microcosm of society are assembled for the sole purpose of participating in a "dialogue" with each other. The first principle of this dialogue is that honesty must exist within the group, everyone must say what they actually believe. This can come about either by the sheer fact of a number of people great enough that superficial cordiality ultimately breaks down, or by a true dedication of the participants to abide by this principle. In addition to a commitment to honesty, the participants

---

27 Ibid.

must have a commitment to what Bohm calls "suspension." That is, one must not suppress one's possibly vehement reactions to others' assumptions, in order that one's own assumptions may be exposed in that response. But one must only follow through and manifest one's emotions, so that their tacit assumptions can be "suspended" as if in thin air, before oneself. One must have a commitment to really look at one's own responses, no matter how emotionally entangled one is by them. This is done because all who are participants are interested in *studying,* and so understanding, themselves.[29]

If everyone expresses what they actually believe on whatever issues the discussion randomly turns to, then they will all make statements that ultimately expose the "assumptions" of their *thought.* Two parties may find each other's statements wrong, even infuriating, and a third party may make yet a different statement confounding the first two and causing them to question the validity of both of their statements. Many may agree with the third, but a further participant or participants may hold yet a different view and thus call the former into question as well. The point is that, all of the assumptions of the members, which reflect the assumptions of society, will be exposed and through conflict with each other they will all be discredited as "*the* truth" or *how it is.* Thus the group will become conscious of the assumptions of "collective thought" upon which society rests. They could only have done this through each other, not realizing in isolation how what each believes is part of a larger but fragmented picture. The "external forces," cease to be in dialogue, because the group is large enough to realize that those *forces* have no independence. It realizes that it is creating those "forces," and that many of the assumptions driving them are contradictory — making for a confused society.[30]

The insight by each of the members into their own assumptions is made possible by the others, and this insight inherently changes one's relationship to those assumptions. They are no longer "fact," just as the "collective thought" of the group no longer seems like a law of nature that demands how each person function in society. At this point, a new horizon opens to the group where the old has been fully realized and the *new* can begin. Exchanges between people become *creative*, not based on old assumptions — but on the present situation. Thus new shared meanings come about, because each person has stopped clinging to restrictive assumptions. The whole attitude or conduct of the group itself may change, as slowly, (albeit in miniature form) a new society comes into being. But it is a society that is conscious of its own "collective thought," in which individuals (through each other) have achieved "proprioception of thought."[31]

This is the kind of revolutionary transformation of the human condition that is presupposed by Marx's so-called "abolition of the family." It is idiotic to imagine that monogamous marriage could simply be done away with as a matter of state policy. People being such as they are now, this cannot but end in disaster. Rather, Marx's understanding of marriage as a form of private property holding is based on his having taken the relationship of man to woman as indicative of the degree of man's metaphysical estrangement from his Nature, in other words his alienation from his truly human Being:

> The direct, natural, and necessary relation of person to person is the *relation of man to woman*. In this *natural* relationship of the sexes man's relation to nature is immediately his relation to man, just as his relation to man is immediately his relation to nature — his own *natural* function… From this relationship one can therefore judge man's whole level of development. It follows from the character of this relationship how much *man* as a *species being*, as *man*, has come to be himself and to comprehend himself; the relation of man to woman is *the most natural* relation of human being to human being. It therefore reveals the extent to which man's *natural* behavior has become *human*, or the extent to which the *human* essence in him

has become a *natural* essence — the extent to which his *human nature* has come to be *nature to him*.[32]

As a follower of Hegel, Marx sees this alienation as a necessary step in a dialectical process whereby man comes to know himself through a history in which his nature is unfolded before him. Marx believes that this estrangement is necessary because of the nature of self-consciousness. Phenomenologically, man himself "establish[es] nature as the mind's world" — nature is the mind's being, but its "externality" confuses man into believing that nature is "outside" of him in the sense of being *separate* from him.[33] This paradox resolves itself in history as Mind (Hegel's *Geist*) reveals its true nature to man through the rise of inequality and oppression in the alienation of labor culminating in the bourgeoisie-proletariat struggle.[34]

Thus *Communism* is not a theory, movement, or regime, but a metaphysical event in which there is an annulment of the estrangement of man from his nature embodied by the annulment of private property, and more abstractly by the annulment of God. In this event the alienated object is drawn back into the self, and the objectified and mechanized world reappears as the manifestation of human consciousness. Freedom and equality which were once taken for granted and lost are now consciously regained and held in the realization that God did not give nature to man, but that man ex-*ist*(s) or is projected outside of himself — together with others — as *nature*.[35] This is the *spectral* revolution that makes Communism a "specter" — no, not just a specter, but *the* specter of human history.

Translators of Karl Marx often occlude the specificity and literality of his references to the *specter* by mistranslating it with a number of

---

32   Robert C. Tucker [Editor], *The Marx-Engels Reader* (New York: W.W. Norton & Company, 1978), 83.

33   Marx, *Economic and Philosophic Manuscripts of 1844*, 125.

34   Ibid., 112.

interpretively loaded terms that they mistake to be equivalent to his usage, for example "phantasmagorical, hallucinatory, fantastic, imaginary" and so forth.[36] With his references to the specter and the spectral, Marx was not merely manipulating the reader with empty "rhetoric, turns of phrase that are contingent or merely apt to convince by striking the imagination."[37] In *Specters of Marx,* Jacques Derrida wants to recover the radically futural promise of Marxism, its spectral possibilities in a movement without organization, party, property, or state, and beyond the (materialist) ontological response of Marx himself to this spectrality, namely his insistence, as well as that of Marxists in general, that the ghost must be "nothing, nothing period (non-being, non effectivity, non-life)…"[38] Marx wants to distinguish the specter (*Gespenst*) from the proper Spirit (*Geist*) of the revolution, and yet the spectral and the spiritual thoroughly contaminate each other in Marx's texts.[39] He still believes in a de-contaminating purification or exorcism of the spectral from out of the spirit.[40] Derrida repeatedly identifies the "difference between specter and spirit" as "a differance."[41] In fact, it is *the* difference of which all others are traces:

> The specter is not only the carnal apparition of the spirit, its phenomenal body, its fallen and guilty body, it is also the impatient and nostalgic waiting for a redemption, namely, once again, for a spirit. The host would be that deferred spirit, the promise or calculation of an expiation. What is this differance? All or nothing. One must reckon with it but it upsets all calculations, interests, and capital.[42]

---

36 Derrida, *Specters of Marx,* 185.

37 Ibid., 186.

38 Ibid., 35.

39 Ibid., 138, 140–141.

40 Ibid., 155.

41 Ibid., 170, 177.

The permanent revolutionary has memories of the future, of a time for ghosts whose extremity lies beyond the "end" qua *telos* of any history.[43] Derrida writes: "Untimely, 'out of joint,' even and especially if it appears to come in due time, the spirit of the revolution is *fantastic and anachronistic through and through.*"[44] Marxism failed when it made common cause with those hunting its specter insofar as it affirmed the dividing line between the ghost and the actuality of utopia by demanding that this line ought to be crossed — as if the coming utopia is not always spectral.[45] The totalitarianism of Marxism arises as a consequence of "an *ontological* treatment of the spectrality of the ghost..."[46] On account of his materialism, Marx in effect joins in with the conspiracy of the nobility and clergy who assemble by the twilight verging on the end of history, in the castle of Old Europe, to set out on a "holy hunt against this specter."[47]

In *Specters of Marx*, Derrida comes closest to the titanic spectral promise of Marx's quest for a worldwide scientific society, which will also be a universal liberation of the human potential, when he contemplates the dramatic figure of Shakespeare's *Hamlet*. Derrida goes so far as to claim that "the only question" that he would like to pose in *Specters of Marx* is the question: "what is the *being-there* of the specter? What is the mode of presence of a specter?"[48] As he later elaborates, this is "the originary question (*die ursprüngliche Frage*), the abyssal question" that bares "on the non-identity to self, on the inadequation and thus the non-presence to self..."[49] What are "spectral forces"?[50] What "spectralizes" is elementally "neither living nor dead, neither

---

43   Ibid., 45.

44   Ibid., 140.

45   Ibid., 47, 45.

46   Ibid., 114.

47   Ibid., 49.

48   Ibid., 46.

49   Ibid., 151.

present nor absent…"[51] Spectrality and ideality are somehow related in Derrida's mind; he claims that the concept of the "irreducible genesis of the spectral" is implicit in the very concept of an "idea."[52] There is an "ideality in the very event of presence" which always already dis-joins what is coming to presence so as to make its apparition possible.[53] Moreover, the ideality of time, its "being-outside-itself" is "obviously the condition of any idealization and consequently of any ideologization and any fetishization, whatever difference one must respect between these two processes."[54]

Explicitly referencing Martin Heidegger, Derrida notes how the "passage of this time of the present comes from the future to go toward the past, toward the going of the gone [*l'en allé*] (*Das Weilen ist der Übergang aus Kunft zu Gang. Das Anwesende ist das Je-weilige*)."[55] The past can be experienced as yet to come.[56] What "seems to be out front, the future, comes back in advance: from the past, from the back."[57] To ask how an event — and in that one should hear *event*uality — comes to pass in this way is to ask: "*What* is a ghost?" It is a question concerning the *effectivity* of a specter, which is disconcerting given that its virtual and insubstantial character as a simulacrum ought to render it ineffective.[58] The comings and goings of a specter manifest the essential — or rather in-essential — character of temporality itself insofar as the absence, non-presence, non-effectivity, inactuality, and virtuality that pervade its apparitions disrupt the order of linear succession wherein past, present, and future are grasped in terms of what

---

51   Ibid., 63.

52   Ibid., 69.

53   Ibid., 94.

54   Ibid., 194.

55   Ibid., 28.

56   Ibid., xix.

57   Ibid., 10.

is deferred to a place before and after what is in "real time."[59] Derrida takes Shakespeare to have epitomized this spectral character of temporality in Hamlet's lament: "The time is out of joint. / O cursèd spite, / That ever I was born to set it right!" This means not only that Time is "disadjusted" in the sense of being "off its hinges" or "off course" but also in the sense of time being "beside itself."[60] It evokes the existential temporality that is the lived context for chronological time.

One way of hearing this phrase calls to mind Prometheus' brother, Atlas, if he were to shrug rather than to *endure* under his burden as the bearer of the celestial spheres that are the gear-works of chronological time: "'Le temps est hors de ses gonds,' time is off its hinges."[61] We can see the specter of Atlas in Derrida's reading of Hamlet as a tragic kingly figure who is cursed by the burden of being destined to put time back into joint, in other words: "to put history, the world, the age, the time *upright*, on the right path…" In Atlas, the sovereign of Plato's doomed *daimonic* kingdom of "Atlantis" (i.e. Realm of Atlas), we are dealing with a struggle against the decline of the time,[62] with the question of Justice in light of the world ages — or the aging of worlds, and the reparation that would be required for a world-historical renaissance. Hamlet declares that "the time is out of joint" at just the moment when he swears together [*conjurer*] with the specter "who is always a sworn conspirator [*conjure*]" from somewhere beneath Shakespeare's world stage or, as it were "from beneath the earth"[63] — where Titans such as Atlas are imprisoned for their faith. As Derrida points out, a "conjuration" is both an oath to take part in a conspiracy against a superior power and a magical incantation or charm intended to summon a spirit.[64]

---

59 Ibid., 48.

60 Ibid., 20.

61 Ibid., 22.

62 Ibid., 23.

63 Ibid., 34.

To redress the wrong of world history—*this*, for Derrida, is the essence of the tragic. Not to redress one or another unfortunate mishap, or to right any particular wrong, but to be aware of what he calls the "pre-originary and properly spectral anteriority of the crime."[65] As soon as we read these words, the Anaximander fragment ought to come to mind. So it should be no surprise that several pages later in *Specters of Marx*, Derrida enters into a sustained meditation on Heidegger's reading of this Presocratic Greek text, a fragment from that primordial epoch in the prehistory of thought which Nietzsche refers to as "the tragic age of the Greeks." It is the age wherein Aeschylus turned Prometheus into the first dramatic persona in recorded history. One of the sole traces of Anaximander's thinking, the fragment concerns the *anachronique* character of Time itself.[66] In Heidegger's translation it reads: "But that from which things arise also gives rise to their passing away, according to what is necessary; for things render justice and pay penalty to one another for their injustice [*adikia*], according to the ordinance of time."[67]

The *adikia* in the fragment does not speak simply of juridical-moral injustice but of its condition of possibility in the very injustice of being—in the way that the world is not going as it ought to go, "something is out of joint" and "all is not right with things."[68] It is not just "something" that is out of joint, but Time—the horizon of being, and this means that the very Being of beings is haunted by the essence of the tragic.[69] We are called to an impossible task—the quest for a utopia founded on a different experience of Time than that which accounts for the violence that we do to one another. Hamlet or any other prince that takes up the mantle of King Atlas is a *tragic* figure

---

65   Ibid., 24.

66   Ibid., 25.

67   Martin Heidegger, "The Anaximander Fragment" in *Early Greek Thinking* (New York: Harper and Row, 1984), 20.

68   Derrida, *Specters of Marx*, 27–28.

because he is cursed with the knowledge that he can and must strive to right the wrong of existence, to bear up under Time's declination. Of course, this is an impossible task, but as Derrida remarks: "here as elsewhere, wherever deconstruction is at stake, it would be a matter of linking an affirmation (in particular a political one), if *there is any*, to the experience of the impossible, which can only be a radical experience of the *perhaps*."[70] The "experience of the impossible" is constitutive of deconstruction.[71] Towards the very end of *Specters of Marx*, Derrida elaborates on this relationship of the impossible to the sociopolitical quest for Justice: "Present existence or essence has never been the condition, object, or the *thing* of justice. One must constantly remember that the impossible is, alas, always possible."[72]

70   Ibid., 42.
71   Ibid., 111.

FREE WILL VS. LOGICAL DETERMINISM

The metaphysical problem of free will is usually defined in terms of whether or not the world is physically deterministic. In *On the Plurality of Worlds*, David Lewis maintains that while *physical* laws may differ from world to world, and while there may be some worlds that are partly or wholly non-physical, *states of affairs in all possible worlds are nonetheless determined by logical laws.*[1] This prohibits contingency with respect to the totality of being: every way that anything could be already is *so* in a completed logical space, and everything that one could ever do is actually done by some counterpart of oneself living at some other causally isolated world. Lewis is not unaware of the potential problem for free will posed by this thesis, but he believes himself to have adequately defeated this objection in Section 2.6 of *On the Plurality of Worlds*, entitled "A Road to Indifference."[2]

In this section, Lewis misconstrues the central force of a hypothetical "indifference" objection, according to which no one will be motivated to do anything in the face of knowing that any thing they

---

1   David Lewis, *On the Plurality of Worlds* (Oxford: Blackwell Publishing, 2003), 91.

could possibly "choose" to do will in fact be done by some parallel world counterpart of theirs. This objection really concerns the impossibility of *novelty* under his maximal ontology, and not merely the psychological question of motivation to act decisively or the lack thereof. With reference to the writings of William James on ontological novelty in respect to the problem of free will, I will question the coherence of Lewis's operative meaning of the terms "causation" and "possibility." I will elaborate on Lewis's "story" metaphor for what he rejects as an impossible ontology, and suggest that only this might allow for the real agent causality that Lewis's essentially mathematical ontology prohibits.

Let me begin by clarifying my point of contention by briefly elaborating on what parts of Lewis's response to a hypothetical "indifference" objection I am *not* concerned to dispute here. Lewis goes on at some length about the "sum total" of "good" and "evil." As indicated by my use of air quotes, it is very problematic what if anything exactly defines "good" and "evil" as so really distinct from one another that one could even begin to *quantitatively* think about a "sum total" of each of them as compared to the other. Lewis also claims that his thesis of the plurality of worlds only poses a problem for a universalist utilitarian morality, one based on a completely altruistic or impersonal imperative to increase the total quantity of good vs. evil.[3] He believes that this is actually a point in favor of his thesis, because such a morality is "a philosophical invention" quite far from "common sense" moralities that concern the good of a person, an emotionally bonded social group, or a nation. I do not particularly care whether Lewis's thesis prohibits *this* kind of morality, and I am quite willing to agree with him that a universalist morality is a false conception that does not speak against his thesis. Furthermore, I am not concerned to dispute his claim that otherworldly evils and goods are just as "good" and "evil" as those of this world that is (indexically) actual for us.[4]

Placing all of that aside, my objection is simply that Lewis's thesis of the maximal plurality of worlds does not allow for any free will worth having, and by "worth having" I mean to suggest that he does not have good grounds for defeating an "indifference" objection. The "indifference" objection that Lewis actually addresses in Section 2.6 is, of course, a hypothetical one that he himself concocts so that he can have a response prepared for anyone that might raise anything like it. However, it seems to me that he misconstrues what the central concern of such an objection would be, perhaps so as to be able to answer it more easily. At issue is not whether we can change the "sum total" of "good" and "evil" in view of the fact that all possibilities, including all possible versions of our own life, are actualized at some world or another. The moral semantics of "good" and "evil" confuse the point here. Rather, a real indifference objection would be that: *I* should be indifferent with respect to my so-called-life if there is *really*, that is *ontologically*, nothing that *I* can *add* to my world or to the lives of those who cohabit it. Whatever meaning the moral terms "good" and "evil" might have is irrelevant to this objection, which could be forwarded based on aesthetic rather than ethical motivations. If they are to be *works of art* — the visionary labors of a *creator* — then in no other possible world do there exist such things to vitally experience, and dynamically respond to, as Shakespeare's plays, Coltrane's jazz, Duncan's dances, Pollock's paintings, or Kubrick's films.

It is a question of *novelty*. I must *be able*, by *my* actions, to transform the world around me in such a way as it could never be transformed were it not for my *decision* to take those actions. Of course, this transformation need not always be according to my intention, and indeed if it *always* were exactly what I wanted, that might pose as great a psychological obstacle to a life worth living. It may be an extremely subtle and hardly noticeable transformation that I effect in the empirical world, and in the large and long view it probably always is. However, it must be *possible* to do something no one has done in just the way that I am contemplating doing it — not anyone in this world of mine, or anyone however like me in any other world that there might ever possibly be, or that there ever has been. Otherwise, I *do* nothing at all, and for that matter "I" have insufficient personal identity to really *be* anyone either.

To be *someone* who makes his or her life what it alone uniquely is, and not the life of another, demands a non-reductionist view of consciousness, one wherein our minds are not ontologically derivative of some more elementary constituents. Whether these simples are taken to be empirically real (as they are in Physicalism) or whether they are constructs of logical possibility is irrelevant. When Lewis says that some of his many worlds contain "spirits" who do not operate according to any physical laws, much less what are taken to be *our* physical laws, he is presumably conceiving of these "spirit" beings as metaphysical simples. Given his reductionism, he would certainly have to do so in order to even attempt to attribute any power of choice to them.

However, if they *are* metaphysical simples, then there seems to be no way that he can conceive of them as ever "doing" anything with respect to each other or to some other objects, unless anything with which each of them could interact already had a logically predetermined propensity-profile for *certain* interactions (and not others). In that case all of the substances with which these "spirits" (or any other would-be-choosers) might interact, are substances whose predetermined propensity-profiles compel the latter to act only according to laws that demarcate a closed system of finite possibilities that are all bound to be actualized "somewhere" at some "time." It seems that on this view, if "I" were one of these "spirits," I would only be discursively responsible for what I do — and not an *ontologically* responsible *agent* of actions that created states of affairs, and brought objects into being.

that could otherwise never have been as I alone was able to will them to be. Metaphysical simples can *create* nothing at all.

Lewis claims that radically isolated causal chains provide real agency for counterparts who are (presently) leading perfectly identical lives (and in some worlds, lives that have already been lived in a perfectly identical way in past cycles or eons of eternal recurrence). He makes this claim in reference to a certain "story" that he adapts for his own purposes:

> A story by Larry Niven even suggests that knowledge of a plurality of worlds might reasonably undermine the will to live. Every decision you ever make is made in all the myriad ways it might be made. It is made one way by you, other ways by your other-worldly counterparts who are exactly like you up to the moment of the decision. Not only difficult and momentous decisions will be made all different ways; but also easy decisions, even decisions too easy to take any thought, like the decision to kill yourself on the spur of the moment for no reason at all. Given that the decision will in any case be made all different ways, what does it matter whether you are one of the ones who makes it one way or one of the ones who makes it another way...[5]

Lewis goes on to qualify his use of Niven's story as a hypothetical "indifference" objection, by pointing out that he is modifying Niven's story in order to do so. Apparently, the original story is about one of two kinds of *physical* parallel universes: (1) parallel universes between which travel is possible, perhaps through worm-holes or time machines; (2) totally inaccessible parallel universes that are posited by Hugh Everett as a solution to the supposedly "mysterious" wave-collapse in quantum theory. Lewis seems to think that it is not clear which of these two types Niven is talking about. On Lewis's view, the "universes" of (1) would only be discrete parts of a *single* possible world. In regard to (2) he makes the following remark: "Niven may be talking about branching worlds, in which one present decider has many futures that are all equally his. If so, I grant his point. That really would make nonsense of decision."[6]

Lewis's criticism of version (2) of the Niven story concerns the manner in which a person's genuine decision-making capacity would be vitiated by there really existing a version of him for each and every decision that *he* could possibly have made. Lewis thinks that this does not pose an agency problem for his thesis of the plurality of worlds because his possible world counterparts are entirely causally isolated from one another. The decisions made by these Lewisian counterparts are supposed to be real choices because they are allegedly radically independent persons. They originate in different worlds. They are not created, together with their worlds, as instantiations of alternative decisions faced by a common predecessor. What I am arguing is that unless contact between worlds *is* possible, as it is on interpretation (1) of Niven's original story, even these counterparts are *not* "deciders" in any real sense that would convince any creatively minded person that life was worth living and that decisions were worth making.

I can well imagine traveling through a worm-hole into an alternate universe where I meet a counterpart of myself who has lived a very similar life, but has or has had somewhat different relationships with counterparts of people with whom I have or have had certain relationships. My presence in his life would change it and, once I traveled back through the worm-hole to my world, my encounter with him would make me reflect on and change the circumstances of my own life as well. Even if these lives were for all intents and purposes *identical*, the *possibility* of meeting my counterpart would allow each of us to act freely in reaction to the other — which, at that point, would cause the direction of our two lives, *and of our two worlds*, to significantly deviate from one another. Only in this case would each of us be ontologically independent agents, as Lewis mistakenly takes his counterparts to be. Lewisian counterparts are rather *effects*, the "cause" (or sufficient reason) of whose actions is determined by the character of an atemporally complete logical space.

On the face of it, and at first glance, Lewis's ontology of maximal possibilities appears very creative (at least compared to other works of analytic philosophy), and so it seems odd to claim that it forecloses every *existentially* significant possibility (and I take the primary meaning of the word "possibility" to be an existential one). However, upon closer scrutiny one should realize that Lewis's ontology is only "creative" in the sense that certain proofs of higher mathematics seem stunning when first discovered, but then grow trivial over time. (Surely, even the Pythagorean theorem seemed "creative" in this sense when it was first discovered.) Lewis places conditions of "size" and "shape" on what could or could not possibly coexist with what within the same possible world, and, by extension, what must be the case at all possible worlds. In so doing, he relies on a mathematical definition of the possible properties and relations that any being could logically have:

> But now there is trouble. Only a limited number of distinct things can coexist in a spacetime continuum. It cannot exceed the infinite cardinal number of the points in a continuum…Our principle [of the conceivability of states of affairs at possible worlds] therefore requires a proviso: 'size and shape permitting.' … Starting with point-sized things that are uncontroversially possible, perhaps because actual, we patch together duplicates of them in great number (continuum many, or more) to make an entire world. The mathematical representations are a book-keeping device, to make sure that the 'size and shape permitting' proviso is satisfied.[7]

Lewis would like to cast his recourse to "mathematical representations" as no more than "a book-keeping device" that is useful for adhering to some intrinsic logical laws of being. However, this manner of *representation*, of *taking* things to be so and so, is the matrix of his ontology. In such an ontology, where mathematics is read into the foundations of all concrete worlds, there "are no gaps in logical space" and so there is no room for contingency in the system as a whole. Lewis states this repeatedly:

> It is futile to want the entire system of worlds to satisfy a condition, because *it is not contingent what conditions the entire system of worlds does or doesn't satisfy*. You might as well want the number seventeen to be prime, or to be even...[8]

> Is it a matter of wants: should I want there to be less evil and more good in total, throughout the worlds? It would be an idle wish, since *the character of the totality of all the worlds is not a contingent matter*. I see no reason why I ought to have so utterly idle and pointless a wish.[9]

Lewis emphasizes that imagination is a poor criterion for defining possible worlds.[10] Things of any significant degree of complexity are usually imagined imprecisely, and so something that is logically impossible may be thought to be possible simply because what it would involve has not been imagined with sufficient clarity. While Lewis emphasizes repeatedly that possible worlds, however bizarre, are not categorically different from our "actual" world in their ontological status (in the reality of their being), he also clearly states that possible worlds, including our own, are essentially of a different kind than the fantastic worlds of story-tellers:

> If worlds were like stories or story-tellers, there would indeed be room for worlds according to which contradictions are true. The sad truth about the prevarications of these worlds would not itself be contradictory. But worlds, as I understand them, are *not* like stories or story-tellers. They are like this world; and this world is no story, not even a true story.[11]

---

8   Ibid., 125; my emphasis.

9   Ibid., 126; my emphasis.

10   Ibid., 90.

Lewis's metaphor of a world as a story-teller's tale, and his warning that the impossible can be imprecisely imagined, suggests what the world might be like if it were not reducible to quantifiable fundamental constituents — if its ontology were not basically *mathematical*. It is worthy of note that the Greek root of the word "mathematical" is *mathesis* — which means "that which can be learned," in other words that which is formulaically anticipatable. On the other hand, *logos*, the Greek root of the word "logic" originally means "discourse" or even "story" and its first philosophical use in reference to the constitution of the cosmos still retained *this* sense. That first use of the notion of "logic" — to refer to dynamically adaptable tactical rules on a cosmic scale — was by Heraclitus, who also called the cosmos "a child at *play*, moving pieces in a game." It may be that any free will worth having requires the world to *indeed* be something like a story-teller's tale — where fundamental ontology allows for the same logically "impossible" phantasmagoria that Lewis attributes to the vagueness of imagination.

In his last years, William James (who was, after all, the brother of a great story-teller) came close to seriously advocating such a view in connection to the problem of free will. In two sections on "Novelty and Causation" in *Some Problems of Philosophy*, James points out that the notion of "causation" primarily derives from our own experience of bringing things into being that we intuitively know could not otherwise have been.[12] Our own acts of origination, our acts of *creation*, are the basis upon which we then only secondarily attribute causes to other beings in nature (first to animistic spirits, then to the gods or God, and finally to material beings or natural laws). To intellectually abstract "causation" from its primary meaning as an immediate experience of the agency of conscious willing beings such as ourselves, and to turn it into an impersonal universal principle, leads to an infinite regress wherein causes collapse into effects of other causes, without a

---

12   William James, *Writings: 1902–1910* (New York: The Library of America, 1987),

first cause being found anywhere within the limits of possible experience. Without a first cause with an ontologically irreducible explanatory power, all causality loses its necessary aspect.

Lewis thinks of the causal power of inner-worldly individuals (who have counterparts at other possible worlds) as a power to *actualize* certain outcomes, not as a power to *create* them. For example, he argues that even if in many possible worlds similar to this one, but slightly different, he completes writing his book while in others he does not, it is impossible for him to take vicarious pleasure in knowing that some of his counterparts complete the book while he does not. Lewis writes: "It matters to me whether I am one of those among my counterparts who labour on, or one of those who quit."[13] The completed books and those that will never be completed already exist in the bounded totality of logical space. Lewis does not allow for an ontologically significant "labour" on his part, as an agent, that would *cause* a book to come into being as an object that otherwise would not be. Note the following two passages:

> I reply that the argument for indifference relies on a false premise…It is not idle to want continued life for yourself; you may have it or not, and you will not get what you want if you make the wrong decision about whether to kill yourself on the spur of the moment.[14]

> 'What is wrong with actualizing evils, since they will occur in some other possible world anyway if they don't occur in this one?' — If you actualize evils, you will be an evil-doer, a causal source of evil. That is something which, if you are virtuous, you do not want to be. Otherworldly evils are neither here nor there. They aren't your evils. Your virtuous desire to do good and not evil… depends causally on what you do.[15]

These passages are subject to internal contradictions. Note Lewis's usage of these phrases: "you may have it or not" unless "you *make* the

---

13   Lewis, *On the Plurality of Worlds*, 126.

14   Ibid., 124–125.

wrong *decision*," because only if "what you *do*" is to "*actualize* evils" will they be "*your* evils," ones that depend on your being "a *causal source* of evil." For Lewis, we are causal "sources" only in the sense that already existing parts of logical space are made (indexically) "actual" through us. I do not see how this non-primitive notion of agent causation does not lead to the same infinite regress of empirical causes that forced Hume to abandon causality and Kant to seek a noumenal basis for personal agency. In that case, Lewis does not allow for "making" any real "decision." Our "choices" collapse into being merely the discursive "effects" of other empirical causes.

We see this again in Lewis's response to an objection raised by Mark Johnston to the effect that Lewis's "egocentric" view of moral action is compromised by Lewis having argued (elsewhere) that we are not strictly unified in our persistence through time, but are each divisible into temporal parts or stages:

> My present stage wants the book to be finished in the fulfillment of *its* present intentions — there's the egocentric part — and that will happen only if the proper sort of causal continuity binds together my present stage with the one that finishes the book. The continuity thus desired is part of the continuity that unifies mereological sums of person-stages into persisting people.[16]

Lewis is saying that even if your personal intentions to "do" *x* and *y* are somehow communicated from person-stage to person-stage, "you" (as defined by the sum of your communicated intentions) are still the "causal source" of *x* and *y*. This is just the kind of intellectually abstracted notion of causality that James believed to have been responsible for Hume's rejection of causality and Kant's artificial imposition of it as a category of pure reason. Interestingly, Lewis explicitly claims to have "taken a Humean view about laws and causation"[17] and "used it instead as a thesis about possibility," though he does not seem to

16   Ibid., 126.

realize the implications of this for agent causality. Such a Humean view requires either rejecting causal agency altogether, or positing a Kantian noumenon. By contrast, William James's insistence on a phenomenologically primitive notion of causation, where agency means the power to effect *novel* outcomes, the power of individuals to really create things and events, leads him towards an ontology wherein there is profound contingency and no complete logical space:

> The melioristic universe is... a pluralism of independent powers. ... Its destiny thus hangs on an *if*, or on a lot of *ifs* — which amounts to saying (in the technical language of logic) that, the world being as yet unfinished, its total character can be expressed only by *hypothetical* and not by *categorical* propositions. (Empiricism, believing in possibilities, is willing to formulate its universe in hypothetical propositions. Rationalism, believing only in impossibilities and necessities, insists on the contrary on their being categorical.)[18]

Lewis's whole thesis of the plurality of worlds is spun out of the premise that philosophical examples involving *possibilia* ultimately require us to assume that when we speak of what is necessarily true we are referring to what *already* obtains at all possible worlds, that what we say is contingently true refers to what *already* obtains at some of them and not others, and what is said to be necessarily false is false because it has no referent at any possible world. On this view, philosophical inquiries that make use of counterfactuals assume the existence of worlds sufficiently similar to our own so as to be different in only the ways relevant to the given example. All of this involves a false notion of "possibility." No *possibility* that already exists in every essential aspect of how it is conceived is any real possibility at all. To speak of possibilities in any coherent sense is to allow, as James does, for *universal* contingency.

An ontology of universal contingency is not possible if Logic is taken to be a real limiting condition on worldhood, as opposed to an intellectual abstraction that is *useful* for coordinating complex projects in the empirical world of experience. In his "Confidences of a Psychical Researcher," James speculated that the paranormal phenomena that he spent twenty-five years researching as a founding member of the American Society for Psychical Research, might turn out to be empirical evidence for an irreducibly illogical aspect of existence.[19] This "bosh" would be the residue of a primordial ontological chaos out of which cosmic order arises only through a long process of evolutionary struggle between willing beings with varying degrees of emergent consciousness. "Laws" might have evolved in fits and starts, as a draw between battling psychical forces, with some of them being selected against and others of them being assimilated — so that the fabric of the cosmos is as ad hoc a patchwork as our DNA (most of which is evolutionary "junk'). In Lewis's terms this would be a battle of story-tellers' imaginations over how the "book of the world" should be written. One would never know what the characters will do next, because there is still no single author whose will has prevailed absolutely over the others.

The persistence of this "bosh" factor, together with emergent order, provides just the kind of razor's edge that is required for free will — a tense balance *between* law-like determinism and real indeterminism. Those of Lewis's possible worlds that are supposed to allow for choosing agents, only feature a rationalist pseudo "indeterminism" defined by propensity-profiles of finite entities that demarcate a completed logical space of "predetermined possibilities." It is beyond the scope of this essay to argue against Lewis's ontology and in favor of something like James's *pluralistic universe* (where "*universe*" properly means the one and only reality). All I have been concerned to suggest is that whatever other merits it may have, the Lewisian ontology does not allow for the kind of free will that defeats an indifference objection. Fundamental and comprehensive logical determination, on the one hand, and allowance for a creativity that makes for meaningfully active engagement in life, on the other, are contradictory demands to make of one and the same ontology.

REWRITING GOD'S PLAN

George Nolfi's 2011 cinematic adaptation of the 1954 short story "Adjustment Team" by Philip K. Dick explores the concept of human freedom in a way that seamlessly intertwines the metaphysical and the metapolitical. *The Adjustment Bureau* is essentially a retelling of Jacob's wrestling match with the unsportsmanlike angel. Not since Franz Kafka penned *The Trial* has there been a more poignant allegory about the struggle between Man and God.

The members of the Adjustment Bureau are angels and their chairman is the Lord. This is made fairly clear at several points in the film. From the very first meeting that David Norris (Matt Damon) has with a member of the Bureau, namely Richardson, it is impressed upon him that the Bureau is there to make sure that everything goes according to plan. This leaves us asking whose plan it is that they are enforcing. Richardson also tells him that he has just seen behind a curtain that he was not even supposed to know existed and that very few humans have ever looked behind. This sets up the author of The Plan as some kind of Wizard of Oz figure — the man behind the curtain, as it were — but even more than that, since the remark about "very few humans" suggests that the Bureau's members are not as "human" as they appear. Then, in the bar, Harry explains to David that they cannot reset people without authorization from "the chairman" whereupon David, appalled and exasperated, asks: "The chairman?" Harry elaborates in these revealing terms: "That's just a name we use. You use many other names."

What other names is he alluding to? Zeus. Jupiter. Jehovah. Allah. Indra. This becomes clearer on the boat ride that they take together. David asks Harry point blank, "Are you an angel?" Harry, somewhat flattered, replies: "We've been called that. We're more like case officers, who live a lot longer than humans." Thompson leaves us with no doubt. He explains to David how these "angels" have controlled human civilizations throughout history on behalf of the chairman, stepping back during two periods wherein they attempted to allow humans to exercise their free will with what he claims were disastrous consequences: the dark ages and then the epoch from World War I to the near destruction of the earth in the Cuban Missile Crisis. Thompson equates the Bureau's enforcement of The Plan with the power of Fate.

Taking this key revelation as our point of departure, what is most fascinating about the film is the way in which it depicts the very finite and fallible character of the divine bureaucracy. Just as the Bible and religious texts of other traditions present us with a hierarchy of angels or gods in service of the most high god or Lord of the gods, in the Adjustment Bureau there is a clear hierarchy—a word, by the way, whose literal meaning is "holy order." The lower echelons have very limited knowledge. David discovers that Richardson cannot tell him why he is not supposed to be with Elise Sellas (Emily Blunt) because neither Richardson nor his assistants are privy to that information. They have to compensate for their lack of knowledge by resorting to bullying tactics and to outright deception.

Harry explains to David that Richardson was "just trying to scare" him when he said that the Bureau members can read everything in his mind, and that he was exaggerating about the effects of a "reset." To read minds, they have to setup thought processes that weigh options and can be mapped out as clear decision trees. Water — whether

in the form of rain or bodies of water — limits their abilities to
"adjust" people and events. Harry even admits that Thompson lied
to David when he claimed that the reason he cannot be with Elise
is that she brings out his reckless side. When Richardson goes in to
see Donaldson, a point is made of the fact that Richardson has never
been in the Archive Room that they enter together: "Have you been
in here before?" "No, of course not." After learning that The Plan is
an illusion and that there have actually been multiple plans rewritten
a dozen times or more, leaving messy fragments from older plans in
place, he confesses to Harry that he has no idea how The Plan can
"just change like that" because, as he puts it: "It's above my pay grade."
At the end we see that "Even Thompson," the "hammer" to whom the
case is kicked up, "has a boss."

The "angel" in whom we see the finitude and fallibility of the Lord's
entire bureaucracy most clearly reflected is Harry. When Richardson
causes a car accident in which a cabbie and another driver are
injured, we see that they are willing to hurt people pretty seriously
to accomplish their ends. Of course, they also cause Elise to sprain
her ankle. But it is in the case of Harry that we learn that outright
murder is also part of their modus operandi. He is responsible for the
death of David's father and brother. Both of them had the potential
to become great men, but The Plan did not call for it. Together with
the death of his mother in the sixth grade — which Harry claims was
"just chance" — David is famous for having overcome these losses on
his way to becoming the youngest congressman elected to the House
of Representatives. Harry feels guilt over these murders that he presided over (one of which was made to look like a drug overdose) even
though he is not supposed to, and he feels as if he owes David. He
admits to David that Bureau members do have emotions, and David
realizes that some have them more than others. Richardson, Harry's
partner, also knows about his guilt over the Norris family deaths. In
one scene, Richardson walks up to Harry as he stands in a tall window
of the Bureau building with a view of the cityscape at night crowned

by the Empire State Building, to tell him that Thompson has finished
the job. Richardson says: "You can't let it get to you. Like it did with his
family. This is the job." Then Harry asks: "You ever wonder if it's right,
I mean, if it's always right?" Richardson replies: "Not like I used to.
Look," and he looks upwards into the night sky as he says this, "chairman has The Plan. We only see part of it." Richardson took the same
attitude when David told him that he must be misreading the Plan or,
if not, then the Plan must be wrong. "Do you know who wrote it?" "I
don't care." "No, you should! You should really show a little respect."
Respect for god.

Instead of showing unquestioning respect for god — or, as it were,
"the chairman" — David earns the respect not only of Harry but ultimately of the chairman himself by trying to force his way past the
enforcers of the divine bureaucracy to seek a direct hearing with the
Lord. As he tries to make it to the Ceder Lake dance rehearsal he
taunts Richardson that his increasingly outrageous use of obstacles
must be causing endless ripples, something the Bureau is supposed
to avoid, and he yells: "I don't care what you put in my way. I'm not
giving up." Later Thompson confronts David with the rhetorical question: "Why do you refuse to accept what should be completely obvious
by now. You've seen what we can do. You can't doubt we are who we
say we are... You can't outrun your fate, David." He means to remind
David that he is dealing with the angels of the Lord. David's response
gives Thompson pause. He stops in his tracks and thinks to himself,
wincing slightly, when David says: "Look, it's not about who you are.
It's about who I am.... I just disagree with you about what my fate is."

When David leaves Elise in the hospital we should not take this as
his giving up with respect to the Bureau, but his putting her lifelong
ambitions and hopes before his own interests. Thompson has, perhaps
deceptively, convinced him that if he stays with her she will wind up
teaching dance to six-year-olds instead of becoming one of the best
dancers in the country and, eventually, one of the world's greatest
choreographers.

Even this does not deter him in the end. He is determined to do "whatever it takes" to get her back. When Harry teaches David how to use the doors, this is a metaphor for what Aldous Huxley called *The Doors of Perception* in a book by that name, after which the band *The Doors* was named. It turns out that he will be able to navigate these "doors" even better than the Bureau because they have a problem with improvisation. Some humans are better at risky creative thinking than they are. This limitation on the power of angels has a long precedent in traditional religious literature. It is his creative vision, together with his determination, that eventually inspires not only Harry but also moves the chairman himself.

This was David's intention. Before he takes Elise through the door at the Statue of Liberty, obviously a profound symbol of the question of metaphysical freedom at the core of the film, he explains to Elise that the Bureau's book says that their relationship is wrong "but what if I can find who wrote it?" On top of Rockefeller Center, in what they think might be their last moment together, David and Elise are confronted by Thompson with these words: "Did you really think you could reach the chairman and change your fate if you did? Or write your own? It doesn't work like that, and I told you why." It turns out that he is wrong and he walks away crestfallen, with a somewhat startled look back at David. Herein we see the inferiority of even the highest of angels, an archangel, in the face of an extraordinary human individual.

In response to a question about whether it was a test, while looking out over Central Park lined by the buildings of Manhattan's upper east and west sides, Harry explains: "In a way. It's all a test, for everybody, even the members of the Adjustment Bureau. David, you risked everything for Elise. And Elise, when you came through that door at the Statue of Liberty you risked everything too. But you inspired me. Seems like you inspired the chairman too." After we learn that the chairman has rewritten The Plan so that the "serious deviation" for which David is responsible can be accommodated, we hear the following closing narration spoken by Harry over a scene of David and Elise walking down 5th Avenue, past Rockefeller Center, which is home to statues of the rebellious Titans Prometheus and Atlas:

> Most people live life on a path we set for them, too afraid to explore any other. But once in a while people like you come along who knock down all the obstacles we put in your way — people who realize that free will is a gift you'll never know how to use until you fight for it. I think that's the chairman's real plan, and maybe, one day, we won't write the plan. You will.

This is a second answer to David's question to Thompson in the vacant concrete lot that is used as a space wherein to interrogate and intimidate him. It is the central question of the film: "Whatever happened to free will?" The Adjustment Bureau, including its chairman, think that a small dose of Elise can be used to inspire David because of the magnetic connection that they feel when they are together on account of the remaining fragments of the many previous plans when they were meant to be together. Yet David cares more about being with her than following the path to the Presidency that his inspired concession speech is supposed to put him on. Despite their detailed knowledge of the significant influence that his father's political interests has on him and the way in which he needs politics to fill the void left by the early losses that he has suffered in life, the angels fail to anticipate and, thereby to control, the full complexity of his psychological makeup. Even the chairman fails at this.

David knows better than god what the future should hold in store for him and, since he is meant to be someone who "really matters," he is also presuming to know better what the future should hold in store for Humanity. The only god that can allow for such creative self-determination on the part of an individual is a finite and fallible god, who can be prevailed upon, and whose relatively unthinking bureaucratic apparatus can be overpowered in such a way as to afford one the possibility of addressing him more directly. The gravity of ethical decisions remains squarely in the hands of exceptional individuals for

CHANGING DESTINY

In Steven Spielberg's film *Minority Report*, based on the short story by Philip K. Dick, Captain John Anderton takes a very scientific attitude towards the precogs and the Precrime program that they make possible. He wants to see the precogs as "pattern recognition filters." We learn about the science behind Precrime methodology at two points in the film. First, when Danny Witwer, the attorney general's representative from the Justice Department, is being given a tour of the facility, and then later in the conversation between Anderton and Dr. Iris Hineman, who is supposed to have "developed precogs, designed the system, and pioneered the interface." The three precogs are floating in a photon milk that acts both as a nutrient supply and a liquid conductor that enhances the images that each of them perceive. Their brain tissue is scanned by means of optical tomography, with white lights pinpointing pulses of neuronal information along the entire length of their headgear. They are drugged with dopamine and endorphins so that they do not feel any pain. Their serotonin levels are also carefully controlled, so that they are kept in a state of sleep that is not too deep.

The three are a hive mind. Arthur and Daschel are twins and they defer to the subconscious guidance of Agatha, who is the one of the three with superior ability. Dr. Hineman tells Anderton that is because Agatha is a female. While the three precogs are, on one level, named after three of the greatest mystery writers — Agatha Christie, Arthur Conan Doyle, and Dashiell Hammett — Agathon also means "the best one" in Greek. Of the three, at least Agatha is still able to see the future without the other two and her precognitive abilities are only augmented by the technological interface. We know that she can do without it, and without the twins, when she guides Anderton through the mall, moment to moment. She also sees or has already seen the future of an Asian lady who happens to pass by, presumably an adulteress, to whom she gives the warning: "He knows. Don't go home."

Later on, Hineman laughs at Anderton's suggestion that she "invented" Precrime. She disabuses Anderton of his view of the precogs as creatures grown in a test tube, entities that he had advised Witwer not to think of as human. It turns out that they are the children of addicts to an impure first generation of the drug Neuroin, to whose new and improved "Clarity" version Anderton himself is addicted, so that he seeks it out from a dealer in the shady sprawl area of D.C. (More on this dealer, momentarily.) Hineman was doing genetic research on these children at the Woodhaven Clinic. It appears that at first she was attempting to treat them. Their severe brain damage had enhanced an apparently latent human ability for extrasensory perception. In particular, they apparently began to be bombarded with precognitive visions in their sleep. These predominately consisted of nightmares of murders being committed and the terrified children would wake screaming in the night or be found clawing away at the wallpaper in some corner of their rooms. Hineman and her colleagues discovered that these dreams were precognitive, in other words that the murders they concerned took place after being foreseen by the children. She admits that, together with Lamar Burgess, she turned these children into test subjects — guinea pigs — and the fact that most of them died before the age of twelve may be on account of what was done to them to develop the supposedly "perfect" system of Precrime.

As in the case of the optical recognition system, the holographic video projections, public advertisements that personally address individual shoppers, animated cereal boxes, the virtual reality parlor where brain-scanning interfaces allow a customer to indulge their fantasies in a full-body suit, and the multi-plane highways for mag-lev smart cars demonstrate that real scientific research by P.K.D. and Spielberg lies behind the film's depiction of precogs. It is that kind of empirical research that William James believed would bring about the next scientific revolution, what he called Psychical Research and what has since come to be widely known as Parapsychology. Parapsychologists use the umbrella term "psi" to refer to both extrasensory perception and psychokinesis (formerly known as telekinesis) in all of their various types. In particular, Dick's story and Spielberg's film adaptation of it draw on five discoveries of parapsychological research: precognitive clairvoyance or remote viewing of the future, enhanced ESP in the dream state, the especially strong psychic bond between twins, childhood trauma as a catalyst of psi ability, and the superior psi abilities of females in general.

Of all of the psi abilities studied by parapsychologists since the days when James and his colleagues at the S.P.R. pioneered the field, the ones for which there is the most overwhelmingly affirmative statistical evidence are the ones that *Minority Report* combines. One of them is to know about future events before they happen and in cases where ordinary inferences are not possible, formally known as precognition. The other is clairvoyance, also known as "remote viewing" or seeing and describing things happening somewhere at a distance without the use of the five known senses.

In the 1970s, in an effort to keep apace with a similar project in the Soviet Union, Russel Targ and Harold Puthoff, two physicists with high security clearances at the Stanford Research Institute, developed a remote-viewing program on contract for the Central Intelligence Agency and the US Department of Defense, one which was used operationally throughout the 1980s for a variety of intelligence and military operations — including antiterrorism and hostage rescue. Targ and Puthoff's book *Mind Reach* gives an overview of the SRI research program and discusses some of its declassified operational successes. Since the disbanding of the unit at the end of the Cold War, a number of other remote viewers have also written books about their experiences in the program. Some have founded private enterprises offering remote-viewing services to Fortune 500 corporations. The dean of the Engineering and Applied Sciences school at Princeton University, Robert Jahn, ran precognition experiments from 1979 to 2003, replicating some of SRI's work on remote viewing and combining this together with precognition in a more rigorously testable way than SRI had done. Statistical meta-analyses of thirty years of data from the PEAR program reveal astronomical odds against chance being responsible for the results, which have since been replicated at a number of other universities. These results have been reported in scientific journals including Foundations of Physics. In the late 1980s, Jahn also co-authored a book on the PEAR program with his research assistant, Brenda J. Dunne, under the title *Margins of Reality: The Role of Consciousness in the Physical World.*

During the 1960s, Dr. Montague Ullman and Dr. Stanley Krippner at the Maimonides Medical Center in New York City headed a project researching extrasensory perception in the dream state. Their results were first published in the 1973 book *Dream Telepathy: Experiments in Nocturnal Extrasensory Perception.* Ullman and Krippner developed a protocol to test whether a sender could telepathically transmit certain images to a receiver who is spatially isolated from the former and who is in a dream state. They found replicable experimental evidence for the fairly old hypothesis advocated by major thinkers such as Schelling and Hegel in the 19th century that psychical ability is strongest in the dream state. The researchers at the Maimonides Center also found strong laboratory evidence for precognitive dreams, which appear to be the most common type of ESP experienced by the average person. Remember that the precogs in *Minority Report* are artificially kept in a perpetual state of a sleep that is not too deep.

Throughout history and in the folklore of many cultures it is reported that twins, especially identical twins, share a psychic bond that
is so strong that, for example, if one suffers an injury the other will
feel it in the very same limb, even if he is at a great distance and not
in any form of sensory communication with his brother. Sometimes
the two will break a leg, the same leg, in precisely the same spot, at
exactly the same time. Remember that the two male precogs, Arthur
and Daschel, are identical twins. In his book Twin Telepathy, the
Brazilian parapsychologist Guy Lyon Playfair collects and discusses
many cases concerning this psychic bond between twin siblings. The
elite scientific establishment of Nazi Germany was intensely interested
in parapsychological phenomena in general and it appears that better
understanding ESP was one of the motivations for the experiments
carried out on identical twins in the concentration camps.

This brings us to another rather grim subject, the connection
between psi ability and traumatic experiences — especially in childhood. The precogs in *Minority Report* were those who survived from
among a much larger group of extremely traumatized children, many
of whom died from the agonizing terror that they suffered first on account of their precognitive nightmares and then at the hands of the
experiments that Hineman and Burgess subjected them to in order
to develop Precrime. Jeffrey J. Kripal, the Newton Rayzor Professor
of Philosophy and Religion and former chair of the Religious Studies
Department at Rice University in Texas, has written about this in a
couple of his books as well as in a recent article. He first broached
the subject in the concluding chapter of *The Serpent's Gift*, where he
discusses the real-world basis for the kind of teenagers with superpowers that we see in the X-Men, and he returns to the subject in
Mutants and Mystics. Kripal raises questions about whether the sterile
and relatively mechanical approach of laboratory parapsychologists
will ever be able to produce the kind of macro-scale psi abilities that
are occasionally displayed by extraordinary individuals in the course
of ordinary life. He notes that the individuals at the center of such

paranormal activity are often young persons, especially adolescents, dealing with some form of trauma.

More often than not, they are also female. The greatest mediums of the 19th century, especially so-called "physical mediums" capable of producing dramatic telekinetic phenomena, were women. One of them, Eusapia Palladino, features prominently in the History of Spiritualism written by Sir Arthur Conan Doyle — the mystery writer who invented Sherlock Holmes and after whom the precog Arthur is named. Unfortunately, suffering from performance anxiety and caving into the expectations of their audience, some of them occasionally cheated and in the eyes of skeptics this discredited the many cases where careful scientific researchers observed legitimate displays of their talents. One female medium that was never caught cheating was Ms. Piper, the woman that William James considered his "white crow" — the single gifted person who more than any other convinced him of the reality of psi. Hineman's claim that, naturally, the most gifted of the precogs is a female reflects this real history of female dominance in psi.

The witch hunts throughout medieval times and as late as the 1600s in places such as Salem probably have some correlation to the fact that women, on average, are more psychically gifted than men. This dark history is alluded to in *Minority Report*, in one of many instances where religious concerns are set in tension with the scientific approach to the Precrime program that Anderton is initially inclined to take. Toward the end of the film, when Lara catches Lamar Burgess inadvertently admitting that he knows about how Ann Lively was "drowned," there is something suggestive of the Puritans about how the light is shining behind Max von Sydow's head to accentuate certain elements of his features, taken together with the accent in his voice when he says "We'll talk about this later. Perhaps tomorrow, I'll come by the cottage." One is subtly reminded of *The Scarlet Letter* or *The Crucible*. During the epoch of the witch burnings, Sarah Marks may have been condemned to death as an adulteress. Instead, in the

2054 timeframe of the film, whose secular value system is basically an extension of our own today, her husband is arrested while her wife is still in bed with her illicit lover. As her husband is "haloed," this protected adulteress is consoled and counseled by the police. The "halo" used by Precrime to immobilize and eventually incarcerate potential perpetrators is, of course, itself one of many references to religious ideas and symbolism in the film. One particularly clever reference to this religious symbol is Anderton's sarcastically spoken remark to Burgess during their final confrontation, "You'll rot in hell with a halo, but people will still believe in Precrime." Significantly, this last exchange between them takes place with the Washington Monument illuminated at night in the background behind Anderton. The titanic obelisk is shown repeatedly, for emphasis, and calls to mind other ancient Egyptian religious symbols adopted by the Masons who founded America, such as the All-Seeing-Eye of Providence shining in the pyramid capstone. The All-Seeing-Eye appears painted onto the forehead of the knowingly laughing old woman in the lobby of Leo Crow's hotel, as her visionary third eye. Agatha's ominous question, repeated throughout the film, is, "Can you see?!"

From the opening scene with the Marks family, through to the end where Lamar is awarded a Civil War pistol, there is a recurring reference to Abraham Lincoln, the place of God and the sacred in the constitutional order of the United States, and the bloodiest battle fought to save the soul of this country supposedly founded on the God-given liberty of the individual. Sarah Marks is helping her son memorize a Civil-War-era speech by Lincoln, which includes the words "remember what was sacred" and "that this nation, under God, shall not perish from the Earth." The mother is thoughtlessly reciting these words while her son cuts out a paper mask of Abe Lincoln, whose eyes are gouged out, and while Sara lies in response to questions asked by her suspicious husband — questions and answers that intercut the Lincoln speech that the mother is helping her son mindlessly memorize. The meaning of this scene is fairly clear. It asks, in light of the overall concerns of the film, whether the founding ideals of this country still mean anything anymore — the ideals enshrined in the Bill of Rights and grounded above all in that pronouncement of the Declaration of Independence that all people are "endowed by their creator with certain inalienable rights, that among these are the right to life, liberty, and the pursuit of happiness."

Specifically, *Minority Report* poses the question of the sacred and the god-given character of the individual liberties threatened by the Precrime program. With particular relevance to the increasingly strong surveillance state of our own time, it compares technological violations of privacy and individual liberty with the psychical violation of free will that the precogs are being used to perpetrate. The Precrime team searches the sprawl district with infrared sensors and robot spiders that crawl into private homes and bedrooms, eye scanning people in the middle of having sex, or in the middle of a heated argument, and terrifying little children. One smirking and gumchewing unnamed Precrime cop, played by Patrick Kilpatrick, is often depicted with the expression of an eager animal and reminds one of the hoodlums turned crooked cops in Kubrick's *A Clockwork Orange*. During the spider-led raid into people's homes this guy answers an indignant mother with the line: "If you don't want your kids to know terror, keep them away from me." It is no wonder that a society where such an invasion of privacy is tolerated is one that would harness a validated psi ability in a way that poses an even more profound threat to individual liberty. Ultimately, Burgess shoots himself with the Civil War revolver gifted to generals at the war's conclusion and whose five accompanying gold-plated bullets were meant "to represent the end of the destruction and death that had rent the country apart for five years." This choice of suicide, rather than the murder of Anderton, ends Precrime and so yet again the Precrime experiment and all it represents is compared to the Civil War on the scale of its challenge to the American ideal of liberty. The deepest question that is being asked is whether free choice is something that an Almighty God can endow us with.

When Anderton is trying to buy the designer drug he's addicted to in the sprawl, under the pretext of a late-night jog, the dealer takes off his glasses and reveals his empty eye sockets as he says: "In the land of the blind, the one-eyed man sees all." This is paradoxical, because he does not even have one eye. The reference to the one eye is metaphorical. It concerns, yet again, the All-Seeing-Eye or the third eye of clairvoyance.[1] It is also a reference to the Oedipus tragedy of Sophocles, where King Oedipus develops the keen psychical vision of a sage after putting his own eyes out in response to his discovery that he has unwittingly committed incest. The specific reference to Oedipus is not as important as the general significance of Sophocles who, together with Aeschylus, is considered among the purest representatives of Greek literature from the archaic age when tragedy was still considered the highest art form, the art form most expressive of the archaic Greek religious worldview, and, as of yet, not matched by any worth comedies. The tragic worldview was one wherein Fate, sometimes equated with the will of Zeus, is taken to be iron clad and the hero is condemned to a tragic death insofar as he attempts to valiantly resist an inevitable but unjust end. *Minority Report* overturns this fatalistic religious worldview, but the implications of this overturning are by no means restricted to Greek fatalism.

The concept of "changing destiny" is at the core of the most religiously charged scene in the film. Danny Witwer, warrant in hand, demands to be taken into the temple, which Anderton has explained to him is off limits to cops: "We keep strict separation." This, in addition of course to its name, demarcates "the temple" of the precogs as a sacred space. The architecture of the vast oracle chamber also emphasizes this. Once inside with the Precrime team, the following exchange ensues when Anderton tells Witwer that it's best not to think of the precogs as human. While handling his rosary, Danny replies: "No, they're much more than that. Science has stolen most of our miracles. In a way, they give us hope. Hope of the existence of the divine. I find it interesting that some people have begun to deify the precogs."

Later on, we see examples of this when Rufus T. Riley, the hacker and computer designer who runs the virtual reality parlor, bows down reverently before Agatha in awe and terror of her knowledge of his sinful thoughts. We also learn that the precogs receive more mail than Santa Claus, who is already replacing Jesus Christ as the focus of the most important holiday or holy day in our culture.

Anderton attempts to quash this religious sentiment on Witwer's part by referring to the precogs as nothing more than "pattern recognition filters," whereupon Danny objects: "Yet you call this room 'the temple.'" Finally, when John tries to dismiss this by saying that it is "just a nickname," Witwer reflects on the fact that "The oracle isn't where the power is anyway. The power's always been with the priests, even if they had to invent the oracle." Anderton is annoyed that his colleagues appear to all be nodding in knowing approval of this observation, especially Jad, the black cop who goes on to say: "Well, come on, chief, the way we work, changing destiny and all, I mean, we're more like clergy than cops."

Anderton sends them back to work and then listens to Witwer apologetically explain that this theologizing is an old habit formed during three years at Fuller Seminary before he went into law enforcement. His father was shot and killed when he was fifteen on the steps of his church and he claims to want to help Anderton prevent crimes like that, and the one that cost John his son, from ever happening again. Anderton takes to calling him "Father Whitwer." Later, this philosophically minded theologian begins to respect Anderton's conviction of his innocence despite the precog prevision and he eventually vindicates Anderton by discovering how Ann Lively's murder was staged by taking advantage of precog "echoes" only to wind up being martyred for his dedication to the truth. He clutches and kisses his rosary as he is shot dead by Lamar Burgess while the precogs are blind.

What does Witwer mean about the relationship between the oracle and the priests and how is this connected to his conviction that there must be a human flaw in what appears to be a perfect system? The oracle consists of the three precogs, and we learn from the tour guide's inane propaganda speech to visiting school children that the public is made to believe that the precogs each have their own bedrooms, televisions, and weight rooms and that "it's really wonderful to be a precog." The reality is that they are prisoners who are being terribly used and abused for their "gift" — a situation that calls for reflection on the German meaning of the word gift, namely poison. In an exchange with Anderton when he first drives her out into the real world, Agatha asks "is it now." We see him still treating her as if she is a machine and she responds, in great pain and sorrow, that she is "tired of the future." The precogs are being drugged up and used against their will and moreover, being used to make people believe that they have no will. The chief priests of Precrime are not the cops who recognize themselves as something like clergy. Burgess and Hineman founded Precrime by distorting the precog abilities, concealing the minority reports, and deceiving people into thinking that the previsions are perfectly accurate. They created a quasi-religious system that suggests we have no free will. The doctrine of this system is reflected in Witwer's initial exchange with Fletcher and Anderton who recite this catechism to Danny in response to his concern that someone might decide not to go through with a crime that the precogs have foreseen. Here is the dialogue.

> Witwer: 'We are arresting individuals who have broken no law.'
> Fletcher: 'But they will, the commission of the crime is absolute metaphysics. The precogs see the future and they are never wrong.'
> Witwer: 'But it's not the future if you stop it. Isn't that a fundamental paradox?'

ANDERTON: 'Yes, it is. You're talking about predetermination, which happens all the time.'

He rolls one of the inscribed balls towards Witwer. 'Why did you catch that?'

WITWER: 'Because it was going to fall.'

ANDERTON: 'You're certain?'

WITWER: 'Yeah.'

ANDERTON: 'But it didn't fall. You caught it. The fact that you prevented it from happening doesn't change the fact that it was going to happen.'

WITWER: 'You ever get any false positives? Someone intends to kill his boss or his wife but they never go through with it. How do the precogs tell the difference?'

ANDERTON: 'Precogs don't see what you intend to do, only what you will do.'

WITWER: 'Then why can't they see rapes, or assaults, or suicides?'

FLETCHER: 'Because of the nature of murder. There's nothing more destructive to the metaphysical fabric that binds us than the untimely murder of one human being by another.'

WITWER: 'Somehow I don't think that was Walt Whitman.'

ANDERTON: 'It's Iris Hineman. She developed precogs, designed the system, and pioneered the interface.'

The word "metaphysical" is deployed twice in this conversation. Witwer's sarcastic reference to Walt Whitman is related to it, since Whitman was the advocate of a poetic "New World Metaphysics" that could not be further from this official doctrine of the Precrime system. The metaphysics in question here is deterministic. Intention is deemed irrelevant, as is the conscientious inner struggle to change one's intended action, and the human individual is analogized with a wooden ball — an object mindlessly following a simple trajectory.

Yet Hineman herself, who is the source of the statement that Fletcher cites as if it were scripture, later explains to Anderton that this veneer of determinism was a deception implemented by her and Lamar Burgess. Some people have alternate futures that result in "minority reports" wherein one precog, Agatha, disagrees with the other two. Technicians like Wally the caretaker are deceived into thinking this vision of an alternate future is an "echo" and they erase the record of it. Anderton is horrified that he may have sent innocent people with alternate futures into the limbo of Containment. There is no "chain of events" that leads "inexorably" to murder, or for that matter any other deed. Even in the case of people who do not have an alternate future or a minority report, such as Anderton himself, knowing your future in advance affords you the chance to change it.

Two powerful examples of this are given in the film. The crux of the first comes across in the exchange between Agatha and John just as Leo Crow walks into his hotel room. Anderton says: "You said so yourself. There is no minority report; I don't have an alternate future. I am going to kill this man." Agatha, who has been repeating pleadingly that he should leave and he can choose for a long time now, finally explains: "You still have a choice. The others never saw their future. You still have a choice!" After wrestling with Crow and then holding him at gunpoint, Anderton hesitates — apparently in response to Agatha's plea — and his watch timer runs out and beeps before he pulls the trigger. He decides to read Crow his rights instead of killing him, after which he discovers that he has been set up and Crow is a patsy. Although Crow grabs Anderton and forces him to pull the trigger, this is not the murder that the precogs saw. Still, it's close enough that we need a better example, and the film ends with one. Here are Anderton's final words to Burgess. Notice how he emphasizes "now," which brings to mind Agatha's question "is it now?" during her first car ride out in the world and Anderton's reply, "Yes, this is all happening right now."

> Lamar, it's over. The question you have to ask is: What are you going to do now. No doubt the precogs have already seen this… You see the dilemma, don't you. If you don't kill me, precogs were wrong and precrime is over. If you do kill me, you go away. But it proves the system works. Precogs were right. So what are you going to do now? What's it worth? Just one more murder. You'll rot in hell with a halo, but people will still believe in Precrime. All you have to do is kill me, like they said you would. Except,

you know your own future, which means you can change it, if you want to. You still have a choice, Lamar. Like I did.

This also confirms that the first example is one where Anderton does defy the prevision, even though Crow still winds up dead. Lamar chooses to shoot himself instead and, as he collapses while asking John for forgiveness, the Precrime team sweeps in to see that the prevision already recorded on the red balls was wrong.

Moreover, it is not simply that John or Lamar had alternate futures that are also predefined, so that it is a matter of choosing between two fixed patterns of action or predetermined versions of the future. John is clearly told that he has no alternate future that the precogs could have seen but he can choose to make one for himself regardless. Once a decision such as this is made, what happens to what would have been? It melts away. This is suggested in the most moving scene of the entire film, when Agatha, sitting in Shawn's room, channels the life that John and Lara could have had with their son but that was melted away by the man who stole him away from the public pool. Lara is in terrible agony towards the end of this mediumistic trance because she feels the truth of it down to the core of her being. It is not a hypothetical life that Agatha is merely imagining, or an alternative future that is going to be lived out by another Shawn in a parallel universe. It is a stolen life. It is what William James would have called an "ambiguous possibility" that was made to dissolve together with all of the people (Shawn's potential children, for example) who would have lived it out. Here's the haunting narrative that Agatha delivers in this séance of sorts:

> There is so much love in this house... Dr. Hineman once said the dead don't die, they look on and help. Remember that, John. ...Shawn. He's on the beach now. Toe in the water. He's asking you to come in with him. He's been racing his mother up and down the sand. There's so much love in this house. He's ten years old. He's surrounded by animals. He wants to be a Vet. You keep a rabbit for him, a bird, a fox. He's in high school. He likes

three. He's at a university. He makes love to a pretty girl named Claire. He asks her to be his wife. He calls here and tells Lara, who cries. He still runs. Across the university and the stadium, where John watches. Oh god, he's running so fast. Just like his daddy. He sees his daddy. He wants to run to him. But he's only six years old and he can't do it, and the other man is so fast. There was so much love in this house.

This is brilliant writing. The way that Shawn running in the university stadium becomes the six-year-old boy trying to run back to his father and away from the kidnapper. The way that Agatha's "There is so much love in this house" turns into "There was so much love in this house." She is able to sense the ruins of a life that could have taken place largely in this house, a family life full of love that was aborted. Traces are left, though. Shades.

The film is posing a compelling yet controversial thesis: for us to be free agents to any degree at all, for us to be individuals ethically responsible for our chosen actions, there cannot be any Almighty God. An Almighty God would be even more all-knowing or omniscient than the precogs were made to seem by the lie that Hineman and Burgess perpetrated when they concealed the minority reports. Any god (lowercase "g") whose existence would be metaphysically compatible with our having a chance to make meaningful choices in life has to be a finite god, without much more precognitive power than Agatha, Art, and Dasch. The same would hold for any other gods or angels in the service of this most powerful god.

Metaphysical liberty cannot be God-given. The very fact of an omniscient God's existence translates into the proposition that all possible futures are already known, which means they already exist, which means that we do not now choose to make them come into being. The idea of God is immoral. We have to choose between God and ethics. This is the most profound implication of *Minority Report*, which anticipates the dawn of a new age wherein the barrier between Science and Religion has been demolished. It will be an age wherein Science is no longer materialistic, mechanistic, and reductionist, and wherein Religion has done away with the unethical idea of God Almighty and has been reconstructed from out of the precondition of all ethical life: the fundamental faith in our chance to make a better future.

NOTES ON THE TAO
OF BRUCE LEE

Bruce Lee was born in San Francisco, California on November 27, 1940, year of the Dragon. He was raised in the thoroughly Westernized British colony of Hong Kong where he attended English schools until the age of eighteen, when he returned to the United States for higher education. During his teenage years in Hong Kong Lee had received training in boxing, which was widely available on account of the British culture of the colony. He could easily have become a light-weight-class boxing world champion. Lee also learned the Western art of fencing from his older brother, who was a fencing champion. Lee, already a boxer, had gotten into numerous street fights with his peers at school, and it is on this account that he sought training in Asian martial arts.

His mother was of half-German ancestry, so the top teachers in Hong Kong refused to teach him, since he was not a full-breed Chinese and they were against teaching martial arts techniques to non-Asians. He had to train privately with the one willing teacher that he did find, since Yip Man's fellow students refused to train with him. When Lee, now empowered with martial arts skills, beat up a boy who turned out to have been the son of a Hong Kong organized crime don, his parents decided he should return to the United States. After a brief stay in his birthplace of San Francisco, he moved to Seattle and studied Drama, Western Philosophy, and Psychology at the University of Washington.

Lee then returned to the San Francisco Bay Area and opened a school in Oakland, where he fought for the right to teach Caucasians, frowned upon in Chinatown at the time. He was concerned with equality of all people regardless of race. According to his wife Linda, Lee viewed himself "as a citizen of the world." In 1967, all of the *sifu* from Chinatown had collectively signed a paper threatening him. He was challenged to a fight, which he won decisively. However, this fight also afforded him a flash of insight that drew together the eclectic influences he had absorbed throughout his life. When he was starting up as a martial arts teacher in Oakland, out of necessity, he worked with teachers from several Asian traditions other than the Wing Chun style of Kung Fu in which he had been predominately trained. These included judo, karate, and taekwondo. Lee decided that his own Wing Chun style and for that matter *all established Martial Arts traditions* were too rigid to be effective under the chaotic real-world conditions of a street fight. He devoted himself to devising a more *scientific* approach to unarmed combat.

Lee studied Newtonian physics, examining how its principles relate to the techniques of European fencing and Western boxing that he learned during his youth in Hong Kong. With a total disrespect for traditional formality and guided solely by the criteria of practicality, flexibility, speed, and efficiency, Lee worked to merge the strongest elements of diverse Asian martial arts traditions together with Western techniques. The latter not only included boxing and fencing, but also an exercise regiment of weight training for strength, running for endurance, and stretching for flexibility. Lee called this "style of no style" *Jeet Kune Do* or "The Way of the Intercepting Strike," and adopted "Using no way as way; having no limitation as limitation" as its motto. These phrases were emblazoned in Chinese calligraphy around the

Taiju, together with arrows depicting the constant flow back and forth between *yin* and *yang*.

At first Lee taught Jeet Kune Do in his schools, but by the end of 1969, he grows concerned that his students look to his art as containing a secret way of special techniques. So in January of 1970 at the height of popularity in Martial Arts world, he closed all of his schools. As he put it in one of his lines in *Longstreet*: "I cannot teach you, only help you to explore yourself—nothing more." He decided to privately train only a handful of students, getting to know each student well enough to help him free himself from his own *psychological* limitations. The Sportsweek in the *Washington Star* printed in Washington, D.C. on August 16, 1970, captures the essence of this period in Lee's career:

> Three of Bruce Lee's pupils, Joe Lewis, Chuck Norris and Mike Stone, have between them won every major karate tournament in the United States at least once. Lewis was Grand National champion three successive years. Lee handles and instructs these guys almost as a parent would a young child. It's like walking into a saloon in the old west and seeing the fastest guy in the territory standing there with notches all over his gun. Then in walks a pleasant little fellow who says: 'How many times do I have to tell you, you're doing it all wrong.' And the other guy listens, intently.

They were listening intently for a reason. Lee's "physical" ability was nearly paranormal. He routinely performed one-finger pushups, on one hand. He could sit elevated in a jackknife position for longer than a half hour, while watching television. He could send opponents flying several feet back from a punch delivered from only one inch away. Lee's sidekicks made recipients feel as if a car had hit them. On one occasion, he was able to strike a formidable karate master opponent sixteen times in a fight that lasted only eleven seconds. The fight ended with Lee knocking him the full length of a handball court. He pushed the body to its limits and he finally found them when he strained his fourth sacral nerve in his back. Although he would defy the expectations of his doctors and rehabilitate himself to being an even better martial artist than he was before the incident, Lee was nonetheless bedridden for six months. He decided to channel his pent-up physical energy mentally, by researching the many volumes on martial arts, philosophy, and motivational psychology that he had collected in his extensive library. He read and reread Buddha, Alan Watts, Karl Rogers, Lao Tzu, Friedrich Pearls, D.T. Suzuki, and Jiddu Krishnamurti. In dialogue with these thinkers, above all Krishnamurti, the bedridden Bruce Lee filled seven notebooks with *The Tao of Jeet Kune Do.*

In this magnum opus, Lee criticizes traditional martial arts forms as "thousands of years of propaganda." Someone bound within the systems of karate, judo, or kung-fu, is incapable of even accurately perceiving the combat actions of a street fight, let alone effectively taking part in one. The training of such a "classical man" consists only of *simulated* combat, wherein flowery forms and artificial techniques are rehearsed ritualistically. Faced with an immediate threat to one's life, it is absurdly impractical to make sure that one is adhering to proper method. Lee demands that students of martial art forget winning or losing, and be prepared to sustain injury and even death in the course of their training. Lee saw it as a farce that judges at martial arts tournaments awarded points for blows that never touched an opponent, based on who would probably have hurt the others. He referred to these rehearsals as "organized despair" and "dryland swimming." Lee was the first martial artist to have taught his student through full contact sparring, borrowing boxing gloves and headgear from Western sports. At the 1967 International Karate Championships at Long Beach, where he was first noticed by Hollywood, Lee introduced this into what were hitherto non-contact martial arts tournaments.

Only in the face of real danger will the martial artist recognize that practicality is the ultimate criterion. This does not mean an "anything goes" recklessness, but the ability to adopt any tool that functions in the simplest and most direct manner to attain one's objective in a given combat situation. For example, in order to respond to an opponent's attack immediately, one must be able to strike from wherever one is, without repositioning. Hooking and swinging techniques from boxing can be usefully adopted by the martial artist to this end. Lee colorfully refers to these unassuming attacking tactics as "the uncrispy stuff."

Patterns of rhythmical classical blocks — such as *katas* of karate — are not suited to the broken rhythm of a street fight. It is not simply that they are not *physically* versatile enough. Stereotyped technique *psychologically* mediates one's relationship to one's opponent, thereby interfering with a direct perception of the combat situation and precluding an immediate response. Consequently, a process of un-conditioning the mind is required in order to replace a "this is the only way" attitude with what Lee calls "choiceless awareness." According to Lee, "awareness has no frontier" whereas "all thought is partial." Systems are established out of fear of uncertainty. So as to be secured against being disturbed by the unexpected, one's relationship to others is fixed within a pattern of conduct. These patterns are sustained by thought, which is a mechanical process whereby memory frames every new experience in terms of old habits and prejudices. It is here that Krishnamurti's influence is most apparent.

Jiddu Krishnamurti, although born and raised in India (another British colony), took an irreverently Western approach to Eastern spirituality. He was an iconoclast who resisted attempts by the Theosophical Society to turn him into an Eastern Messiah. He advocated individual authenticity and open-minded, dynamic creativity against what he saw as the backwards fascination of certain Westerners with the guru-worship and obscurantist ritualism that held Indian society in a spiritual straightjacket. Krishnamurti taught that outward revolution aimed at a sane world society beyond intercultural warfare was only attainable through freeing the mind from all cultural conditioning, by cultivating an intense awareness wherein Thought's conceptualizing function becomes transparent to itself.

Krishnamurti's "method" for this involved the *aporia* of Socratic dialogue. He referenced Socrates repeatedly and had mocking contempt for Eastern sitting meditation.

Agreeing with Krishnamurti, Lee explains that there is a different kind of *knowing* than the piecemeal knowledge afforded by the thinking intellect. It is clear that Lee does not mean a mere regress to animal instinct, since cultivating such "intuition" also means "to destroy your own impulses caused by the instincts of self-preservation." We see this juxtaposition of a call to retrieve something like animal instinct together with a transcendent teaching of reconciliation with death, in this famous scene from *Longstreet* where Bruce Lee (L) has his student (S) on the ground in a choke hold, and the following exchange ensues. It centers on the Taoist imagery of water as a metaphor for the yielding, dynamic strength of the formless:

L: What is your instinct?
S: To pray.
L: In this position, your arms are useless.
S: Yeah. (coughing)
L: Can you kick or stomp me?
S: (coughing) No.
L: Then, if you wish to survive, what do you do?
S: I don't know.
L: Bite.
S: Bite?!
L: Are we not animals?
(Lee releases him, checks if he's ok.)
S: Bite, huh?
L: Biting is efficient in close quarters. But don't make a plan of biting. That
   is a very good way to lose your teeth.
S: There is so much to remember.
L: If you try to remember you will lose. Empty your mind. *Be formless.*
   Shapeless. Like water. Now you put water into a cup, it becomes the cup.
   Put it into a teapot, it becomes the teapot. Now water can flow, or creep, or
   drip, or crash. Be water, my friend.

> S: Yeah, why don't I just stand in front of Bull and recite that to him, maybe he'll faint — or drown.
>
> L: When is it?
>
> S: Tomorrow.
>
> L: You are not ready.
>
> S: I know.
>
> L: Like everyone else, you want to learn the way to win, but never to accept the way to lose. To accept defeat, to learn to die is to be liberated from it. So when tomorrow comes you must free your ambitious mind, and learn the art of dying.

Lee calls for the cultivation of immediate intuition through non-judgmental introspective observation, wherein an alert and sharply focused consciousness beyond the limits of thought becomes aware of the limitations that deliberative thought has placed on oneself. This cannot be done in monastic isolation. It requires interpersonal relationship, which is "a process of self-revelation." The other is "the mirror in which you discover yourself." Even at an ontological level "to be is to be related." One can only become aware of one's unconscious conditioning by observing one's reactions in living relationship with others, and then subjecting these reactions to "a continuous state of inquiry without conclusion" which dissolves the judgmental convictions upon which they are based. Of course, Lee is by no means suggesting a sacrifice of oneself through uncritical empathy with various willful dogmatists. While it is important not to "start from a conclusion" in relating to an other, the person to whom one relates may be far from capable of also setting aside "comparison and condemnation." A relationship that is unmediated in both directions is possible only among free spirits, but establishing a relationship to the other that is at least unmediated on one's own end helps one to defeat opponents by being less rigidly conditioned by unconsciously held beliefs than they are:

> When real feeling occurs, such as anger or fear, can the stylist express himself with the classical method, or is he merely listening to his own screams and yells? Is he a living, expressive human being or merely a patternized

mechanical robot? ...Is his chosen pattern forming a screen between him and the opponent and preventing a 'total' and 'fresh' relationship?[1]

Jeet Kune Do is "the Way of the Intercepting Strike" because the delay in the opponent's attacks on account of his psychological conditioning affords one's unconditioned mind the chance to decipher it and allows one time for *interception*. The opponent gives himself away through his psychological deliberation and lack of versatility in his actions.

Lee hung this motto on the wall of his Los Angeles school: "Man, the living creature, the creating individual, is always more important than any established style or system." We should couple it with these lines from the *Tao of Jeet Kune Do*: "Classical forms dull your creativity, condition and freeze your sense of freedom. ... When one is not expressing himself, he is not free. ... But in classical style, *system* becomes more important than the man!" A student of Drama as much as of Philosophy, Lee was the first person to view martial art first and foremost as *art*, not merely in the sense of *techne* or "crafts" artistry but in the fullest sense of *poesis*:

> The aim of art is to project an inner vision into the world, to state in aesthetic creation the deepest psychic and personal experiences of a human being. It is to enable those experiences to be intelligible and generally recognized within the total framework of an ideal world... We must employ our own souls through art to give a new form and meaning to nature or the world.[2]

This is unquestionably a Western development of Eastern traditions that, as we have seen, Lee has already deconstructed as "traditions." Lee's own work as the Hollywood director, choreographer, and screenplay writer of *Way of the Dragon* (1972), *Enter the Dragon* (1973), and the uncompleted *Game of Death* attests to his own artistic ability. In *Game of Death* he symbolically represents the steps in finding one's

---

1   Bruce Lee, *The Tao of Jeet Kune Do* (California: Ohara, 1975), 15.

own way in martial arts, until one attains the style of no style. He chooses the Buddhist temple of Pope Ju Saw as his shooting location. On the site a thirty-three-meter-high Buddha statue (caste in one mold, with 150 tons of bronze, the largest such standing figure in all of Asia) stands in front of a five-story pagoda. In his role as the protagonist, Lee takes on advocates of different styles at every level and, having no fixed style of his own, is able fit in with each and defeat them according to their limitations. A green bamboo whip that he uses at one point represents flexibility, the pliable adaptability needed in order to change with change. His character wears a one-piece yellow tracksuit rather than a traditional uniform, because while it is comfortable and flexible it has no affiliation with any style. Very aware of how camera angles worked in fight scenes, Lee was a perfectionist on the film set, choreographing all of the fights and reshooting them many times. Lee's footage from the uncompleted original version of *Game of Death* is considered by many "the most graceful and dynamic presentation of the human form in hand-to-hand combat ever captured on film."

As in the Western tradition of fine arts, he recognizes that "Art calls for complete mastery of techniques" but that to produce a work of creative genius — a genuine *work of art* — the artist must be able to use his disciplined skill to channel the limitless source of the unconscious and irrational. This insight lies at the heart of how Jeet Kune Do approaches training in diverse techniques, just as a great painter studies many styles diligently before breaking out of his schooling:

> Having 'no form,' then, does not mean having no 'form.' Having 'no form' evolves from having form. 'No form' is the higher, individual expression. *No cultivation* does not really mean the absence of any kind of cultivation. What it signifies is a cultivation by means of non-cultivation. To practice cultivation through cultivation is to act with conscious mind.[3]

The liberated, authentic individual and the creative genius in touch with the wellspring of the unconscious mind are one and the same: "Art reaches its greatest peak when devoid of self-consciousness. Freedom discovers man the moment he loses concern over what impression he is making or about to make." According to Lee, "Artistic skill" is only one "step in psychic development," and "artistic perfection" cannot be attained until: "An artist's expression is his soul made apparent, [behind] his schooling... behind every motion, the music of his soul is made visible." Lee laments that the martial arts have hitherto stunted the kind of psychic development of the individual that we see in the fine arts, where training in technique is only a preparatory tool for creative self-expression:

> The second-hand artist blindly following his sensei or sifu accepts his pattern. As a result, his action and, more importantly, his thinking become mechanical. His responses become automatic, according to set patterns, making him narrow and limited.[4]

> In combative arts, it has been the problem of ripening. This ripening is the progressive integration of the individual with his being, his essence. This is possible only through self-exploration in free expression, and not in imitative repetition of an imposed pattern of movement.[5]

However, this is not simply a case of the adoption of "Western" values over Eastern ones. Bruce Lee has an understanding of artistic creativity that surpasses that of both monotheistic and materialistic Western aesthetic theorists and that emerges from out of the core of Eastern spirituality. In a 1972 interview with his leading biographer, John Little, Lee made it clear that he not only had no religious affiliation whatsoever, but that he did not believe in God at all. Rather than postulating "God" or the "Absolute" as the unconscious source tapped by the creative genius, Lee understands that: "Art reveals itself in psychic

---

4   Ibid., 22.

understanding of the inner essence of things and gives form to the relation of man with *nothing*, with the nature of the absolute." This inversion of "the nature of the absolute" into *nothing* is significant not only as a critique of the Judeo-Christian-Islamic worldview, but also as a Buddhist modification of the Taoist understanding of nature. In *The Tao of Jeet Kun Do* Lee describes the non-referential self-expression of the true (martial) artist as "Zen" and he follows the Zen masters in their fusion of *Tao* and *Shunyata*. He describes "thusness — what is" in terms that are clearly Taoist: "Thusness does not move, but its motion and function are inexhaustible." At the same time, Lee equates this "is-ness, or...suchness" in "its nakedness" with "the Buddhist concept of emptiness."

To some extent, this leads Lee in the same direction as it led the Japanese Zen masters, namely beyond Taoist naturalism and Buddhist pacifism and on to the Heraclitean view that "Life is combat." There are lines in *The Tao of Jeet Kune Do*, where the influence of D.T. Suzuki is clear: "Jeet Kune Do teaches us not to look backward once the course is decided upon. It treats life and death indifferently."[6] This kind of decisionism is the exception and does not sit well with Lee's over-whelming influence on personal expressiveness arrived at through "a continuous state of inquiry without conclusion."[7] He realizes that a true relationship to *nothingness*, wherein one has the "insight [that] one's original nature is not created" — in effect that there is no fixed human nature endowed by God or anything else — does not nihilisti-cally negate the individual, but frees one for creative self-expression: "Creation in art is the psychic unfolding of the personality, which is rooted in the *nothing*. Its effect is a deepening of the personal dimen-sion of the soul."[8] Martial *art* cultivates fearlessness for this honest en-counter with the Abyssal, and it in turn expresses the creative power

6   Ibid., 12.

7   Ibid., 19.

unleashed through the destruction of retarding and constraining beliefs that takes place when one enters the life-giving Void: "The void is all inclusive, having no opposite. ... It is a living void, because all forms come out of it and whoever realizes the void is filled with life and power and the love of all beings."[9]

Again, this does not mean surrendering to one's opponents. The two purposes of using one's natural tools in Jeet Kune Do are "to overcome your own greed, anger, and folly" *and* "to destroy the opponent in front of you — annihilation of things that stand in the way of peace, justice and humanity."[10] Since Lee advocates the self-deconstruction of all judgmental and prejudicial fixed beliefs, by "the way of peace, justice and humanity" he cannot mean any definite ideology but rather the "annihilation" of *all ideologies* "that stand in the way" of a free society dedicated to the creative self-expression of individuals in dynamically open relationship to one another.

Unlike the early Taoists and orthodox Buddhists, whose apolitical pacifism opened a vacuum that has allowed Asians to be dominated by collectivist tyranny for most of their history, Lee shares the classical Greek concern with a just society. However, unlike most Greeks, with the possible exception of Heraclitus, Lee recognizes that Justice is not an absolute form, a universal concept come down from on high that instantiates itself in this imperfect world of relativity and change. Instead, a just society can only be grounded in an encounter with Nothingness and a consequent recognition of the artificial, provisional character of all forms. This means a society that has "annihilated" faith in the Abrahamic God, and one wherein Tao*ism* and Buddh*ism* have deconstructed themselves through their own deepest insights.

---

9   Ibid., 7.

PHILOSOPHY, SCIENCE, AND ART

The attempt to define Philosophy as a discipline distinct from Science and Art, one justified by its unique type of productivity, is Gilles Deleuze's central concern in *What Is Philosophy?* Philosophy, Science, and Art all aim at establishing order in the face of Chaos — or *infinite variability* — by some means other than the insulation of mere opinion.[1] Whereas the sciences crystallize the field of experience into functions of *variables* and the arts break up an accretion of clichés by cultivating chaos in the form of *varieties* of percepts and affects, philosophers produce conceptual personae whose *variations* cut planes of consistency through Chaos. In the following, I argue that on the contrary, the unity of Philosophy/Science may be discerned with a view to the aesthetic nature of conceptual personae. Deleuze himself makes observations that undermine his tripartite disciplinary distinctions. My ultimate aim is to demonstrate that, on Deleuze's own terms, we can see the partial observers of science and the aesthetic figures of art as ultimately indistinguishable from conceptual personae.

---

1   Gilles Deleuze, *What Is Philosophy?* (New York: Columbia University Press,

Deleuze does not accept Martin Heidegger's idea that Philosophy has irretrievably disintegrated into the disparate empirical sciences and that a scientific *thinking* that could reflectively regulate technical endeavors, would require some irreducibly *aesthetic* insight. He refers to talk of "the death of metaphysics" or "the overcoming of philosophy" as "tiresome, idle chatter," and he concludes that "even if it is called something else" *philosophy* persists insofar as there is still "a time and place for creating concepts."[2] The "concept" belongs to philosophy alone.[3]

Deleuze identifies two types of inseparability distinctive of concepts. Firstly, on account of both the conditions of historical genesis enfolded within it and its insufficiency to grasp the totality of its present situation, each concept relates to (it does *not* "refer" to) concepts other than itself. Second, while the components that constitute a concept are somewhat distinct, at their threshold they neighbor each other in a zone of ultimate indiscernibility that renders them analytically inseparable and confers the concept that they collectively constitute with its endoconsistency.[4] These zones of indiscernibility also deny concepts any conditions of reference.[5] Each concept is that point at which its coincident components accumulate and condense into a certain consistency.[6] Deleuze also describes this development of concepts as the emergence of "centers of vibrations" that "resonate" rather than refer.[7] Moreover these vibrations are not measurable in terms of mathematical magnitude; the concept "has no number."[8]

Consequently, Deleuze claims that there are no concepts in science, which is strictly concerned with the conditions of states of

2   Ibid., 9.

3   Ibid., 34.

4   Ibid., 19.

5   Ibid., 143.

6   Ibid., 20.

7   Ibid., 23.

affairs in terms of propositions and functions.[9] The elements of these scientific functions are *functives*, which are at work in different forms in sciences as diverse as physics, where they are explicitly mathematical, and biology, where they are the functions of lived states.[10] Unlike the philosophical concept, scientific functions consist of individual features that can be categorized into variable species under one or another constant genus.[11] Confusing concepts with propositions that can be linked together, as in logicians' "infantile idea of philosophy," is what leads to the mistaken belief that there are scientific concepts.[12] Unlike concepts, propositions are concerned with the referential relationship between bodies extensionally situated in states of affairs.[13] This is a relationship between independently isolable *variables* or convertible units, whose clean separation admits of them being "varied" or interchangeable.[14] A state of affairs grasped in terms of scientific propositions is in turn a complex variable expressing a relationship between two or more variables.[15]

Unlike independent variables that interlock into states of affairs like pieces of a jigsaw puzzle, philosophical concepts resonate with one another on what Deleuze alternatively calls a "plane of consistency" or "the plane of immanence of concepts."[16] One cannot simply add a new component to a concept without causing the whole concept to breakup, or catalyzing a radical change that transforms it into a different concept addressing problems of a different order.[17] The concept

---

9   Ibid., 33.

10   Ibid., 117, 151.

11   Ibid., 20.

12   Ibid., 22.

13   Ibid.

14   Ibid., 23.

15   Ibid., 122.

16   Ibid., 35.

is not an aggregate. Its *whole* is more than the sum of its parts.[18] It is a unity of diversity that may be disturbed in such a way as it crystallizes into a new unity; it has a wholeness that remains open to catalytic change.[19] This means that the plane of consistency is not a concept of (the) concepts (to be found on it). If it were, the concepts would lose their genuine singularity and planar openness and instead become universals that are closed off — therefore dead, incapable of conjuring events and summoning us to them.[20] The relationship of concepts to their plane is rather that of events to their horizon. The plane is an event horizon, but a horizon independent of different observers rather than relative to them. It is what grants the concept its independence of the visible state of affairs through which it manifests.[21] Strictly speaking, neither can it be thought in the way that a concept can, nor is it even a method that defines and precedes proper thinking in terms of concepts.[22]

Rather, according to Deleuze, the plane of immanence is what allows one "to find one's bearings in thought."[23] Concepts are intensive features of absolute dimension encountered in the context of this non-conceptual field of understanding, which must always already be scoped out for them.[24] This calls to mind the image of someone with his hands outstretched as he makes his way through a dark but familiar room, where the walls and furniture are intuited before making contact with them as if by an unfocused and invisible searchlight. Indeed, Deleuze describes the "diagrammatic features" of the plane of consistency as dimensions of fractal (not co-ordinate) directionality

---

18   Ibid., 50.

19   Ibid., 35.

20   Ibid.

21   Ibid., 36.

22   Ibid., 37.

23   Ibid., 73.

that can only be intuited.[25] Deleuze goes so far as to suggest that this occult background of philosophical thought, which only intuition can access, is of the order of dreamlike esoteric experiences that may be classed as pathological and irrational (from an academic or scholastic standpoint).[26] Deleuze evokes the image of a desert whose dunes are always in motion to help us understand this space that concepts come to populate, for a time.[27]

That which lies beyond conceptual understanding is Chaos. For Deleuze the Chaos into which thought plunges is not an absence of determinations. Rather, it is characterized by the transformation of immeasurable determinations at what he calls "infinite speed" so that they vanish almost as soon as they take shape "without consistency or reference, without [discernable] consequence."[28] Deleuze calls to mind the Buddhist notion of *Shunyata* when he describes Chaos as "a void that is not a nothingness."[29] In other words, Being is the *virtual*. This is also Deleuze's view of the irrational in Nature as "infinite variabilities" that we need "just a little order" to protect ourselves from.[30]

Deleuze asks, "what would *thinking* be if it did not constantly confront chaos?"[31] The plane of immanence, which allows for the creation of concepts, is a section of Chaos — i.e. a cross-section that

---

25 Ibid., 39–40.

26 Ibid., 41. "Precisely because the plane of immanence is prephilosophical and does not immediately take effect with concepts, it implies a sort of groping experimentation and its layout resorts to measures that are not very respect-able, rational, or reasonable. These measures belong to the order of dreams, of pathological processes, esoteric experiences, drunkenness, and excess. We head for the horizon, on the plane of immanence, and we return with bloodshot eyes, yet they are the eyes of the mind. Even Descartes had his dream. To think is always to follow the witch's flight."

27 Ibid., 41.

28 Ibid., 42, 118.

29 Ibid., 188.

30 Ibid., 201.

slices through Chaos.[32] Deleuze identifies what he calls "conceptual personae" as the points of view that stand between Chaos and the diagrammatic features of the plane, as well as between the plane and the concepts that it allows to take shape on the plane. [33] In other words, it is a conceptual persona that first and foremost "plunges into the chaos" to extract from it both the diagrammatic features of the plane and its intensional features — both the horizon for concept-formation and the groups of concepts related by their mutual possibility within *this* horizon.[34] He compares this "constructivism" to "a throw of dice" in "a very complex game."[35] This means that although at times Deleuze lays out personalistic, diagrammatic, and intensive elements involved in philosophy as if they were co-equal functions, the personalistic features determine the diagrammatic and intensive ones.[36]

A philosopher's name is actually a pseudonym for his conceptual personae, and Deleuze suspects that "The face and body of philosophers shelter these personae who often give them a strange appearance, especially in the glance, as if someone else were looking through their eyes."[37] For Deleuze, the "idiot" popularized by Dostoevsky — the *private* man of the *cogito* — is Descartes' conceptual persona.[38] Deleuze also cites the examples of "the Socrates of Plato," "the Antichrist" and "the Dionysus of Nietzsche" among others.[39] Deleuze takes Nietzsche to have worked with more conceptual personae, of both a sympathetic

---

32 Ibid., 42.

33 Ibid., 75.

34 Ibid.

35 Ibid.

36 Ibid., 77.

37 Ibid., 64, 73.

38 Ibid., 64. In the guise of the question "Descartes goes mad in Russia?" Deleuze draws a connection between the conceptual personae of the old and new *idiot*, as exemplified by Descartes' doubter in search of absolute mathematical certainty and Dostoevsky's underground man who wills a return of the absurdly incomprehensible (Deleuze 62, 63)

and antipathetic nature, than any other thinker. Deleuze points out that it is almost a rule that sympathetic personae can never fully free themselves from their antipathetic shadow (or "ape" in the case of Zarathustra) to emerge into pure positivity.[40] For two personae to even be able to encounter each other in a hostile manner they have to be functioning on the same plane.[41] Nietzsche's sympathetic personae include Dionysus, Zarathustra, and the Superman whose arrival he heralds. His antipathetic ones are Christ, the Priest, the Last Men, and even Socrates (a conceptual persona appropriated from Plato).[42]

Although, for this reason, many have seen Nietzsche as a poet or mythmaker, his conceptual personae are neither historical figures nor literary heroes (or villains). By means of them he populates the plane of immanence that he lays out — life as *will to power* — with many new concepts, such as: "forces," "value," "becoming," "life," "eternal return," *"ressentiment"* and "bad conscience."[43] It is also with reference to Nietzsche that Deleuze volunteers one of his most illuminating definitions of what he means by evoking a conceptual "horizon" as a metaphor for the plane of consistency — namely that one plane or another is a bounded field that opens up certain determinate "modes of existence or possibilities of life."[44] Conceptual personae are, in turn, not "invented" in a facile manner so much as they are "brought to life."[45]

Deleuze claims that the personal names affixed to diverse scientific propositions — such as the Pythagorean theorem, Cartesian coordinates, Hamiltonian number, etc. — are not conceptual personae, but *partial observers* that extract *prospects* from sentences in relation to

---

40 Ibid., 76.

41 Ibid., 77.

42 Ibid., 65.

43 Ibid.

44 Ibid., 72.

a particular axis of reference.[46] These partial observers—even in quantum mechanics—are not indicative of subjectivism, they attest to a truth of the relative and not a relativity of truth.[47] They are the postulation of a monadic perceptive and experiential capacity to be affected to things studied, without which those things could not be studied.[48] Deleuze also wants to differentiate the conceptual personae of philosophy from the *psychosocial types* studied by the sciences—especially psychology and sociology.[49] He cites the work of Simmel and Goffman on identifying certain of these psychological types that are functions of a structured social field, such as the stranger, the exile, the migrant, the transient, the native, and the homecomer.[50] Deleuze takes these psychosocial types to be "only physical and mental" in nature, whereas conceptual personae are "spiritual."[51] Psychosocial types may help us assess the relationship of conceptual personae to the epoch in which they manifest, but the way in which the personae are in a realm of pure thought above (or beneath), beyond, and determinative of a historical milieu *qua* a state of affairs observable by social science, is taken by Deleuze to mean that conceptual personae and psychosocial types never merge.[52]

Conceptual personae allegedly not only differentiate philosophy from science, but also from the arts. Deleuze attempts to draw a clear distinction between the personae of philosophy and the figures of art. Unlike conceptual personae, which are "the powers of concepts," aesthetic figures are supposed to be "the powers of affects and percepts." Deleuze draws an analogy between the way that the great aesthetic figures of literature (Melville's Captain Ahab), painting (David's Marat),

---

46 Ibid., 24.

47 Ibid., 129–130.

48 Ibid., 130, 155.

49 Ibid., 67.

50 Ibid.

51 Ibid., 68.

sculpture (Michelangelo's David), and music (Strauss' Zarathustra) produce affections and perceptions that go beyond those ordinarily experienced, and the way that conceptual personae allow us to think beyond ordinary opinions.[53] This analogy is based on a parallelism of distinction. Deleuze does not at all belittle art by comparison to philosophy. He claims that while such powerful contemplative artists as Hölderlin, Rimbaud, Kafka, Artaud, and Melville are in one sense only "half" philosophers, they are "also much more than philosophers."[54]

So long as its materials — stone, canvas, chemical color — last, art preserves by means of them and so artworks are also the subject of a concern for preservation that is unique to them among all things.[55] This unique concern for preservation of the work of art is on account of an at least tacit acknowledgement that what is enfolded within it is a compound of *percepts* and *affects*, concentrated sensations that have their own manner of being, their own existential capacity to affect — even in the absence of human observers — by means of perceptions encoded within them.[56] This understanding of art in terms of percept and affect blurs the boundary between works of art and natural becomings: "The artist is a seer, a becomer..."[57] Deleuze claims that through his relationship with Moby Dick, Captain Ahab enters into a becoming-whale that allows him to *really* have perceptions of the sea — a nonhuman landscape of nature — and the whale for his part has a compound of sensations that involve him in a non-human *becoming* "ocean."[58] Deleuze wants to differentiate the zone of indiscernibility here from that at work within philosophical concepts, a non-distinction and reversion of human and animal wherein

---

53   Ibid., 65.

54   Ibid., 67.

55   Ibid., 163.

56   Ibid., 164.

57   Ibid., 171.

"something or someone is ceaselessly becoming-other."[59] This does not allow aesthetic figures to grasp heterogeneity in an absolute form the way that conceptual personae do.[60] Sensory becoming only expresses otherness in a striking way.[61]

The work of art confronts opinion by strategically marshalling the destructive force of chaos. The artist does not face a blank canvas or an uncarved block; she is always already confronted by a coagulation of clichés that must be painted out or chiseled away.[62] These clichés are the attempts of opinion to resist chaos, but they are too feeble and faltering to secure us from a collapse into the abyss. So the artist draws on chaos to produce a composition of sensations that defies every opinion, every past attempt at art that has been assimilated and uprooted.[63] Deleuze uses the term "chaosmos" — borrowed from James Joyce — to refer to this composed chaos wherein chaotic variability has been transformed into a *chaoid* variety that allows for a sensory encounter with chaos.[64]

By contrast, whether it transforms the chaotic variability into a determinist calculus — where a future state is supposed to be able to be determined from a present one — or whether enough of chaos is allowed in to only admit of a calculus of statistical probabilities, science does not aim at the retrieval of chaos. Rather, the scientist at least tacitly filters chaos out of a framework of constants, limits, and coordinate axes of mathematical spatio-temporality.[65] This referenced chaos becomes "Nature" qua object of empirical research — by contrast with the natural non-human becomings at work in art.[66] The

---

59   Ibid., 173, 177.

60   Ibid., 177.

61   Ibid.

62   Ibid., 204.

63   Ibid.

64   Ibid., 204–205.

65   Ibid., 205.

sciences slow down the infinite into a "freeze-frame" that allows for propositional thought to penetrate matter, turning the virtual into a finite quantity of movement, force, or energy bounded by the parameters of a universal constant (e.g. the speed of light) so that it congeals into the formulaic mold of a frame of reference.[67]

Yet there are numerous instances throughout *What Is Philosophy?* where Deleuze undermines his sharp disciplinary distinction between philosophy, science, and art. Some of his remarks readily lend themselves to deconstructing this distinction altogether. Deleuze sees Art, Science, and Philosophy as the three daughters of Chaos, like the three muses. He dubs them "Chaoids." They produce realities out of Virtuality.[68] Yet, interestingly, the parallelism and tripartite distinction between them is undermined by the ontological priority that Deleuze assigns to the *chaoid* of philosophy. Concepts are not principles governing the reasonable association of ideas or things; they are "mental objects determinable as real beings."[69] Concepts cut a plane of immanence through chaos, like a cross section that gives chaos an intellectually conceivable consistency — a "mental chaosmos" which is "a chaoid state par excellence."[70] This plainly asserts that the chaoid of philosophy sets the standard for those of art and science.[71] It contradicts Deleuze's claim elsewhere[72] that philosophy is not superior to science and art.

Bearing this in mind, let us look at Deleuze's admission that the relationship between philosophy, science, and art is not merely an extrinsic interdisciplinary one.[73] There is also an *intrinsic* relationship between the three on the basis of which we not only see how they

---

67 Ibid., 118–119.

68 Ibid., 208.

69 Ibid., 207.

70 Ibid., 208.

71 Ibid.

72 Ibid., 8.

would need each other,[74] but why his claim that they are distinct at all must really be called into question. One example of this "intrinsic type of interference" is "when concepts and conceptual personae seem to leave a plane of immanence that would correspond to them, so as to slip in among the functions and partial observers, or among the sensations and aesthetic figures, on another plane; and similarly in the other cases." While on the one hand Deleuze claims that "these slidings are so subtle, like those of Zarathustra in Nietzsche's philosophy" or when "partial observers introduce into science sensibilia that are sometimes close to aesthetic figures," he admits that it can bring us to "find ourselves on complex planes that are difficult to qualify…mixed planes" constituted by "interferences that cannot be localized."[75] Most significantly, Deleuze sees that it is here where "concepts, sensations, and functions become undecidable, at the same time as philosophy, art, and science become indiscernible," that they extend a common shadow out of chaos and into the future — the specter of the "people to come."[76]

Deleuze also equates the artist and the philosopher, or views them as interchangeable, at two crucial points when he is talking about bringing forth "the new people and earth in the future." The first passage is explicitly in the context of discussing Heidegger: "He got the wrong people…the race summoned forth *by art or philosophy* is not the one that claims to be pure but rather an oppressed, bastard, lower, anarchical, nomadic, and irremediably minor race…"[77] The second passage reads: "*The artist or the philosopher* is quite incapable of creating a people, each can only summon it with all his strength. A people can only be created in abominable sufferings, and it cannot be concerned with art or philosophy. But *books of philosophy and works of art* also contain their sum of unimaginable sufferings that forewarn

---

74 Ibid., 218.

75 Ibid., 217.

76 Ibid., 218.

of the advent of a people."[78] Later, when he discusses the twists and turns of language employed by the writer to wrest percepts from perceptions and sensation from opinion, Deleuze hopes that this attempt to make language vibrate is being made "in view…of that still-missing people."[79]

In a passage on conceptual personae and aesthetic figures, Deleuze admits that, "the two entities do… often pass into each other," because sometimes the "plane of composition of art and the plane of immanence of philosophy can slip into each other."[80] As examples he cites how the literary figure of Don Juan becomes a conceptual persona for Kierkegaard, and how the Zarathustra figure that was already a mythical-religious figure (of the Persians) and a musical-theatrical figure for Mozart (Sarastro in *The Magic Flute*), is transformed into a conceptual persona by Nietzsche, only to once again become a great musical figure in the composition of Richard Strauss.[81]

Furthermore, Deleuze uses a definitively aesthetic term, actually *the* definitive term of aesthetic judgment, namely "taste," to describe the faculty of co-adaptation that unifies the three basic functions of philosophy: Reason's laying out of the plane, the Imagination of conceptual personae, and the manner in which Understanding grasps Chaos through the creation of concepts.[82] This is to subsume reason and rational understanding under the imaginative faculty that cannot properly be distinguished from taste. Deleuze explicitly says: "Taste is this power, this being-potential of the concept: it is certainly not for 'rational or reasonable' reasons that a particular concept is created…"[83]

In a later passage Deleuze calls into question the endowment of concepts "with the prestige of reason" and the association of aesthetic

---

78   Ibid., 110. My emphasis.

79   Ibid., 176.

80   Ibid., 66.

81   Ibid.

82   Ibid., 77.

figures with "the night of the irrational and its symbols" and the "spiritual life," remarking that "disturbing affinities appear" between them that elude such a clear-cut distinction.[84] So again we see that conceptual personae are not on a level with the diagrammatic features of the plane or the intensive features of concepts, but as they emerge out of a creative act of aesthetic judgment they are determinative of these features at a point when the latter are still inchoate — determinative in the sense of endowing them with their *aesthetic* coherence.

Deleuze himself says of this type of aesthetic judgment: "It is as in painting: there is a taste according to which even monsters and dwarves must be well made... that their irregular contours are in keeping with a skin texture or with a background of the earth as germinal substance with which they seem to fit."[85] If there were any doubt, shortly thereafter he repeats: "The same goes for the taste for concepts."[86] Deleuze further elaborates on the aesthetic character of the criteria of judgment in Philosophy when he claims that a philosophical work should not be rejected as "false" (as it is by scholastics or analysts) but only as uninteresting or unremarkable and therefore unimportant.[87] Flimsy concepts and those that are too rigidly reduced to a framework are both uninteresting.[88]

Taken on his own terms, there is really no ground on which Deleuze can maintain that the creation of concepts involves a "specifically philosophical taste" as opposed to aesthetic judgment. He is mistaken to conclude that profoundly disturbing "correspondences [between aesthetic figures and conceptual personae] do not rule out there being a boundary, however difficult it is to make out."[89] There is no boundary.

---

84 Ibid., 91.

85 Ibid., 78.

86 Ibid.

87 Ibid., 82–83.

88 Ibid., 83.

GOTHAM GUARDIAN

Among the neo-pagan American Pantheon of the Justice League, Batman has always had a unique place. He hails neither from a crystalline alien planet of supermen, nor from an equally exotic hidden island utopia. He certainly was not raised in Kansas, like Clark Kent, and he does not work in the hallowed halls of Washington, like Diana Prince. Bruce Wayne is a native son of the grittiest, most powerful and most corrupt city-state on Earth, *Gotham* — the archetypal image of New York City, a modern Babylon or Rome. He was not endowed by birth with the magical powers of a cryptic super-race that render him virtually invulnerable. His extraordinary abilities are born of long hard training and self-discipline, and many confrontations with an all-too-palpable mortality. Finally, Batman is not a star-spangled, heaven-sent Apollonian emissary of Truth, Justice, and the American Way. He is of one cloth with the benighted world, in the shadows of which he stealthily works. His work often pits him against the authorities as an elusive bane of those who have proclaimed themselves officers of Law and Order. The atmosphere of his world is that of our own — a milieu where the difference between organized crime and legal order is rarely clear, so that even the noblest man must resort to mass deception and terrorism in his thankless task of protecting the decent.

Like any tale that taps into symbols and themes of archetypal power and significance, the Batman mythos has developed a life of its own. In my view, however, its many iterations culminated in the masterpiece trilogy of Christopher Nolan. During my doctoral studies a Marxist colleague of mine who dressed up as Bane for Halloween claimed that Nolan's "Batman is a fascist." I immediately understood what he meant and replied that he was paying a great compliment to fascism. Perhaps he will think otherwise of Ben Affleck's rendition of Batman, given that the actor's stance on Islam is closer to Bane's than to that of the Dark Knight. The release of *Dawn of Justice* is an opportunity for those of us who have protested that "Ben Affleck is not our Batman" to reflect on the ethos of an Übermensch willing to be hated because he is something more than a hero.

When Bruce Wayne, still in his Chinese prison cell, first hears of the League of Shadows from Ducard and dismissively identifies them as vigilantes, Ducard replies, "No, no. A vigilante is a man lost in his quest for gratification. He can be destroyed or locked up. But if you make yourself more than just a man, if you devote yourself to an ideal, and if *they* can't stop you, then you become something else entirely." Later, during the final test in Bruce's training, Ducard says: "You have to become a terrible thought. A wraith. *You have to become an idea!*" What Nolan is referring to here is "Justice" — with a capital J — as a Platonic ideal or idea (Greek *eidos*) above or beyond the plane of transient worldly manifestations.

Christopher Nolan's Batman films sketch out the broad contours of a multi-tiered organized crime syndicate that has effectively become a de facto world government. At the *lowest* level are old-time mafia bosses like Carmine Falcone and Salvatore Moroni and a variety of new-wave gang leaders and drug dealers who each manage their own territories and are grouped in some cases according to race or ethnicity. Lacking any real economic expertise, the first tier of organized criminals must turn to experts in high finance in order to manage their collective investments. Mr. Lau of Hong Kong represents this financier class, and it is significant that he is in turn trying to invest in Wayne Enterprises on their behalf. If a CEO like Earl had still been running Wayne Enterprises, Lau's business deal with the corporation would probably have gone through. While Earl was at the helm of Wayne Enterprises he had departed radically from Thomas Wayne's philanthropic vision for the corporation by becoming involved in heavy arms manufacture, as represented by the microwave emitter chemical-agent-dispersal unit designed for desert warfare. At the same time, Earl tried to take the company public so as to raise capital from big investors in the arms industry. Bruce ultimately saves his family business from taking this course, but only after Nolan has given us an idea of the second tier of organized crime: *the military-industrial corporation*, which views the first tier of organized criminals as legitimate "no questions asked" investors.

These first two tiers consist of weak-minded people who lack a fearless commitment to principles that they would not violate at any cost. Their ultimate aim is lining their wallets. Most organized criminals hatch their plots to gain something, but this also means that they live in fear of all they have to lose. Both the gangsters and the military-industrial corporatists are glorified thieves. Consequently, more disciplined and intelligent men with well-considered plans and long-term projects find them easy to manipulate. Among this third class of organized criminals are experts in mind control and psychological warfare, such as Dr. Crane (Scarecrow) and his handler Henri Ducard, as well as Ras Al Ghul's daughter, the disciple who was her protector, Bane, and the Islamists that he recruits as his "liberation army."

Crane, an unethical scientist, manipulates the drug dealing activities of the first level of criminals in order to carry out nefarious psychological experiments. Crane is in turn Ducard's pawn. Ducard controls at least part of the international trafficking that brings various illicit substances from Asia to Gotham. Meanwhile, the infrastructure of Gotham has been so badly corrupted that Ducard's men can infiltrate every level of it, to the point of stealthily acquiring classified special weapons designed and manufactured by the military-industrial corporatists. The League of Shadows is not merely after profit. In fact, Bane's rabble-rousing leadership of the Occupy Wall Street movement in *The Dark Knight Rises* demonstrates the essentially anti-Capitalist character of the cult. Although it skillfully makes use of mobsters, militarist corporatists, and unethical scientists and technocrats, it is ultimately a cult of "true believers" who reject materialism and creature comforts. That is also what lies behind its thinly veiled association with radical Islam. This means that even these Assassins can be manipulated. Only the Joker cannot be.

The Joker is not after money, or for that matter any other logically comprehensible advantage or materially definable gain. In *The Dark Knight*, Christopher Nolan shows us this through both Alfred's anecdote about the bandit he chased in the forests of Burma and the Joker's own dramatic decision to burn his half of the laundered money. The former clearly foreshadows the latter. Alfred explains to Bruce that Batman hammered the underworld "to the point of desperation, and in their desperation they turned to a man they didn't fully understand." Bruce then echoes what Ducard said about criminals in *Batman Begins*, namely that: "Criminals aren't complicated." Bruce thinks that they are all after something and they just need to figure out what the Joker wants. Alfred disagrees: "With respect Master Wayne, perhaps this is a man *you* don't fully understand either." He then tells the story about the Bandit. Bruce asks Alfred why the Bandit would have stolen the stones just to throw them away. Alfred replies: "Well, because he thought it was good sport, because *some* men [Nolan focuses the camera on the Joker's face on TV] aren't looking for anything logical like money. They can't be bought, bullied, reasoned, or negotiated with. Some men just want to watch the world burn." Later, when in the predawn hours Bruce, still half dressed as Batman, is sitting by the window of his apartment overlooking Gotham and contemplating whether he is responsible for Rachel's death, he asks Alfred: "That bandit, in the forest in Burma, did you catch him?" Alfred replies "Yes." Bruce asks "How?" Alfred's ominous response once again references fire: "We burned the forest down."

The two references to the Bandit who wanted to watch the world burn and who forces his pursuers to burn a forest down to apprehend him, frame the scene where the Joker sets fire to the money he's extorted from the mobsters and gangsters that he has turned into his playthings. As he burns the mountain of cash the Joker says to one of the gangsters: "All you care about is money, this town deserves a better class of criminal. I'm gonna give it to them. Tell your men they work for me now. This is *my* city." The gangster retorts that his men "won't work for a *freak*," whereupon the Joker delivers one of his most revealing lines in *The Dark Knight*: "Why don't we cut you up and feed you to your pooches. Then we'll find out how loyal everybody really is. It's not about *money*, it's about *sending a message: EVERYTHING BURNS!*"

The word "mob" has a dual meaning in Nolan's Batman films. It is not only a reference to the organized crime syndicate that rules Gotham, but also to the masses who allow it to do so. As the Joker recognizes, the people of Gotham are utterly hypocritical. Even though they want law enforcement to hunt down Batman as an outlaw vigilante, and are ready to put him in prison once he turns himself in, they are happy to use him when they really need him. Most of them view him as just as *freakish* and "crazy" as the Joker, and moreover as the catalyst for the "craziness" that has come over Gotham. They share the mob's wish to just go back to the way things were in the old days. Harvey Dent's impassioned plea at the press conference, to the effect that while things are indeed "worse than ever" it is "always darkest just before the dawn" has no effect on them. They do not appreciate him reminding them that although the Batman is an outlaw, the people of Gotham, who have so far been happy to let Batman clean up their streets, are really demanding that he turn himself in because they are scared of a terrorist madman.

The Joker's "social experiment" with the two ferries rigged with explosives is an attempt to demonstrate the validity of his thesis that "when the chips are down, these uh, these 'civilized' people, *they'll eat each other.*" Although this appears to fail, the Joker still makes his point through his "ace in the hole." Both Gordon and Batman agree that the Joker was right to think that if the people of Gotham were to find out what he had turned Harvey into, their spirit would break and they would give up all hope in the good. The only way they can avert this outcome is to cover up the truth that the public cannot handle. This shows that even Harvey Dent's criticism of Democracy is too weak. Recall the exchange between Bruce, his Russian ballerina date, Rachel, and Harvey in a restaurant towards the beginning of *The Dark Knight*:

NATASCHA (prima Russian ballerina): How could you want to raise children in a city like this.

BRUCE: Well, I was raised here, I turned out ok.

DENT: Is Wayne Manor even in the city limits?

BRUCE: The pallisades, sure. You know, as our new DA you might want to figure out, uh, where your jurisdiction ends.

NATASCHA: I'm talking about the kind of city that idolizes a masked vigilante.

DENT: Gotham city is proud of an ordinary citizen standing up for what's right.

NATASCHA: Gotham needs heroes like you, elected officials, not a man who thinks he is above the law.

BRUCE: Exactly, who appointed the Bat Man?

DENT: We did. All of us who stood by and let scum take control of our city.

NATASCHA: But this is a democracy, Harvey.

DENT: When their enemies were at the gates, the Romans would suspend democracy and appoint one man to protect the city, and it wasn't considered an honor, it was considered a public service.

RACHEL: Harvey, the last man that they appointed to protect the Republic was named Caesar, and he never gave up his power.

DENT: Ok, fine. You either die a hero or you live long enough to see yourself become the villain. Look, whoever the Bat Man is he doesn't want

to do this for the rest of his life, how could he? Batman is looking for
someone to take up his mantle.

NATASCHA: Someone like you, Mr. Dent?

DENT: Maybe, if I'm up to it.

He is *not* up to it, and since both Gordon and Batman agree that
Dent is Gotham's finest, it turns out that *no one* is up to it. For most
of *The Dark Knight*, Batman believes that Dent is the "real hero" that
he "can never be." Bruce sees his own fight against organized crime
as provisional, and hopes to be able to create the conditions whereby
a public official of a democratic government can take up the struggle
through more legitimate means. Rachel clearly influenced Bruce into
taking this view. Towards the opening of *Batman Begins* she preaches
the virtues of an impartial Justice system over vigilante vengeance,
and while Bruce initially responds that "your system is broken" he
ultimately tells Ducard that the man he is supposed to execute "should
be tried." Ducard replies: "By who? Corrupt bureaucrats? Criminals
mock society's laws. You know this better than most." This *was* Bruce's
view, but he has come around to seeing things Rachel's way.

Yet in the end we see that Rachel makes excuses to break her
promise to Bruce, betraying him to be with Dent — whose character
she grossly misjudges as being superior to that of Batman. When
Alfred explains to her why Bruce and Dent agree that Batman should
not turn himself in, she completely misses the point of what he means
by saying that Bruce is not being a hero. She leaves a letter with him
whose contents consist of an appalling betrayal of Bruce. Alfred decides to withhold the letter and then ultimately to burn it altogether,
which Nolan shows us as one of the montages over Gordon's closing
narration in *The Dark Knight*. The juxtaposition of that image together
with this narration is intended to suggest that Rachel was just another
member of the mob. Bruce blinded himself to her true character (or
lack thereof) because without his love for her he would be *so* alone.
Alfred burns the letter so that this sudden realization of almost total

loneliness will not endanger Batman's compassion for the people of Gotham.

Whether or not Nolan will admit it publicly, one moral of his film is that a Caesar is not only justified under certain circumstances, but that the suspension of democracy need not be temporary. Lucius Fox was mistaken to believe that it is wrong for one man (or a few) to have as much power as the sonar cellular spying system has given Batman, and Bruce Wayne was wrong to think that he had to delegate this power to Fox and then allow him to destroy the machine after only a single use. *The Dark Knight* explores why democracy is a misguided political system altogether. In this closing narration we see the total inversion of Gordon and Wayne's initial belief that Dent is the true hero and Batman only a temporary stopgap. Dent's heroism is a lie that Batman, who is far more than a hero, decides must be maintained for the citizens' own good. Ras Al Ghul was right that "theatricality *and deception* are powerful weapons," and Batman learns that it is sometimes necessary to use both. Here is the dialogue and narration of *The Dark Knight*'s devastating last scene:

GORDON: Thank you.

BATMAN [after having fallen]: You don't have to thank me.

GORDON: Yes, I do.

The Joker won. Harvey's prosecution, everything he fought for, undone. Whatever chance you gave us of fixing our city, dies with Harvey's reputation. We bet it all on him. the Joker took the best of us and tore him down. People will lose hope.

BATMAN: They won't. They must never know what he did.

GORDON: Five dead. Two of them cops. You can't sweep that up.

BATMAN: But the Joker cannot win. Gotham needs its true hero [he turns Two Face's head over to the Harvey side]. You either die a hero or you live long enough to see yourself become a villain. I can do those things, because I'm not a hero, unlike Dent. *I* killed those people. That's what I can be.

GORDON: No, you *can't*, you're *not*.

BATMAN: I'm whatever Gotham needs me to be. Call it in.

GORDON [giving a speech before Dent's portrait]: 'A hero, not the hero we
  deserved, but the Hero we needed, nothing less than a Knight, shining.'
[Gordon's closing narration, over images of him breaking down the Bat
  signal, and the cops chasing Batman...]
GORDON: They'll hunt you.
BATMAN: *You'll* hunt me. *You'll* condemn me. Set the dogs on me, because
  that's what *needs* to happen. Because sometimes Truth isn't good enough
  [OVER THE IMAGE OF ALFRED BURNING RACHEL'S LETTER],
  sometimes people deserve more, sometimes people deserve to have their
  faith rewarded.
GORDON'S SON: Batman. Batman! Why's he running, dad?
GORDON: Because we have to chase him...
Gordon's son: He didn't do anything wrong.
GORDON: ...because he's the hero Gotham *deserves*, but not the one it
  needs right now. So we'll hunt him, because he can take it, because he's
  not our hero, he's a silent *Guardian*, a watchful protector — a dark knight.

Beautiful, terrible — but only the way a myth, a modern legend can
be, right? On the contrary, that is what the mob believes and what The
Cosmic Joker who manipulates them wants you to believe. Nolan gives
us a hint that he knows otherwise. The card Joker tacks to corpses of
the Batman copycats reads: "Will the real Batman please stand up."

In the closing narration of *The Dark Knight*, with its reference to
the "guardian" and the noble lie, it becomes clear that Nolan is pro-
moting a new interpretation of the idea of Guardianship that we find
in Plato's *Republic* — the most antidemocratic political text in the history of Philosophy. The basic problem of the *Republic* is set forth in
the parable of "the Ring of Gyges," from 358a–362b in Book II.[1] This
thought experiment is provided as a means to strengthen the argument of Thrasymachus that might makes right, with which *Republic*
opens in Book I before going on to counter this view for the rest of
the text. Gyges is a Lydian shepherd who, in the midst of a terrible
thunderstorm and earthquake, finds the subterranean tomb of a giant

---

1   Plato, *The Republic of Plato* (New York: Basic Books, Perseus Books Group,

in a crevice that has just cracked open the Earth. There are many marvelous things in the tomb but the giant himself is naked except for a ring, which Gyges removes and slips onto his own finger before leaving the chamber. Later, he discovers that whenever he turns this ring inward he becomes invisible, because others discuss him as if he is not there. He uses this power to have sex with the Queen and murder her husband, installing himself as the King of Lydia.

Plato asks, if there were two such rings, one being given to what we take to be a just man and the other to an unjust man, would not nearly everyone at least privately think of the just man as a fool if he did not go about raping and plundering with impunity, if he did not, in effect, behave exactly as the unjust man does (and would do even more efficaciously with such a ring)? In an annex to the Gyges parable, Plato sharpens the question. Putting aside the ring, what if the state of affairs in the world were such that the man who only seems just in order to profit thereby were to be rewarded for his veiled injustice at every turn, whereas the just man would be taken by the many to be unjust and on that account hunted down and subjected to every variety of torture before in the end being crucified, then who could honestly say he would prefer to be a just man rather than a man who in the eyes of the many only seems just? Bruce Wayne's extraordinary wealth, honored position as "the Prince of Gotham," and his cunning intellect, afford him something like the Ring of Gyges — he could be the seemingly just man, being celebrated as a philanthropist while getting away with all kinds of dastardly deeds or at least living the callow life of a playboy. Instead, he chooses to be a feared, hated, hunted, vigilant guardian who protects those who persecute him and who cannot expect a hero's reward.

The famous or infamous passages on the so-called "philosopher king" as Guardian of the city-state appear from 497b–503b of the *Republic*.[2] I say so-called "philosopher king" because Plato (quite scandalously for his time) thinks that female philosophers are also fit to be Guardians. Three main points are emphasized in these core passages.

The first is that, Plato is fully convinced that philosophers cannot quietly retire from politics because they distain its rampant corruption. Philosophers will inevitably be victimized by unjust governments and perhaps martyred. Moreover, given that philosophers who contemplate ideals and are purified through long abiding in a transcendent state, if they turn their efforts to ordering the affairs of the world they would tend to reflect the archetypal patterns within their soul in the re-structured city-state as if in a mirror. In the absence of this, Plato is fully convinced that men of lesser intuition and understanding will always make themselves miserable through bringing about one or another unjust regime as a reflection of their own inner discord. Although the philosopher would rather keep to himself and his peers in a life of quiet contemplation, taken together these two facts make it incumbent upon him or her to protect lesser men from their own folly and to temper the violence that these men suffer at each other's hands by taking up statecraft as a public service.

Secondly, to the contrary of the view of those who think that Plato is naively engaging in an idle meander through the land of make-believe, if one reads these passages one finds several times both an insistence that such a regime should actually be implemented and a repeated acknowledgment that although this would be very difficult, and would be vociferously opposed by the mob, it is nonetheless not impossible.

Third and finally, one finds that Plato recognizes that the implementation of such a regime cannot be accomplished through reformist half-measures, but will require a radical revolution that wipes out the prevailing corruption before supplanting it with a more just social order. Like a master craftsman, the Guardian is a "painter of regimes" who will not accept anything less than a blank canvas or "a tablet... which, in the first place, they would wipe clean." They "would rub out one thing and draw in another...mixing and blending...ingredients" for a new "image of man."

Needless to say, such a revolution will be resisted by the mob who are incapable of understanding that it is for their own good, and that even those of them who are killed in the course of it will benefit by being reincarnated into a more just society. Therefore, a certain measure of deception will be necessary in order for the Guardians to forward their noble-minded project. This is the aspect of the doctrine of Guardianship in the *Republic* that is most evidently alluded to in Nolan's use of the Batman mythos to critique democracy. In the course of the *Republic*, Plato offers us two principal examples of the role that a "noble lie" might play in establishing a just social order.

The concept is introduced at the core of the so-called "myth of the metals" recounted from 413a–417b, with the key passage being at 414c: "Could we...somehow contrive one of those lies that come into being in case of need, of which we were just now speaking, someone noble lie to persuade, in the best case, even the rulers, but if not them, the rest of the city?"[3] The second reference comes at 457a–462c in the context of proposals as to how to coerce compliance with controversial Eugenics and population control policies, with this striking pronouncement as its fulcrum at 459d: "It's likely that our rulers will have to use a throng of lies and deceptions for the benefit of the ruled. And, of course, we said that everything of this sort is useful as a form of remedy."[4]

The content of these noble lies might not seem to have much in common with the noble lie that Batman decides to have Commissioner Gordon tell the people of Gotham, but their form is the same. In all cases, the noble lie is really about using deception or trickery as a way to fool people into becoming something that they would not otherwise have been capable of becoming. It is a way of crossing over and

---

3   Ibid., 93.

redefining the boundaries of the possible, like pretending to hold a child who is just learning to tread water in the deep end of the pool but holding him so lightly that he is already really keeping himself afloat but would still drown if he were made aware of this. Or, in a more sinister example, it is like forcing people you want to protect to face a false enemy so that they will build their strength in earnest and be more prepared for a real enemy that you know will arrive later.

The message of Hermes, the Trickster, may bring new boundaries decreed by Heaven, but only because he already crossed the old ones or brought people to cross them.[5] He is the god of the threshold.[6] Although he upsets the established social order, Hermes is most decidedly *not* the god of democracy; he will align himself with any number of different (and even opposed) political systems for strategic reasons.[7] He is known to play both sides, perhaps to provoke them into a *generative* strife. It appears that the Hermes archetype is not only at work in the Joker, but also in the response that the Joker's apparent victory elicits from the Dark Knight. In fact, the Batman and the Joker are an alchemical conjunction of opposites with tremendous transformative potential. A majority of Gothamites and most of the police force want to go back to a time before Batman, and the city's organized criminals think that the "craziness" the Joker has unleashed is just too much. Yet, as Alfred explains to Bruce, he "crossed the line first" and as the Joker explains to Batman, "there is no going back." Hermes has crossed the boundaries and calls forth a new order out of Chaos.

A good student of Plato recognizes that "do not unto others as you would not want others to do unto you" is a principle as necessary for maintaining the cohesion of a gang of criminals as it is for governing a city-state. It is based on the lowest common denominator of

---

5   Lewis Hyde, *Trickster Makes This World* (New York: Farrar, Straus, and Giroux, 2010), 7.

6   Ibid., 7–8.

self-interest, not on any contemplation of a moral ideal. Furthermore, it falsely assumes that most people are able to make a contract of their own free will, and to recognize each other as equal partners in such a contract.

When Batman decides that he must tell a Platonic noble lie, when he realizes that his proper role is as a republican Guardian and not as the hero of a democracy sustained through a social contract, something of the Trickster's dynamism has transformatively insinuated itself into his character as well. To recognize this, in the compelling context of Nolan's films, is to better discern the esoteric Hermetic dimension of the Platonic project. Truth lies beyond the limits of the possible, such that the instauration of Justice makes impossible demands of allegedly "conservative" but unprincipled hypocrites. "You must be joking," they say — to which the only answer is for the real Batman to stand up.

BIBLIOGRAPHY

Adorno, Theodor (1983) "Notes on Kafka" in *Prisms* (MA: MIT Press).

Alexander, John B. (2011) *UFOs: Myths, Conspiracies, and Realities* (New York: St. Martin's Press).

Aristotle (1995) *The Complete Works of Aristotle*. Two Volumes. (Princeton, NJ: Princeton University Press). Barnes, Jonathan [Translator].

Ayoub, Mahmoud (1988) "The Speaking Qur'an and the Silent Qur'an" in *Approaches to the History of the Interpretation of the Quran*, Andrew Rippin Ed. (New York: Oxford University Press).

Barnes, Jonathan (1971) *Early Greek Philosophy* (New York: Penguin Books).

Barlas, Asma (2002) *"Believing Women" in Islam* (Austin: University of Texas Press).

Benjamin, Walter (1969) "Franz Kafka: On the Tenth Anniversary of His Death," in *Illuminations* (New York: Schocken Books).

Blascovich, Jim and J. Bailenson (2011) *Infinite Reality: The Hidden Blueprint of our Virtual Lives* (New York: William Morrow).

Bohm, David (1996) *On Dialogue* (London: Routedge).

Breton, André (1972) *Manifestoes of Surrealism* (Ann Arbor, MI: University of Michigan Press).

Brod, Max [Editor] (1991) *The Blue Octavo Notebooks by Franz Kafka* (Cambridge: Exact Change).

Clack, Brian R. (1999) *An Introduction to Wittgenstein's Philosophy of Religion* (Edinburgh: Edinburgh University Press).

Cohen, Peter (1991) *The Architecture of Doom* (First Run Features).

COMETA (2003) *Les OVNI et La Défense: A quoi doit-on se preparer?* (France: Éditions du Rocher).

Cook, Nick (2001) *The Hunt for Zero Point* (London: Random House).

Crowe, Michael J. (2009) *The Extraterrestrial Life Debate: Antiquity to 1915* (University of Notre Dame).

Dawood, N.J. (1995) *The Koran* (New York: Penguin Classics).

Deleuze, Gilles (1994) *What Is Philosophy?* (New York: Columbia University Press).

Derrida, Jacques (1994) *Specters of Marx* (New York: Routledge).

D'Este, Sorita (2005) *Artemis: Virgin Goddess of the Sun & Moon — A Comprehensive Guide to the Greek Goddess of the Hunt* (London: Avalonia Press).

D'Este, Sorita and David Rankine (2009) *Hekate: Liminal Rites: A study of the rituals, magic and symbols of the torch-bearing Triple Goddess of the Crossroads.* (London: Avalonia Press).

Dodd, Bill (2003) "The case for a political reading" in *The Cambridge Companion to Kafka*. [Edited by Julian Preece] (Cambridge, UK: Cambridge University Press).

Ellis, Richard (1998) *Imagining Atlantis* (New York: Alfred A. Knopf, Inc.).

Evans-Wentz, W.Y. (1960) *The Tibetan Book of the Dead* (New York: Oxford University Press).

Evola, Julius (1992) *The Yoga of Power: Tantra, Shakti, and the Secret Way* (Rochester, VT: Inner Traditions International).

Farrell, Joseph P. (2004) *Reich of the Black Sun: Nazi Secret Weapons and the Cold War Allied Legend* (Kempton, IL: Adventures Unlimited Press).

Farrell, Joseph P. (2006) *The SS Brotherhood of the Bell* (Kempton, IL: Adventures Unlimited Press).

Farrell, Joseph P. (2008) *The Nazi International* (Kempton, IL: Adventures Unlimited Press).

Farrell, Joseph P. (2010) *Roswell and the Reich: The Nazi Connection* (Kempton, IL: Adventures Unlimited Press).

Farrell, Joseph P. (2011) *Saucers, Swastikas, and Psyops* (Kempton, IL: Adventures Unlimited Press).

Fulcanelli (1999) *The Dwellings of the Philosophers* (Boulder, CO: Archive Press).

Godwin, Joscelyn (1996) *Arktos: The Polar Myth in Science, Symbolism, and Nazi Survival* (Kempton, IL: Adventures Unlimited Press).

Goffman, Erving (1959) *The Presentation of Self in Everyday Life* (New York: Doubleday).

Griffin, Roger (2007) *Modernism and Fascism: The Sense of a Beginning under Mussolini and Hitler* (New York: Palgrave Macmillan).

Grözinger, Karl Erich (1994) *Kafka and Kabbalah* (New York: Continuum).

Hamilton, Edith (1998) *Mythology* (New York: Back Bay Books).

Hansen, George P. (2001) *The Trickster and the Paranormal* (Xlibris Corporation).

Havelock, Eric (1982) *Preface to Plato* (Belknap Press).

Hegel, G.W.F. (1998) "Lectures on Fine Art" in *The Origins of Modern Critical Thought: German Aesthetics and Literary Criticism from Lessing to Hegel*. Edited by David Simpson. (New York: Cambridge University Press).

Heidegger, Martin (1984) "The Anaximander Fragment" in *Early Greek Thinking* (New York: Harper and Row).

Heidegger, Martin (2009) *Logic as the Question Concerning the Essence of Language* (Albany: State University of New York Press).

Hoagland, Richard C. and Mike Bara (2009) *Dark Mission: The Secret History of NASA* (Port Townsend, WA: Feral House).

Hunt, Linda (1991) *Secret Agenda: The United States Government, Nazi Scientists, and Project Paperclip, 1945–1990* (St Martin's Press).

Hyde, Lewis (2010) *Trickster Makes This World* (New York: Farrar, Straus, and Giroux).

Ibn Kathir, Hafiz (2000) *Tafsir* (Dar-us-Salam Publications).

Jacobson, Annie (2015) *Operation Paperclip: The Secret Intelligence Program That Brought Nazi Scientists to America* (New York: Little, Brown and Company).

James, William (1987) *Writings: 1902–1910* (New York: The Library of America).

Jaynes, Julian (1990) *The Origin of Consciousness in the Breakdown of the Bicameral Mind* (New York: Mariner Books).

Jung, Carl Gustav (1972) "On the Psychology of the Trickster Figure" in Paul Radin, *The Trickster: A Study in American Indian Mythology* (New York: Schocken Books).

Jung, Carl Gustav (1979) *Flying Saucers* (New York: Princeton University Press).

Kafka, Franz (1996) *The Trial*. Translated by Willa and Edwin Muir with an Introduction by Georg Steiner. (New York: Schocken Books).

Kahn, Charles H. (1999) *The Art and Thought of Heraclitus* (New York: Cambridge University Press).

Kant, Immanuel. *Critique of Pure Reason* (New York: Cambridge University Press, 1998).

Kant, Immanuel. *Groundwork of the Metaphysics of Morals* in *Practical Philosophy* (New York: Cambridge University Press, 2006).

Kean, Leslie (2010) *UFOs: Generals, Pilots, and Government Officials Go On the Record* (Harmony Books).

Kenny, Anthony (2002) *The Wittgenstein Reader* (Oxford: Blackwell Publishing).

Levenda, Peter (2002) *Unholy Alliance: A History of Nazi Involvement with the Occult* (New York: Continuum).

Lewis, David (2003) *On the Plurality of Worlds* (Oxford: Blackwell Publishing).

Lubicz, R.A. Schwaller de (1978) *Symbol and the Symbolic: Ancient Egypt, Science, and the Evolution of Consciousness* (Vermont: Inner Traditions).

Malcolm, Norman (1994) *Wittgenstein: A Religious Point of View* (Ithaca, New York: Cornell University Press).

Marx, Karl (1988) *The Economic and Philosophic Manuscripts of 1844 and the Communist Manifesto* (New York: Prometheus Books).

Miller, A.V. and N.J. Findlay (1971) *Hegel's Philosophy of Mind* (New York: Oxford University Press).

Miller, A.V. (1977) *Hegel's Phenomenology of Spirit* (New York: Oxford University Press).

Mills, M.L. (1971) *Early Greek Philosophy and the Orient* (Oxford: Carendon Press).

Merleau-Ponty, Maurice (1968) *The Visible and the Invisible* (Evanston: Northwestern University Press).

Nasr, Seyyed Hossein and Mehdi Aminrazavi [Editors] (1999) *An Anthology of Philosophy in Persia: Volume 1* (New York: Oxford University Press).

Nietzsche, Friedrich (1968) *The Will to Power* (New York: Random House).

Nietzsche, Friedrich (1974) *The Gay Science* (New York: Vintage Books).

Nietzsche, Friedrich (1984) *Human, All Too Human*. Marion Faber [Translator.] (University of Nebraska Press).

Nietzsche, Friedrich (1990) *Twilight of the Idols & the Anti-Christ*. R.J. Hollingdale [Translator]. (New York: Penguin Books).

Nietzsche, Friedrich (1995) *Thus Spoke Zarathustra*. Walter Kaufmann [Translator.] (New York: The Modern Library).

Nietzsche, Friedrich (1995) *The Birth of Tragedy* (New York: Dover Publications).

Nietzsche, Friedrich (1998) *Philosophy in the Tragic Age of the Greeks* (Washington, D.C.: Regnery Publishing).

Nietzsche, Friedrich (2000) *The Basic Writings of Nietzsche* (New York: Random House).

Nietzsche, Friedrich (2001) *The Pre-Platonic Philosophers* (Chicago: University of Illinois Press).

Nietzsche, Friedrich (2003) *Writings from the Late Notebooks*. Rüdiger Bittner [Editor and Translator.] (New York: Cambridge University Press).

Parmenides (2000) *Fragments* (Toronto: University of Toronto Press).

Plato (1999) *The Collected Dialogues of Plato* (Princeton, NJ: Princeton University Press). Hamilton, Edith and Huntington Cairns [Translators].

Plato (1991) *The Republic of Plato* (New York: Basic Books, Perseus Books Group). Allan Bloom [Translator].

Sartre, Jean-Paul (2007) *Existentialism Is a Humanism* (New Haven: Yale University Press).

Schoch, Robert M. (1999) *Voices of the Rocks: A Scientist Looks at Catastrophes and Ancient Civilizations* (New York: Harmony Books).

Schur, David (1998) *The Way of Oblivion: Heraclitus and Kafka* (Cambridge, MA: Harvard University Press).

Singer, P.W. (2010) *Wired for War: The Robotics Revolution and Conflict in the 21st Century* (New York: Penguin Books).

Spinoza, Benedict de (1994) *A Spinoza Reader: The Ethics and Other Works*. Edwin Curley [Editor and Translator.] (Princeton, NJ: Princeton University Press).

Taimni, I.K. (2001) *The Science of Yoga: The Yoga Sutras of Patanjali in Sanskrit with Transliteration in Roman, Translation and Commentary in English* (Wheaton, IL: The Theosophical Publishing House).

Taylor, Richard P. (2002) "Order in Pollock's Chaos" in *Scientific American* (December).

Tucker, Robert C. (1978) *The Marx-Engels Reader* (New York: W.W. Norton & Company).

Vallée, Jacques (1993) *Passport to Magonia* (Chicago: Contemporary Books).

Verbrugghe, Gerald P. and John M. Wickersham (2000) *Berossos and Manetho, Introduced and Translated: Native Traditions in Ancient Mesopotamia and Egypt* (Ann Arbor: University of Michigan Press).

Wadud, Amina (1999) *Qur'an and Woman: Rereading the Sacred Text from a Woman's Perspective* (New York: Oxford University Press).

Warlick, M.E. (2001) *Max Ernst and Alchemy: A Magician in Search of Myth* (Austin, TX: University of Texas Press).

Wessell, Leonard P. (1984) *Prometheus Bound: The Mythic Structure of Karl Marx's Scientific Thinking* (Baton Rouge: Louisiana State University Press).

Wilde, Lyn Webster (2000) *On the Trail of the Women Warriors: The Amazons in Myth and History* (New York: St. Martin's Press).

Wilson, Colin and Rand Flem-Ath (2002) *The Atlantis Blueprint* (New York: Random House).

Witkowski, Igor (2003) *The Truth About the Wunderwaffe* (Farnborough, England: European History Press).

Wittgenstein, Ludwig (1972) *On Certainty* (New York: Harper & Row).

Wittgenstein, Ludwig (1979) *Notebooks 1914–1916* (Chicago: University of Chicago Press).

Wittgenstein, Ludwig (1980) *Culture and Value* (Chicago: University of Chicago Press).

Wittgenstein, Ludwig (2001) *Philosophical Investigations: The German text, with a revised English translation* (Oxford: Blackwell Publishing).

Wittgenstein, Ludwig (2003) *Tractatus Logico-Philosophicus* (New York: Barnes and Noble).

Wittgenstein, Ludwig (2007) *Zettel* (Berkeley: University of California Press).

INDEX

OTHER BOOKS PUBLISHED BY ARKTOS

	The Myth of the Blood
	Notes on the Third Reich
	The Path of Cinnabar
	Recognitions
	A Traditionalist Confronts Fascism
GUILLAUME FAYE	*Archeofuturism*
	Archeofuturism 2.0
	The Colonisation of Europe
	Convergence of Catastrophes
	Ethnic Apocalypse
	A Global Coup
	Sex and Deviance
	Understanding Islam
	Why We Fight
DANIEL S. FORREST	*Suprahumanism*
ANDREW FRASER	*Dissident Dispatches*
	The WASP Question
GÉNÉRATION IDENTITAIRE	*We are Generation Identity*
PAUL GOTTFRIED	*War and Democracy*
PORUS HOMI HAVEWALA	*The Saga of the Aryan Race*
LARS HOLGER HOLM	*Hiding in Broad Daylight*
	Homo Maximus
	Incidents of Travel in Latin America
	The Owls of Afrasiab
RICHARD HOUCK	*Liberalism Unmasked*
A. J. ILLINGWORTH	*Political Justice*
ALEXANDER JACOB	*De Naturae Natura*
JASON REZA JORJANI	*Iranian Leviathan*
	Prometheus and Atlas
	World State of Emergency
VINCENT JOYCE	*The Long Goodbye*
RODERICK KAINE	*Smart and SeXy*

OTHER BOOKS PUBLISHED BY ARKTOS

OTHER BOOKS PUBLISHED BY ARKTOS

Made in the USA
Monee, IL
29 January 2024

52562238R20310